Patricia Smith's

DOLL VALUES

Antique to Modern

Eleventh Edition

COLLECTOR BOOKS

A Division of Schroeder Publishing Co., Inc.

Searching For A Publisher?

We are always looking for knowledgeable people considered experts within their fields. If you feel that there is a real need for a book on your collectible subject and have a large comprehensive collection, contact us.

COLLECTOR BOOKS
P.O. Box 3009
Paducah, Kentucky 42002-3009

CREDITS

Gloria Anderson, Chaye "Sara" Arotsky, Doris Blake, Candy Brainard, Elizabeth Burke, Barbara Earnshaw-Cain, Betty Chapman, Sharon Caldwell, Susan Capps, John C. Connell, Lee Crane, Sandra Cummins, Renie Culp, Ellen Dodge, Marie Ernst, Debbie Fellanz, Albert Fossat, Frasher Doll Auctions (Rt. 1, Box 72, Oak Grove, MO 64075), Maureen Fukushima, Green Museum, Susan Giradot, Pat Grady, Pat Graff, Lee Nell Haye, Nell Hudson, Kathy & Steve Humphries, Phyllis Huston-Kates, Floyd & Gracie James, Marcia Jarmush, Cris Johnson, Roger Jones, Jo Keelen, Lawton Dolls (548 North First Street, Turlock, CA 95380), Theo Lendley, Charlene Lopez, Kris Lundquist, Margaret Mandel, Jeannie Mauldin, Marge Meisinger, Ellyn McCorkell, Chris McWilliams, Arthur Michnevitz, A. Pidd Miller, Peggy Millhouse, June Murkins, Jeannie Nespoli, Randy Numley, Christine Perisho, "Flip" Phelps, Kathy Riddick, Shirley's Doll House (P.O. Box 99, Wheeling, IL 60090), Virginia Sofie, Pat Sparks, David Spurgeon, Karen Stephenson, Startzel's, Beth Summers, Martha Sweeney, Phyliss Teague, Betty Todd, Carol Turpin, Turn of Century Antiques (1421 Broadway, Denver, CO 80210), Kathy & Don Tvrdik, Jane Walker, Ann Wencel, Mary Williams, Patricia Wood (17517 NE 92nd Ave., Battle Ground, WA 98604), Glorya Woods, Jeanne Venner.

ON THE COVER

Upper right: 13½" Gebruder Heubach, mold #5636, with glass eyes, open/closed mouth, and two lower teeth. Laughing with cheek dimples. Fully jointed body. $1,500.00. *Courtesy Turn of Century Antiques.*

Lower left: 11" Simon & Halbig oriental doll with beautiful bisque. Original and in mint condition. $2,200.00. *Courtesy Turn of Century Antiques.*

Lower right: 17" Scarlett made by Robin Woods, 1992–1993. Wears a beautiful floral gown with chiffon overskirt. Carries a basket of flowers. $285.00.

Book and cover design by Karen Geary

PRICES

This book is divided into "Antique" and "Modern" sections, with the older dolls in the first section and the newer dolls in the second section. To make a quick reference, each section alphabetically lists the dollmaker, type of material or name of doll. (Example: Bye-Lo or Kewpie.) An index is provided for locating a specific doll.

In antique dolls, the uppermost concern is the condition of the head and body. It is also important for the body to be correct to the doll. An antique doll must be clean, nicely dressed and ready to place into a collection. It must have no need of any repair for it to bring book price. An all original doll with original clothes, marked shoes and original wig will bring a lot more than list price. Boxes are very rare and also will bring a higher price for the doll.

In modern dolls, the condition of the doll is the uppermost concern in pricing. An all original modern doll in excellent condition will bring a much higher price than listed in this price guide. A doll that is damaged, without original clothes, soiled and dirty, will bring far less than the top price listed. The cost of doll repairs and cleanup has soared, so it is wise to judge the damage and estimate the cost of repairs before you attempt to sell or buy a damaged doll. An excellent reference concerning storing and restoring is *Dolls – Preserve and Restore Your Collection* by Kathy Tvrdik (6415 S.W. 27th Street, Topeka, KS 66614).

For insurance reasons, it is very important to show the "retail" price of dolls in a price guide and to try to be as accurate as possible. The "retail" price can be referred to as "replacement cost" so that insurance companies or postal services can appraise a damaged or stolen doll for the insured, and the collectors can judge their own collections and purchase adequate amounts of insurance.

No one knows your collection better than yourself and in the end, when you consider a purchase, you must ask yourself if the doll is affordable to you and whether you want it enough to pay the price. You will buy the doll, or pass it up – it is as simple as that!

Prices shown are for dolls that are clean, undamaged, well-dressed and in overall excellent condition. Many prices are also listed for soiled, dirty, and redressed dolls.

Antique and Older Dolls

Right: 16" rare mold number 220 by Kestner on chunky toddler body. Sleep eyes and open mouth. Left: 15" "Fany" by Armand Marseille. Closed pouty mouth, sleep eyes, and on jointed toddler body. Marked "Fany/DRGM A 4 M 230." 16" - $5,700.00; 15" - $4,500.00. *Courtesy Frasher Doll Auctions.*

Henri Alexandre dolls were made from 1889 to 1891 only. The dolls have closed mouths with a white space between the lips, fat cheeks, and early French bodies with straight wrists. (Also see under "Phenix" section.)

18" - $6,250.00; 22" - $7,200.00; 25" - $7,500.00.

Mark:

ALL BISQUE – FRENCH

French all bisque dolls are jointed at the necks, shoulders and hips. They have slender arms and legs, glass eyes and most have kid-lined joints. Most of the heads have sliced pates with tiny cork inserts. French all-bisque dolls have finely painted features with outlined lips, well-tinted bisque, and feathered eyebrows. They can have molded-on shoes, high-top boots with painted toes, high-top buttoned boots with four or more painted straps. They can also be barefooted or just have stockings painted on the legs.

Any French bisque should be in very good condition, not have any chips, breaks, or hairline cracks to bring the following prices. *Allow much more for original clothes;* less for damage or repairs.

Bare Feet: 5" - $1,200.00; 8" - $1,850.00; 10" - $2,600.00.

Bru Type with glass eyes: Five-strap boots. Outlined lips. (See photo in Series 3, pg. 25.) 5" - $1,800.00. **Painted eyes:** 5" - $850.00 up.

Jointed Elbows: 5½" - $2,400.00; 8½" - $3,300.00.

Jointed Elbows and Knees: 6" - $3,000.00; 8" - $3,800.00.

Marked E.D., F.G.: Or other French makers. Glass eyes, bare feet. Allow more for original clothes. 7–8" - $2,300.00–2,500.00.

S.F.B.J., UNIS: Or other late French all bisques. Painted eyes. 5" - $525.00; 7" - $750.00.

Swivel Neck: (Socket head) Molded shoes or boots. 7" - $1,350.00; 7" repaired - $650.00; 8" - $2,100.00; 8" repaired - $975.00.

3½" and 4½" French-type dolls with glass eyes, closed mouths, and slim bodies. Both have kid-lined swivel necks. The tall one has original gloves and painted white socks to above the knees. Each - $975.00 up. *Courtesy Shirley's Doll House.*

German-made all bisque dolls run from excellent to moderate quality. Prices are for excellent quality and condition with no chips, cracks, breaks, or hairlines. Dolls should be nicely dressed and can have molded hair or wig. They generally have painted-on shoes and socks. Allow much more for original clothes. Circa 1880s–1930s.

Bathing dolls: See that section.

Black or brown dolls: See that section.

French types: 1880s–1910. Slender dolls with one-piece body and head. Usually wire or peg-jointed shoulders and hips. Closed mouth. Allow much more for original clothes. (Many are in regional costumes.) **Add more for unusual color boots,** such as gold, yellow, or orange. All in good condition. **Glass eyes:** Open or closed mouth. 4" - $285.00; 5–6" - $350.00. **Swivel neck:** Closed mouth. 4" - $375.00; 5–6" - $500.00; 8½" - $900.00; 10" - $1,300.00. **Bent at knees:** 6" - $200.00. **Jointed knees and/or elbows:** 6" - $1,950.00; 8" - $2,550.00. **Jointed knees and/or elbows with swivel waist:** 6" - $2,650.00; 8" - $3,200.00. **Swivel waist only:** 6" - $2,000.00. **Painted eyes, swivel neck:** Open or closed mouth. Painted one-strap shoes. 4" - $200.00; 6" - $350.00; 8" - $475.00; 10" - $675.00.

Glass eyes, one-piece body and head: (Sometimes legs.) Ca. 1880–1913. Excellent bisque, open/closed mouth, sleep or set eyes, good wig, and nicely dressed. Molded one-strap shoes. Allow more for unusual footwear such as yellow boots, multi-strap boots. 3" - $225.00; 5" - $275.00; 6" - $345.00; 7" - $400.00; 8" - $485.00; 9" - $600.00; 10" - $750.00; 12" - $875.00. **Bent at knees:** 6" - $285.00. **Mold #100, 125, 161, 225 (Alt, Beck, & Gottschalck):** 1911 on. Chubby body and limbs. 5" - $225.00; 6½" - $300.00; 8" - $450.00; 10" - $700.00. **Mold #130, 150, 168, 184, 257, 602, 790 (Bonn or Kestner):** Painted blue or pink stockings, one-strap black shoe: 4" - $235.00; 6" - $325.00. 7" - $350.00; 8" - $425.00; 9" - $575.00; 10" - $750.00; 11" - $975.00; 12" - $1,250.00. **Mold #155, 156 (smile):** 6" - $450.00. **Swivel neck:** 5½" - $600.00; 7" - $800.00. **Mold #160:** Molded hair. 5½" - $325.00. **Mold #168:** 9" - $365.00. **Mold #790:** 5½" - $475.00.

Painted eyes, one-piece body and head: (Sometimes legs.) Ca. 1880–1913., 1921–1932. Molded hair or wig, open or closed mouth, painted-on shoes and socks. Dressed or undressed. All in good

8" marked "83/150/18." Has open/closed mouth, sleep glass eyes, molded-on shoes and socks. Made by Kestner of Germany. $425.00.

condition. Allow more for unusual footwear such as yellow boots. 1½–2" - $85.00; 4–5" - $175.00; 6½" - $225.00; 8" - $300.00; 10" - $750.00. **Swivel neck:** 2" - $145.00; 4" - $245.00; 6½" - $285.00; 8" - $350.00. **Swivel neck with molded hat:** 4" - $900.00. **Black stockings, tan slippers:** 6" - $375.00. **Ribbed (shirred) hose :** 4½" - $185.00; 6" - $365.00; 8" - $565.00. **Molded hair:** 4" - $175.00; 6½" - $350.00. **Early very round face:** 7" - $2,300.00. **Mold #130, 150, 160, 168, 184, 208, 602 (Kestner):** 5" - $250.00; 6" - $300.00; 7" - $350.00; 8" - $425.00; 9" - $600.00; 10½" - $825.00; 12" - $1,200.00.

Glass eyes, swivel neck: Pegged or wired joints, open or closed mouth, molded-on shoes or boots and stockings. All in good condition. Allow more for unusual footwear such as yellow boots, multi-strap boots. Very good quality. 3" - $275.00; 4" - $325.00; 5½" - $500.00; 7" - $675.00; 8" - $775.00; 9" - $895.00; 10" - $1,100.00. **Mold**

4" and 3½" figures with one-piece bodies and heads. Wire jointed hips and shoulders. Molded-on underclothes. Both marked "Germany." Tall one also has "3/0" and "30" on the legs. 4" - $150.00; 3½" - $135.00. *Courtesy Shirley's Doll House.*

#130, 150, 160, 208, 602 (Kestner): 4" - $500.00; 6" - $600.00; 8" - $900.00; 10" - $1,300.00. **Simon & Halbig or Kestner types:** Closed mouth, excellent quality. 5" - $925.00; 6" - $1,350.00; 8" - $2,100.00; 10" - $2,750.00. **Jointed knees:** 5½–6½" - $2,900.00. **In original factory case or box with clothes and accessories:** 5" - $3,500.00. **Bare feet:** 5" - $1,600.00; 7½" - $2,400.00. **Early round face:** 6" - $850.00; 8" - $1,250.00. **#184 Kestner:** Sweet face, solid color boots. 4–5" - $700.00; 8" - $1,600.00. **Mold #881, 886, 890 (Simon & Halbig):** Painted high top boots with 4 or 5 straps. 4½" - $725.00; 7½" - $1,200.00; 9¼" - $1,500.00. **Long stockings:** Above knees. Can be black, blue, green, or yellow. Perfect condition. 4½" - $775.00; 6½" - $900.00.

Flapper: One-piece body and head, thin limbs. Fired-in tine bisque. Wig, painted eyes, painted-on long stockings, one-strap painted shoes. 6" - $300.00; 8" - $425.00. **Molded hair:** 6" - $350.00; 8" - $450.00. **Later (1920s–1930s): Pink bisque:** Wire joints, molded hair, painted eyes. 4" - $70.00. **Molded hat:** 4" - $285.00 up. **Aviatrix:** 5" - $250.00. **Swivel waist:** 4½" - $350.00. **Molded cap with rabbit ears:** 4½" - $385.00. **Medium quality bisque/artist workmanship:** 5" - $150.00; 7–8" - $250.00.

Molded-on clothes or underwear: Ca. 1890s. Jointed at shoulders only or at shoulders and hips. (Molded-on hat or bonnet are listed below.) **Painted eyes:** Molded hair, molded shoes or bare feet. Excellent artist workmanship. No cracks, chips, or breaks. 4½" - $150.00; 6" - $300.00. (See photo in Series 5, pg. 11.) **Glass eyes:** 5" - $385.00; 7" - $525.00. **Medium to poor quality:** 3" - $85.00; 4" - $100.00; 6" - $140.00.

Molded-on hat or bonnet: In perfect condition. 5–6½" - $365.00 up; 8–9" - $500.00 up. **Stone (porous) bisque:** 4–5" - $135.00; 6–7" - $165.00. **Glass eyes:** 5½" - $450.00; 8" - $600.00. **Swivel neck, early round face:** 7" - $2,300.00.

Marked with maker: (S&H, JDK, A.B.G., mold #369. See photo in Series 9, pg. 9.) Closed mouth, early fine quality face. 8" - $2,000.00; 10" - $2,400.00 up. **Same, with open mouth:** Later quality bisque. 6" - $500.00; 8" - $900.00; 10" - $1,100.00. **K✧R:** 8" - $1,300.00 up.

Hertel, Schwab: See that section.

Limbach Mold #573, 620, etc: Marked with three-leaf clover. 5" - $85.00. **Swivel neck:** 6" - $200.00. **One-piece body and head:** 6" - $150.00. **Glass eyes:** 5" - $150.00; 8" - $265.00. **Baby:** 5" - $95.00; 7" - $130.00; 12" - $400.00.

Schmidt, Bruno: Baby, mold #425. 6" - $235.00.

Mold 415: Aviator with molded-on goggles and cap. 3½" - $250.00; 5" - $400.00; 7" - $525.00.

Pink bisque: 1920s and 1930s. Jointed shoulders and hips. Painted features. Can have molded hair or wig. Excellent condition. 2–3" - $45.00; 4–5½" - $65.00.

Bow loop in hair: 3" - $60.00; 7" - $85.00.

Wrestler (so called), some mold #102: (See photo in Series 7, pg. 10.) Considered French. Fat thighs, arm bent at elbow, open mouth (can have two rows of teeth) or closed mouth. Stocky body, glass eyes, socket head, individual fingers or molded fists. All in good condition. **Painted boots:** 6" - $1,200.00; 8" - $1,600.00; 9" - $2,100.00. **Bare feet:** 5–6" - $1,700.00. **Long painted stockings to above knees:** 6½" - $1,600.00; 8" - $1,900.00. **Jointed elbows and knees:** (See photo in Series 7, pg. 6.) 6" - $1,750.00; 8" - $2,000.00. **Jointed shoulders only:** (See photo in Series 9, pg. 9.) Painted-on two- or three-strap boots, painted eyes, round early face. 6" - $565.00.

Immobilies: Figures with no joints. **Child:** 3" - $50.00 up. **Adults:** 5" - $1,400.00 up. **Santa:** 4" - $125.00. **Child with animal on string:** 4" - $125.00 up.

ALL BISQUE – BABIES

All bisque babies were made in both Germany and Japan, and dolls from either country can be excellent quality or poor quality. Prices are for excellent painting and quality of bisque. There should be no chips, cracks, or breaks. Dressed or nude - 1900; bent limbs - after 1906.

Germany (Jointed necks, shoulders and hips): Wigs or painted hair. **Glass eyes:** 4" - $200.00; 5" - $245.00; 7" - $365.00; 9" - $600.00. **Painted eyes:** 3½" - $85.00; 5" - $140.00; 6½" - $200.00; 8½" - $325.00.

Germany (Jointed at shoulders and hips only): Well-painted features, free-formed thumbs and many have molded bottle in hand. Some have molded-on clothes. 3½" - $65.00; 5" - $120.00.

Germany (character baby): Jointed shoulders and hips, molded hair, painted eyes with character face. 4" - $175.00; 6" - $250.00. **Glass eyes:** 4" - $350.00; 6" - $450.00. **Mold #830, 833, and others:** 8" - $525.00 up; 11" - $1,000.00 up. **Swivel neck, glass eyes:** 6" - $675.00; 10" - $1,200.00 up. **Swivel neck, painted eyes:** 6" - $375.00; 8" - $500.00; 10" - $750.00.

Germany (toddler) #369, 372: Jointed neck, glass eyes, perfect condition. 7" - $725.00; 9" - $1,000.00; 11" - $1,400.00 up.

"Candy Babies": (Can be either German or Japanese.) Ca. 1920s. Generally poorly painted with high bisque color. Were given away at candy counter with purchase. 4" - $25.00; 6" - $40.00.

Pink bisque baby: Ca. 1920s. Jointed at shoulders and hips, painted features and hair, bent baby legs. 2" - $20.00; 4" - $65.00; 8" - $100.00.

Mold #231: (A.M.) Toddler with open mouth, glass eyes. 9" - $1,400.00 up.

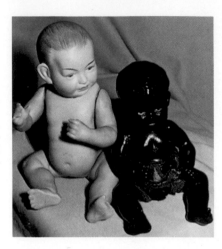

Left: 8" all bisque baby on five-piece bent limb baby body with painted hair and eyes. Right: 6½" baby made of clay like material with painted features and molded hair. One-piece body and head, jointed at hips and shoulders. Marked "A.T." in triangle. 8" - $425.00; 6½" - $350.00. *Courtesy Frasher Doll Auction.*

ALL BISQUE – CHARACTERS

All bisque dolls with character faces or stances were made both in Germany and Japan. The German dolls have finer bisque and workmanship of the painted features. Most bisque character dolls have jointed shoulders only, with some having joints at the hips. A very few have swivel heads. They can have molded-on shoes or be barefooted. Prices are for dolls with no chips, cracks, hairlines or breaks.

8" all bisque Bye-Lo twins. One-piece body and head, sleep eyes. Original. Each - $725.00. *Courtesy Turn of Century Antiques.*

Baby Bo Kaye: Made by Alt, Beck & Gottschalck. Marked with mold **#1394.** 5" - $1,400.00; 7" - $1,800.00.

Baby Bud: Glass eyes, wig: 6–7" - $650.00 up.

Baby Darling, Mold #497, Kestner #178: (Allow more for toddler body.) **Swivel neck, glass eyes:** 5" - $450.00; 9" - $800.00. **One-piece body, painted eyes:** 7" - $425.00; 9" - $625.00; 11" - $825.00 up.

Baby Peggy Montgomery: Made by Louis Amberg. Marked with paper label. 4" - $425.00; 6" - $600.00.

Bonnie Babe: Made by Georgene Averill. Has paper label. 5" - $700.00; 7" - $900.00. **Molded-on clothes:** 6" - $950.00.

Bye-Lo: Made by J.D. Kestner. Has paper label. Jointed neck, glass eyes, solid dome. 4" - $525.00; 6" - $685.00. **Jointed neck, wig, glass eyes:** 5" - $650.00; 8" - $1,200.00. **Painted eyes, molded hair, one-piece body and head:** 5" - $285.00; 7" - $500.00. **Immobilies:** "Salt" and "Pepper" on back or stomach. 3-3½" - $350.00. **One piece:** Various poses. 3" - $350.00.

Campbell Kids: Molded-on clothes, "Dutch" hairstyle. 5" - $245.00.

Chin-Chin: Made by Heubach. 4½" - $325.00. Poor quality: 4½" - $150.00.

Didi, Fefe (Fifi), Chi Chi, Mimi, Veve (Vivi): Made by Orsini. 5–6" - $1,200.00 up. **Painted eyes:** $675.00 up.

Googly: 1911 on. **Glass eyes:** 4" - $385.00, 6" - $600.00. **Painted eyes:** 4" - $300.00; 6" - $475.00. **Glass eyes, swivel neck:** 6" - $650.00; 8" - $1,000.00. **Jointed elbow and/or knees:** (See photo in Series 9, pg. 88.) 6" - $2,600.00; 7–7½" - $3,200.00. **Marked with maker:** Example K✿R. 6½" - $2,600.00 up. **#217, 501, and others:** 4" - $465.00; 6" - $625.00. **#182, 292:** Swivel neck. 4" - $585.00; 6" - $785.00.

Grumpy Boy: Marked "Germany." 4" - $140.00. Marked "Japan": 4" - $50.00.

Happifats: 5" boy or girl. Each - $345.00 up.

Hebee or Shebee: 5" - $500.00. (See photo in Series 5, pg. 11; Series 7, pg. 9.)

Heubach: Molded hair, side glance eyes. Molded ribbon or bows: 7" - $775.00; 9" - $950.00. Wigged: 7" - $950.00.

Bunny Boy or Girl figurine: By Heubach. 5" - $365.00; 8½" - $675.00.

Little Imp: Has hooved feet. 6½" - $475.00.

Kestner: Marked mold **#257, 262,** etc. **Baby:** Glass eyes, swivel head. 9–10" - $1,000.00. **One piece body and head:** 5½–6½" - $300.00.

Max and Moritz: Kestner. See All Bisque – Comic Character. (See photo in Series 7, pg. 12.)

Medic: One piece, uniform molded-on, carries case. (See photo in Series 7, pg. 9.) 3½–4" - $175.00.

Mildred (Prize Baby) #880: 1913. 7" - $1,500.00; 8½" - $1,800.00.

Orsini: Head tilted to side, made in one piece and hands hold out dress. 4" - $500.00; 6" - $750.00.

Our Fairy: Molded hair and painted eyes. (See photo in Series 7, pg. 81.) 9–10" - $1,700.00. **Wig and glass eyes:** 9–10" - $2,000.00.

Our Mary: Has paper label. 5" - $465.00.

Peek-a-boo: By Drayton. 5" - $285.00.

Peterkin: 5" - $275.00; 9" - $525.00.

Peterkin, Tommy: Horsman. 4" - $275.00.

Queue San Baby: Various poses. **Germany:** 5½" - $225.00. **Japan:** 4" - $70.00–90.00.

Scootles: Made by Cameo. 6" - $700.00 up.

Sonny: One-piece body and head. Made by Averill. 5" - $500.00 up. **Glass eyes, swivel neck:** 6–7" - $1,400.00.

Tynie Baby: Made by Horsman. **Glass eyes:** 6" - $1,000.00; 9" - $1,700.00. **Painted eyes:** 6" - $565.00.

Wide Awake Doll: Germany: 7½" - $325.00. Japan: 7½" - $125.00.

ALL BISQUE – NODDERS

"Knotters" are called "nodders" since when their heads are touched, they "nod." The reason they should correctly be called "knotters" is due to the method of stringing. The string passed through a hole in the head and knotted. They can also be made with cutouts on the bodies to take a tiny rod that comes out of the side of the neck. Both styles were made in Germany and Japan, circa 1920s.

Santa Claus or Indian: 6" - $145.00–175.00.

Teddy Bear: 5" - $165.00.

Other Animals: Rabbit, dog, cat,

etc. 3½–5" - $35.00–75.00. **Molded-on clothes:** 4" - $125.00 up.

Comic Characters: 3½–5" - $65.00–235.00 up.

Children/Adults: Made in Germany. 4½–5½" - $35.00–145.00.

Japan/Nippon: 3½" - $20.00; 4½" - $40.00.

Sitting Position: 5" - $150.00 up; 9" - $245.00 up.

ALL BISQUE – JAPANESE

All bisque dolls from Japan vary a great deal in quality. They are jointed at shoulders and may have other joints. Good quality bisque is well painted with no chips or breaks. (Also see All Bisque – Characters and Nodder sections.)

Marked Nippon: The mark "Nippon" ceased in 1923. 4" - $35.00; 6" - $55.00.

"Betty Boop": Bobbed hair style, large painted eyes to side, and one-piece body and head. 4" - $40.00; 6–7" - $65.00.

Child: With molded clothes. 4½" - $30.00; 6" - $45.00.

Child: 1920s and 1930s. Pink or painted bisque with painted features. Jointed at shoulders and hips. Has molded hair or wig. Excellent condition. 3" - $15.00; 4–5" - $27.50; 7" - $45.00 up. **Bow loop in hair:** 4" - $20.00; 7" - $45.00.

Comic Characters: See All Bisque – Comic Characters section.

Occupied Japan: 3½" - $25.00; 5" - $35.00; 7" - $50.00.

Immobilies: Figurines with no joints. (Add 50% more if German.) **Bride & groom cake top:** 6–6½" - $100.00. **Children:** 3–4" - $10.00–20.00; 6–7" - $25.00–45.00. **Teddy Bears:** 3" - $50.00 up. **Indians, Dutch, etc:** 2½" - $25.00 up. **Santa Claus:** 3½" - $65.00 up. **Adults:** 5" - $70.00. **Child with animal on string:** 3½" - $65.00 up.

Bent leg baby: May or may not be jointed at hips and shoulders. Very nice quality. 3½–5" - $30.00–70.00.

Bye-Lo copy: (See photo in Series 6, pg. 12.) 3½" - $95.00, 5" - $145.00. **Medium to poor quality:** 3½–5" - $6.00–45.00.

7" all bisque children marked "Made in Japan." Both have painted molded-on clothes. Each - $60.00. *Courtesy Glorya Woods.*

Annie Rooney, Little: Made in Germany. 4" - $250.00; 7" - $450.00.

Betty Boop: With musical instrument. Made in Japan. 3½" - $50.00 up.

Betty Boop: Fleisher Studios. Made in Japan. 3½" - $30.00 up.

Dick Tracy: Made in Germany. 5" - $185.00.

Made in Japan: Paint washes off easily. 3–4½" - $25.00 up.

Jackie Coogan: Japan. 6½" - $150.00.

Katzenjammer Kids: 4" - $55.00 each ; 6" - $130.00 each. **Mama:** 4" - $60.00; 8" - $110.00. **Papa:** 4" - $65.00; 8" - $165.00. **Uncle Ben:** 4" - $60.00, 8" - $125.00.

Max or Moritz: K☼R, 5–5½". Each - $1,800.00 up.

Mickey Mouse: Walt Disney. 5" - $175.00 up. **With musical instrument:** $200.00 up.

Minnie Mouse: Walt Disney. $200.00 up.

Moon Mullins and Kayo: 4" Mushmouth (black), Uncle Willie, Aunt Mamie, Little Egypt, Emmy, and Lord Plushbottom. Each - $70.00 up.

Orphan Annie: 3½" - $60.00. **Nodder:** $70.00 up.

Mr. Peanut: Made in Japan. 4" - $30.00.

Our Gang: Boys: 3½" - $50.00. Girls: 3½" - $60.00.

Popeye: 3" - $125.00 up.

Rare 3½" "Munchkin" flower from the *Wizard of Oz* movie. Comes with different hair and flower colors but molded-on clothes are nearly the same. $145.00 up. *Courtesy Ellen Dodge.*

Seven Dwarfs: Walt Disney. 3½". Each - $85.00 up.

Skeezix: 3½" - $75.00.

Skippy: (See photo in Series 6, pg. 13.) 5" - $110.00.

Snow White: Japan. 5½" - $100.00. **Boxed with Dwarfs:** $625.00 up. (See photo in Series 6, pg. 13.) Germany: $800.00.

Three Bears/Goldilocks: Japan: Boxed set. $325.00 up. Germany: $600.00.

ALL BISQUE – PAINTED BISQUE

Painted bisque has a layer of paint over the bisque which has not been fired. The color can be washed off or can come off with the glue of a wig. These dolls have molded hair, painted features, painted-on shoes and socks, and are jointed at shoulders and hips. All should be in good condition with no paint chips.

Boy or Girl: German: 3" - $25.00; 4½–5" - $55.00-60.00. Japan: 3" - $15.00; 5" - $25.00.

Baby: Germany: 3½" - $50.00; 5" - $60.00. Japan: 3" - $15.00; 5" - $30.00.

Alt, Beck & Gottschalck was located at Nauendorf, Germany, near Ohrdruf, as a porcelain factory from 1854. It is not known when they started making dolls. The firm was the maker of both the **"Byelo"** baby and **"Bonnie Babe"** for the distributor, George Borgfeldt. The leading authorities in Germany, and now the United States, have assigned nearly all the turned-head dolls as being made by Alt, Beck & Gottschalck, with the bodies being made by **Wagner & Zetzsche.** It is claimed that this firm produced dolls with tinted bisque and molded hair (see that section of this book), as well as wigged turned head and shoulder head dolls and also dolls made of china. There is a vast variation to the eyebrows among these dolls. Prices are given for just one eyebrow style. (Also see All Bisque section.)

Marks:

Babies: After 1909. Open mouth, some have pierced nostrils, bent leg baby body and are wigged. Prices will be higher if on toddler body or has flirty eyes. Allow more for toddler body. Clean, nicely dressed and with no cracks, chips or hairlines. 12" - $375.00; 16" - $500.00; 21" - $800.00; 26" - $1,600.00.

Child #1361, 1362, 1367, etc.: Socket head on jointed composition body, sleep or set eyes. No crack, chips or hairlines. Clean and nicely dressed. 12–13" - $350.00; 18" - $465.00; 23" - $550.00; 26" - $675.00; 32" - $1,000.00; 36" - $1,300.00; 40–42" - $2,000.00.

Character child or baby: Ca. 1910 on. Socket head on jointed composition body, glass or painted eyes, open mouth.

33" "Sweet Nell" with large sleep eyes and open mouth. Marked "1362 A.B.G." $1,050.00 up. *Courtesy Turn of Century Antiques.*

Nicely dressed with good wig or molded hair with no hairlines, cracks or chips. **#630:** 22" - $2,400.00. **#911, 916:** Closed mouth. 20" - $2,400.00. **#1322, 1352, 1361:** 12" - $365.00; 15" - $485.00, 18" - $565.00, 22" - $825.00. **#1357, 1358, 1359:** Molded center part hair, bun , and molded ribbon. Deep dimples. Wide open/closed mouth. **Painted eyes:** 15" - $600.00; 20" - $1,850.00. **Glass eyes:** 15" - $965.00; 20" - $2,300.00. **#1362 "Sweet Nell":** (See photo in Series 9, pg. 166.) 16" - $675.00; 20" - $975.00. **In box:** 27" - $1,250.00 up. **#1367:** 15" - $475.00; 19" - $725.00.

Turned shoulder head: 1880s. Bald head or plaster pate. Kid body with bisque lower arms. All in good condition with no chips, hairline and nicely dressed. Dolls marked "DEP" or "Germany" date after 1888. Some have the Wagner & Zetzsche mark on head or paper label inside top of body. Some mold numbers include: **639, 698, 784, 870,**

890, 911, 912, 916, 990, 1000, 1008, 1028, 1032, 1044, 1046, 1064, 1123, 1127, 1142, 1210, 1234, 1235, 1254, 1288, 1304. Glass eyes, closed mouth: (Allow more for molded bonnet or elaborate hairdo.) 12–13" - $550.00; 16" - $725.00; 18" - $950.00; 22" - $1,200.00; 26" - $2,000.00. **Glass eyes, open mouth.** 16–17" - $385.00; 21" - $525.00; 25" - $675.00. **Painted eyes, open mouth:** 14" - $250.00; 20" - $400.00. **Painted eyes, closed mouth:** 14" - $385.00; 20" - $550.00.

Bisque shoulder head: 1880s. Molded hair, cloth or kid body, bisque lower limbs. No damage and nicely dressed. Same mold numbers as turned shoulder head dolls above. (Allow much more for molded bonnet or hat.) **Painted eyes, closed mouth:** 15" - $345.00; 18" - $475.00; 22" - $550.00. **Glass eyes, closed mouth:** 15" - $700.00; 18" - $875.00; 22" - $1,000.00. **Painted eyes, open mouth:** 15" - $225.00; 21" - $400.00. **Glass eyes, open mouth:** 15" - $400.00; 21" - $850.00.

Glazed china shoulder head: 1880s. Blonde or black hair, china limbs (or leather), cloth body and nicely dressed with no damage. **Mold #784, 786, 1000, 1003, 1008, 1028, 1032, 1046, 1142, 1144, 1210.** May also have mark ✗ or *№.*. 15" - $350.00; 19" - $425.00; 23" - $775.00.

Louis Amberg & Sons were in business from 1878 to 1930 in New York City and Cincinnati, Ohio.

Prices are for dolls in perfect condition, with no cracks, chips or breaks, clean and nicely dressed. (Allow more for original clothes and wig.)

Marks:

L.A. & S. 1926

22" "Baby Peggy Montgomery" with closed smiling mouth, dimples, sleep eyes, and original wig with bangs. Bisque shoulder head on kid body with bisque lower arms. Marked "1924/L.A.&S. N.Y./Germany 50-983/2." $2,800.00. *Courtesy Elizabeth Burke.*

A^MBER_G
DOLLS
THE WORLD
STANDARD
MADE
IN
U.S.A.

AMBERG
L.A. & S. 1928

Baby Peggy (Montgomery): 1923 and 1924. Closed mouth, socket head. **Mold #973 (smiling) or 972 (solemn):** 17" - $2,400.00; 22" - $2,800.00.

Baby Peggy mold #983 or 982: Shoulder head. 17" - $2,400.00; 23" - $2,800.00.

Baby Peggy: All bisque. 3½" - $400.00; 5" - $650.00.

Baby Peggy: 1923. Composition head and limbs with cloth body. Painted eyes with molded lower eyelids. Closed mouth with visible teeth or painted teeth. Molded brown short bobbed hairdo or mohair wig. 14" - $325.00; 17" - $500.00; 21" - $700.00.

Baby, mold #88678: Cloth body. 16–17" - $1,200.00; 25" - $1,600.00.

Charlie Chaplin: 1915–1920s. Portrait head of composition with painted features, composition hands, cloth body and legs. Black suit and white shirt. Cloth tag on sleeve or inside seam of coat. Marked "Amberg. Essamay Film Co." (See photo in Series 1, pg. 79.) 13–14" - $485.00; 20" - $765.00.

Newborn Babe: Bisque head with cloth body and can have celluloid, composition or rubber hands. Lightly painted hair, sleep eyes, closed mouth with protruding upper lip. 1914 and reissued in 1924. Marks: "L.A.&S. 1914/**G45520** Germany." Some will be marked "L. Amberg and Son/**886**" and some will be marked "Copyright by Louis Amberg." (See photo in Series 7, pg. 15.) 8" - $365.00; 11" - $425.00; 14" - $500.00; 18" - $825.00.

Newborn Babe: Open mouth version. Marked "L.A.&S. **371**." 10" - $400.00; 15" - $450.00.

Mibs: Marked "L.A.& S. 1921/ Germany" and can have two different paper labels with one "Amberg Dolls/ Please Love Me/I'm Mibs," and some with the same label, but does not carry the name of Amberg. Molded hair with long strand down center of forehead. Composition head and limbs with cloth body,

painted eyes. All in good condition. (See photo in Series 6, pg. 17.) 12" - $550.00; 16–17" - $850.00.

Mibs: All bisque. May be marked "1921" on back and have paper label with name. 3½" - $250.00; 5" - $425.00.

Sue (Edwina, Peggy, or "It"): 1928. All composition with painted features, molded hair and with a waist that swivels on a large ball attached to the torso. Jointed shoulders, neck and hips. Molded hair has side part and swirl bangs across forehead. Marked "Amberg/Pat. Pen./L.A.&S." (See photo in Series 6, pg. 17.) 14" - $425.00

Twist bodies (Tiny Tots, Teenie Weenies): 1926, 1928. All composition with swivel waist made from large ball attached to torso. Boy or girl with molded hair and painted features. Tag attached to clothes: "An Amberg Doll/Body Twist/ Pat. Pend. #32018." 7½–8½" - $180.00.

Vanta Baby: 1927. Composition head and limbs with fat legs. Cloth body, spring strung, sleep eyes, open/closed mouth with two teeth. Made to advertise Vanta baby garments. Marked "Vanta Baby-Amberg (or L.A.&S.)" 18" - $265.00; 23" - $375.00. **Same but with bisque head, glass eyes, open mouth:** (See photo in Series 6, pg. 17.) 18" - $1,100.00; 24" - $1,700.00. **Glass eyes, closed mouth:** 18" - $1,400.00; 24" - $2,000.00.

Amfelt Art Dolls: Cloth bodies with cloth or felt limbs and metal disk joints. Fingers are stitched with free standing thumb. Various materials, such as composition and papier maché, were used for the heads. Doll clothes and bonnets were made of felt. 15" - $350.00; 18" - $475.00; 22" - $585.00.

Armand Marseille made the majority of their dolls after the 1880s and into the 1920s, so they are some of the most often found dolls today. The factory was at Koppelsdorf, Germany. A.M. marked dolls can be of excellent to very poor quality. The finer the bisque and artist workmanship, the higher the price. This company also made a great many heads for other companies, such as George Borgfeldt, Amberg (Baby Peggy), Hitz, Jacobs & Kassler, Otto Gans, Cuno & Otto Dressel, etc. They were marked with "A.M." or full name "Armand Marseille."

Prices are for perfect dolls with no chips, cracks, breaks or hairline cracks. Dolls need to be clean and nicely dressed.

Mold #370, 326, 309, 273, 270, 375, 376, 920, 957: Kid or kidaleen bodies, open mouths. 12" - $165.00; 16" - $185.00; 20" - $265.00; 22" - $385.00; 25" - $475.00.

Mold #390, 266, 300, 310, (not "Googly"), 384, 390N, 391, 395: Socket head, jointed body and open mouth. 14" - $200.00; 17" - $285.00; 19" - $350.00; 23" - $485.00; 26" - $600.00; 29" - $725.00; 32" -

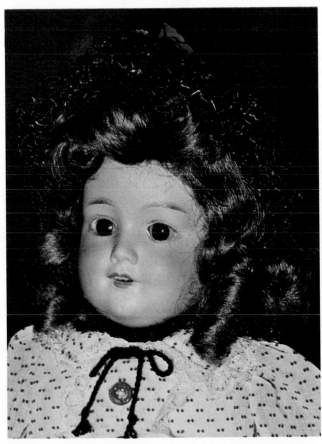

17" "Baby Betty" with jointed composition child body. Made for Butler Bros. in 1912. Marked "Baby/0½/Betty/D.R.G.M." $600.00.

This is a very beautiful example of a 16" Armand Marseille #390. Has open mouth and sleep eyes with hair lashes. On fully jointed body. Excellent quality bisque. $285.00. *Courtesy Kathy Riddick.*

$850.00; 36" - $1,200.00; 42" - $2,000.00. **Closed mouth:** 6" - $200.00; 8" - $300.00. **Crude body:** 8" - $150.00; 10" - $245.00. **Jointed body:** 8" - $245.00; 10" - $300.00. **Flapper:** 5-piece body with long painted stockings. 9" - $265.00.

Large Sizes Marked Just A.M.: Jointed bodies, socket head and open mouths. 32"- $1,300.00; 35" - $1,500.00; 40" - $2,000.00.

Mold #1776, 1890, 1892, 1893, 1894, 1896, 1897 (which can be a shoulder head or have a socket head); **1898, 1899, 1901, 1902, 1903, 1908, 1909, 3200:** Kid or kidaleen body, open mouth. (See below for prices if on composition bodies.) 10" - $165.00; 14" - $225.00; 17" - $345.00; 20" - $385.00; 24" - $475.00; 27–28" - $675.00. **On composition jointed body:** 10" - $300.00; 14" - $350.00; 17" - $525.00; 20" - $600.00; 24" - $700.00; 28" - $800.00; 32" - $975.00; 36" - $1,300.00.

Alma, Floradora, Mabel, Lilly, Lissy, Darling, My Dearie, My Girlie, My Playmate, Sunshine, Dollar Princess, Duchess, 3700, 14008: 1890s. Kid or kidaleen body. 12" - $200.00; 15" - $265.00; 18" - $345.00; 22" - $365.00; 26" - $485.00; 30" - $900.00. **On composition body:** 15" - $350.00; 19" - $465.00; 24" - $575.00; 27" - $775.00; 32" - $1,000.00.

Queen Louise, Beauty, Columbia, Jubilee, Majestic, My Companion, Pansy, Princess, Rosebud, Sadie: Kid or kidaleen body. 14" - $275.00; 17" - $425.00; 22" - $500.00; 25" - $600.00; 28" - $700.00; 32" - $950.00 up. **On composition body:** 12" - $225.00; 15" - $300.00; 18" - $500.00; 22" - $550.00; 26" - $650.00; 29" - $875.00; 30" - $1,000.00; 34" - $1,200.00.

#2000: Kid or kidaleen body, glass eyes. 14" - $725.00; 17" - $900.00. **Jointed body:** 14" - $900.00; 17" - $1,100.00.

Babies (infant style): Some from 1910; others from 1924. Can be on composition bodies, or have cloth bodies with curved or straight cloth legs. (Add $100.00–150.00 more for toddler babies.)

Mold #340, 341, 345: With closed mouth. **My Dream Baby**, also called **Rock-A-Bye Baby**. Made for the Arranbee Doll Co. **Composition body:** 6–7" - $175.00; 9" - $235.00; 12" - $350.00; 14" - $425.00; 16" - $500.00; 20" - $600.00; 24" - $875.00; 28" - $1,100.00. **Toddler:** 20" - $700.00; 25" - $1,000.00.

Mold #345, 351: With open mouth. Same as above, but some will also be marked **"Kiddiejoy"** or **"Our Pet."** 7–8" - $185.00; 10" - $250.00; 14" - $475.00; 20" - $685.00; 28" - $1,200.00.

Mold #340, 341 or 345, 347, 351: Twin puppets in basket - $650.00 up. Hand puppet, single doll - $350.00 up.

Mold #341, 345, 351 ("Kiddiejoy" or "Our Pet"): With fired-on black or brown color. See Black section. (See photo of #345 in Series 5, pg. 17.)

Babies, mold #256, 259, 326, 327, 328, 329, 360, 750, 790, 900, 927, 970,

971, 975, 980, 984, 985, 990, 991, 992, 995, 996, 1321, 1330, 1330A, 1333: 1910 on. (Add $100.00–150.00 for toddler bodies or flirty eyes.) 9" - $265.00; 12" - $375.00; 14" - $550.00; 17" - $675.00; 20" - $775.00; 23" - $850.00. **Same mold numbers, but painted bisque:** 13–14" - $225.00; 17" - $350.00; 20" - $450.00; 23" - $600.00.

Character Babies: 1910 on. (Add $100.00–150.00 for toddler body.) Composition jointed body. Can have open mouth or open/closed mouth.

Mold # 225: 1916. Baby, toddler. (Also see child.) Glass eyes, upper and lower teeth. 16" - $3,200.00; 19" - $3,800.00.

Mold #233: 9" - $265.00; 13" - $525.00; 16" - $650.00; 19" - $800.00.

Mold #248, 251 with open/closed mouth: 12" - $1,600.00; 15" - $1,750.00. **Open mouth:** 15" - $850.00.

Mold #327, 328: 9" - $250.00; 13" - $400.00; 17" - $575.00; 21" - $750.00.

Mold #346: 17" - $685.00; 22" - $750.00; 25" - $875.00.

Mold #347: 15" - $500.00; 18" - $685.00.

Mold #352: (See photo in Series 7, pg. 18.) 9" - $250.00; 14" - $425.00; 17" - $600.00; 25" - $1,100.00.

Mold #355: A. Eller/3K. Closed mouth, sweet face. 11–12" - $575.00; 16" - $745.00.

Mold #362: 10" - $265.00; 16" - $600.00; 20" - $800.00.

Mold #410: Two rows of teeth, some are retractable. 15" - $1,200.00; 17" - $1,500.00; 22" - $1,750.00.

Mold #518: 15" - $550.00; 21" - $650.00.

Mold #506A, 560A: 12" - $485.00; 14" - $625.00; 19" - $900.00.

Mold #560, 570: Open/closed mouth. 6½" - $250.00; 12" - $500.00; 16" - $1,500.00; 20" - $1,850.00.

Mold #550, 580, 590: (See photos in Series 1, pg. 48; Series 4, pg. 18; Series 7, pg. 19.) **Open/closed mouth:** 12–13" -

11½" toddler with sleep eyes, open/closed mouth, and molded tongue. On five-piece composition body. Also can be on fully jointed body (increase value with this kind of body). Marked "A.M. 251/G.B./Germany/A.0M./D.R.G.M. 248." $1,600.00. *Courtesy Turn of Century Antiques.*

$1,200.00; 16" - $1,600.00; 20" - $2,000.00. **Open mouth:** 12" - $625.00; 18" - $950.00.

Mold #750: Character face. Rare. 14" - $1,350.00; 17" - $2,000.00.

Mold #920: Cloth body, shoulder head. 21" - $985.00 up.

Mold #970: 18" - $575.00; 22" - $825.00; 26" - $1,050.00.

Baby Gloria (Mold #240): (See photo in Series 5, pg. 18.) 10" - $365.00; 15" - $525.00; 17" - $950.00; 22" - $1,200.00.

Baby Phyllis: Heads by Armand Marseille. Painted hair, closed mouth. 12" - $425.00; 17" - $650.00; 21" - $1,100.00.

Baby Florence: 12" - $550.00; 16" - $825.00; 19" - $1,300.00.

Baby Betty: 1890s. Jointed composition child body, but few heads found on bent limb baby body. (See photo in Series 8, pg. 20.) 13" - $400.00; 17" - $600.00; 20" - $700.00. **Kid body:** 15" - $225.00; 18" - $475.00.

Fany Baby: Mold #231 along with incised "Fany." Can be baby, toddler or child. With wig: 16" - $4,500.00; 20" - $6,000.00.

Fany Baby: Mold #230 along with incised "Fany." Molded hair. 16" - $5,000.00; 19"- $6,400.00; 24" - $8,000.00.

Just Me: Mold #310. See Googly section.

Melitta: (See photo in Series 8, pg. 20.) **Baby:** 16" - $550.00; 19" - $750.00. **Toddler:** 20" - $1,000.00; 25" - $1,500.00.

Character Child: 1910 on. May have wig, molded hair, glass or intaglio painted eyes and some will have fully closed mouths while others have open/closed mouth. For these prices, doll must be in excellent condition and have no damage.

10" "Just Me" with painted bisque. Has closed mouth and sleep, googly eyes made of glass. All original. Shown with 13½" Kestner, mold #260. It has sleep eyes, mohair wig, and jointed "flapper" body. 10" - $1,200.00; 13½" - $975.00. *Courtesy Turn of Century Antiques.*

10" "Baby Gloria" has painted molded hair, sleep eyes, deep cheek dimples, and open mouth with two upper teeth. Body and limbs are cloth with composition hands. Original dress tagged "Baby Gloria/RBL/New York." $365.00. *Courtesy Glorya Woods.*

Mold #225 (Little Mary): Open mouth with two rows of teeth. Glass eyes. (See photo in Pat Smith's *Armand Marseille 1865–1925* book, pg. 133.) 15" - $3,500.00; 18" - $4,000.00.

Mold #250: 12" - $650.00; 16" - $850.00; 19" - $1,200.00.

Mold #251 with open/closed mouth: 16" - $1,800.00; 19" - $2,100.00. **Open mouth:** 16" - $950.00.

Mold #340: 15" - $2,850.00.

Mold #345: (See photo in Series 5, pg. 17.) 11–12" - $1,100.00; 16" - $1,900.00.

Mold #350: Socket head, glass eyes, closed mouth. 9" - $950.00; 16" - $2,000.00; 24" - $3,600.00.

Mold #360: 14" - $465.00; 18" - $850.00.

Mold #372 "Kiddiejoy": Kid body, molded hair, glass eyes. (See photo in Series 5, pg. 18.) 12" - $465.00; 16" - $600.00; 18" - $850.00; 22" - $1,200.00.

Mold #400: Glass eyes, socket head and closed mouth. (See photo in Series 8, pg. 21; Series 9, pg. 22.) 12" - $1,600.00; 14" - $2,200.00; 17" - $2,950.00; 20" - $3,400.00.

Mold #401, 449: Painted eyes, socket head and closed mouth. (See photo for #401 in Series 3, pg. 39.) 9" - $485.00; 16" - $1,200.00; 19" - $1,600.00.

Mold #450: Socket head, glass eyes and closed mouth. 14" - $725.00; 17" - $1,000.00; 21" - $1,700.00.

Mold #500, 520: Molded hair, intaglio eyes, open/closed mouth. (See photo for #500 in Series 3, pg. 39.) 9" - $450.00; 17" - $1,100.00; 22" - $1,700.00.

Mold #500, 520, 620, 630, 640: Wigged, glass eyes and open/closed mouth. **Composition, jointed body:** 9" - $600.00; 16" - $1,300.00; 20" - $1,800.00. **Same, with kid body:** 16" - $1,000.00; 20" - $1,500.00.

Mold #550, 600, 640: (See photo in Series 7, pg. 19 and Series 8, pg. 21.) **Molded hair, painted eyes:** 12" - $950.00; 16" - $1,600.00. **Glass eyes:** 12" - $1,800.00; 16" - $3,000.00; 18" - $3,400.00. **Closed mouth, dimples:** 15" - $1,800.00.

Mold #570, 590 with open mouth: (See photos in Series 4, pg. 18; Series 7, pg. 19.) 10" - $485.00; 16" - $900.00. **Open/closed mouth:** 17" - $2,000.00.

Mold #700: (See photo in Series 8, pg. 21 and Series 9, pg. 23.) **Glass eyes:** 12" - $2,000.00; 14–15" - $3,000.00; 17" - $3,500.00. **Painted eyes:** 15" - $2,000.00.

Mold #701, 709, 711: Glass eyes, closed mouth, sweet expression. 9" - $1,100.00; 16" - $2,700.00.

Mold #800, 820: Child. Glass eyes, open/closed mouth. (See photos in Series 6, pg. 21; Series 8, pg. 21; Series 10, pg. 23.) 13" - $1,500.00; 16" - $2,200.00; 20" - $2,850.00.

20" closed mouth character girl with painted bisque five-piece body. Has sleep eyes with hair lashes. Original, circa 1930. Marked "A. 449 M." $1,400.00.

Mold #950: Painted hair and eyes, open mouth. 12" - $675.00; 16" - $1,000.00.

Character marked only "A.M.": Closed mouth. (See photo in Series 4, pg. 17.) **Intaglio eyes:** 17" - $4,600.00. **Glass eyes:** 18" - $5,200.00.

Googly: See Googly section.

Black/Brown Dolls: See that section.

Adult Lady Dolls: 1910–1920s. Adult face with long, thin jointed limbs. Knee joint is above knee area.

Mold #300: 10" - $1,400.00; 14" - $1,800.00.

Mold #400, 401 with closed mouth: 10" - $1,400.00; 15" - $2,300.00; 18" - $2,600.00. **Open mouth:** 10" - $800.00; 15" - $1,200.00; 18" - $1,500.00.

Mold #800: Lady with thin face, closed mouth, and glass eyes. High heel feet. (See photo in Doll Values 10, pg. 23.) 9" - $985.00; 12" - $1,200.00.

Painted bisque, mold #400, 401, 449: 15" - $800.00; 18" - $1,000.00.

Painted bisque, mold #242, 244, 246, etc.: 15" - $400.00; 19" - $650.00; 26" - $950.00.

Biscoloid, mold #378, 966, etc.: Like painted bisque but material under paint more plastic type. 16" - $500.00; 18" - $725.00.

ARNOLD, MAX

Max Arnold made dolls from 1876 into the 1920s in Germany.

Mark:

M.O.A.
(for Max Oscar Arnold)

Child: Marked **150, 200,** or just M.O.A. **Excellent bisque:** 12" - $400.00; 15" - $545.00; 21" - $725.00; 23" - $845.00; 30" - $1,250.00. **Poor to medium bisque:** 15" - $165.00; 20" - $300.00; 24" - $450.00. **Baby:** 12" - $165.00; 16" - $285.00; 19" - $500.00.

20" with open mouth and fully jointed body. Clothes may be original. Marked "MOA" inside star with "200/Welsh/Made in Germany" under it. $300.00. *Courtesy Jeanne Venner.*

A.T.

A. Thuillier made dolls in Paris from 1875 to 1893 and may be the maker of the dolls marked with "A.T." A.T. marked dolls can be found on wooden, jointed composition or kid bodies and can range in sizes from 14" to 30". The dolls can have closed mouths or open mouths with two rows of teeth. The following prices are for marked A.T. dolls on correct body, clean, beautiful face, dressed nicely and with no damage, such as a hairline

cracks, chips or breaks. (See photos in Series 7, pgs. 21–22.)

Marks:

A.T. N°3
A N°6 T
A. 8 T.

Closed mouth: Jointed composition body. (See photos in Series 7, pg. 21–22; Series 8, pg. 23.) 14" - $37,000.00; 16" - $42,000.00; 19" - $48,000.00; 24" - $52,000.00.

Kid body, closed mouth: Bisque lower arms. 16" - $42,000.00; 19" - $48,000.00; 23" - $50,000.00.

Open mouth: Jointed composition body. (See photos in Series 9, pg. 24; Series 10, pg. 25.) 15" - $11,000.00; 18" - $14,500.00; 22" - $19,000.00; 26" - $25,000.00.

26" with closed mouth and on French jointed, fashion-style body. Silk faille dress and hat original. Marked "A. 12 T." $58,000.00. This quality and all original - $68,000.00. *Courtesy Frasher Doll Auctions.*

AVERILL, GEORGENE (MADAME HENDREN)

Georgene Averill used the business names of Madame Georgene Dolls, Averill Mfg. Co., Georgene Novelties and Madame Hendren. Averill began making dolls in 1913 and designed several for George Borgfeldt.

First prices are for extra clean dolls. Second prices for dolls with chips, craze lines, dirt, or missing some or all of the original clothes.

Baby Georgene or Baby Hendren: 1918 on. Composition/cloth and marked with name on head. (Add more if tagged and mint in box.) Original. (See photo in Series 4, pg. 23.) 16" - $250.00, $70.00; 22" - $300.00, $85.00; 26" - $400.00 up, $100.00.

Baby Yawn: Composition with closed eyes and yawn mouth. 15" - $450.00, $150.00; 18" - $600.00, $200.00.

Body Twist Dolls: 1927. Composition with large ball joint at waist, painted hair and features. 13–14" - $425.00, $90.00.

Bonnie Babe, mold #1368-140 or 1402: 1926. Bisque head, cloth body, open mouth/two lower teeth, molded hair and composition arms/or hands. 15" - $1,000.00; 18" - $1,300.00; 24" - $1,900.00 up. **Celluloid head:** 15–16" - $725.00 up. **Composition body, bisque head:** (See photo in Series 8, pg. 11.) 10" - $985.00; 15" - $1,500.00.

Bonnie Babe: All bisque. See All Bisque section.

Cloth Dolls: 1930s. Mask face with painted features, yarn hair, cloth body. First price for clean dolls; second for soiled dolls.

Characters: Such as **Becassine,** etc. 1950s. Must be mint. (See photo in Series 7, pg. 24; Series 8, pg. 24.) 13–14" - $450.00 up.

International: (See photos in Series 5, pg. 22; Series 9, pg. 27.) 12" - $95.00, $20.00; 15" - $165.00, $60.00; 20" - $265.00.

One of Georgene Averill's animal dolls of the 1930s. Cloth body and limbs. Note the "Raggedy Ann" style lower legs. Felt hands and black feet. Plush and velvet ears. The head is composition painted white with the features painted on. Long tail felt jacket suggest he may be a character from "Alice in Wonderland." $600.00 up. *Courtesy Ellen Dodge.*

Children: (Add more if mint in box.) 12" - $90.00; $30.00; 15" - $165.00, $70.00; 20" - $285.00, $80.00; 22" - $325.00, $100.00; 26" - (See photo in Series 9, pg. 27.) **Musical:** 16" - $250.00, $70.00. **Brownies:** 14" - $200.00, $70.00. **Scout:** (See photo in Series 7, pg. 23.) 14" - $250.00, $80.00.

Tear Drop Baby: One tear painted on cheek. 16" - $325.00, $60.00.

Animals: 1930s on. Must be mint. **B'rer Rabbit, Fuzzy Wuzzy, Nurse Jane, Uncle Wiggily, etc.:** (See photos in Series 7, pg. 25; Series 8, pg. 25; Series 9, pg. 27.) 18" - $600.00 up. **All bisque cat (mold #891) and dog (mold #890):** Jointed shoulder, neck, and hips. Glass eyes, modeled-on booties. 5–6" - $1,800.00 up; 10–11" - $2,800.00 up.

Children: Composition, cloth body. Perfect and original. 14–15" - $250.00, 18" - $375.00; less than mint - $145.00. **Scout, Pirate, Brownie, Storybook (Little Boy Blue, Mother Goose, Captain Kidd, etc.):** 14" - $300.00, $100.00; 18" - $500.00, $200.00. **"Patsy" type:** 14" - $285.00, $100.00.

Comic Characters (Alvin, Little Lulu with round face, fat cheeks, **Nancy, Sluggo, Tubby Tom):** 1944–1951. All cloth with mask faces and painted features. 14" - $500.00. **Little Lulu:** In rare cowgirl outfit. 14" - $585.00.

12" composition skier and skater, designed by Harriet Flanders for Georgene Averill, were on the market in 1937. This size has painted eyes; larger sizes have sleep eyes. Molded hair along with tufts of flossy yarn hair. Both are original. Each (in this mint condition) - $245.00. *Courtesy Ellyn McCorkell.*

Dolly Dingle: (For Grace Drayton) All cloth. 12" - $400.00, $90.00.

Dolly Record: 1922. Composition with record player in back. (See photo in Series 10, pg. 26.) 26" - $550.00, $250.00.

Googly: Composition/cloth. 12" - $250.00, $70.00; 14" - $325.00, $100.00; 16" - $465.00, $150.00.

Indian, Cowboy, Sailor, Soldier, Scout, Pirate: Composition/cloth, molded hair or wig, sometimes yarn hair, painted features. (See Indian photo in Series 1, pg. 57.) 10" - $145.00, $35.00; 14" - $385.00, $100.00.

Krazy Kat: 1916. Felt, unjointed. (See photo in Series 6, pg. 27.) 14" - $350.00, $85.00. 18" - $500.00, $125.00.

Snookums: 1927. Composition/cloth. Smile face, character from George McManus's "The Newlyweds." 14" - $375.00, $100.00.

Vinyl Head, Laughing Child: With oil cloth body. 26" - $185.00, $70.00.

13½" "Indian" by Georgene Averill. All cloth and original. Inset lashes, painted face mask, and yarn hair.

Whistling Dan: 1925–1929. Sailor, cowboy, policeman, child, etc. (See photo in Series 6, pg. 26.) 14" - $250.00, $85.00; 16" - $300.00, $100.00.

Whistling Rufus/Nell: Black doll. Whistles well. (See photo in Series 10, pg. 27.) 14" - $425.00, $125.00.

Whistling Dolly Dingle: 14" - $425.00, $125.00.

Babies, Infant Types: 1920s. Composition/cloth, painted hair, sleep eyes. 15" - $185.00, $80.00; 20" - $265.00, $100.00; 24" - $350.00, $145.00.

Lenci types: Circa late 1920s. Flocked type faces, cloth body, rest composition. Felt and organdy costumes. Stamped on back "Genuine Madame Hendren Doll/Made in U.S.A." Dress tagged. 15" - $000.00; 18" - $000.00.

27" "Katrinka." Unusually large size. She is a product of Georgene Novelties and made in United States. Mask face with painted features, inset lashes, yarn hair, floral print body, and wooden shoes. $400.00. *Courtesy Susan Giradot.*

Bisque heads for Baby Bo-Kaye were made by Alt, Beck & Gottschalck in 1925. Celluloid heads were made in Germany, and composition heads were made in the U.S. by Cameo Doll Company. Designer of the doll was Joseph L. Kallus, owner of Cameo Doll Co. (See photo in Series 8, pg. 26; Series 9, pg. 28.)

Bisque head, mold #1307-124, 1394-30, 1407: Molded hair, open mouth, glass eyes, cloth body, composition limbs. In overall good condition with no damage. 17" - $2,800.00; 20" - $3,100.00.

Celluloid head: Same as bisque head description. 13" - $400.00; 16" - $750.00.

Composition head: Same as above description. 14" - $550.00. Light craze: 16" - $425.00. Cracks and/or chips: 16" - $125.00.

All bisque: 5" - $1,400.00; 7" - $1,800.00.

BAHR & PROSCHILD

Bahr & Proschild operated at Ohrdruf, Germany from 1871 into the late 1920s. They also made celluloid dolls (1910).

Marks:

Character Baby: 1909 on. Bent limbs, sleep eyes, wigged and open mouths. Allow $100.00–150.00 more for toddler body. Clean, nicely dressed and no damage.

Baby, mold #592: 12" - $675.00. **Toddler:** 12" - $850.00.

Mold #585, 586, 587, 604, 620, 624, 630, 678, 619, 641: 14" - $485.00; 17" - $650.00; 20" - $750.00; 24" - $950.00. **Toddler:** 9–10" - $600.00; 16" - $865.00; 19" - $1,100.00.

Mold #169: 12" - $500.00; 18" - $800.00; 22" - $975.00.

Character Child: Can be on fully jointed composition body or toddler body. Ca 1910. Nicely dressed, clean, no damage. Can have molded hair or be wigged.

Mold #526 and other 500s, 2072, or marked B.P. baby body: 1910. Open/closed mouth. 14" - $3,200.00; 18" - $4,100.00.

Mold # in 200 and 300 series: Now attributed to Bahr & Proschild. **Child, open mouth:** Circa 1880s. Full cheeks, jointed composition body. Can be on French body. Prior to recent findings, these dolls were attributed to Kestner.

Mold #204, 224, 239, 246, 273, 274, 275, 277, 281, 286, 289, 293, 297, 309, 325, 332, 340, 379, 394, etc.: 1880s. Same as previous listing. **Five-piece body:** 8" - $350.00. **Fully jointed body:** 8" - $350.00. 10" - $500.00; 14" - $675.00; 17" - $750.00; 20" - $850.00; 23" - $1,000.00. **Kid bodies, open mouth:** 16" - $400.00; 18" - $550.00; 24" - $675.00.

Mold # in 200 or 300 series, closed mouth: Circa 1880. Same as above. **Dome head** or **"Belton type,"** socket head on composition or kid body with bisque shoulder plate. 12" - $1,600.00; 16" - $2,000.00; 21" - $2,600.00; 24" - $3,200.00.

Mold #224: Light cheek dimples. Open mouth, large glass eyes. Looks very much like Simon & Halbig. 16" - $950.00; 22" - $1,300.00.
Mold #360: Character face with "long" look, glass eyes, full cheeks. 22" - $1,250.00. **Open mouth:** 25" - $1,500.00.
Mold #2025: Painted eyes, closed mouth: 16" - $1,500.00. **Glass eyes:** 19" - $4,000.00.
Mold #2072, child: Closed mouth, glass eyes. (See photo in Series 10, pg. 29.) 18" - $3,800.00. **Toddler:** 22" - $4,350.00.

Adorable 13" Bahr & Proschild toddler. Character with open mouth and two upper teeth. Unusual size. $1,600.00. *Courtesy Barbara Earnshaw-Cain.*

BATHING DOLLS

Bathing dolls of the 1920s can be in any position, including standing on a base. They are all bisque and will have painted-on bathing costumes or be nude. They were made in Germany and some in the United States. Prices are for dolls with no damage, chips or breaks. Must be clean.
Excellent quality bisque and artist workmanship, painted eyes: 3" - $250.00; 6" - $400.00; 9" - $525.00 up. **Glass eyes:** 5" - $400.00; 6" - $650.00. **Swivel neck:** 5" - $675.00; 6" - $725.00. **With animal:** 5½" - $1,500.00 up. **Two modeled together:** 4½–5½" - $1,600.00 up. **Holding one leg up:** 5" - $450.00 up.

Both arms raised in air: 5" - $600.00 up. **Molded ballet slippers:** 7½" - $450.00 up. **Molded-on Grecian beaded swimsuit:** 6" - $900.00 up. **Mohair wig, knees crossed:** 7" - $600.00 up. **Sitting on boat:** 7½" - $950.00 up.
Marked Japan: Fair quality of bisque and workmanship. Some pebbling worn off. 3" - $75.00; 5–6" - $100.00; 9" - $175.00. **Unusual or with animal:** 4" - $250.00; 6" - $350.00.
Ederle, Gertrude: In diving pose. (See photo in Series 7, pg. 26.) 8" - $700.00; 13" - $1,450.00; 18" - $1,850.00.

3" bathing beauties wearing two-piece bathing suits on fish. Both have brown hair. One has a series of numbers. Each - $45.00.

BELTON-TYPE

"Belton-type" dolls are not marked or will just have a number on the head. They have a concave top to a solid uncut head with one to three holes for stringing and/or plugging in wig. The German dome heads have a full round solid uncut head, but some of these may even have one or two holes in them. (See photo in Series 7, pg. 28.) This style doll was made from 1875 on, and most likely a vast amount of these dolls were actually German made, although they must be on a French body to qualify as a "Belton-type." Since these dolls are found on French bodies, it can be assumed the German heads were made for French firms.

Prices are for nicely dressed dolls with excellent quality bisque with **closed or open/closed mouths.** Bodies are French with straight wrists and no damage.

French style face, #124, 125, 136, 137, 191, etc.: Five-piece body: 8" - $800.00. **Jointed body:** 8" - $1,400.00; 12" - $2,000.00; 14" - $2,250.00; 17" - $2,800.00; 20" - $3,200.00; 23" - $3,500.00; 26" - $4,000.00.

Bru look: 16" - $2,600.00; 20" - $3,000.00.

German style face: 10" - $1,300.00; 12" - $1,400.00; 14" - $1,600.00; 16" - $1,800.00; 21" - $2,200.00; 25" - $2,500.00. **Five-piece body:** 8" - $800.00.

#200 and #300 series: See Bahr & Proschild section.

14" Belton-type with open/closed mouth with white space between lips. Straight wrist French body. Beautiful pale bisque. Outlined pale lips. $2,250.00. *Courtesy Turn of Century Antiques.*

14" Belton-type with closed mouth. Three stringing and wig plug holes. Jointed body with unusual painted-on high top boots. Original and a very cute doll. $2,450.00. *Courtesy Turn of Century Antiques.*

BERGMANN, C.M.

Charles M. Bergmann made dolls from 1889 at both Waltershausen and Friedrichroda, Germany. Many of the Bergmann heads were made for him by other companies, such as Simon & Halbig, Kestner, Armand Marseille and others.

Marks:

C.M. BERGMANN

S. & H
C.M. BERGMANN
Waltershausen
Germany

Child: 1880s into early 1900s. On fully jointed composition bodies and open mouth. (Add $100.00 more for heads by Simon & Halbig.) 10" - $325.00; 15" - $375.00; 19" - $450.00; 24" - $600.00; 28" - $800.00; 34" - $1,200.00; 42" - $1,800.00.

Elenore: Open mouth. Marked "CMB/SH." 18" - $650.00.

Character Baby: 1909 and after. Socket head on five-piece bent limb baby body. **Open mouth:** 10" - $325.00; 14" - $425.00; 18" - $575.00; 21" - $700.00.

Baby, mold #612: Open/closed mouth. 14" - $1,400.00; 18" - $2,000.00.

Lady doll: Adult-style body with long thin arms and legs. "Flapper-style" doll. 12" - $650.00; 15" - $800.00; 19"- $1,450.00.

19½" with open mouth, painted upper and lower lashes. On fully jointed body. Marked "C.M. Bergmann/Waltershausen/Germany/1916/2½." $465.00. *Courtesy Kathy Riddick.*

B.F.

The French dolls marked "B.F." were made by Ferte (Bébé Ferte.) Some collectors refer to them as Bébé Française by Jumeau. They are now being attributed to Danel & Cie who also used the Bébé Française trademark. They have closed mouths and jointed French bodies with most having straight wrists. (See photos in Series 4, pg. 28 and Series 10, pg. 32.)

Marks:

$$B \, 6 \, F$$

Child: 12" - $2,800.00; 14" - $3,400.00; 16" - $3,800.00; 19" - $4,400.00; 25" - $5,200.00; 28" - $6,300.00.

B.L.

Dolls marked "B.L." are referred to as "Bébé Louvre," but they most likely were made by Alexandre Lefebvre, who made dolls from 1890 and by 1922 was part of S.F.B.J. (See photo in Series 7, pg. 30; Series 8, pg. 31; Series 9, pg. 34.) Allow more if all original. 12" - $2,200.00; 18" - $4,200.00; 21" - $4,600.00; 25" - $5,200.00; 27" - $5,500.00.

15" with large paperweight eyes and closed mouth. On jointed French body. Marked "B.5.L." $3,400.00. *Courtesy Virginia Sofie.*

Black or brown dolls can have fired-in color or be painted bisque, composition, cloth, papier maché and other materials. They can range from very black to a light tan and also be a "dolly" face or have Black features.

The quality of these dolls varies greatly and prices are based on this quality. Both the French and Germans made these dolls. Prices are for undamaged, nicely dressed and clean dolls.

Alabama: See Cloth Doll section.

All bisque: Glass eyes, one-piece body and head. 4–5" - $385.00 up.

All bisque: Glass eyes, swivel head. 5–6" - $500.00 up.

All bisque: Painted eyes, one-piece body and head. 5" - $245.00. **Swivel head:** 5" - $500.00. **French type:** 4" - $350.00 up.

All bisque marked with maker (S&H, JDK, etc.): 6½–7" - $1,400.00 up.

Armand Marseille (A.M.) #341 or 351: (See photo in Series 8, pg. 32.) 10" - $350.00; 13" - $565.00; 16" - $825.00; 20" - $1,100.00. **#362, 396, 513, 518:** 15–16" - $775.00; 21" - $950.00. **#390, 390n:** (See photo in Series 6, pg. 39.) 16" - $485.00; 19" - $725.00; 23" - $875.00; 28" - $1,000.00. **#451, 458 (Indians):** 9" - $285.00; 12" - $465.00. **#970, 971, 992, 995 (Baby or Toddler):** 9–10" - $265.00; 14" - $550.00; 18" - $875.00. **#1894, 1897, 1912, 1914:** 12" - $325.00; 14" - $550.00.

Baby Grumpy: Made by Effanbee. 10" - $265.00; 16" - $450.00. Craze, dirty: 10" - $95.00; 16" - $125.00.

Bahr & Proschild #277: Open mouth. 12" - $700.00; 16" - $1,650.00.

Bruckner: See Cloth section.

Belton-type: Closed mouth. 12" - $1,800.00; 15" - $2,700.00.

Bru Jne: 19" - $26,000.00 up; 23" - $35,000.00 up.

Bru (circle dot or Brevette): 16" - $24,000.00 up; 19" - $29,000.00 up.

Bubbles: Made by Effanbee. 17" - $425.00; 22" - $650.00. Craze, dirty: 17" - $100.00; 22" - $200.00.

Bye-Lo: 16" - $3,000.00 up.

Candy Kid: 12" - $285.00. Craze, dirty: 12" - $125.00.

Celluloid: All celluloid. (Add more for glass eyes.) 10–12" - $200.00 up; 15" - $350.00; 18" - $600.00. **Celluloid shoulder head, kid body:** (Add more for glass eyes.) 17" - $350.00; 21" - $450.00.

Chase, Martha: 24" - $7,400.00; 28" - $9,200.00.

Cloth: See Cloth Doll section.

Composition: Made in Germany. Glass eyes, sometimes flirty. 12" - $325.00; 15" - $565.00; 19" - $750.00; 24" - $950.00 up.

E.D.: Open mouth: 16" - $2,300.00; 22" - $2,900.00.

F.G.: Open/closed mouth. 17–18" - $3,800.00. **Fashion:** Kid body, swivel neck. 14" - $2,400.00; 17" - $3,800.00.

Fashion: Swivel neck, original. 16" - $14,600.00. **Shoulder head:** Original. 16" - $6,000.00.

French, unmarked or marked "DEP": (See photo in Series 7, pg. 33.) **Closed mouth, bisque head:** 11–12" - $1,800.00 up; 15" - $3,400.00; 20" - $4,400.00. **Closed mouth, painted bisque:** 15" - $975.00; 20" - $1,200.00. **Open mouth, bisque head:** (See photo in Series 7, pg. 33.) 10" - $600.00; 15" - $1,300.00; 22" - $2,400.00. **Open mouth, painted bisque:** 15" - $600.00; 20" - $900.00. **With Black features:** 18" - $4,600.00 up.

French marked "SNF": Celluloid. 14" - $350.00; 18" - $600.00.

Frozen Charlotte/Charlie: 3" - $145.00; 6" - $250.00; 8–9" - $350.00. **Jointed shoulder:** 3" - $200.00; 6" - $350.00.

German, unmarked: Open mouth, bisque head: 10" - $500.00; 13" - $650.00; 15" - $850.00. **Open mouth, painted bisque:** 14" - $300.00; 18" - $500.00. **Closed mouth, bisque head:** 10–11" - $300.00; 14" - $400.00; 17" - $525.00; 21" - $800.00. **Closed mouth, painted bisque:** 16" - $350.00; 19" -

$500.00. **Black features:** 15" - $3,000.00; 18" - $3,800.00.

Hanna: Made by Schoenau & Hoffmeister. 8" - $350.00; 10–12" - $465.00; 15" - $650.00; 18" - $850.00.

Heinrich Handwerck: Open mouth. 18" - $900.00; 22" - $1,200.00; 25" - $1,500.00.

Heubach, Gebruder: Sunburst mark. **Boy:** Eyes to side, open/closed mouth. 12" - $2,500.00 up. **#7657, 7658, 7668, 7671:** 9" - $1,450.00; 13" - $1,800.00. **#7661, 7686:** 10" - $1,200.00; 14" - $2,700.00; 17" - $3,900.00.

Heubach Koppelsdorf, #320, 339 350: 10" - $425.00; 13" - $585.00; 18" - $800.00; 21" - $1,000.00 up. **#399:** Allow more for toddler. (See photo in Series 2, pg. 32; Series 5, pg. 28; Series 8, pg. 32.) 10" - $400.00; 14" - $600.00; 17" - $800.00. **Celluloid:** 14" - $300.00; 17" - $575.00. **#414:** 9" - $385.00; 14" - $775.00; 17" - $1,250.00. **#418 (grin):** 9" - $675.00; 14" - $900.00. **#444, 451:** 9" - $400.00; 14" - $700.00. **#452:** Brown. Can be Spanish, Gypsy, Moor, etc. 7½" - $375.00; 10" - $475.00; 15" - $675.00. **#458:** 10" - $465.00; 15" - $700.00. **#463:** 12" - $600.00; 16" - $950.00. **#1900:** 14" - $500.00; 17" - $600.00.

Kestner, J.D.: #134: 10" - $575.00; 14" - $925.00. **#237, 245 Hilda:** 14" - $3,400.00; 17" - $5,200.00; 20" - $6,200.00; 24" - $7,100.00.

Kestner, J.D.: Child, no mold number. **Open mouth:** 12" - $425.00; 16" - $600.00. **Closed mouth:** 14" - $625.00; 17" - $950.00. **Five-piece body:** 9" - $285.00; 12" - $350.00.

Jumeau: Tete Jumeau, open mouth: 10" - $2,200.00; 15" - $2,800.00; 18" - $3,200.00; 23" - $3,800.00. **Tete Jumeau, closed mouth:** (See photo in Series 10, pg. 37.) 15" - $4,900.00; 18" - $5,100.00; 23" - $6,200.00. **E.J:** Closed mouth. 15" - $7,200.00; 17" - $8,300.00; 19" - $8,700.00. **Character:** Very character face. All very rare. 20" - $90,000.00.

13½" Jumeau with open mouth and antique costume. On marked Jumeau body. Stamped "Tete Jumeau." $2,450.00.
Courtesy Turn of Century Antiques.

Jumeau type, open mouth: (See photo in Series 2, pg. 48; Series 7, pg. 33.) 12" - $1,200.00; 15" - $2,300.00; 19" - $3,700.00. **Jumeau type, closed mouth:** 12" - $2,600.00; 15" - $3,600.00; 19" - $4,800.00.

Kammer & Reinhardt (K✦R): Child, no mold number. 7½" - $445.00; 14" - $675.00; 17" - $875.00. **#100:** (See photo in Series 6, pg. 38.) 10" - $650.00; 14" - $1,000.00; 17" - $1,500.00; 19" - $1,800.00. **#101, painted eyes:** 15" - $2,200.00. **#101, glass eyes:** 17" - $4,400.00. **#114:** (See photo in Series 7, pg. 35.) 13" - $4,400.00. **#116, 116a:** 15" - $3,200.00; 19" - $3,900.00. **#126 baby:** (See photo in Series 5, pg. 28.) 12" - $750.00, 18" - $1,200.00. **#126 toddler:** 18" - $1,600.00.

Kewpie ("Hottentot"), bisque: 4" - $400.00; 5" - $565.00; 9" - $985.00. **Papier maché:** 8" - $265.00. **Composition:** 12" - $400.00; 15" - $725.00.

Konig & Wernicke (KW/G): 18" - $800.00.

Kühnlenz, Gebruder, mold #34-17, 44-16, etc.: (See photo in Series 10, pg. 38.) **Open mouth:** 10" - $450.00; 15" - $700.00. **Closed mouth:** 15" - $900.00; 18" - $1,800.00.

Moss, Leo: Papier maché head and lower limbs. Molded hair or wig. Inset glass eyes. Closed mouth, full lips, brown twill body. Excelsior filled. With or without tear on cheek. 1920s. 21" - $7,400.00; 27" - $8,800.00.

Papier maché: Black features. (See photo in Series 9, pg. 39.) 8" - $275.00; 13" - $525.00; 17" - $825.00. **Others:** 15" - $325.00; 22" - $685.00.

16" with open mouth, heavy feathered eyebrows, and curly wig. Old jointed body, old clothes. Marked "S&H 1009." Shown with 8" on five-piece body. Open mouth, glass eyes, painted shoes, knee high stockings. Made by Gebruder Kühnlenz and marked "34.17." 16" - $1,600.00; 8" - $650.00. *Courtesy Frasher Doll Auctions.*

Paris Bébé: (See photo in Series 10, pg. 36.) 16" - $4,600.00; 19" - $5,500.00.

Parson-Jackson, baby: 13" - $450.00. **Toddler:** 14" - $575.00.

Recknagel: Marked "R.A." May have mold **#138.** 16" - $725.00; 22" - $1,400.00.

Schoenau & Hoffmeister, #1909: (See photo in Series 5, pg. 29.) 16" - $475.00; 19" - $725.00.

Scowling Indian: (See photo in Series 6, pg. 41.) Medium to poor quality: 10" - $350.00; 13" - $450.00. Excellent quality: Probably by Simon and Halbig. 15" - $1,350.00; 21" - $2,800.00.

Scootles, composition: 15" - $650.00 up. **Vinyl:** 14" - $250.00; 19" - $450.00; 27" - $550.00.

21" "Scowling/Frowning Indian" with open mouth and jointed body. Excellent quality. Very rare size. Clothes and wig are possibly original. $2,800.00. *Courtesy Turn of Century Antiques.*

19" with Black features. Sleep eyes, full lips with six teeth. On jointed body. Marked "1358 Simon & Halbig/Germany/ S&H 6." (See #1368 in Series 6, pg. 37.) $7,200.00. *Courtesy Frasher Doll Auctions.*

Simon & Halbig, #639: 14" - $6,800.00; 18" - $10,000.00. **#729, open mouth:** Smiling. 17" - $3,800.00 up. **#739, closed mouth:** (See photo in Series 6, pg. 38.) 17" - $2,400.00; 22" - $3,300.00. **#939, closed mouth:** (See photo in Series 5, pg. 28.) 18" - $3,700.00; 21" - $4,600.00. **#939, open mouth:** (See photo in Series 7, pg. 34.) 17" - $1,400.00; 21" - $2,300.00. **#949, closed mouth:** 18" - $3,200.00; 21" - $4,000.00. **#949, open mouth:** 18" - $1,500.00; 27" - $3,400.00. **Kid body:** 18" - $1,300.00; 21" - $1,750.00; 27" - $2,100.00. **#969, open mouth:** Puffed cheeks. (See photo in Series 10, pg. 37.) 18" - $1,700.00. **#1009, 1039, 1079:** (See photo in Series 8, pg. 35.) **Open mouth:** 12" - 1,300.00; 16" - $1,600.00; 19" - $2,000.00. **Pull string, sleep eyes:** 19" - $2,300.00. **#1248, open mouth:** 15" - $850.00; 18" - $1,100.00.

#1302, closed mouth: Glass eyes, very character face. **Black:** 18" - $6,850.00. **Indian:** Sad expression. 18" - $7,400.00. **#1303 Indian:** Man or woman. Thin face. 16" - $6,900.00; 21" - $7,000.00. **#1339, 1358, 1368:** 16" - $5,800.00; 20" - $7,200.00. **#1368:** (See photo in Series 6, pg. 37.) 13" - $3,700.00; 16" - $5,700.00; 18" - $6,700.00.

S.F.B.J., #226: 16" - $2,900.00. **#301 or 60, open mouth:** 10" - $465.00; 14" - $650.00. **#301 or 60, closed mouth:** 10" - $675.00; 14" - $1,200.00. **#235, open/ closed mouth:** 15" - $2,600.00; 17" - $2,950.00. **#34.29, open mouth:** 17" - $4,700.00; 23" - $5,500.00.

Sarg, Tony: Mammy doll. Composition/cloth. (See photo in Series 8, pg. 36.) 18" - $575.00 up.

S.P. mark: Toddler, glass eyes, open mouth: 16" - $650.00.

19½" with sleep eyes, original mohair wig, and five-piece bent limb baby body. Open mouth with thick lips. Two upper teeth and tongue. Marked "252 S&Q Germany." $1,650.00. *Courtesy Frasher Doll Auctions.*

Steiner, Jules, "A" series: Open mouth: 13" - $4,300.00; 16" - $4,800.00; 19" - $5,400.00. **Closed mouth:** 18" - $5,900.00; 22" - $6,500.00. **"C" series:** 18" - $5,750.00; 21" - $5,900.00.

Stockinette: Oil-painted features. Excellent condition. 16" - $3,000.00; 22" - $3,500.00.

S & Q, #251: 9" - $600.00; 15" - $2,000.00. **#252 baby:** 20" - $1,650.00. Child: 20" - $1,800.00.

UNIS, #301 or 60: Open mouth. 13" - $450.00; 16" - $800.00.

Bonnet dolls date from the 1880s to the 1920s. They can be all bisque or have cloth or kid bodies. The lower limbs can be china, leather, or stone bisque. Most were made in Germany, but some were made in Japan. Also see under Goebel, Googly, and Recknagel sections.

All bisque: One-piece body and head, painted or glass eyes. Germany. 5" - $175.00; 7" - $235.00; 8" - $285.00; 10" - $375.00. **With swivel neck, glass eyes:** Germany. 5" - $325.00; 7" - $400.00 up.

Bisque head: Excellent bisque. Glass eyes, hat or bonnet, molded hair.

Five-piece papier maché, kid, or cloth body: 7" - $185.00; 9" - $300.00; 12" - $425.00; 15" - $650.00; 18" - $1,000.00; 21" - $1,250.00. **Fully jointed composition or kid or cloth body with bisque lower arms:** 7" - $225.00; 9" - $365.00; 12" - $485.00; 15" - $725.00; 21" - $1,200.00. **Molded shirt or top:** 15" - $825.00; 21" - $1,350.00.

Stone bisque: (See photo in Series 10, pg. 38.) 8–9" - $165.00; 12" - $225.00; 15" - $385.00; 18" - $600.00; 21" - $850.00.

Googly: See that section.
Japan: 8–9" - $85.00; 12" - $135.00.

3" all bisque flapper dolls were made in Germany. Legs are wired on, and arms have elastic ball sockets. (Doll dressed in red has no hat or bonnet.) Each - $200.00–265.00. *Courtesy Virginia Sofie.*

The "Bonnie Babe" was designed by Georgene Averill in 1926 with the bisque heads being made by Alt, Beck & Gottschalck and the cloth bodies made by the K & K Toy Co. (NY). The dolls were distributed by George Borgfeldt. The doll can have cloth body and legs or composition arms and legs with cloth body.

Marks: "Copr. by Georgene Averill/Germany/1005/3652" and sometimes "1368."

All bisque: See the All Bisque section.

Bisque head: Crooked smile, open mouth. 10" - $465.00; 14" - $950.00; 17" - $1,250.00; 21" - $1,500.00; 23" - $1,700.00; 25" - $1,950.00.

Celluloid head: 10" - $400.00; 16" - $675.00.

Composition body: Bisque socket head. 9" - $1,150.00; 15" - $1,500.00.

Right: 17" "Bonnie Babe" with open mouth, crooked smile, and two lower teeth. Fully marked. Left: 17" Kestner #226 with open mouth. Both have painted hair. "Bonnie Babe" - $1,250.00; Kestner #226 - $800.00. *Courtesy Turn of Century Antiques.*

BORGFELDT, GEORGE

George Borgfeldt imported, assembled, and distributed dolls in New York. The dolls that he carried or had made ranged from bisque to composition. Many dolls were made for him in Germany. Many heads were made for this firm by Armand Marseille.

Marks:

G.B.

Child, mold #325, 327, 329, or marked "G.B.": 1910–1922. Fully jointed composition body, open mouth. No damage and nicely dressed. 10" - $235.00; 13" - $400.00; 15" - $525.00; 17" - $550.00; 20" - $625.00; 22" - $725.00; 25" - $950.00 up.

Baby: 1910. Five-piece bent limb baby body, open mouth. 10" - $225.00; 14" - $400.00; 17" - $500.00; 22" - $700.00; 27" - $1,200.00 up.

Babykins: Made for G. Borgfeldt by Grace S. Putnam. Round face, glass eyes, and pursed lips. 1931. 14" - $950.00 up; 17" - $1,400.00 up.

Boudoir dolls are also called "flapper" dolls and were most popular during the 1920s and early 1930s, although they were made through the 1940s. Very rarely is one of these dolls marked with the maker or country of origin, but the majority were made in the United States, France and Italy.

The most desirable boudoir dolls are the ones from France and Italy. (Lenci, especially. See that section.) These dolls will have a silk or velvet painted face mask, an elaborate costume, and be of excellent quality.

The least expensive ones have a full or half-composition head, some with glass eyes, and the clothes will be stapled or glued to the body.

Boudoir dolls: Finely oil-painted features, excellent clothes. **Excellent quality:** 16" - $300.00 up; 28" - $475.00 up; 32" - $500.00 up. **Average quality:** 16" - $125.00; 28" - $185.00; 32" - $245.00. **Undressed:** 28–32" - $85.00. **With glass eyes:** 28–32" - $585.00 up. **Miniature:** 15" - $325.00.

Boudoir dolls: With composition head, stapled or glued-on clothes. No damage, and original clothes. 15" - $95.00; 28" - $165.00; 32" - $185.00.

Lenci: See that section.

Smoking doll: (See photo in Series 3, pg. 46; Series 5, pg. 32.) **Cloth:** 16–17" - $285.00 up; 25" - $465.00 up. **Composition:** 25" - $245.00 up; 28" - $375.00 up.

Printed-on clothes: 27" - $350.00 up. **Harem girl:** Has turban with spit curls around face. From lower torso to ankles, wears wide stuffed harem pants of colored material. 27" - $600.00 up.

13" Art Deco boudoir doll with adult head, sculptured eyes, and ¾ length slim limbs. Wax over composition or papier maché. Short body made of very smooth muslin. Legs have painted-on stockings to thighs and molded high heel feet. From 1920s. Excellent condition. $275.00.

25" smoking boudoir doll with cigarette missing. Composition head with tuft of mohair on forehead. Very classic face. Corduroy body and limbs with matching stapled-on cap. $465.00. *Courtesy Susan Giradot.*

Bru dolls will be marked with the name Bru or Bru Jne, Bru Jne R. Some will have a circle and dot or a half circle and dot. Some have paper labels – see marks. Prices are for dolls with no damage at all, very clean, and beautifully dressed. Add $2,000.00 up for all original clothes and marked shoes.

Marks:

BEBE BRU BTE SGDG

BEBE
BREVETE SDGD
PARIS

18" with open/closed mouth and molded tongue. Kid body with kid over wood upper limbs. Wood lower legs and bisque lower arms. Marked "Bru Jne 6" on head and shoulders. Shown with two 9½" hat stands of wood and papier maché. Doll - $18,000.00; stands, each - $150.00. *Courtesy Frasher Doll Auctions.*

Closed mouth, all kid body: Bisque lower arms. 15" - $9,000.00; 17" - $13,000.00; 23" - $24,000.00; 25" - $27,000.00.

Bru Jne: Ca. 1880s. Kid over wood, wood legs, bisque lower arms. 10–11" - $18,000.00; 12–13" - $16,000.00; 15" - $14,000.00; 18" - $18,000.00; 21" - $22,000.00; 24" - $26,000.00; 25" - $26,000.00; 28" - $32,000.00; 30" - $35,500.00. **All wood body:** 17" - $14,000.00; 20" - $20,000.00. **Key wound music box:** 16½" - $22,000.00.

Circle dot or half circle: Circa 1870s. Open/closed mouth, very slightly parted lips with molded or painted teeth. Kid body, bisque lower arms. 13" - $15,000.00; 15" - $18,000.00; 19" - $22,000.00; 24" - $26,000.00; 27" - $29,000.00; 30" - $36,000.00. **Key wound music box:** 16½" - $20,000.00.

21" with closed mouth. Very pretty face and bisque for this late doll. Composition body is fully jointed. Clothes may be original. Head marked "Bru Jne R #9." Original - $11,500.00; redressed - $8,800.00. *Courtesy Barbara Earnshaw-Cain.*

Breveté: Circa 1870s. Swivel head, closed mouth with space between lips, full cheeks. Kid body, bisque lower arms. Sticker or stamp on body, size number on head. 13" - $16,000.00; 18" - $19,500.00; 22" - $24,500.00.

Bru Jne R., closed mouth: 18" - $9,000.00; 22" - $9,200.00.

Bru Jne R., open mouth: 1890s. Jointed composition body. First price for excellent quality bisque and second for poor quality bisque. 12" - $2,300.00, $1,600.00; 14" - $6,800.00, $4,300.00; 16" - $7,500.00, $5,000.00; 19" - $8,000.00, $6,000.00; 23" - $8,800.00, $6,800.00.

Walker body: Throws kiss. 17" - $7,000.00; 21" - $7,700.00; 25" - $8,500.00.

Nursing Bru: 1878–1899. Operates by turning key in back of head. **Early, excellent quality:** 14" - $6,800.00 up; 17" - $8,800.00; 20" - $9,600.00. **Fair quality:** 15" - $5,800.00; 18" - $6,400.00. **High color, late S.F.B.J. type:** 15" - $5,000.00; 18" - $5,900.00.

Breathing, crying, kissing: (See photo in Series 7, pg. 41.) 19" - $16,000.00; 24" - $18,000.00.

Head of rubber/gutta percha: Original. Bru Jne R face, jointed body. Marked "Gomme Durée." 17" - $9,800.00. Redressed: $8,200.00.

Bru marked shoes: Size #1 to 4 (for 12–16" dolls) $600.00–800.00. Size #5 to 10 (for 17–25" dolls) $500.00–600.00. Size #11 to 12 (for 26–30" dolls) $800.00–1,000.00.

12" #1 circle dot ⊙ Bru. Open/closed mouth with slightly painted teeth. Original dress and wig. Very rare tiny size. $15,000.00. *Courtesy Ellen Dodge.*

17" beautiful nursing Bru with open mouth. Ball inside head with key lever in back of head that compresses the ball to resemble "nursing." Kid body, bisque lower arms. This early model is all original. $8,800.00. *Courtesy Ellen Dodge.*

Very rare pair of Bucherer dolls as the characters "Mutt and Jeff." Both have metal ball-jointed bodies with composition heads and limbs. Heavy lead feet help them stand well. The jointing can be seen through the torn clothing. Bucherer made a variety of dolls including regular people, comic figures, baseball players, and clowns in 1921. 6–7" - $285.00–600.00. (This pair is valued over $1,200.00.) *Courtesy John C. Connell.*

BYE-LO

The Bye-Lo baby was designed by Grace Storey Putnam, distributed by George Borgfeldt, and the cloth bodies were made by K & K Toy Co. of New York. The bisque heads were made by Kestner, Alt, Beck & Gottschalck and others. The all bisque dolls were made by Kestner. The dolls date from 1922. Most dolls have celluloid or composition hands. Prices are for undamaged, clean and nicely dressed dolls.

Marks:

**1923 by
Grace S. Putnam
Made in Germany
7372145**

**Copy. By
Grace S. Putnam**

**Bye-Lo Baby
Pat. Appl'd For**

Bisque head: Allow more for original clothes and pin. 8" - $500.00; 10" - $500.00; 12"- $585.00; 15" - $925.00; 17–18" - $1,300.00. **Black:** 16" - $3,000.00 up.

Mold #1415, smiling mouth: Very rare bisque with painted eyes. 14–15" - $5,000.00 up. **Composition head:** 14–15" - $900.00 up.

Socket head: Bisque head on five-piece bent limb baby body. 14–15" - $1,500.00; 17" - $1,900.00.

Composition head: 1924. 10–11" - $345.00; 13–14" - $450.00; 16–17" - $650.00.

Painted bisque: With cloth body, composition hands. 10" - $275.00; 14" - $450.00; 16" - $575.00.

Schoenhut, wood: 1925. Cloth body, wooden hands. 14–15" - $1,700.00 up.

All celluloid: 6" - $200.00. **Celluloid head/cloth body:** 10–11" - $350.00; 13–14" - $465.00.

All bisque: See All Bisque section, Characters.

Vinyl heads: Early 1950s. Cloth/stuffed limbs. Marked "Grace Storey Putnam" on head. 16" - $250.00.

Honey Child: Bye-Lo look-alike made by Bayless Bros. & Co. in 1926. 16" - $325.00; 20" - $465.00.

Wax Bye-lo: Cloth or sateen body. 15–16" - $2,000.00 up.

Basket with blanket and extra clothes: Five babies in basket, bisque heads: 12" - $4,400.00 up. Composition heads: 12" - $2,700.00 up.

Mold #1418, Fly-Lo Baby (Baby Aero): Bisque head, cloth body, celluloid hands, glass eyes. Closed mouth, deeply molded hair. Very rare. (See photo in Series 10, pg. 45.) 10" - $3,800.00; 13" - $5,000.00; 16" - $5,600.00. Composition head: 14" - $900.00.

Background: Bye-Lo babies with sleep eyes. 14½" and 13" head circumferences. (Doll on right has tagged gown.) Foreground, in basket: 5" all-bisque baby with painted eyes. Beside it is a 4" tall jointed Snow Baby of very good quality. 14½" - $585.00; 13" - $585.00; 5" - $395.00; 4" - $450.00. *Courtesy Turn of Century Antiques.*

Catterfelder Puppenfabrik of Germany made dolls from 1902 until the late 1930s. The heads for their dolls were made by various German firms, including Kestner.

Marks:

$$\frac{\underset{219}{CP}}{5}$$

$$\underset{Deponiert}{\underset{201/40}{CP}}$$

Catterfelder
Puppenfabrik
45

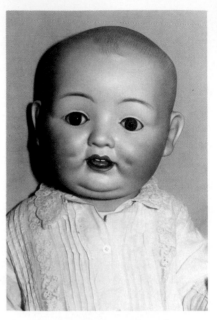

27" with sleep eyes, open mouth, two upper teeth, and tremble tongue. On baby body. Marked "C.P. 208 G. 5 S. Deponiert." $1,300.00. *Courtesy Frasher Doll Auctions.*

Child: Ca. 1900s. Composition jointed body. Open mouth. **Mold #264:** Or marked "C.P." 18" - $650.00; 24" - $900.00; 35" - $2,000.00.

Character child: 1910 or after. Composition jointed body, closed mouth, and painted eyes. Can be boy or girl with character face. **Mold #207:** (See photo in Series 9, pg. 48.) 15–16" - $5,300.00; 20" - $7,000.00. **Mold #212, 215**: 16" - $4,800.00; 20" - $5,200.00. **Mold #217:** Rare. 24" - $9,300.00. **Mold #219:** 16" - $3,850.00; 20" - $4,600.00. **Glass eyes:** 22" - $6,300.00. **Mold #220: Glass eyes.** 17" - $7,300.00.

Babies: 1909 or after. Wig or molded hair, five-piece bent limb baby body, glass or painted eyes. Add more for toddler body.

Mold #200, 201, 207, 208, 209, 262, 263, 264: (See photo of #208 in Series 5, pg. 37.) 15" - $545.00; 17" - $650.00; 21" - $850.00; 24" - $1,000.00; 27" - $1,300.00.

CELLULOID DOLLS

Celluloid dolls date from the 1880s into the 1940s when they were made illegal in the United States because they burned or exploded if placed near an open flame or heat. Some of the makers were:

United States: Marks Bros., Irwin, Horsman, Averill, Parsons-Jackson, Celluloid Novelty Co.

France: Societe Industrielle de Celluloid (Sisoine), Petitcollin (eagle symbol), Societe Nobel Française (SNF in diamond), Jumeau/Unis (1950s), Neumann & Marx (dragon symbol).

Germany: Rheinische Gummi und Celluloid Fabrik Co. (turtle mark), Minerva (Buschow & Beck) (helmet symbol), E. Maar & Sohn (3 M's mark), Adelheid Nogler Innsbruck Doll Co. (animal with spread wings and a fish tail, in square), Cellba (mermaid symbol). **Poland:** P.R. Zask ("ASK" in triangle). **England:** Cascelloid Ltd. (Palitoy).

Prices for perfect, undamaged dolls.

All celluloid baby: 1910 on. **Painted eyes:** 8" - $75.00; 12" - $125.00; 14" - $175.00; 16" - $185.00; 19–20" - $300.00; 24" - $350.00; 26" - $450.00. **Glass inset eyes:** 14" - $200.00; 16" - $265.00; 20" - $425.00; 24" - $485.00. **Bye-Lo:** See that section.

All celluloid child dolls, painted eyes: Made in Germany. Jointed at neck, shoulders and hips. 6" - $40.00; 8" - $65.00; 12" - $100.00; 15" - $185.00; 18" - $350.00 up. **Jointed at neck and shoulders only:** 5" - $20.00; 7" - $40.00; 9–10" - $75.00. **Glass eyes:** 13" - $200.00; 15" - $300.00; 17–18" - $450.00. **Marked "France":** 8" - $150.00; 10" - $200.00; 16" - $300.00; 19" - $550.00 up.

All celluloid with molded-on clothes: Jointed at shoulders only. (See photo in Series 9, pg. 49.) 4" - $50.00; 6" - $65.00; 8" - $115.00.

All celluloid immobilies: No joints. 4" - $20.00; 6" - $35.00.

All celluloid Black dolls: See Black or Brown dolls section.

Carnival Dolls: Feathers glued to body and/or head. Some with top hats. (See photo in Series 7, pg. 45.) 7–8" - $50.00; 12–14" - $100.00; 17–18" - $175.00 up.

Celluloid shoulder head: 1900–1912. Germany. Molded hair or wigged. Painted eyes, open or closed mouth. Kid, kidaleen, or cloth bodies. Can have any material for arms. 13–14" - $165.00 up; 16" - $200.00 up; 19" - $375.00. **Glass eyes:** 13–14" - $200.00; 16" - $300.00; 19" - $450.00; 23" - $500.00.

Celluloid socket heads: Made in Germany. Glass eyes. (Allow more for flirty eyes). Ball-jointed body or five-piece

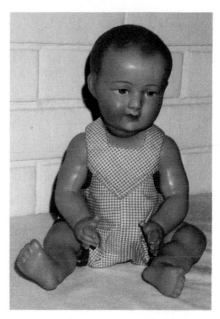

14" all celluloid baby with painted features and molded hair. Romper may be original. Made for Petitcollin and marked "85 France" with the eagle head mark. Circa 1927–1935. $175.00. *Courtesy Pat Graff.*

bodies. Open or closed mouths. 14" - $300.00; 18" - $425.00; 20" - $500.00; 25" - $700.00.

Celluloid/Plush: Early 1910s. Teddy bear body. Can have half or full celluloid body with hood half head. 12" - $650.00; 14" - $785.00; 17" - $925.00.

Bye-Lo: 4–4½" - $165.00; 6" - $200.00.

Jumeau: Marked on head, jointed body. (See photo in Series 4, pg. 41.) 12" - $400.00; 15" - $500.00.

Heubach Koppelsdorf, mold #399 (brown or black): See Black or Brown Dolls section.

Hitler youth group: (See photo in Series 5, pg. 39; Series 6, pg 53.) 8–9" - $175.00.

Kruse, Käthe: All original. 14" - $475.00; 17" - $675.00.

Kammer & Reinhardt (K✿R), mold #406, 700: Child or baby. (See

photo in Series 4, pg. 40.) 14"- $400.00.
#701: 14" - $975.00. **#714 or 715:** 16" -
$700.00. **#717:** 16" - $500.00; 20" - $700.00.
#728, 828: 16" - $500.00; 20" - $700.00.
Toddler: 15" - $650.00. **#826, 828, 406,
321, 255, 225: Baby:** 12" - $200.00; 14" -
$400.00; 17" - $550.00; 20" - $650.00. **Child:**
14" - $350.00; 16" - $550.00; 20" - $650.00;
23" - $750.00.

Kewpie: See that section.

**Konig & Wernicke (K&W), tod-
dler:** 15" - $325.00; 19" - $500.00.

Japan: 4" - $20.00; 7" - $35.00; 10–11" -
$50.00; 14" - $100.00; 17" - $200.00; 19" -
$325.00; 22" - $400.00.

Max and Moritz: 7", each - $275.00 up.

Parsons-Jackson: (See photo in
Series 7, pg. 44.) **Baby:** 12–13" - $185.00;
13–14" - $285.00. **Toddler:** 14–15" -
$385.00. **Black:** 13–14" - $485.00.

19" celluloids with green, brown, and
blue sleep eyes. Clothes on the two
standing dolls may be original. All have
turtle marks. Each - $375.00 up. *Courtesy Turn
of Century Antiques.*

CHAD VALLEY

Chad Valley dolls usually will have a
felt face and all velvet body that is jointed
at the neck, shoulders and hips. They can
have painted or glass eyes and will have a
mohair wig. First prices are for those in
mint condition. Second prices are for
dolls that are dirty, worn or soiled and/or
do not have original clothes.

Marks: "Hygienic Toys/Made in England by/Chad Valley Co. Ltd."

"The Chad Valley Hygienic
Textile/Toys/Made in England."

Child with painted eyes: 9–10" -
$150.00, $50.00; 12" - $265.00, $100.00;
15" - $450.00, $185.00; 18" - $600.00,
$250.00.

Child with glass eyes: 14" -$550.00,
$165.00; 16" - $700.00, $200.00; 18" -
$725.00, $300.00.

Child representing Royal Family:
Four in set: **Princess Elizabeth,
Princess Margaret Rose, Prince
Edward, Princess Alexandra.** All four
have glass eyes. (See photos in Series 5,
pgs. 39–40; Series 10, pg. 50.) **Prince
Edward as Duke of Kent:** 15" - $1,500.00,
$600.00; 18" - $1,700.00, $700.00. **As Duke
of Windsor:** 15" - $1,500.00, $600.00; 18" -
$1,700.00, $700.00. **Others:** 15" - $1,400.00
up, $500.00; 18" - $1,500.00 up, $500.00.

**Characters (Long John Silver,
Captain Bly, Policeman, Train Con-
ductor, Pirate, Fisherman, etc.):** Glass
eyes. (See photo in Series 6, pg. 56.) 18" -
$1,000.00 up, $325.00; 20" - $1,300.00 up.
Painted eyes: 18" - $850.00; 20" - $1,000.00.

Storybook Dolls: Snow White: 17" -
$1,000.00. **Dwarfs:** 9½" - $650.00 each.
Red Riding Hood: 14" - $650.00. **Ding
Dong Dell:** 14" - $675.00. **My Elizabeth,
My Friend:** 14" - $750.00.

Ghandi/India: 13" - $700.00 up,
$200.00. **Rahma-Jah:** (See photo in
Series 9, pg. 53.) 26" - $950.00.

Animals: Cat: 12" plush - $200.00 up; 6" cloth - $95.00 up. **Dog:** 12" plush - $250.00 up. **Bonzo:** Cloth dog with painted eyes almost closed and smile. 4" - $200.00; 13" - $400.00. Eyes open: 5½" - $265.00; 14" - $565.00.

14" "Duchess and Duke of Kent." Cloth with felt faces, velvet bodies, glass eyes, and mohair wigs. Both are original and tagged "Made in England." Each - $1,500.00. *Courtesy Frasher Doll Auctions.*

CHALK CARNIVAL DOLLS

15" chalk carnival dolls from the 1930s. On the left is Snow White; on the right, a more common figure. Snow White - $125.00; Others - $75.00.

Martha Jenks Chase of Pawtucket, Rhode Island, began making dolls in 1893, and they are still being made by members of the family. They all have oil painted features and are made of stockinette and cloth. They will be marked "Chase Stockinette" on left leg or under the left arm. There is a paper label (often gone) on the backs with a drawn head, shown here. The words "Stockinette Doll" may also appear on brim of hat.

Mark:

The older Chase dolls are jointed at the shoulders, hips, knees and elbows; the newer dolls are jointed at the shoulders and hips with straight arms and legs. Some after 1920 have sateen bodies. Prices are for very clean dolls with only minor wear.

Older Dolls:

Babies: 15" - $600.00; 18" - $775.00; 23" - $900.00. Hospital used: 23" - $350.00; 28" - $500.00.

Child: Molded bobbed hair. 12– 13" - $1,250.00; 15" - $1,600.00; 20" - $2,000.00; 23" - $2,300.00. **Solid dome, painted hair:** 14" - $500.00; 17" - $650.00; 20" - $750.00; 24" - $850.00. **Rare hairdo:** Such as molded oil-painted hair pulled back into bun, two sausage curls around face. 16" - $10,000.00 up.

Lady: 15" - $1,900.00; 18" - $2,200.00; 22" - $2,500.00. Life size, hospital used: $1,800.00.

Man: 16" - $2,200.00; 23" - $2,600.00. Life size: $2,000.00.

Black: 23" - $7,900.00 up; 27" - $9,500.00 up.

Alice In Wonderland: 16" - $1,500.00.

Frog Footman: 16" - $2,000.00 up.

Mad Hatter: 16" - $2,100.00 up.

Duchess: 16" - $1,900.00 up.

Tweedledum: 16" - $2,200.00 up.

George Washington: (See photo in Series 10, pg. 52.) Mint: 26" - $5,000.00 up. Played with: $2,200.00.

Chase Type: Child. 14" - $1,000.00 up; 19" - $1,600.00 up.

Newer Dolls:

Babies: 14" - $200.00; 16" - $275.00; 20" - $425.00.

Child, boy or girl: 14" - $265.00; 16" - $365.00.

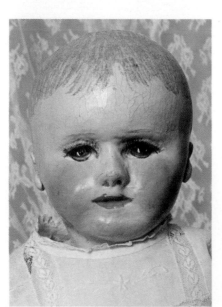

20" stockinette with molded face, oil-painted features, applied ears, and brush stroked hair. Cloth body with treated (oil painted) limbs. 1890s. $750.00 up. *Courtesy Turn of Century Antiques.*

Almost all china heads were made in Germany between 1840 and the 1900s. Most have black hair, but blondes became popular by the 1880s. By 1900, one out of every three dolls was blonde. China dolls can be on a cloth or kid body with leather or china limbs. Generally, these heads are unmarked, but a few will have a number and/or "Germany" on the back shoulder plate. Prices are for clean dolls with no cracks, chips, or repairs on a nice body and nicely dressed. Also see Huret/Rohmer under "Fashions" and Alt, Beck & Gottschalck.

Alice In Wonderland: Snood, head band. (See photo in Series 1, pg. 75.) 12" - $250.00; 16" - $450.00; 20" - $785.00. **With flange neck:** Motschmann style body. 9" - $1,600.00; 12" - $2,600.00; 14" - $2,900.00.

Alice In Wonderland

Adelina Patti: 1860s. Center part, roll curl from forehead to back on each side of head and "spit" curls at temples and above exposed ears. 14" - $365.00; 18" - $525.00; 22" - $600.00.

Adelina Patti

Bald Head/Biedermeir: Ca. 1840. Has bald head, some with top of head glazed black, takes wigs. (See photo in Series 7, pg. 48.) **Excellent quality:** 12" - $500.00; 14" - $900.00; 18" - $1,250.00. **Medium quality:** 10–12" - $300.00; 14" - $500.00; 18" - $675.00. **Glass eyes:** 16" - $1,600.00; 21" - $2,200.00.

Bald Head/Biedermeir

18½" bald china of the Sevres or KPM style. Brown painted eyes, closed smile mouth. Cloth body with china lower limbs and bare feet. Rare china. Circa 1850. $2,800.00. *Courtesy Turn of Century Antiques.*

Bangs: Full across forehead. 1870s. **Black hair:** 14" - $250.00; 17" - $425.00; 20" - $525.00. **Blondes:** 15" - $275.00; 20" - $550.00; 23" - $650.00.

Brown eyes: (See photo in Series 5, pg. 43; Series 8, pg. 51.) Painted eyes, can be any hairstyle and date, but usually has short, "flat top" Civil War hairdo. 11" - $425.00; 15" - $625.00; 18" - $1,100.00; 22" - $1,300.00; 26" - $1,800.00.

Brown hair: Early hairdo with flat top or long sausage curls around head. Center part and smooth around face. 16" - $2,700.00; 20" - $3,600.00. **With bun:** 16-17" - $4,000.00 up.

Bun: 1830s–1840s. China with bun, braided or rolled and pulled to back of head. Usually has pink luster tint. Cloth body, nicely dressed, undamaged. (See photo in Series 3, pg. 54; Series 10, pg. 55.) Prices depend upon rarity of hairdo and can run from $700.00–6,000.00.

Bun Hairdo

Early hairdo: Also see "Wood Body." 7" - $1,300.00 up; 14" - $1,800.00 up; 17" - $2,500.00 up; 23" - $3,200.00 up. **Double bun or any fancy bun:** 17" - $3,700.00; 23" - $5,200.00.

Common Hairdo

Common hairdo: Called "Lowbrow" or "Butterfly." Made from 1890, with most being made after 1900. Black or blonde hair. Wavy hairdo, center part with hair that comes down low on forehead. Also see "Pet Names." 8" - $80.00; 12" - $145.00; 14" - $165.00; 17" - $200.00; 21" - $265.00; 25" - $345.00. **With jewel necklace:** 14" - $225.00; 20" - $325.00. **With molded-on poke bonnet:** 8" - $165.00; 13" - $225.00. **Open mouth:** 14" - $465.00; 18" - $850.00.

Child: Swivel neck. China shoulder plate. May have china lower limbs and torso. 12" - $2,450.00.

Child or Boy: Short black or blonde hairdo, curly with partly exposed ears. 14" - $250.00; 20" - $600.00.

Covered Wagon: 1840s. Hair parted in middle with flat hairstyle and has sausage-shaped curls around head. 8" - $185.00; 12" - $285.00; 15" - $550.00; 18" - $650.00; 22" - $900.00; 35–36" - $1,100.00 up.

Countess Dagmar: Pierced ears. 16" - $625.00; 19" - $900.00.

Covered Wagon   **Countess Dagmar**

Curly Top: 1845–1860s. Ringlet curls that are loose and over entire head. (See photo in Series 4, pg. 48.) 16" - $550.00; 20" - $950.00.

Currier & Ives: (See photo in Series 4, pg. 48.) 14" - $475.00; 19" - $665.00.

Curly Top   **Currier & Ives**

Dolly Madison: 1870–1880s. Loose curly hairdo with modeled ribbon and bow in center of the top of the head. Few curls on forehead. 14" - $365.00; 18" - $550.00; 21" - $585.00; 24" - $625.00; 28" - $800.00.

Dolly Madison

Early Marked China (Nuremberg, Rudolstadt, etc.): 16" - $2,600.00 up; 18" - $3,000.00 up.

Fancy Hairstyles: Flared sides, rolls of hair over top of head, long hair cascading down back, ringlet curls around face and full exposed ears. (See photos in Series 4, pg. 46; Series 9, pg. 57.) 14" - $500.00 up; 17" - $600.00 up; 21" - $750.00 up.

Flat Top, Civil War: 1850–1870s. Black hair parted in middle, smooth on top with short curls around head. 6–7" - $95.00; 12" - $185.00; 14" - $250.00; 17" - $300.00; 20" - $350.00; 24" - $425.00; 26" - $500.00; 30" - $700.00; 35" - $800.00. **Swivel neck:** 14" - $800.00 up; 21" - $1,500.00 up. **Molded necklace:** 21" - $700.00.

Flat Top, Civil War (1850–1870)

20" "Dolly Madison" with cloth body and china lower limbs. She is rare because of her pierced ears. This hairdo comes in blonde and black. With pierced ears - $850.00. *Courtesy Turn of Century Antiques.*

French: China shoulder head, painted eyes, cut pate with cork, wigged, fashion kid body. (See Fashions, Huret type.) 16" - $3,500.00; 19" - $4,400.00.

Glass eyes: 1840–1870s. Can have a variety of hairdos. 14" - $2,600.00; 18" - $3,600.00; 23" - $4,200.00.

Hat or bonnet: Molded on. 13" - $3,200.00; 16" - $4,000.00.

High Brow: 1860–1870s. Like Covered Wagon, but has very high forehead, smooth on top with a center part, curls over ears and around base of neck, and has a very round face. 14" - $475.00; 20" - $725.00; 24" - $925.00.

Highland Mary: (See photo in Series 7, pg. 50.) 16" - $425.00; 19" - $500.00; 23" - $600.00.

Highland Mary

Japanese: 1910–1920s. Can be marked or unmarked. Black or blonde and can have a "common" hairdo, or have much more adult face and hairdo. 12" - $125.00; 14" - $185.00.

Jenny Lind: Hair pulled back in bun. 16" - $1,800.00.

Jenny Lind

Kling: Number and bell. 13" - $365.00; 16" - $450.00; 20" - $750.00.

Man or boy: Excellent quality, early date, side part hairdo. Brown hair. 14" - $1,900.00; 17" - $2,600.00; 21" - $3,100.00 up.

Man hairdo with side part

Man or boy, glass eyes: (See photo in Series 4, pg. 45; Series 10, pg. 55.) 15" - $2,300.00; 17" - $3000.00; 21" - $3,800.00.

Man: Coiled, graduated size curl hairdo. 16" - $1,500.00; 20" - $2,000.00.

Man hairdo with curls

Mary Todd Lincoln

Mary Todd Lincoln: Has snood. 15" - $550.00; 19" - $850.00. Blonde with black snood: 18" - $1,700.00.

Morning Glory: Long neck, narrow at chin, wide at eyes. Very high forehead, brush strokes around face. Hair very flat, pulled back. Exposed ears. 21" - $5,600.00.

Open mouth: 1906. Common hairdo. Rare. 15" - $475.00 up; 19" - $875.00 up.

Pet Names: 1905. Same as "Common" hairdo with molded shirtwaist with the name on front: **Agnes, Bertha, Daisy, Dorothy, Edith, Esther, Ethel, Florence, Helen, Mabel, Marion, Pauline.** (See photo in Series 5, pg. 44; Series 9, pg. 59.) 8–9" - $125.00; 14" - $200.00; 16" - $225.00; 19" - $265.00; 22" - $300.00; 25" - $425.00.

19" with hairdo pulled back into small cascade of banded curls. Deep shoulder plate with three sew holes. Protruding pierced ears. $925.00. *Courtesy Turn of Century Antiques.*

Pierced ears: Can have a variety of hairstyles (ordinary hairstyle, flat top, curly, covered wagon, etc.) 14" - $485.00 up; 18" - $700.00 up. **Rare hairstyles:** 14" - $1,200.00 up; 18" - $1,800.00 up.

Snood, combs: Applied hair decoration. 14" - $650.00; 17" - $800.00. Grapes in hairdo: 18" - $1,850.00 up.

Sophia Smith: Straight sausage curls ending in a ridge around head rather than curved to head. 14" - $2,300.00; 18" - $3,200.00.

Sophia Smith   Spill Curls

Spill curls: With or without headband. Many individual curls across forehead and over shoulders. Forehead curls continued to above ears. 14" - $425.00; 18" - $800.00; 22" - $900.00; 27" - $1,100.00.

Swivel flange neck: 8–9" - $1,800.00 up; 12" - $2,600.00 up.

Unusual: Such as gray hair, long thin face, downcast eyes, molded eyelids. Marked, such as "Nuremberg." (See Series 3, pg. 55; Series 6, pg. 59.) 17" - $3,400.00.

Whistle: Has whistle holes in head. 14" - $575.00; 18" - $750.00.

16" glass-eyed Greiner style china doll with fully exposed ears. Old cloth body and limbs. $1,500.00. *Courtesy Ellen Dodge.*

Wood body: Articulated with slim hips, china lower arms. 1840-1850s. Hair pulled back in bun or coiled braids. 6" - $1,200.00; 8" - $1,500.00; 12" - $1,650.00 up; 15" - $1,800.00 up; 18" - $3,600.00 up. **Same with Covered Wagon hairdo:** 8" - $775.00; 12" - $985.00; 16" - $1,400.00.

Young Queen Victoria: 16" - $1,600.00; 21" - $2,000.00; 25" - $3,200.00.

CLOTH DOLLS

Alabama Indestructible Doll: All cloth with head molded and painted in oils, painted hair, shoes and stockings. Marked on torso or leg "Pat. Nov. 9, 1912. Ella Smith Doll Co." or "Mrs. S.S. Smith/Manufacturer and dealer/The Alabama Indestructible Doll/Roanoke, Ala./Patented Sept. 26, 1905 (or 1907)." Prices are for clean dolls with only minor scuffs or soil. Allow more for mint dolls. **Child:** 16" - $1,700.00; 22" - $2,300.00. **Baby:** 14" - $1,500.00; 21" - $2,000.00. **Barefoot baby:**

Rare. 22" - $2,800.00. **Black child:** 18" - $6,200.00; 23" - $6,800.00. **Black baby:** 20" - $6,200.00.

Art Fabric Mills: See Printed Cloth Dolls.

Averill Mfg. Co.: See Averill section.

Babyland: Made by E.I. Horsman from 1904 to 1920. Marked on torso or bottom of foot. Oil-painted features, photographic features or printed features. With or without wig. All cloth, jointed at shoulders and hips. First price for extra clean, original dolls; second price for dolls in fair condition that show wear and have slight soil. Allow more for mint dolls. **Oil-painted features:** 13" - $775.00, $250.00; 15" - $850.00, $350.00; 18" - $950.00, $400.00; 22" - $1,100.00, $500.00; 28" - $1,600.00, $800.00. **Black oil-painted features:** 14" - $800.00, $300.00; 17" - $1,100.00, $550.00; 20" - $1,400.00,

$575.00; 26" - $2,000.00; $950.00. **Photographic face:** 14–15" - $550.00, $225.00; 19" - $950.00, $400.00. **Black photographic face:** 14–15" - $650.00, $275.00; 19" - $1,000.00; $450.00. **Photographic face, 1930s–1960s:** (See Series 10, pg. 59.) Mint and original. 15" - $250.00. Played with, little soil. 15" - $100.00. **Printed:** 16" - $285.00, $95.00; 20" - $575.00, $125.00; 23" - $785.00, $250.00. **Black printed:** 16" - $400.00, $150.00; 20" - $700.00, $200.00; 23" - $925.00, $325.00.

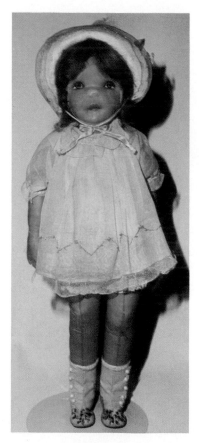

Back row: 25" Art Fabric and 24" "Flaked Rice." Both with printed-on underclothes. Front row: 17" with printed-on clothes and bow in hair. 12" "Blue Boy" with printed-on clothes. 25" - $225.00; 24" - $300.00; 17" - $200.00; 12" - $145.00. *Courtesy Turn of Century Antiques.*

21" "Bye Bye Kiddie" by Alta & Bauer. Plain muslin body with head and limbs coated with paint-like coating. Oil-painted features. Painted design on boots. Very pug nose makes an indentation at eye line. One-piece teddy slip matches dress. Original. $300.00.

Topsy-Turvy: Two-headed doll. One black, other white. Oil painted: $650.00. Printed: $400.00.

Beecher (Missionary Babies): 1893–1910. Stuffed stockinette, painted eyes, needle sculptured features. Originated by Julia Jones Beecher of Elmira, N.Y., wife of Congregational Church pastor. Dolls made by sewing circle of church and all proceeds used for missionary work, so dolls can also be referred to as "Missionary Babies." Have looped wool hair. Extra clean: 15" - $2,800.00; 21" - $5,900.00. Slight soil and wear: 15" - $1,300.00; 21" - $2,400.00. **Black:** Extra clean: 15" - $3,000.00; 21" - $6,000.00 up. Soil and wear: 16" - $1,600.00; 23" - $2,900.00. **Beecher type:** 19" - $2,100.00.

Bing Art: By Bing Werke of Germany, 1921–1932. All cloth, all felt, or composition head with cloth body. Molded face mask, oil-painted feature, wig or painted hair, can have pin joints on cloth body, seams down front of legs, mitt hands with free formed thumbs. (See photo in Series 9, pg. 61.) **Painted hair, cloth or felt:** Unmarked or "Bing" on sole of foot. 10" - $600.00; 15" - $700.00. **Wig:** 10" - $350.00; 15" - $550.00. **Composition head:** 7–8" - $150.00; 12" - $185.00, 15" - $250.00.

Bruckner: Made for Horsman from 1901–on. Cloth with mask face stiffened and printed. Marked on shoulder "Pat'd July 8, 1901." Clean: 13–15" - $300.00 up. Soil and wear: 13–15" - $100.00. **Black:** Clean: 13–15" - $400.00 up. Soil and wear: 13–15" - $180.00.

Chad Valley: See that section.

Chase, Martha: See that section.

Columbian Doll: Ca. 1890s. Sizes 15–29". Stamped "Columbian Doll/Manufactured by/Emma E. Adams/Oswego Centre/N.Y." After 1905–1906, the mark was "The Columbian Doll/ Manufactured by/Marietta Adams Ruttan/Oswego, NY." All cloth with painted features and flesh-painted hands and feet. Stitched fingers and toes. (See photo in Series 5, pg. 63;

20" primitive clown with excelsior-filled cloth body and limbs. Canvas-like material head is oil painted. Felt boots and hat. $200.00.

Series 9, pg. 62.) Extra clean: 16" - $4,600.00; 20" - $6,200.00. Fair, with slight scuffs or soil, repainted: 15" - $2,700.00; 23" - $3,200.00. **Columbian type:** 16" - $1,500.00 up; 22" - $2,500.00 up.

Comic Characters: Extra clean: 16" - $625.00 up. Soil and wear: 16" - $200.00 up.

Deans Rag Book Dolls: Golliwogs (Black): (See photo in Series 6, pg. 65.) 12" - $300.00; 14" - $450.00. **Child:** 10" - $300.00; 15" - $625.00; 17" - $825.00. **Printed face:** 10" - $95.00; 15" - $150.00; 17" - $225.00. **Mask face:** Velvet and cloth body and limbs. 12" - $125.00; 18" - $265.00; 24" - $385.00; 30" - $475.00; 34" - $565.00; 40" - $695.00.

Drayton, Grace: Dolly Dingle. 1923 by Averill Mfg. Co. Cloth with printed features, marked on torso. 11" - $400.00; 15" - $550.00. **Two faced or two headed (one at each end):** 16" - $695.00. **Chocolate Drop:** 1923 by Averill. Brown cloth with printed features and three tufts of yarn hair. 11" - $445.00; 16" - $625.00. **Hug Me Tight:** By Colonial Toy Mfg. Co. in 1916. One-piece printed cloth with boy standing behind girl. 12" - $250.00; 16" - $350.00. **Kitty-puss:** All cloth, cat face, wired posable limbs and tail. 16" - $425.00. **Peek-A-Boo:** Made by Horsman in 1913–1915. All cloth with printed features. 8" - $140.00; 10" - $185.00; 12" - $225.00.

40" Dean Rag doll with oil-painted modeled face mask. Rest of the body is cloth and velvet. Mohair waved hair and "fur" trimmed accents. In her arms is a 12" version of the same doll. Shown with a 42" "Raggedy Andy" by Knickerbocker. 40" - $695.00; 12" - $185.00; "Raggedy Andy" - $525.00. *Courtesy Turn of Century Antiques.*

Embroidered features, primitive: Home made, all cloth, yarn, lamb's wool or painted hair. **White:** 16" - $265.00 up; 20" - $485.00 up. **Black:** 15" - $365.00 up; 19" - $825.00 up.

Fangel, Maud Toursey: 1938 on. All cloth with printed features. Can have printed cloth body or plain body without "undies." Mitt-style hands with free-formed thumbs. Marked "M.T.F. 1938." (See photo in Series 5, pg. 58.) **Child:** "Snooks," "Sweets," "Peggy Ann," "Rosy," and others. Must be near mint condition. 9" - $375.00; 12" - $600.00; 15" - $700.00; 18" - $800.00. **Baby:** 14" - $525.00; 17" - $750.00.

Farnell's Alpha Toys: Marked with label on foot "Farnell's Alpha Toys/Made in England." (See photo in Series 6, pg. 58.) **Child:** 14" - $465.00; 16" - $575.00. **Baby:** 14" - $400.00; 17" - $500.00. **King George VI:** 16" - $1,250.00. **Palace Guard/Beefeater:** 16" - $650.00. **Boudoir dolls:** Adult face. 26–28" - $1,000.00.

Georgene Novelties: See Averill, Georgene section.

Kamkins: Made by Louise Kampes. 1928–1934. Marked on head or foot, also has paper heart-shaped label on chest. All cloth with molded face mask and painted features, wigs, boy or girl. Extra clean: 20" - $1,600.00; 25" - $2,000.00. Slight wear/soil: 20" - $800.00; 25" - $1,000.00.

Kewpie Cuddles: See Kewpie section.

Krueger, Richard: New York, 1917 on. All cloth, oil-painted mask face, yarn or mohair wig, oil cloth body. Clean and original. Marked with tag "Krueger, N.Y. Reg. U.S. Pat. Off. Made in USA. **Child:** 13" - $115.00; 16" - $150.00; 20" - $200.00. **Character:** 1940. Such as Pinocchio. 15–16" - $350.00 up.

Kruse, Käthe: See that section.

Leather dolls: 1890s on. Made in Germany. Oil-painted features, painted hair. **Lady:** Cloth body. 16" - $1,850.00. **Child or baby:** All leather, oil-painted features, jointed 10" - $950.00; 16" - $1,800.00.

Lenci: See Lenci section.

Liberty of London Royal Dolls:
Marked with cloth or paper tag. Flesh-colored cloth faces with stitched and painted features. All cloth bodies. 10" Royal Portrait dolls from 1939 include Queen Mary, King George VI, Queen Victoria and Princess Elizabeth. (See photo in Series 7, pg. 53) Extra clean: 10" - $150.00. Slight wear/soil: 10" - $60.00. **Other historical or coronation figures:** Extra clean: 10" - $150.00. Slight wear/soil: 10" - $60.00.

Madame Hendren: See Averill section.

Mammy style Black dolls: All cloth with painted or sewn features. **Circa 1910–1920s:** 10" - $150.00; 14" - $245.00; 17" - $425.00. **Circa 1930s:** 15" - $165.00 up.

Missionary Babies: See Beecher in this section.

Mollye: See Mollye in Modern section.

Mother's Congress Doll: Patented Nov. 1900. All cloth, printed features and hair. Mitt-style hands without formed thumbs. Designed and made by Madge Mead. Marked with cloth label "Mother's Congress Doll/Children's Favorite/Phila-delphia, Pa./Pat. Nov. 6, 1900." Extra clean: 17" - $900.00 up; 25" - $1,100.00 up. Slight soil: 17" - $400.00; 22" - $500.00. **Oil-painted faces and hair:** Unidentified, cloth body and limbs. 22" - $700.00; 27" - $950.00.

Philadelphia Baby: Also called "Sheppard Doll." Made by J.B. Sheppard in late 1890s to early 1900s. Stockinette covered body with painted cloth arms and legs. Modeled cloth head is painted. (See photo in Series 9, pg. 64.) Extra clean: 22" - $4,200.00. Slight soil and wear: 22" - $2,800.00. Very worn: 22" - $1,400.00.

Petzold, Dora: Germany, 1920s. Pressed paper head, painted features, wig, stockinette body filled with sawdust, short torso. Soft stuffed arms, free-formed thumbs, stitched fingers. Legs have formed calves. (See photo in Series 7, pg. 139.) 18" - $600.00; 22" - $800.00; 25" - $900.00.

Poir, Eugenie: 1920s, made in New York and France. All cloth body with felt face and limbs or can be all felt. Painted

Left: 23" American made all-cloth doll with oil-painted features and sewn on mohair wig, Muslin body with stitch jointed shoulders, elbows, hips, and knees. Original. Right: 23" "Philadelphia Baby" by J.B. Sheppard & Co. All stockinette with pressed, oil-painted head and lower limbs. Molded eyelids, stitched fingers and toes. All cloth - $625.00; "Philadelphia Baby" - $2,500.00 up. *Courtesy Frasher Doll Auctions.*

features, majority of eyes are painted to the side, mohair wig. Stitched four fingers together with free-standing thumb. Unmarked except for paper label. Extra clean: 17" - $675.00; 23" - $900.00. Slight soil and wear: 17" - $350.00; 23" - $400.00. **Photographic faces:** (Also see Babyland in this section) Extra clean: 16" - $600.00. Slight soil and wear: 16" - $250.00.

Printed Cloth Dolls: 1903 on. All cloth with features and/or underwear and clothes printed. These dolls are cut and sew types. (See photos in Series 4, pg. 53; Series 5, pg. 46; Series 10, pg. 62.) **Rastus, Cream of Wheat:** 18" - $145.00. **Aunt Jemima:** Set of four dolls. $100.00 each; **Printed-on underwear (Dolly Dear, Merry Marie, Flaked Rice, etc.):** Cut: 7" - $100.00; 16" - $175.00; 19" - $200.00. Uncut: 7" - $125.00; 16" - $200.00; 19" - $275.00. **Boys and girls with printed outer clothes:** Circa 1903. Cut: 9–10" - $100.00; 14" - $200.00; 19" - $325.00. Uncut: 9" - $125.00; 14" - $200.00; 19" - $300.00. **Black boy or girl:** 17" - $450.00; 21" - $625.00. **Brownies**: By Palmer Cox in 1892. 8" - $100.00; 14" - $200.00. **George/Martha Washington:** Art Fabric in 1901. Cut: $450.00. Uncut: Set of four - $850.00. **Punch and Judy:** 14" - $425.00 pair. **St. Nicholas/Santa Claus:** Marked "Pat. Dec. 28, 1886. Made by E.S. Peck, NY." One arm stuffed with toys and other arm holds American flag. Cut: 15" - $325.00. Uncut: 15" - $600.00.

Raynal: Made in France by Edouard Raynal. 1920s. Cloth body and limbs (sometimes has celluloid hands), felt mask face with painted features. Eyes painted to side. Marked on soles of shoes or will have necklace imprinted "Raynal." Original clothes generally are felt, but can have combination felt/organdy or just organdy. (See photo in Series 5, pg. 123.) Extra clean: 16" - $550.00; 21" - $775.00. Slight soil and wear: 16" - $225.00; 21" - $375.00.

Rollinson dolls: Molded cloth with painted features, head and limbs. Molded hair or wig. Designed by Gertrude F. Rollinson, made by Utley Doll Co. Marked with a stamp of doll in a diamond and printed around border "Rollinson Doll Holyoke, Ma." (See photo in Series 7, pg. 52.) **Molded hair:** Extra clean: 21" - $1,200.00 up. Slight soil and wear: 21" - $500.00. **Wigged by Rollinson:** Extra clean: 18" - $1,600.00 up, 23" - $2,000.00. Slight soil and wear: 20" - $700.00; 26" - $900.00. **Toddler with wig:** 18" - $1,800.00.

Smith, Mrs. S.S.: See Alabama in this section.

Soviet Union: 1920–1930s. (See photo in Series 8, pg. 57.) All cloth with stockinette hands and head. Molded face mask with painted features. Dressed in regional costumes. Marked "Made in Soviet Union." Extra clean: 10" - $145.00,

26½" Soviet stockinette doll with typical bound legs. Arms are stitched together in folded position. Molded features are oil painted. Clothes tag is printed in Cyrillic. All original. $700.00. *Courtesy Patricia Woods.*

14" - $250.00; 18" - $400.00. Slight soil and wear: 10" - $40.00; 14" - $85.00. **Tea cozies:** (See photo Series 8, pg. 57.) Doll from waist up with full skirt that is placed over teapot to keep contents warm. 17" - $185.00; 22" - $300.00; 28" - $400.00.

Steiff: See Steiff section.

Walker, Izannah: Made in 1870s and 1880s. Modeled head with oil- painted features, applied ears, cloth body and limbs, painted-on boots. Brushstroke or corkscrew curls around face over ears. Hands and feet are stitched. Marked "Patented Nov. 4, 1873." (See photo in Series 9, pg. 62.) Very good condition: 17" - $18,000.00; 20" - $28,000.00. Fair condition: 17" - $8,000.00; 20" - $12,000.00. Poor condition: 17" - $2,500.00; 20" - $3,400.00.

Two vertical curls in front of ears: Very good condition: 20" - $23,000.00 up; 26" - $28,000.00 up. Fair condition: 20"- $15,000.00; 26" - $19,000.00.

Wellings, Norah: See Wellings section.

Wellington: 1883 on. All stockinette, oil-painted features, lower limbs. Features are needle sculpted. Hair is painted. Has distinctive buttocks; rounded. Label on

21" Russian tea cozy with wonderful character smiling face. Arm bent and sewn to braid. Molded stockinette face and arms; the rest is cloth. Heavily batted quilted skirt (no torso or lower limbs) to put over teapot. This example - $385.00.

back: "Pat. Jan. 8, 1883." Excellent condition: 22–23" - $15,000.00 up. Fair to poor condition: 22–23" - $6,000.00 up.

COMPOSITION DOLLS – GERMANY

Most German manufacturers made composition-headed dolls as well as dolls of bisque and other materials. Composition dolls were made in Germany before World War I, but the majority were made in the 1920s and 1930s. They can be all composition or have a composition head with cloth body and limbs. Prices are for excellent quality and condition.

Child: All composition with wig, sleep/flirty eyes, open or closed mouth and jointed composition body. Unmarked or just have numbers. 14" - $245.00; 18" - $375.00; 21" - $500.00; 24" - $600.00.

Marked: Name of company (or initials). 14" - $300.00; 18" - $475.00; 25" - $600.00; 28" - $750.00.

Baby: All composition, open mouth. 14" - $185.00; 16" - $345.00; 19" - $450.00. **Toddler:** 18" - $485.00; 22" - $625.00.

Baby: Composition head and limbs with cloth body, open mouth, sleep eyes. 16" - $200.00; 22" - $300.00; 27" - $485.00.

Painted Eyes, child: 14" - $165.00; 18" - $275.00. **Baby:** 14" - $165.00; 18" - $300.00.

Shoulder Head: Composition shoulder head, glass eyes, wig, open or closed mouth, cloth or kidaleen body with composition arms (full arms or lower arms only with cloth upper arms), and lower legs. May have bare feet or modeled boots. Prices for dolls in extra clean condition and nicely dressed. Unmarked. (Also see Wax Section.) Excellent quality: Extremely fine modeling. 12" - $400.00; 16" - $500.00; 21" - $700.00; 24" - $750.00; 29" - $975.00.

Average quality: May resemble a china head doll. 12" - $165.00; 14" - $200.00; 17" - $250.00; 22" - $325.00; 25" - $365.00; 29" - $500.00; 36" - $725.00.

Painted Hair: 10" - $165.00; 15" - $250.00; 19" - $475.00.

Swivel Neck: On composition shoulder plate. 14" - $450.00; 17" - $600.00; 23" - $750.00.

CRECHE

The early creche figures had gesso-over-wood head and limbs and wire frames with fabric covered bodies. These figures have extremely fine detailed heads with carved hair or fine curly wigs. They have inset glass eyes. On later figures, terra cotta replaced the gesso and the eyes were painted, with a few still having glass eyes.

Older creche: 1790s. Gesso over wood or all wood. **Woman:** 13" - $400.00; 20" - $800.00. **Man:** 13" - $600.00; 20" - $900.00. **Child:** 11" - $300.00; 14" - $450.00.

Later creche: 1820s. Made with terra cotta. **Woman:** 13" - $195.00; 20" - $295.00. **Man:** 13" - $225.00; 20" - $300.00. **Child:** 11" - $150.00; 14" - $185.00.

13" early creche figure made of gesso over wood. Painted features. Original. $765.00. *Courtesy Turn of Century Antiques.*

Chambre Syndicates des Fabricants de Jouets et Jeux et Engins Sportif. One member was Societe du Caoutchouc Manufacture.
Child: Closed mouth. Excellent quality bisque. Allow more for original clothes. 12" - $925.00; 16" - $1,300.00.

12" bisque shoulder head with cloth body and bisque lower limbs. Beautiful face with large glass eyes and unusual modeled, painted mouth. Darker line between lips. Original clothes. Made by C.S.F.J. which had over 47 doll/toy manufacturers in its syndicate. This particular doll was made by Societe du Cautchouc, circa 1895. #4, marked with inverted triangle (▽). $1,100.00. *Courtesy Kathy Riddick*

DE FUISSEAUX

This wonderful 21" character was made by De Fuisseaux in Baudour, Belgium, circa 1910. Painted eyes, closed mouth. Kid body with bisque lower arms. Marked "F.2." $6,000.00. *Courtesy Virginia Sofie.*

Many French and German dolls bear the mark "DEP" as part of their mold marks, but the dolls referred to here are marked *only with the* DEP *and a size number.* They are on French bodies with some bearing a Jumeau sticker. The early 1880s DEP dolls have fine quality bisque and artist workmanship, and the later dolls of the 1890s and into the 1900s generally have fine bisque, but the color will be higher, and they will have painted lashes below the eyes with most having hair eyelashes over the eyes. The early dolls will have outlined lips but the later ones will not. Prices are for clean, undamaged and nicely dressed dolls.

Marks:

DEP
10

27" made from Jumeau mold. Sleep eyes and open mouth. On French jointed body. Incised "DEP." $2,100.00. *Courtesy Turn of Century Antiques.*

Open mouth: 12" - $700.00; 14" - $875.00; 18" - $1,200.00; 21" - $1,500.00; 25" - $1,900.00; 30" - $2,500.00; 35" - $3,400.00. **Open mouth, very Jumeau looking, red check marks:** 18" - $1,600.00; 23" - $2,100.00; 30" - $3,200.00.

Closed mouth: 14" - $2,500.00; 18" - $3,300.00; 25" - $4,000.00; 28" - $4,500.00. Unusually fine example: 18" - $3,900.00; 28" - $5,000.00 up.

Walking, kissing (open mouth): 16" - $1,300.00; 19" - $1,700.00; 22" - $1,900.00; 26" - $2,500.00.

20" with French body and voice box cryer. Has very Jumeau look. Upper hair lashes, painted lower ones. Open mouth with outlined lips. Original wig. Clothes may be original. Doll marked "DEP 8." Wig marked "Cheveux naturel Paris, France." $1,400.00. *Courtesy Kathy Riddick.*

Doll house man or woman: With molded hair/wig and painted eyes. 6–7" - $160.00–230.00.

Children: All bisque: 3½" - $80.00, 5!/2" - $125.00. Bisque/cloth: 3½" - $95.00; 5!/2" - $150.00.

Man or woman with glass eyes and wigs: 6–7" - $400.00–465.00.

Man or woman with molded hair: Glass eyes. 6–7" - $400.00.

Man with mustache: (See photo in Series 6, pg. 70.) 5½–6½" - $165.00–250.00.

Grandparents, old people, or molded-on hats: 6–7" - $265.00 up.

Military men: Have mustaches. Original. (See photo in Series 8, pg. 128; Series 9, pg. 68.) 6–7" - $600.00 up. **Molded helmet:** 6–7" - $725.00 up.

Black man or woman: Molded hair, all original. 6–7" - $465.00.

Chauffeur: Molded cap. 6–7" - $275.00 up.

Swivel neck: Wig or molded hair. 6–7" - $700.00 up.

China glaze with early hairdos: (See photo in Series 8, pg. 62.) 4–5" - $300.00-385.00. **Low brow/common hairdo:** 1900s and after. $65.00–125.00.

Wonderful 6" doll house "chef" in original box. Early round face, closed mouth, and glass eyes. Box is marked 1889. This example - $600.00. *Courtesy Jane Walker.*

DRESSEL, CUNO & OTTO

Cuno & Otto Dressel operated in Sonneberg, Thuringia, Germany and were sons of the founder. Although the firm was in business in 1700, they are not listed as dollmakers until 1873. They produced dolls with bisque heads or composition over wax heads, which can be on cloth, kid, or jointed composition bodies. Some of their heads were made for them by other German firms, such as Simon & Halbig, Heubach, etc. They registered the trademark for "Jutta" in 1906 and by 1911 were also making celluloid dolls. Prices are for undamaged, clean and nicely dressed dolls.

Marks:

C.O.D.

C.O.D. 49 D.E.P.
Made in Germany

Babies: 1910 on. Marked "C.O.D." but without the word "Jutta." Allow more for toddler body. 12" - $325.00. 15" - $425.00; 18" - $585.00; 24" - $785.00.

Child: 1893 on. Jointed composition body. Open mouth. 15" - $365.00; 18" - $465.00; 23" - $525.00; 25" - $600.00; 30" - $1,200.00; 35" - $2,100.00.

Child: Shoulder head or turned head on jointed kid body. Open mouth. 16" - $325.00; 20" - $695.00; 24" - $775.00.

Jutta baby: 1910–1922. Open mouth. Five-piece bent limb body. 12" - $425.00; 14" - $500.00; 17" - $650.00; 20" - $800.00; 24" - $1,300.00; 27" - $1,700.00.

Jutta toddler: 8" - $575.00; 14" - $665.00; 17" - $900.00; 20" - $1,100.00; 24" - $1,500.00; 26" - $1,800.00.

Jutta child: Marked with "Jutta" or with **S&H #1914, #1348, #1349, etc.:** 1906–1921. (See photo in Series 8, pg. 67.) 13" - $425.00; 15" - $550.00; 19" - $685.00; 23" - $825.00; 25" - $925.00; 30" - $1,200.00; 38–39" - $2,500.00.

Lady doll: 1920s. Flapper with adult face, closed mouth. On five-piece composition body with thin limbs and high heel feet. Hoses painted on entire leg. Original clothes. Marked **#1469.** (See photo in Series 8, pg. 66.) 14" - $3,800.00; 16" - $4,200.00. Redressed or nude: 14" - $2,700.00; 16" - $3,300.00.

Character dolls: 1909 and after. Closed mouth. Molded hair or wig. May be glazed inside head. **Painted eyes:** 12" - $1,700.00; 14" - $2,200.00; 17" - $2,800.00; 22" - $3,200.00. **Glass eyes:** 14" - $2,400.00; 17" - $3,000.00; 22" - $3,400.00; 24" - $3,500.00.

Character dolls: Marked with letter and number, such as **B/4, A/2, or A/16.** Jointed child or toddler body, painted eyes, closed mouth. No damage, ready to display. 12" - $1,400.00; 15–16" - $2,500.00; 18" - $2,800.00.

Composition: 1870s. Shoulder head, glass or painted eyes, molded hair or wig. Cloth body with composition limbs with molded-on boots. Will be marked with Holz-Masse:

19½" with turned shoulderhead and open mouth. On kid body with bisque lower arms. $695.00. *Courtesy Turn of Century Antiques.*

With wig: Glass eyes. 14" - $250.00; 16" - $325.00; 24" - $425.00. **Molded hair:** 13" - $250.00; 17" - $400.00; 24" - $565.00.

Portrait dolls: 1896. Such as **Uncle Sam, The Farmer, Admiral Dewey, Admiral Byrd, Old Rip, Witch, etc.** Portrait bisque head, glass eyes, composition body. Some will be marked with a **"D"** or **"S."** Heads made for Dressel by Simon & Halbig. Prices for clean, undamaged and originally dressed. **Military dolls:** (See photo in Series 6, pg. 72) 9" - $750.00; 13" - $1,600.00; 16" - $2,000.00. **Old Rip, Farmer or Witch:** 9" - $725.00; 13" - $1,400.00; 16" - $1,700.00. **Uncle Sam:** 9" - $825.00; 13" - $1,500.00; 16" - $2,000.00. **Buffalo Bill:** 10–12" - $765.00. **Father Christmas:** 10–12" - $1,500.00 up.

Fur covered: Glued on body/limbs. 8–9" - $175.00; 12" - $265.00.

E.D.

E. Denamur of Paris made dolls from 1885 to 1898. The E.D. marked dolls seem to be accepted as being made by Denamur, but they could have been made by E. Dumont, Paris. Composition and wood jointed bodies. Prices are for excellent quality bisque, no damage and nicely dressed.

Closed or open/closed mouth: 15" - $2,300.00; 17" - $2,900.00; 22" - $3,400.00; 25" - $3,800.00; 28" - $4,400.00; 32" - $5,000.00.

Open mouth: 16" - $1,600.00; 18" - $1,800.00; 22" - $2,300.00; 25" - $2,700.00.

Black: Open mouth. 18" - $2,600.00; 24" - $3,200.00.

Marks:

$$E\,6\,D$$

E5D
DEPOSE

20" with closed mouth. On jointed body with straight wrists. Clothes and wig may be original. Marked "E.D." $3,000.00.

Fleischmann & Bloedel of Fürth, Bavaria; Sonneberg, Thuringia; and Paris, France was founded in 1873 and making dolls in Paris by 1890. The company became a part of S.F.B.J. in 1899. Dolls have composition jointed bodies and can have open or closed mouths. Prices are for dolls with excellent color and quality bisque, no damage and nicely dressed.

Marks:

EDEN BÉBÉ PARIS

Closed or open/closed mouth: Pale bisque. 15" - $2,400.00; 18" - $2,850.00; 22" - $3,100.00; 26" - $3,800.00.

Closed mouth: High color bisque. Five-piece body. 12" - $1,200.00; 15" - $1,400.00; 18" - $1,700.00; 22" - $2,000.00; 26" - $2,500.00.

Open mouth: 15" - $1,200.00; 18" - $2,000.00; 22" - $2,400.00; 26" - $3,000.00.

Walking, kissing doll: Jointed body with walker mechanism, head turns and one arm throws a kiss. Heads by Simon & Halbig using mold **#1039** (and others). Bodies assembled by Fleischmann & Bloedel. Price for perfect, working doll. 21" - $1,800.00 up.

18" with large paperweight eyes. Open/closed mouth with space between lips. Has an "F.G." look. Marked "Eden Bébé 1." $2,850.00. *Courtesy Frasher Doll Auctions.*

ELLIS, JOEL

Joel Ellis made dolls in Springfield, Vermont, in 1873 and 1874 under the name Co-operative Manufacturing Co. All wood jointed body has tenon and mortise joints, arms are jointed in same manner. The hands and feet are made of pewter. Has molded hair and painted features.

Springfield Wooden Doll: It must be noted that dolls similar to the Joel Ellis ones were made in Springfield, Vt. also by Joint Doll Co. and D.M. Smith & Co. They are very much like the Joel Ellis except when standing the knee joint will be flush

with the method of jointing not showing. The hips are cut out with the leg tops cut to fit the opening, and the detail of the hands is not as well done. Prices are also for Mason-Taylor dolls. (See example under Bonnet dolls.)

Fair condition: Does not need to be dressed. 11" - $575.00; 13" - $750.00.

Excellent condition: 13" - $950.00 up; 15" - $1,300.00 up.

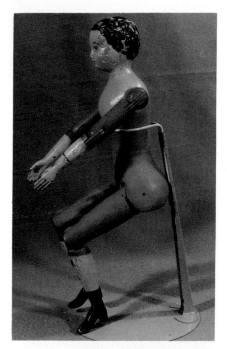

12" Joel Ellis doll that is all wood with tendon and mortise joints and metal hands and feet. $950.00. *Courtesy Startzel's.*

FASHION AND FORTUNE DOLLS, FRENCH

These "adult" style dolls were made by a number of French firms from about 1860 into the 1930s. Many will be marked only with a number or have a stamp on the body, although some of the stamps/labels may be the store from where they were sold and not the maker. The most available fashion doll seems to be marked F.G. dolls. Prices are for dolls in perfect condition with no cracks, chips, or repairs and in beautiful old or newer clothes made of appropriate age materials.

Articulated wood: Marked or unmarked. Or blown kid bodies and limbs. Some have bisque lower arms. 16" - $6,600.00 up; 20" - $8,500.00 up.

Articulated: Marked or unmarked. With bisque lower legs and arms with excellent modeling detail. 16" - $8,500.00 up; 22" - $9,500.00 up.

Marked "Bru": (Also see Smiling Mona Lisa in this section.) 1860s. Round face, swivel neck, glass eyes: (See photo in Series 6, pg. 79.) 14" - $2,900.00; 17" - $4,400.00; 20" - $5,300.00 up. **Wood body:** 14" - $4,700.00.

Marked "Huret": Bisque or china glazed shoulder head, kid body with bisque lower arms. **Painted eyes:** 15" - $5,400.00; 18" - $6,500.00. **Glass eyes:** 14" - $6,000.00; 17" - $7,400.00. **Wood body:** 15" - $6,750.00 up; 18" - $8,600.00 up. **Gutta percha body:** 16" - $9,500.00 up; 19" - $12,000.00 up. **Portrait adult lady:** Painted eyes, articulated body with metal hands. (See photo is Series 4, pg. 64.) 20" - $12,000.00.

Huret Child: 16" - $24,000.00 up; 20" - $28,000.00 up.

Marked "Rohmer": (See photo in Series 7, pg. 65 and Series 8, pg. 71.)

Bisque or china glazed shoulder head (can be jointed). Kid body with bisque lower arms (or china). **Glass eyes:** 16" - $6,600.00; 19" - $10,500.00; **Painted eyes:** 16" - $6,200.00; 19" - $9,000.00. **Wood body:** 15" - $7,000.00; 18" - $11,000.00.

Unmarked Rohmer or Huret type: Painted eyes. 16" - $5,000.00; 20" - $5,800.00; 26" - $7,000.00. **Wire controlled flat glass sleep eyes:** 27" - $12,000.00. **Painted black hair:** Kid body. 16" - $3,900.00.

Marked "Jumeau": Will have number on head and stamped body. (See photo in Series 7, pg. 79.) **Portrait-style head:** 15" - $3,000.00; 18" - $5,200.00; 21" - $6,000.00; 24" - $6,800.00. 27" - $7,400.00. **Wood body:** 15" - $5,600.00; 18" - $8,600.00 up; 24" - $10,000.00 up.

Marked "Jumeau": Swivel head. 13–14" - $2,800.00; 17" - $3,400.00; 21" -

23" Bru fashion with bisque swivel shoulder head, cobalt blue eyes, original wig, and old clothes. $4,000.00 up. *Courtesy Barbara Earnshaw-Cain.*

25½" with swivel neck on bisque shoulder-plate. Smiling mouth and all kid body. Marked "Depose K" on forehead and back of head. (Now attributed to Bru as maker.) $6,400.00. *Courtesy Frasher Doll Auctions.*

$3,800.00. **Wood body:** Bisque limbs. 17" - $5,400.00; 21" - $6,500.00. **Very large eyes:** 11–12" - $2,200.00; 15–16" - $2,600.00.

Marked "F.G.": 1860 on. All kid body, one-piece shoulder and head. Glass eyes: 11" - $975.00; 13" - $1,100.00; 16" - $1,500.00. Painted eyes: 11" - $800.00; 13" - $1,100.00; 16" - $1,400.00.

Marked "F.G.": 1860 on. All kid body (or bisque lower arms), swivel head on bisque shoulder plate. Glass eyes: 12" - $1,600.00; 14" - $2,500.00; 17" - $3,000.00; 21" - $3,500.00; 26" - $4,400.00. **Black:** 14" - $2,900.00; 18" - $4,000.00.

Marked "F.G.": Gesland cloth-covered body with bisque lower arms and legs. Early face. 15" - $5,400.00; 18" - $6,400.00; 23" - $6,800.00; 26" - $7,400.00.

Marked "F.G.": Gesland cloth-covered body with composition or papier maché lower arms and legs. 15" - $4,000.00; 18" - $4,800.00; 23" - $5,200.00; 26" - $5,600.00.

Smiling "Mona Lisa": After 1866. Now being referred to as made by Bru. (See photo in Series 8, pg. 72; Series 9. pg. 74.) Kid body with leather lower arms, stitched fingers or bisque lower arms. Swivel head on bisque shoulder plate. Marked with letter (example: E, B, D, etc.) Allow more for wood body or arms. 12" - $2,600.00; 15" - $3,800.00; 18" - $5,000.00; 22" - $5,500.00; 26" - $6,400.00; 29" - $9,400.00.

Unmarked with numbers only: Kid body with one-piece bisque head and shoulder. Extremely fine quality bisque, undamaged. Glass eyes: 12" - $1,200.00; 14" - $1,400.00; 22" - $2,200.00. Painted eyes: 14" - $950.00; 17" - $1,400.00; 22" - $1,800.00. **Swivel neck:** Bisque shoulder plate. Glass eyes, kid body. Extremely fine quality bisque and undamaged. 12" -

$2,200.00; 14" - $2,500.00; 16" - $2,900.00; 18" - $3,400.00. **Black:** 14" - $1,800.00 up. **Wood or twill over wood body:** 14" - $3,700.00; 17" - $4,400.00.

Unmarked: Medium to fair quality. **One-piece head and shoulder:** 11" - $550.00; 15" - $725.00–1,000.00. **Swivel head:** On bisque shoulder plate. 16" - $1,000.00; 20" - $1,700.00 up.

Marked E.B. (E. Barrois): 1854–1877. (See photo in Series 7, pg. 67.) Allow more for bisque or wood arms. Glass eyes: 16" - $3,400.00; 20" - $4,900.00. Painted eyes: 17" - $3,000.00; 21" - $3,700.00. **China glaze:** (See photo in Series 8, pg. 73.) 16" - $6,000.00.

Marked "Simone": Glass eyes: 20" - $5,700.00; 24" - $6,800.00.

Factory original fashion clothes: Dress: $600.00 up. Wig: $300.00 up. Cape: $300.00 up. Boots: $250.00 up. Boots marked by maker: $500.00 up.

18" French fashion doll with swivel head on bisque shoulderplate and kid body. Cobalt blue eyes, original wig, and antique outfit. $3,400.00. *Courtesy Barbara Earnshaw-Cain.*

13" Simone type fashion with glass eyes. Body is wood articulated with tenon joints at shoulders, elbows, hips, and knees. Lower arms are bisque. Old costume and wig. $7,000.00. *Courtesy Frasher Doll Auctions.*

Fortune dolls: French fashion type head with swivel neck, kid body. Open mouth, painted or glass eyes. Underskirt formed by many folded papers written in French. (See photo in Series 5, pg. 62; Series 8, pg. 82.) 18" - $3,000.00 up. **Closed mouth:** 18" - $4,800.00 up. **Wooden (German):** Tuck comb of mid-19th century. 17½" - $3,400.00 up.

F.G. BÉBÉ/GESLAND

F. Gaultier (earlier spelled Gauthier) is the accepted maker of the F.G. marked dolls. These dolls are often found on the cloth-covered or all composition bodies that are marked "Gesland." The Gesland firm was operated by two brothers. One of them had the initial "F" (1887–1900).

Marks:

(1887–1900)

F. 8 G.

(1879–1887 Block Letter Mark)

Child with closed mouth (scroll mark): Excellent quality bisque, no damage and nicely dressed. 7–8" - $750.00; 12" - $1,200.00; 15" - $2,600.00; 17" - $3,000.00; 20" - $3,200.00; 23" - $3,600.00; 25" - $4,200.00; 30" - $4,900.00. **High face color:** No damage and nicely dressed. 14" - $1,200.00; 16" - $1,700.00; 19" - $1,900.00; 22" - $2,200.00; 25" - $2,600.00.

Child with open mouth (scroll mark): Excellent quality bisque, no damage and nicely dressed. 10–12" - $650.00; 15" - $1,700.00; 17" - $1,900.00; 20" - $2,200.00; 23" - $2,600.00; 27" - $3,000.00. **High face color:** Very dark lips. No damage, nicely dressed. 14" - $1,200.00; 16" - $1,700.00; 19" - $1,900.00; 22" - $2,200.00; 25" - $2,600.00.

Marked "F.G. Fashion": See Fashion section.

Child on marked Gesland body: (See photo is Series 6, pg. 80; Series 8, pg. 80.) Bisque head on stockinette over wire frame body with composition limbs. Closed mouth: 16" - $5,000.00; 19" - $5,500.00; 25" - $6,200.00. Open mouth: 17" - $2,600.00; 21" - $3,000.00; 26" - $3,900.00.

17" with large glass eyes and closed mouth. On French jointed body with straight wrists. Marked "F.G." in scroll. $3,000.00. *Courtesy Turn of Century Antiques.*

Block letter (so called) F.G. child:
1879–1887. Closed mouth, chunky composition body, excellent quality and condition. 12–13" - $3,900.00; 16–17" - $4,750.00; 19–21" - $5,100.00; 23–24" - $5,500.00; 26–27" - $6,000.00; 34" - $7,000.00. **Gusseted kid body:** Bisque swivel head on bisque shoulder plate, bisque lower arms. 17" - $4,900.00; 21" - $5,200.00; 26" - $6,000.00.

Boy: Kid body, painted eyes, and closed mouth. Painted brown hair. (See photo in Series 8, pg. 75.) 12" - $1,800.00 up.

9" with trousseau, circa 1887–1900. Never played with condition. Marked "F.G." in scroll. Trousseau set - $3,500.00. *Courtesy Turn of Century Antiques.*

FRENCH BÉBÉ, MAKER UNKNOWN

A variety of French doll makers produced unmarked dolls from the 1880s into the 1920s. These dolls may only have a head size number or be marked "Paris" or "France." Many of the accepted French dolls that have a number are now being attributed to German makers and it will be questionable for some time.

Unmarked French Bébé: Closed or open/closed mouth, paperweight eyes. Excellent quality bisque and artistry on French body. Prices for clean, undamaged and nicely dressed dolls.

16" unknown French child with closed mouth and large expressive eyes. Appears to be all original. Marked "189." $3,000.00. *Courtesy Turn of Century Antiques.*

Early desirable, very French-style face: Marks such as "J.D." (maker probably J. DuSerre. See photo in Series 8, pg. 71), "J.M. Paris," numbers only, and "H.G." (probably made by Henri & Granfe-Guimonneau. See photo in Series 6, pg. 99). 14" - $10,000.00; 18" - $19,000.00 up; 22" - $24,000.00 up; 26" - $27,000.00 up.

Jumeau or Bru style face: May be marked "W.D." or "R.R." (See photo in Series 8, pg. 76.) 15" - $3,200.00; 18" - $4,400.00; 21" - $4,800.00; 24" - $5,300.00; 27" - $5,900.00.

Excellent quality, closed mouth: Unusual face. Molds such as **F.1, F.2, J, #137, 136, etc.** (See photo in Series 8, pg. 79.) 10" - $1,900.00; 15" - $4,500.00; 18" - $5,000.00; 23" - $6,000.00; 27" - $8,000.00.

Standard French-looking head: Excellent bisque, closed mouth. 15" - $3,000.00; 18" - $4,000.00; 23" - $4,800.00.

Medium quality: May have poor painting and/or blotches to skin tones. 16" - $1,300.00; 21" - $1,800.00; 26" - $2,200.00.

Excellent quality, open mouth: 1890s and later. Will be on French body. 15" - $1,800.00; 18" - $2,300.00; 22" - $2,500.00; 25" - $3,200.00.

Open mouth, high face color: 1920s. May have five-piece papier maché body. 16" - $650.00; 20" - $825.00; 24" - $1,000.00.

14" unknown French doll with paperweight glass eyes and open mouth. On chunky 1920s style toddler body. Marked "0" on lower neck and "4" on back of body. $600.00. *Courtesy Sharon Caldwell.*

Cute 12" unmarked French Bébé with caracul wig and full closed mouth. On early straight wrist French body. Has pale bisque. Dress and undies may be original. $1,900.00. *Courtesy Barbara Earnshaw-Cain.*

Freundlich Novelty Company operated in New York from 1923. Most of their dolls have a cardboard tag and will be unmarked or may have name on the head, but no maker's name.

Baby Sandy: 1939–1942. All composition with molded hair, sleep or painted eyes. Marked "Baby Sandy" on head. (See photo in Series 6, pg. 85.) **Excellent condition:** No cracks, craze or chips. Original or appropriate clothes. 8" - $185.00; 12" - $245.00; 16" - $350.00 up; 19" - $650.00. **With light crazing:** Clean, may be redressed. 8" - $85.00; 12" - $100.00; 16" - $125.00; 19" - $200.00.

General Douglas MacArthur: Circa 1942. Portrait doll of all composition with painted features. Molded hat. Jointed shoulders and hips. (See photo in Series 6, pg. 85.) **Excellent condition:** Original. 16" - $265.00; 18" - $325.00. **Light craze:** Clothes dirty. 16" - $100.00; 18" - $125.00.

Military dolls: Circa 1942 on. All composition with painted features and molded-on hats. Can be woman or man – W.A.V.E, W.A.A.C., sailor, Marine, etc. (See photo in Series 5, pg. 65; Series 6, pg. 85.) **Excellent condition:** Original and no crazing. 16" - $250.00 up. **Light craze:** Clothes in fair condition. 16" - $95.00.

Pinocchio: Composition and cloth with molded hair. Painted features with bright red cheeks. Large eyes, moderate size nose, and open/closed mouth. Tongue molded on one side of mouth. Tagged "Original as portrayed by C. Collodi." 16" - $400.00 up.

15" "Baby Sandy" from 1939. Made of all composition with sleep eyes, open smile mouth, and molded hair. All original. $350.00. *Courtesy Jeannie Mauldin.*

Storybook dolls: Orphan Annie/ Sandy, Red Riding Hood/Wolf/Grandma, etc. 9–12" - $250.00–400.00.

Ventriloquist Doll (Dummy Dan): (See photo in Series 7, pg. 73.) Looks like Charlie McCarthy. 15" - $145.00; 21" - $350.00 up.

FROZEN CHARLOTTE AND CHARLIE

Frozen Charlotte and Charlie figures can be china, partly china (such as hair and boots), stone bisque or fine porcelain bisque. They can have molded hair, have painted bald heads or take wigs. The majority have no joints, with hands extended and legs separate (some are together). They generally come without clothes and they can have painted-on boots, shoes and socks or be barefooted.

It must be noted that in 1976 a large amount of the 15½–16" "Charlie" figures were reproduced in Germany and their quality is excellent. It is almost impossible to tell that these are reproductions.

Prices are for doll figures without any damage. More must be allowed for any with unusual hairdos, an early face or molded eyelids or molded-on clothes.

All china: Glazed with black or blonde hair, excellent quality of painting and unjointed. 2" - $55.00; 5" - $110.00; 7" - $150.00; 9" - $235.00; 10" - $250.00. **Bald head with wig:** 6" - $125.00; 8" - $150.00; 10" - $200.00. **Charlie:** Molded black hair, flesh tones to neck and head. (See photo in Series 3, pg. 67.) 12" - $300.00; 14" - $475.00; 17" - $650.00. **All pink luster:** 12" - $475.00 up. Luster to

head and neck only: $350.00. Blonde: 14–15" - $500.00 up.

Untinted bisque (Parian): Mold-ed hair, unjointed. 4" - $150.00; 7" - $185.00.

Untinted bisque: 1860s. Molded hair, jointed at shoulders. 4" - $160.00; 7" - $250.00.

Stone bisque: Unjointed, molded hair, medium to excellent quality of painting. 4" - $45.00; 8" - $65.00.

Black Charlotte or Charlie: Unjointed, no damage. 3" - $150.00; 5" - $250.00; 7" - $350.00. Jointed at shoulders: 4" - $225.00; 7" - $425.00.

Molded headband or bow: Excellent quality: 5" - $200.00; 8" - $300.00. Medium quality: 5" - $125.00; 8" - $165.00.

Molded-on clothes, shorts, or bonnet: Unjointed, no damage and medium to excellent quality. (See photo in Series 4, pg. 33.) 3" - $285.00; 6" - $450.00; 8" - $525.00.

Dressed in original clothes: Unjointed Charlotte or Charlie. No damage and in overall excellent condition. 5" - $135.00; 7" - $185.00.

Jointed at shoulder: Original clothes and no damage. (See photo in Series 2, pg. 75.) 6" - $150.00; 8" - $235.00.

Molded-on, painted boots: Unjointed, no damage. 5" - $185.00; 7" - $250.00. Jointed at shoulders: 5" - $225.00; 7" - $325.00.

Unique hairdo and boots: 5" - $325.00.

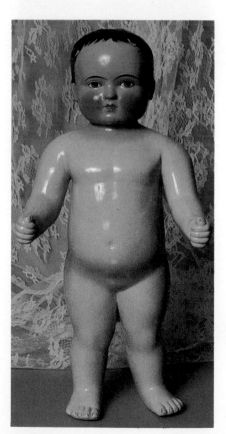

15½" "Frozen Charlie" with pink fleshtones on head and neck. Wide spread legs, molded hair, and painted features. $600.00. *Courtesy Turn of Century Antiques.*

Fulper Pottery Co. of Flemington, N.J. made dolls from 1918–1921. They made children and babies and used composition and kid bodies.

Marks:

Made in U.S.A.

Child: Fair to medium quality bisque head painting. No damage, nicely dressed. **Composition body, open mouth:** 14" - $300.00; 16" - $450.00; 20" - $600.00. **Kid body, open mouth:** 15" - $325.00; 17" - $425.00; 21" - $550.00.

Child: Poor quality (white chalky look, may have crooked mouth and be poorly painted.) **Composition body:** 16" - $225.00; 21" - $325.00. **Kid body:** 16" - $175.00; 21" - $275.00.

Baby: Bent limb body, open mouth. Near excellent to medium quality bisque. No damage and dressed well. Good artist work on features. 15" - $525.00; 18" - $625.00; 25" - $900.00. **Toddler:** Has toddler jointed or straight leg body. 18" - $775.00; 26" - $1,100.00.

Baby: Poor quality bisque and painting. 16" - $160.00; 25" - $400.00. **Toddler:** 18" - $325.00; 26" - $650.00.

GANS & SEYFARTH

Dolls with the "G.S." or "G & S" were made by Gans & Seyfarth of Germany who made dolls from 1909 into the 1930s. Some dolls will be marked with the full name.

Child: Open mouth, composition body. Good quality bisque, no damage and nicely dressed. (See photo in Series 9, pg. 82.) 12" - $350.00; 15" - $550.00; 18" - $675.00; 20" - $750.00; 25" - $850.00; 30" - $1,100.00.

Baby: Bent limb baby body. Perfect condition and nicely dressed. (Add more for toddler body.) 15" - $400.00; 18" - $585.00; 22" - $700.00; 25" - $800.00.

G.D.

9" with closed mouth and five-piece body. Glass eyes with no painted lashes. Head is marked "Paris/G.D. Made by Henri Delcroix for Granjean." Body on lower back is marked with "G.D." in diamond. 9" - $600.00; 15" - $1,250.00; 18" - $1,600.00. *Courtesy Kathy Riddick.*

Left: 15" has bisque head with pierced nostrils on cloth body. Signed "Arthur A. Gerling/Made in Germany." Right: 9½" "Bye-Lo" with sleep eyes, cloth body, and celluloid hands. 15" - $695.00; 9½" - $500.00. *Courtesy Turn of Century Antiques.*

GERMAN DOLLS, MAKER UNKNOWN

Some of these unmarked dolls will have a mold number and/or a head size number and some may have the mark "Germany."

Closed mouth child: 1880–1890s. Excellent bisque. No damage and nicely dressed. **Jointed composition body:** 12" - $850.00; 16" - $1,400.00; 21" - $1,900.00; 25" - $2,600.00. **Kid or cloth body:** May have slightly turned head. Bisque lower arms. 12" - $575.00; 15" - $800.00; 20" - $1,200.00; 24" - $1,400.00; 26" - $1,600.00.

26" bisque shoulderhead with kid body, sleep eyes, open mouth, and wood turned lower arms. Marked "1500-4½-Germany." $475.00. *Courtesy Arthur Michnevitz.*

Open mouth child: Late 1880s to 1900. Excellent pale bisque, glass eyes. No damage and nicely dressed. **Jointed composition body:** 12" - $185.00; 15" - $285.00; 20" - $450.00; 23" - $550.00; 26" - $650.00; 30" - $900.00. **Kid body:** Excellent quality bisque. Bisque lower arms. 15" - $175.00; 20" - $300.00; 23" - $425.00; 26" - $550.00.

Open mouth child: 1888–1920s. With very "dolly" type face. Overall excellent condition. **Jointed composition body:** 12" - $150.00; 15" - $175.00; 18" - $285.00; 22" - $400.00; 25" - $525.00; 28" - $675.00; 32" - $750.00. **Kid body:** 12" - $125.00; 15" - $150.00; 18" - $200.00; 22" - $350.00.

Belton type: May have **mold #132, 136, 137, 138, etc.** Composition jointed body, glass eyes. **Open mouth:** 12" - $1,400.00; 15" - $1,900.00; 20" - $2,800.00; 24" - $3,200.00. **Closed mouth:** Excellent quality. 16" - $2,600.00; 19" - $3,200.00; 26" - $4,200.00.

Molded hair: See that section.

All bisque: See All Bisque – German section.

Infants: Bisque head, molded/painted hair, cloth body with composition or celluloid hands, glass eyes. No damage. 10–12" - $325.00; 15" - $500.00; 18" - $625.00.

Babies: Solid dome or wigged, five-piece baby body, open mouth. Nicely dressed and no damage. (Allow more for closed or open/closed mouth or very unusual face and toddler doll.) **Glass eyes:** 8–9" - $265.00; 14" - $475.00; 17" - $600.00; 22" - $765.00. **Painted eyes:** 8–9" - $185.00; 14" - $300.00; 17" - $400.00; 22" - $650.00. **Toddler:** 14" - $550.00; 17" - $625.00.

Bonnet or hat: See Bonnet Doll section.

8½" "Max and Moritz" with bisque heads, painted features, and five-piece composition bodies. Painted-on shoes and socks. Maker unknown. "Max" is marked "31"; "Moritz" is "32." Pair - $1,500.00. *Courtesy Ellen Dodge.*

Tiny unmarked doll: Head is of very good quality bisque. Glass eyes, open mouth. On five-piece papier maché or composition body. No damage. 6" - $250.00; 9" - $365.00; 12" - $425.00. Jointed body: 6" - $300.00; 9" - $450.00; 12" - $525.00. **Poorly painted:** 6" - $100.00; 9" - $145.00; 12" - $200.00.

Tiny doll: Closed mouth, jointed body. 6" - $350.00; 9" - $500.00; 12" - $650.00. Five-piece body: 6" - $250.00; 9" - $350.00; 12" - $425.00.

Character child: Unidentified, closed mouth, **very character face.** May have wig or solid dome. Glass eyes, closed or open/closed mouth. Excellent quality bisque. No damage, nicely dressed. 16" - $3,200.00 up; 20" - $4,000.00 up.

Character: Mold **#128, 134,** and others of this quality. Closed mouth. Glass eyes: 16" - $7,500.00 up; 22" - $10,000.00 up. Painted eyes: 16" - $6,000.00 up; 22" - $8,500.00 up. **Mold #111:** (See photo in Series 8, pg. 82.) Glass eyes: 22" - $22,000.00 up. Painted eyes: 21" - $13,000.00 up. **Mold #163:** 16" - $1,000.00.

American Schoolboy: (so called) Side part painted hair swept across forehead like bangs. Glass eyes, closed mouth. **Jointed composition body:** 10–12" - $550.00, 16" - $700.00. **Kid or cloth body:** 10–12" - $450.00; 16" - $600.00; 20" - $750.00.

Left: 25" with open mouth on fully jointed body. Factory original clothes and wig. Incised "101." Right: 26" nun made by Armand Marseille. On jointed body. Marked "390 A-9-M." 25" - $525.00; nun - $545.00. *Courtesy Frasher Doll Auctions.*

GLADDIE

Gladdie was designed by Helen Jensen in 1929. The German-made doll was distributed by George Borgfeldt. The cloth body has composition limbs, and the head has glass eyes. (See photos in Series 5, pg. 69; Series 6, pg. 92; Series 7, pg. 79.)

Ceramic style or biscaloid head: 16–17" - $1,000.00; 19–20" - $1,300.00 up. **Unusual:** Teeth rest on molded tongue. (See photo in Series 6, pg. 92.) 20" - $2,000.00.

Bisque head, mold #1410: 16–17" - $4,400.00; 19–20" - $5,500.00; 25–26" - $6,800.00.

18" "Gladdie" with painted ceramic head, open/closed mouth, sleep eyes, and molded hair. Marked "Gladdie/copyright by/Helen W. Jensen." $1,100.00.

The Goebel factory has been operating since 1879 and is located in Oeslau, Germany. The interwoven W.G. mark has been used since 1879. William Goebel inherited the factory from his father, Franz Detlev Goebel. About 1900, the factory only made dolls, dolls heads and porcelain figures. They worked in both bisque and china glazed items.

Child: 1895 and later. Open mouth, composition body, sleep or set eyes with head in perfect condition, dressed and ready to display. 5–6" - $200.00; 14" - $300.00; 18" - $500.00; 22" - $600.00.

Child: Open/closed mouth, wig, molded teeth, shoulder plate, kid body, bisque hands. 17" - $850.00; 20" - $1,000.00.

Child: Rare. Deeply molded hair; may have molded bows. Intaglio eyes, open/closed mouth, smile, jointed body. (See photo in Series 7, pg. 80.) 12" - $1,800.00; 15" - $3,200.00; 17" - $4,000.00.

Character: After 1910. Molded hair that can be in various styles, with or without molded flowers or ribbons, painted features and on five-piece papier maché body. No damage and nicely dressed. 7" - $345.00; 9" - $475.00; 12" - $600.00.

Character baby: After 1909. Open mouth, sleep eyes and on five-piece bent limb baby body. No damage and nicely dressed. 13" - $425.00; 16" - $550.00; 19" - $725.00; 24" - $900.00. Toddler: 14" - $550.00; 17" - $725.00; 22" - $950.00.

Molded-on bonnet: Closed mouth, five-piece papier maché body, painted features and may have various molded-on hats or bonnets and painted hair. 7" - $375.00; 9" - $500.00; 12" - $600.00.

Marks:

(1920–1950)

(1920–1950)

Round wings
(1940–1956)

Squared off wings
(1957–1959)

W. GERMANY

(1960–1963)

GOEBEL
W. GERM

(1964–1970)

GOEBEL®
W. Germany

(1970–1979)

GOEBEL®
W. Germany

(1984–1991)

GOEBEL
GERMANY

(1991 on)

Bisque head with glass or set eyes to the side, closed smiling mouth, impish or watermelon-style mouth, original composition or papier maché body. Molded hair or wigged. 1911 and after. Not damaged in any way and nicely dressed.

All bisque: See All Bisque section.

Armand Marseille, #200: (See photo in Series 8, pg. 21.) 8" - $1,300.00; 12" - $2,000.00. **#210:** 8" - $2,000.00; 12" - $2,800.00. **#223:** 7" - $825.00; 10" - $1,000.00. **#240, 241:** (See photos in Series 3, pg. 35; Series 5, pg. 72.) Three tufts of molded hair, glass eyes. 10–11" - $2,000.00; 13" - $2,400.00. **#248:** 9" - $1,000.00. **#252:** Kewpie type baby. (See photo in Series 5, pg. 72.) 8" - $1,000.00; 12" - $1,900.00. **#253, 353:** 7" - $800.00; 9" - $1,200.00; 12" - $1,400.00. **#254:** 10" - $1,000.00. **#255–#310 (Just Me), fired-in color:** 7–8" - $1,000.00; 10–11" - $1,500.00 up; 13" - $2,000.00 up. **#310,** **painted bisque:** 8" - $700.00; 12"- $1,200.00. **#320:** Glass eyes: 9" - $1,200.00. Painted eyes: 6" - $750.00; 8" - $900.00. **#323, fired-in color:** 7" - $900.00; 10–11" - $1,250.00; 13" - $1,500.00. On baby body: 10" - $900.00; 14" - $1,300.00. **Painted bisque baby:** 9" - $400.00; 14" - $650.00. **#325:** 7" - $700.00; 12" - $975.00.

B.P. (Bahr & Proschild), #686: 10" - $2,400.00; 13" - $3,000.00 Baby: 14" - $1,600.00. **#401:** 6" - $675.00.

Demalcol: (See photo in Series 7, pg. 82.) 10" - $525.00; 14" - $725.00.

Elite: See end of this section.

Hansi: "Gretel." Molded hair, shoes and socks. Made of composition and celluloid-type material called "prialytine." (See photo in Series 8, pg. 87.) 12" - $3,200.00.

Hertel Schwab: See that section.

Heubach Einco: 9–10" - $4,600.00; 15" - $7,200.00; 17" - $8,000.00.

6" all-bisque googly with closed smile mouth and swivel neck. Painted-on shoes and socks. Marked "200 A 10/0 M. Germany DGRM 243." $1,300.00. *Courtesy Jane Walker.*

12" with round googly eyes and closed smile mouth. On fully jointed body. Marked "Demalcol 5/0." $600.00. *Courtesy Frasher Doll Auctions.*

Heubach (marked in square): 9" - $950.00; 13" - $1,800.00. **#8556:** 15" - $8,000.00 up. **#8676:** 7" - $750.00; 10" - $1,100.00. **#8995:** Glass eyes. 9" - $2,500.00. **#9056:** Full bangs, hair rolled under around head. 8" - $1,000.00 up; 12" - $1,300.00 up. **#9573:** 7" - $825.00; 9" - $1,500.00; 12" - $1,800.00. **#9578, 11173:** Called "Tiss Me." (See photos in Series 6, pg. 96; Series 9, pg. 89.) 8" - $1,500.00; 12" - $1,800.00. **Winker:** One eye painted closed. (See photo in Series 8, pg. 85.) 10" - $1,800.00. **#9743:** Sitting. Wide open/ closed mouth, top knot, and "star" shaped hands. 5" - $550.00.

Heubach Koppelsdorf: (See photo in Series 6, pg. 96) **#260–264:** 7" - $400.00; 10" - $500.00. **#291:** Dimples, lower lip sucked up under upper lip. Glass eyes. 7" - $1,500.00. **#318:** 9" - $1,300.00; 14" - $2,100.00. **#319:** 7" - $675.00, 11" - $1,300.00. **#417:** 7" - $550.00; 13" - $1,250.00.

Kestner, #111: Jointed body. (See photo in Series 8, pg. 8.) 10" - $2,900.00; 14" - $3,400.00.

Kestner, #163, 165: This number now attributed to **Hertel Schwab.** 13" - $4,600.00; 15" - $5,400.00. **#172–173:** Attributed to **Hertel Schwab.** 11" - $3,200.00; 14" - $4,300.00. **#217, 221:** (See photo in Series 8, pg. 85.) 6" - $1,200.00; 10" - $3,600.00; 12–13" - $4,500.00; 14" - $5,000.00; 16" - $5,500.00; 17" - $5,700.00.

Kammer & Reinhardt (K✿R): Five-piece body. 9" - $2,600.00. **#131:** 7" - $2,600.00; 10" - $5,200.00; 14" - $7,200.00.

Kley & Hahn (K&H), #180: 15" - $2,800.00; 17" - $3,500.00.

Oscar Hitt: 14" - $6,000.00; 17" - $8,000.00.

Our Fairy: See All Bisque section. (See photo in Series 7, pg. 81.)

P.M. (Otto Reinecke), #950: 6" - $950.00; 8" - $1,200.00; 12–13" - $1,600.00; 15–16" - $1,800.00 up.

8" very cute small mold #243, which generally is an oriental Kestner. Sleep googly eyes, open/closed mouth with slightly molded tongue. Original mohair wig. $1,050.00. *Courtesy Turn of Century Antiques.*

12" toddler, Kestner mold #221. Glass eyes with eyebrows arched toward forehead. On jointed toddler body. All factory original. $4,500.00. *Courtesy Turn of Century Antiques.*

S.F.B.J., #245: (See photo in Series 6, pg. 96) Five-piece body: 8" - $1,500.00. Fully jointed body: 12" - $2,600.00; 15" - $4,800.00 up.

Steiner, Herm: 9" - $900.00; 12" - $1,100.00.

Composition face: Very round composition face mask or all composition head with wig, glass eyes to side and closed impish watermelon-style mouth. Body is stuffed felt. In original clothes. (See photo in Series 10, pg. 86.) **Excellent condition:** 8" - $450.00; 12" - $650.00; 14" - $850.00; 16" - $1,000.00; 20" - $1,400.00. **Fair condition:** Cracks or crazing, nicely redressed. 7" - $165.00; 11" - $300.00; 13" - $450.00; 15" - $525.00; 19" - $750.00. **Composition head:** Can have plain cloth or corduroy stuffed body. Celluloid disc eyes: Made during World War II. (One maker was Freundlich.) 16" - $115.00; 20" - $145.00.

Painted eyes: Composition or papier maché body with painted-on shoes and socks. Bisque head with eyes painted to side, closed smile mouth and molded hair. Not damaged and nicely dressed. **A.M. 320, Goebel, R.A., etc.:** 6" - $365.00; 8" - $525.00; 10" - $645.00; 12" - $725.00. **Heubach, Gebruder:** 7–8" - $475.00 up.

Disc eyes: Bisque socket head or shoulder head with molded hair (can have molded hat/cap), closed mouth and inset celluloid discs in large googly eyes. (See photo in Series 8, pg. 85; Series 10, pg. 86.) 10" - $1,000.00; 14" - $1,200.00; 17" - $1,500.00; 21" - $1,900.00. **Black:** 12" - $1,550.00.

Molded-on military hat: Marked **"Elite."** (See photo in Series 5, pg. 71; Series 7, pg. 82; Series 8, pg. 86.) 12" - $2,400.00; 16" - $3,400.00. **Japanese soldier:** 12" - $3,000.00. **Two faced:** 12" - $4,000.00.

GREINER

Ludwig Greiner of Philadelphia, PA, made dolls from 1858 into the late 1800's. The heads are made of papier maché, and they can be found on various bodies. Some can be all cloth; many are homemade. Many have leather arms or can be found on Lacmann bodies that have stitched joints at the hips and the knees and are very wide at the hip line. The Lacmann bodies will be marked "J. Lacmann's Patent March 24th, 1874" in an oval. The Greiner heads will be marked "Greiner's Patent Doll Heads/Pat. Mar. 30, '58." Also "Greiner's/Improved/Patent Heads/Pat. Mar. 30, '58." The later heads are marked "Greiner's Patent Doll Heads/Pat. Mar. 30, '58. Ext. '72."

Greiner doll: Can have black or blonde molded hair, blue or brown painted eyes and be on a nice homemade cloth body with cloth arms or a commeri-

26" 1872 Greiner with deeply molded eyelids and natural hollows in eyes. Original and tagged. $750.00. *Courtesy Turn of Century Antiques.*

cal cloth body with leather arms. Dressed for the period and clean, with head in near perfect condition with no paint chips and not repainted.

With '58 label: 18" - $525.00; 24" - $775.00; 27" - $850.00; 30" - $1,000.00; 35" - $1,400.00; 38" - $1,700.00. **With chips/flakes or repainted:** 17" - $350.00; 23" - $450.00; 26" - $550.00; 29" - $675.00; 34" - $775.00; 37" - $850.00.

With '72 label: 19" - $475.00; 22" - $550.00; 27" - $700.00; 32" - $1,000.00. **With chips/flakes or repainted:** 19" - $250.00; 22" - $350.00; 27" - $450.00; 32" - $525.00.

Glass Eyes: 22" - $2,000.00; 27" - $2,500.00. **With chips/flakes or repainted:** 22" - $975.00; 27" - $1,200.00.

Unmarked: Circa 1850. So called "Pre-Greiner." Papier maché shoulder head, cloth body can be home made. Leather, wood or cloth limbs. Painted hair, black eyes with no pupils. Glass eyes, old or original clothes. **Good condition:** 19" - $1,400.00; 27" - $1,800.00; 32" - $2,000.00. **Fair condition:** 19" - $500.00; 27" - $700.00; 32" - $900.00.

H

Dolls with an "H" mark are attribiuted to Halopeau (France), circa 1882. They have outlined eyes, blushed eyelids, open/closed mouths with white space between lips, and original human hair wigs. Original French bodies are of composition and wood with straight wrists. (See photos in Series 2, pg. 77; Series 3, pg. 72; Series 7, pg. 84; Series 10, pg. 88.) 19–20" - $75,000.00; 24–25" - $85,000.00. Unmarked: 20" - $28,000.00; 26" - $36,000.00.

HALF DOLLS

Half dolls can be made of any material including bisque, papier maché and composition. Not all half dolls were used as pincushions. They were also used for powder box tops, brushes, tea cozies, etc. Most date from 1900 into the 1930s. The majority were made in Germany, but many were made in Japan. Generally, they will be marked with "Germany" or "Japan." Some have numbers; others may have the marks of companies such as William Goebel or Dressel, Kister & Co.

The most desirable are the large figures, or any size for that matter, that have both arms molded away from the body or are jointed at the shoulder. Allow more if marked by maker. Very rare half figures can cost from $800.00 to $2,000.00.

Arms and hands extended: Prices can be higher depending on detail and rarity of figure. Marked; china or bisque. 3" - $145.00 up; 5" - $285.00 up; 8" - $650.00 up; 12" - $950.00 up.

Arms extended: Hands attached to figure. China or bisque: 3" - $75.00; 5" - $115.00; 8" - $160.00. Papier maché or composition: 5" - $35.00; 7" - $85.00.

Bald head, arms away: 4" - $145.00 up. Arms attached: 4" - $75.00 up.

Common figures: Arms and hands attached. China: 3" - $22.00; 5" - $35.00; 8" - $45.00. Papier maché or composition: 3" - $20.00; 5" - $30.00; 8" - $40.00.

Jointed shoulders: China or bisque: 5" - $145.00; 8" - $245.00; 10" - $325.00. Papier maché: 4" - $60.00; 7" - $100.00.

Wax over papier maché: 4" - $55.00; 7" - $100.00.

Children or men: 3" - $85.00; 5" - $125.00; 7" - $175.00. Jointed shoulders: 3" - $100.00; 5" - $145.00; 7" - $225.00.

Japan marked: 3" - $20.00; 5" - $35.00; 7" - $55.00. **Germany marked:** 3" - $150.00 up; 5" - $300.00 up; 7" - $600.00 up.

7½" pin holder or powder box. Fine porcelain and excellent quality. $65.00. *Courtesy Glorya Woods.*

1½" half doll of excellent quality. Made in Germany. Has both arms and hands molded to body. $45.00 up.

12" "Marie Antoinette" with base. Holds fan and has delicate sleeve detail. Incised with the Goebel bee symbol/"W G 5." Shown with 6" senorita marked "10016." 12" - $425.00; 6"- $300.00. *Courtesy Frasher Doll Auctions.*

Heinrich Handwerck began making dolls and doll bodies in 1876 at Gotha, Germany. The majority of their heads were made by Simon & Halbig. In 1897 they patented, in Germany, a ball jointed body #100297 and some of their bodies will be marked with this number.

Mold numbers include: **12x, 19, 23, 69, 79, 89, 99, 100, 109, 118, 119, 124, 125, 139, 152, 189, 199, 1001, 1200, 1290.**

Sample mold marks:

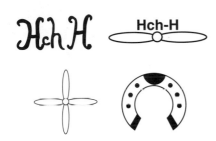

Child, no mold number: After 1885. Open mouth, sleep or set eyes, on ball jointed body. Bisque head with no cracks, chips or hairlines, good wig and nicely dressed. 14" - $400.00; 16" - $485.00; 19" - $550.00; 23" - $675.00; 25" - $750.00; 32" - $1,250.00; 36" - $1,450.00; 41–42" - $2,400.00. **Child with mold marks:** 12" - $450.00; 14" - $475.00; 17" - $525.00; 21" - $650.00; 24" - $725.00; 28" - $985.00; 32" - $1,400.00; 35–36" - $1,650.00; 42" - $3,200.00; 45" - $4,200.00.

Kid body: Bisque shoulder head, open mouth. All in good condition and nicely dressed. 16" - $295.00; 19" - $385.00; 25" - $500.00; 27" - $700.00.

Mold #79, 89: With closed mouth. 14" - $1,600.00; 17" - $1,950.00 up; 21" - $2,300.00 up.

Mold #189: With open mouth. 14" - $465.00; 17" - $825.00; 21" - $975.00.

Bear: Bisque head on teddy bear body of silver/blue mohair. 14" - $650.00 up.

27" Heinrich Handwerck with sleep eyes, and open mouth. On fully jointed body. Marked "119 Handwerck." $950.00. *Courtesy Turn of Century Antiques.*

Max Handwerck started making dolls in 1900 and his factory was located at Waltershausen, Germany. In 1901, he registered "Bébé Elite" with the heads made by William Goebel. The dolls from this firm are marked with the full name, but a few are marked with "M.H."

Child: Bisque head, open mouth, sleep or set eyes, on fully jointed composition body, no damage and nicely dressed. **Mold #283, 287, 291, etc.:** 16" - $375.00; 20" - $475.00; 24" - $575.00; 28" - $850.00; 32" - $1,000.00; 40" - $2,200.00.

Bébé Elite: Bisque heads with no cracks or chips, sleep or set eyes, open mouth. Upper teeth and smile. Can have a flange neck on cloth body with composition limbs or be on bent leg composition baby body. (See photo in Series 7, pg. 88.) 15" - $450.00; 21" - $675.00. **Toddler:** 17" - $700.00; 22" - $900.00; 26" - $1,300.00. **Socket head on fully jointed body:** 17" - $625.00; 21" - $850.00.

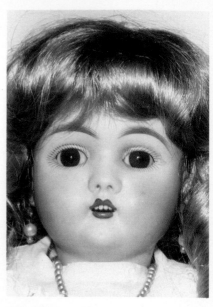

17" Max Handwerck with open mouth and on fully jointed body. Stamped in red "Handwerck." $375.00. *Courtesy Kathy Riddick.*

HERTEL, SCHWAB & CO.

Hertel, Schwab & Co. has been recognized by the German authors Jurgen and Marianne Cieslik as the maker of many dolls that were attributed to other companies all these years. There does not seem to be a "common denominator" to the Hertel, Schwab doll lines and any style can be included. As of 1993, collectors believe that this company made heads of very poor to finest quality for major Germany dollmakers.

Babies: Bisque head, molded hair or wig, open or open/closed mouth, sleep or painted eyes, bent limb baby body. Good condition with no damage.

Mold #125, 127 ("Patsy"): 14" - $900.00; 17" - $1,300.00.

Mold #126 ("Skippy"): 12" - $1,000.00; 15" - $1,300.00.

Mold numbers: 130, 136, 142, 150, 151, 152, 153, 154: 10" - $425.00; 15" - $575.00; 17" - $675.00; 20" - $825.00; 23" - $900.00; 26" - $1,000.00.

Child: Bisque head, painted or sleep eyes, closed mouth, jointed composition body, no damage and nicely dressed.

#119, 134, 140, 141, 149: 16" - $4,900.00; 18" - $6,000.00; 23" - $8,400.00.

#154, closed mouth: 16" - $2,500.00; 22" - $2,900.00. **Open mouth:** 18" - $1,200.00; 22" - $1,600.00.

#169, closed mouth: 18" - $3,400.00; 22" - $3,800.00. **Toddler:** 22" - $4,200.00; 26" - $5,200.00. **Baby:** Open mouth. 21", $1,300.00; 24" - $1,500.00.

All bisque: One-piece body and head, glass eyes, closed or open mouth. All in perfect condition.

Prize Baby, #208: Late 1920s. 6" -
$325.00; 8" - $550.00.
   Swivel neck: (See #222 below.) 6" -
$450.00; 8" - $700.00; 10" - $800.00.
   Googly: Large, side glance sleep or
set eyes. Wig or molded hair. Closed
mouth, no damage and nicely dressed.
   #163, 164, 165: 12" - $3,000.00; 15" -
$5,600.00. **Baby:** 13" - $3,300.00. **Toddler:**
15" - $5,900.00.
   #168: Looks like Campbell Kid.
Open/closed mouth: 16" - $6,300.00.
Two-faced: 15" - $7,000.00.
   #172: 14–15" - $6,300.00.
   #173: 12" - $3,200.00; 14" - $4,000.00.
   #189: 8" - $750.00.
   #217: 7½" - $800.00.
   #222 (Our Fairy): Painted eyes,
molded hair. 5½" - $625.00; 9–10" -
$1,450.00; 12" - $1,800.00 up. **Wig, glass
eyes:** 9–10" - $1,750.00; 12" - $2,300.00 up.
Baby: 16" - $4,600.00. **Toddler:** 16" -
$5,200.00.

23" baby with mold #152 is now being
attributed to Hertel & Schwab. (Once considered a Kestner.) Solid dome with brush
stroke hair. On five-piece bent limb baby
body. $900.00 *Courtesy Turn of Century Antiques.*

HEUBACH, GEBRÜDER

   The Heubach Brothers (Gebrüder)
made dolls from 1863 into the 1930's at
Lichte, Thuringia, Germany. They started
producing character dolls in 1910.
Heubach dolls can reflect almost every
mood and are often found on rather
crude, poor quality bodies, and many are
small dolls.
   Character dolls: Bisque head,
open/closed or closed mouth. Painted
eyes (allow more for glass eyes). Kid,
papier maché or jointed composition
bodies. Molded hair or wig. No damage
and nicely dressed.
   Marked "Heubach": No mold number. Open/closed mouth, deep dimples.
(See photo in Series 9, pg. 98.) 20" -
$4,850.00; 30" - $7,900.00.

Marks:

   #1017: Baby-faced toddler with open
mouth. 18" - $1,400.00; 22" - $1,700.00; 28" -
$2,150.00.
   #2850, 8058: Open/closed mouth,
two rows teeth. Molded braided hair,
blue ribbon bow. 16" - $9,600.00 up; 20" -
$11,000.00 up.

#5636: Laughing child. Two lower teeth, intaglio painted eyes. 9" - $900.00; 12" - $1,200.00. **Glass eyes:** 12" - $1,500.00; 16" - $2,200.00.

#5689: Open mouth, smiling. Glass eyes. (See photos in Series 5, pg. 82; Series 7, pg. 90.) 16" - $1,800.00; 18" - $2,200.00; 23" - $2,400.00.

#5730 (Santa): 14" - $1,500.00; 17" - $2,300.00; 24" - $2,500.00.

#5777, 7307, 9355 (Dolly Dimples): Ball-jointed body. (See photo in Series 5, pg. 93; Series 9, pg. 97.) 12–13" - $2,200.00; 16" - $2,600.00; 22" - $3,300.00; 24" - $3,500.00.

#6692: Shoulder head, smiling, intaglio eyes. 15" - $950.00 up.

#6736, 6894: Laughing, wide open/closed mouth, molded lower teeth. 10" - $950.00; 16" - $1,900.00.

12" Gebrüder Heubach with glass eyes, closed mouth, two painted teeth, and deep cheek and chin dimples. Mold #7307. $1,650.00. *Courtesy Jane Walker.*

18" Gebrüder Heubach "Santa" with glass sleep eyes and open smiling mouth. On fully jointed body. Old clothes. $2,300.00. *Courtesy Barbara Earnshaw-Cain.*

#6894, 6898, 7759: Baby, closed mouth, pouty. (See photo in Series 6, pg. 107.) 5" - $235.00; 6½" - $325.00; 9½" - $500.00; 12–13" - $700.00.

#6896: Pouty, jointed body. 16" - $900.00; 20" - $1,200.00.

#6969, 6970, 7246, 7248, 7347, 7407, 7602, 7802, 8017, 8420: Pouty boy or girl, jointed body, painted eyes. (See #6970 in Series 9, pg. 97.) 6½" - $350.00; 10" - $650.00; 12" - $950.00; 15" - $1,200.00; 21" - $2,800.00. **Glass eyes:** 12" - $2,200.00; 14" - $2,600.00; 17" - $3,200.00; 20" - $3,700.00; 24" - $4,200.00. **Toddler, painted eyes:** 21" - $2,600.00; 25" - $3,200.00. **Toddler, glass eyes:** 20" - $2,900.00; 24" - $4,500.00.

#7134: See #7634.

#7172, 7550: 15" - $1,600.00.

#7307: Deep cheek dimples, glass eyes, and closed mouth. 12" - $1,650.00; 16" - $1,900.00.

#7448: Open/closed mouth, eyes half shut. 15" - $2,850.00.

#7602: Painted eyes and hair. Long face pouty. Closed mouth. (See photo in

Series 9, pg. 98.) 16" - $2,000.00; 20" - $2,700.00 up. **Glass eyes:** 16" - $2,600.00; 20" - $3,200.00.

#7604: Laughing expression. Jointed body, intaglio eyes. 10" - $525.00; 12" - $675.00; 14" - $800.00. **Baby:** 14" - $675.00. **Walker:** Key wound. 14" - $1,600.00.

#7606: Open/closed mouth. 14" - $950.00; 20" - $1,350.00.

#7616: Open/closed mouth with molded tongue. Socket or shoulder head. **Glass eyes:** 12" - $1,500.00; 16" - $2,000.00.

#7620: Open/closed mouth, dimples, protruding ears. 20" - $1,500.00.

#7622, 8793, 76262: Molded hair, intaglio eyes. Closed mouth, light cheek dimples. (See photos in Series 7, pg. 91; Series 9, pg. 100.) 14" - $1,600.00; 16" - $2,000.00. **Pouty:** 14" - $985.00; 17" - $1,300.00.

#7623: Molded hair, intaglio eyes, open/closed mouth, molded tongue, on bent limb baby body. (See photo in Series 5, pg. 80.) 12" - $850.00; 16" - $1,300.00. **Jointed body:** 15" - $1,600.00; 21" - $2,200.00.

#7634, 7134: Crying, squinting eyes. Wide open/closed mouth. 14" - $1,000.00; 16" - $1,500.00.

#7636: 10" - $800.00; 13" - $1,000.00.

#7644: Slight smiling mouth, open/closed mouth, or can be laughing. Socket or shoulder head, small intaglio eyes. 14" - $900.00; 17" - $1,200.00.

#7665, 8724: Smile expression. 16" - $1,800.00.

#7666: Squinting eyes, crooked smile. 16" - $3,600.00 up.

#7661, 7686: Wide open/closed mouth, deeply molded hair. 14" - $2,500.00; 17" - $3,900.00.

#7669, 7679: Walker doll. Laughing expression with open/closed mouth, glass eyes. (See photo in Series 10, pg. 95.) 11–12" - $1,000.00; 15" - $1,600.00; 18" - $2,400.00.

7668, 7671: See Black or Brown Doll section.

#7679: Whistler with socket head. (See photo in Series 8, pg. 75.) 11" - $800.00; 15" - $1,200.00; 17" - $1,600.00.

#7684: Screamer with molded tongue, painted eyes. Large open/closed mouth, wrinkles between eyes. 12" - $1,100.00; 16" - $1,900.00; 18" - $2,400.00.

#7701: Pouty with intaglio eyes. 16" - $1,500.00; 19" - $1,900.00.

#7711: Open mouth, jointed body. 12" - $395.00; 15" - $900.00; 22" - $1,300.00.

#7743: Girl singing. 16" - $4,000.00.

#7745, 7746: Wide open/closed mouth, two painted lower teeth, molded hair. **Baby or toddler:** 16" - $2,200.00.

#7748: Protruding ears, open/closed mouth, two lower teeth, dimples, painted laughing eyes partly closed. Row of baby fat on back of neck. Chunky **toddler** body. 16" - $5,400.00 up.

#7751: Squinting eyes, open/closed mouth modeled as yawn. Molded hair, jointed body. 15" - $3,400.00; 18" - $4,200.00.

#7759: See #6894.

#7763: Same description as #7768, 7788.

#7764: Wide open/closed mouth, intaglio eyes to side, deeply sculptured hair, large molded bow. Five-piece body or **toddler** body. 14" - $1,300.00 up; 17" - $2,000.00 up.

#7768, #7788 ("Coquette"): Tilted head, molded hair and can have ribbon modeled into hairdo. (See photos in Series 7, pg. 93; Series 8, pg. 97.) 8½" - $485.00; 10" - $750.00; 15" - $1,100.00. **Swivel neck:** 8" - $565.00; 10" - $885.00. **All bisque:** 9" - $1,450.00 up.

#7781 baby: Squinted eyes, wide yawn mouth. 15" - $1,800.00.

#7820: Boy with molded hair, intaglio eyes. Open/closed mouth with two painted upper teeth. Slight smile, cheek dimples. 14" - $3,000.00; 17" - $3,800.00.

#7849: Closed mouth, intaglio eyes. 14" - $850.00.

Rare 17" adult portrait doll by Heubach, mold #7926. Slender bisque face. Head turned slightly right on shoulder plate. Cloth body with composition lower limbs. $3,400.00. *Courtesy Frasher Doll Auctions.*

#7851: Same description as #7764. Cloth body, composition limbs. 12" - $1,200.00.

#7852, 7862, 119: Braids coiled around ear (molded), intaglio eyes. (See photo in Series 8, pg. 96.) 16" - $5,400.00 up; 18" - $5,800.00 up.

#7853: Shoulder head, down cast eyes. 14" - $1,650.00; 16½" - $1,850.00.

#7865: 14" - $3,000.00.

#7911: Grin. 15" - $1,300.00.

#7925, 7926 (Adult): Painted eyes: 15" - $3,000.00 up; 18" - $3,400.00. **Glass eyes:** 17" - $4,000.00.

#7958: Deeply modeled hair and bangs. Dimples, open/closed mouth, intaglio eyes. 15" - $3,600.00; 18" - $4,200.00.

#7959: Intaglio eyes, molded-on bonnet, deeply molded hair, open/closed mouth. 17" - $3,800.00; 21" - $4,600.00 up.

#7975 (Stuart Baby): Glass eyes, removable porcelain bonnet. 11–12" - $1,800.00.

#7977, #7877, 8228 (Stuart Baby): Molded baby bonnet. Painted eyes. (See photo in Series 7, pg. 93.) 10" - $1,100.00; 12" - $1,600.00; 14" - $2,200.00; 16" - $2,800.00. **Glass eyes:** 12" - $2,000.00, 14" - $2,500.00; 16" - $3,000.00.

#8035: Boy with molded hair, painted eyes, and jointed body. Long cheeks, short chin, full lips (closed mouth). 16–17" - $9,000.00 up.

#8050: Lightly modeled hair, intaglio eyes, open/closed laugh mouth with two rows of teeth. 17" - $2,900.00. **Smiling girl:** Molded hairbow. 15" - $3,500.00; 18" - $6,000.00.

#8053: Round cheeks, closed mouth, painted eyes to side, large ears. 19" - $3,800.00.

#8058: Laughing expression. Open/closed mouth, two rows teeth, painted eyes, molded hair with ribbon around head. 16–17" - $9,000.00 up.

#8145: Toddler with closed smile mouth. Eyes painted to side. Painted hair. 16" - $1,600.00 up; 20" - $2,000.00 up.

Adorable 8" Gebrüder Heubach twins, mold #8192. Sleep eyes, open mouth. On five-piece toddler bodies. Each - $625.00. *Courtesy Turn of Century Antiques.*

#8191: Smiling openly. Jointed body. 12" - $1,000.00; 14" - $1,200.00; 17" - $1,500.00.

#8191: "Dolly" style face, glass eyes, open mouth. Composition jointed body. (See photos in Series 1, pg. 141; Series 4, pg. 86.) 14" - $525.00; 17" - $625.00; 22" - $765.00.

#8192: Open/closed smiling mouth with tongue molded between teeth. (See photo in Series 6, pg. 109.) 9" - $525.00; 12" - $800.00; 16" - $1,300.00; 23" - $2,000.00. **Open mouth, glass eyes:** 15" - $825.00; 18" - $1,400.00; 23" - $2,000.00.

#8197: Deeply molded curls. Molded loop for bow. Pretty face with closed mouth and full lips. Shoulder head, kid body, bisque lower arms, composition legs. 16–17" - $9,200.00 up.

#8316: Smiling expression. Open/closed mouth, molded teeth, wig. **Glass eyes:** 16" - $3,500.00 up; 19" - $4,700.00 up. **Painted eyes:** 14" - $1,000.00 up.

#8381 (referred to as "Princess Juliana"): Closed mouth, pensive expression, painted eyes, molded hair, ribbon around head with bow, exposed ears. 16" - $8,000.00 up.

#8420: Pouty type, painted eyes. (See photo in Series 9, pg. 99.) 14" - $750.00; 17" - $825.00. **Glass eyes:** 9" - $825.00; 14" - $1,400.00; 16" - $1,600.00; 19" - $2,600.00.

#8459, 8469: Wide open/closed laughing mouth, two lower teeth, glass eyes. (See photo in Series 6, pg. 109.) 12" - $2,600.00; 15" - $3,200.00.

#8850: Molded tongue sticking out. Intaglio eyes. 14" - $1,050.00. Glass eyes: 14–15" - $1,400.00.

#8555: Shoulder head, painted bulging eyes. (See photo in Series 8, pg. 97.) 14" - $4,900.00.

#8556: Bulging painted eyes to side and looking down. Very puckered small mouth. Deeply molded hair with top knot. Hair wave near front and onto forehead. 12" - $2,000.00; 16" - $2,800.00.

#8556: Open/closed mouth, two rows teeth, molded hair, ribbon. 18" - $8,400.00; 21" - $9,200.00.

#8590: Closed mouth, puckered lips. 14" - $1,400.00; 17" - $1,900.00. Baby: 14" - $1,200.00; 16" - $1,500.00.

#8596: Smile, intaglio eyes. 14" - $825.00; 16" - $1,000.00.

#8648: Extremely pouty closed mouth, intaglio eyes to side. 20" - $2,800.00; 24" - $3,600.00.

#8724: See #7665.

#8774 ("Whistling Jim"): Eyes to side and mouth modeled as if whistling. (See photo in Series 7, pg. 92.) 12" - $750.00; 14" - $985.00; 17" - $1,450.00.

#8868: Molded hair, glass eyes, closed mouth, very short chin. (See photo in Series 7, pg. 92.) 16" - $2,000.00; 20" - $2,600.00.

#8991: Molded hair, painted eyes to side, open/closed mouth with molded tongue, protruding ears. **Toddler body:** 9" - $1,500.00; 15" - $2,600.00. **Kid body:** 12–13" - $1,200.00.

#8995: Smile, large round glass eyes. Top knot on back of molded hair. Hair molded like flaps over ears. 13" - $2,700.00.

#9141: Winking. Glass eyes: 9" - $1,400.00. Painted eyes: 7-8" - $950.00.

#9145: Intaglio eyes to side. Molded hair. Open/closed mouth. **Toddler body:** (See photo in Series 10, pg. 94.) 22" - $7,000.00.

#9189: Same description as #7764 but no bow in molded hair. Cloth body, composition limbs. 11–12" - $1,000.00.

#9355: Shoulder head. 17" - $950.00; 23" - $1,600.00.

#9457, 9467 (Indian): 14" - $2,400.00; 17" - $3,800.00.

#9891: Molded-on cap, intaglio eyes. **Aviator:** 12–13" - $1,600.00. **Sailor:** 12–13" - $1,300.00. **Farmer:** 12–13" - $1,100.00.

#10532: Open mouth, jointed body. 10" - $450.00; 14" - $700.00; 17" - $950.00; 20" - $1,300.00.

#10586, 10633: Child with open mouth, jointed body. (See #10586 in Series 7, pg. 93.) 16" - $650.00; 19" - $800.00; 23" - $1,000.00.

#11173 (Tiss-Me): Glass eyes, five-piece body, pursed closed mouth with large indented cheeks. 8" - $1,600.00 up; 12" - $1,900.00.

Child with dolly-type face (non-character): Open mouth, glass sleep or set eyes. Jointed body, bisque head with no damage. Nicely dressed. 14" - $450.00; 16" - $550.00; 19" - $750.00; 24" - $950.00; 27" - $1,100.00.

Googly: See that section.

Indian portrait, #8467: Man or woman. 14" - $4,600.00 up.

Babies or Infants: Bisque head, wig or molded hair, sleep or intaglio eyes, open/closed pouty-type mouths.

#6894, #6898, #7602: 6" - $265.00; 8" - $350.00; 12" - $450.00; 15" - $550.00; 17" - $725.00; 22" - $1,000.00; 25" - $1,300.00; 27" - $1,700.00.

#7604: Laughing expression. 12–13" - $800.00.

#7745, 7746: Rare. Has laughing expression. 15–16" - $4,400.00 up.

#7959, molded bonnet: Deep modeling to pink or blue bonnet. Molded hair to front and sides of face. 11–12" - $2,000.00 up.

#7975: See #7977 "Stuart Baby."

Animals: Bisque head on five-piece body or fully jointed body. Usually smiling with painted teeth. 9" - $1,100.00 up.

Walking: Key wind. Price depends on head used. 15" - $900.00 up.

13" Gebrüder Heubach toddler with glass eyes, open/closed mouth, and molded tongue. Key wind walker. All original. Shown with a 4½" all bisque with swivel neck and glass eyes. Toddler - $2,600.00; bisque - $450.00. *Courtesy Turn of Century Antiques.*

Ernst Heubach began making dolls in 1887 in Koppelsdorf, Germany. Marks of this firm can be the initials "E.H." or the dolls can be found marked with the full name, Heubach Koppelsdorf, or:

Child, #250, 275, 302 etc.: After 1888. Jointed body, open mouth, sleep or set eyes. No damage and nicely dressed. 8" - $200.00; 10" - $245.00; 14" - $275.00; 18" - $425.00; 22" - $500.00; 26" - $600.00; 30" - $875.00; 38" - $1,250.00.

Child: Kid or cloth body with bisque lower arms, bisque shoulder head, some turned head, open mouth. No damage and nicely dressed. 14" - $200.00; 20" - $300.00; 24" - $400.00; 30" - $700.00. **Painted bisque:** 8" - $145.00; 12" - $175.00.

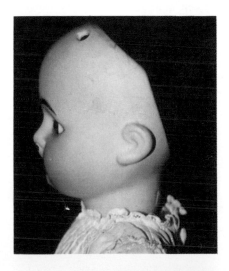

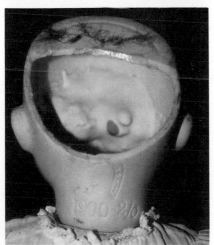

Very rare and unusual 16" nursing doll made by Ernst Heubach of Koppelsdorf, Germany. Large glass eyes and very round open mouth. Nursing mechanism unknown. On French jointed body. Original clothes and wig. Photos at right shown the cut of the cork pate. $1,400.00.
Courtesy Susan Capps.

Babies, #300, 320, 330, 342, etc.: 1910 and after. Five-piece bent limb baby body. Open mouth with some having wobbly tongue and pierced nostrils. Sleep eyes. No damage and nicely dressed. Allow more for toddler body. (See photo in Series 4, pg. 88.) 6" - $200.00; 10" - $285.00; 14" - $425.00; 16" - $500.00; 19" - $600.00; 25" - $900.00.

#300, 320: Fully jointed body. 18" - $525.00; 23" - $675.00.

Baby, #267: Typical baby with open mouth but has flirty eyes and metal eyelids that drop down over eyes. 14" - $485.00; 17" - $600.00; 20" - $785.00; 24" - $900.00. **Painted bisque:** 10" - $125.00; 16" - $245.00. **Toddler:** 16" - $400.00.

Infant: 1925 and after. Molded or painted hair, sleep eyes, closed mouth, flange neck bisque head on cloth body with composition or celluloid hands. No damage and nicely dressed.

#338, 340: 14" - $675.00; 16" - $750.00.

#339, 349, 350: 9½" - $365.00; 12" - $450.00.

#320, 335, 339, 340, 349, 350, 399: See Black or Brown Doll section.

Character child: 1910 on. Molded hair, painted eyes and open/closed mouth. No damage. **#261, 262, 271, 330 and others:** 12" - $500.00; 16" - $975.00; 18" - $1,100.00; 20" - $1,400.00.

INNOVATION NOVELTY

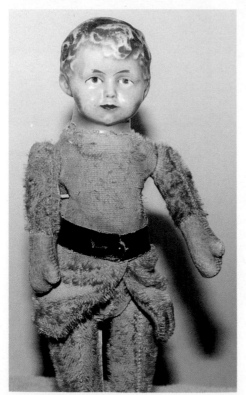

17¼" with composition head and painted features. Disc-jointed mohair bear style body that is straw stuffed. Felt hands and feet. Black oil cloth band around waist holds on the "suit tails." He originally had another band around neck for coat top. Made in 1916 by Innovation Novelty Mfg. Co., Inc. of New York. Marked "Sam-407" on head. In this condition - $400.00.
Courtesy Susan Giradot.

Jullien marked dolls were made in Paris, France from 1875 to 1904. The heads will be marked Jullien and a size number. In 1892, Jullien advertised "L'Universal" and the label can be found on some of his doll bodies. (See photo in Series 7, pg. 96.)

Child, closed mouth: Paperweight eyes. French jointed body of composition and papier maché with some having wooden parts. Undamaged bisque head. Excellent condition. 12" - $2,200.00; 14" - $2,700.00; 16" - $3,700.00; 18" - $4,000.00; 22" - $4,400.00; 25" - $5,000.00; 28" - $5,400.00. **Open mouth:** 15" - $1,300.00; 17" - $1,700.00; 20" - $1,800.00; 22" - $2,200.00; 25" - $2,600.00.; 29" - $3,200.00. **Poor quality, high color:** 15" - $1,000.00; 20" - $1,600.00; 22" - $1,700.00; 25" - $2,000.00; 29" - $2,500.00.

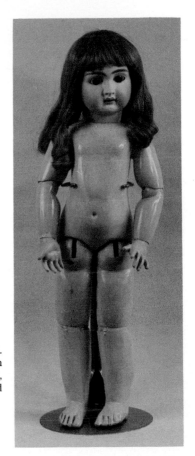

16" with French jointed body with bisque head. Note: French knees lack detail and are flush with lower legs. German bodies have rolls, dimples, and detail at the knee area. Marked "Jullien." $3,700.00.

Known Jumeau Sizes: 0 - 8–9"; 1 - 10"; 2 - 11"; 3 - 12"; 4 - 13"; 5 - 14–15"; 6 - 16"; 7 - 17"; 8 - 19"; 9 - 20"; 10 - 21–22"; 11 - 24–25"; 12 - 26–27"; 13 - 29–30".

Tete Jumeau, closed mouth: 1879–1899 and later. Marked with red stamp on head and oval sticker on body. Paperweight eyes, jointed body with full joints or jointed with straight wrists. Pierced ears with larger sizes having applied ears. No damage at all to bisque head, undamaged French body, dressed and ready to place into collection. (Allow more for original clothes and marked shoes.) 9–10" - $4,000.00 up; 12" - $3,200.00; 14" - $3,400.00; 16" - $3,800.00; 18" - $4,100.00; 20" - $4,300.00; 22" - $4,600.00; 24" - $5,000.00; 28" - $5,800.00; 30" - $6,100.00; 34" - $7,000.00; 36" - $7,400.00.

Tete Jumeau, open mouth: Not incised "1907." May or may not have number. Will have marked Jumeau body. (See photo in Series 8, pg. 103, Series 9, pg. 105–107.) 16" - $2,400.00; 21" - $3,000.00; 24" - $3,300.00; 27" - $3,500.00; 30" - $3,900.00.

1907 Jumeau: Incised "1907," sometimes has the Tete Jumeau stamp. Sleep or set eyes, open mouth, jointed French body. No damage, nicely dressed. 14" - $1,600.00; 16" - $2,400.00; 19" - $2,700.00; 22" - $3,000.00; 25" - $3,400.00; 29" - $3,900.00; 34" - $4,650.00.

Tete Jumeau: Adult body, closed mouth. (See photo in Series 5, pg. 87.) Allow more for original clothes. 19–20" - $5,800.00; 25" - $6,400.00. **Open mouth:** (See photo in Series 9, pg. 104.) Allow more for original clothes. 14" - $2,000.00; 16" - $2,500.00; 19" - $2,800.00; 20" - $3,000.00; 22" - $3,200.00; 24" - $3,400.00; 28" - $3,900.00; 30" - $4,300.00; 34" - $4,700.00.

E.J. child: Circa early 1880s. Head incised "Depose/E. 6 J." Paperweight eyes, closed mouth, jointed body with straight wrist (unjointed at wrist). Larger dolls will have applied ears. No damage to head or body and nicely dressed in excellent quality clothes. 10" - $5,400.00 up; 14" - $5,700.00; 16" - $6,200.00; 18" - $6,400.00; 22" - $7,300.00; 26" - $8,500.00 up. **Tete style (later dolls):** 18" - $5,000.00; 24" - $6,400.00; 27" - $7,600.00.

E.J. child: Mark with number over the E.J. (Example: $E.^6J.$) 17–18" - $11,000.00; 22–23" - $18,000.00.

E.J./A child: 19" - $16,000.00; 22" - $20,000.00; 26" - $28,000.00 up.

Depose Jumeau, incised: 1880. Head will be incised "Depose Jumeau" and body should have Jumeau sticker. Closed mouth, paperweight eyes and on jointed body with straight wrists, although a few may have jointed wrists. No damage at all and nicely dressed. 15" - $5,300.00; 18" - $6,000.00; 22" - $7,000.00; 25" - $7,600.00.

Long Face (Triste Jumeau): 1870s. Closed mouth, applied ears, paperweight eyes and straight wrists on Jumeau marked body. Head is generally marked with a size number. No damage to head or body, nicely dressed. 20–21" -

22" E.J. with beautiful almond-shaped eyes and closed mouth. On French body with straight wrists. $7,300.00. *Courtesy Barbara Earnshaw-Cain.*

28" Tete Jumeau with unusual face. Applied ears and has "long" face and short chin. On fully jointed Jumeau body Shown in original trunk/shipping case. With trunk/case - $7,400.00. *Courtesy Barbara Earnshaw-Cain.*

$20,000.00 up; 25–26"- $24,000.00 up; 29–30" - $28,000.00 up; 33–34" - $32,000.00.

Portrait Jumeau: 1870s. Closed mouth, usually large almond-shaped eyes. Jointed Jumeau body. Head marked with size number only. Body has Jumeau sticker or stamp. Allow more for original clothes. 10" - $5,500.00; 12" - $5,700.00; 15" - $6,400.00; 21" - $7,900.00; 25" - $11,000.00; 28" - $15,000.00. **Very early almond-shaped eyes:** 12" - $5,900.00; 15–16" - $7,000.00; 19" - $8,500.00; 24" - $12,500.00.

Phonograph Jumeau: Bisque head with open mouth. Phonograph in body. No damage, working and nicely dressed. 20" - $8,000.00; 25" - $10,000.00 up.

Wire Eye (Flirty) Jumeau: Lever in back of head operates eyes. Open mouth, jointed body, straight wrists. 18" - $6,800.00; 21" - $8,200.00; 26" - $9,600.00.

Walker: Open mouth. 20" - $2,600.00; 24" - $3,000.00. **Throws kisses:** 20" - $2,800.00; 24" - $3,200.00.

21½" Jumeau with sleep eyes and open mouth on French walking body. $3,000.00. *Courtesy Frasher Doll Auctions.*

Celluloid head: Incised "Jumeau." (See photo in Series 3, pg. 85.) 14" - $625.00 up.

Mold #200 series: Examples: **201, 203, 205, 208, 211, 214, 223.** *Very character faces* and marked "Jumeau." Closed mouth. No damage to bisque or body. (See photo in Series 6, pg. 116; Series 7, pg. 100.) 16" - $32,000.00 up; 20" - $52,000.00 up. **At auction:** Original dressed African with scowl lines - $115,000.00. Smiling woman - $120,000.00.

Mold #230 series: Circa 1906. Open mouth. 14" - $1,200.00; 16–17" - $1,500.00; 20" - $1,800.00 up.

S.F.B.J. or UNIS: Marked along with Jumeau. No damage to head and on French body. Open mouth: 16" - $1,400.00; 20" - $1,800.00. Closed mouth: 16" - $2,400.00; 20" - $3,000.00.

Two-faced Jumeau: Two different faces on same head – one crying and one smiling. Open/closed mouths, jointed

19" with large almond-shaped eyes and applied ears. On marked Jumeau jointed body with straight wrists. Marked "E.J. 8." $6,400.00. *Courtesy Turn of Century Antiques.*

body. No damage and nicely dressed. 15" - $9,000.00 up.

Fashion: See Fashion section.

Mold #221: Circa 1930s. Small 10" dolls will have a paper label "Jumeau." Adult style bisque head on five-piece body with painted-on shoes. Closed mouth and set glass eyes. Dressed in original ornate gown. No damage and clean. 10–11" - $700.00 up.

Mold #306 ("Princess Elizabeth"): Jumeau made after formation of Unis and mark will be "Unis/France" in oval and "71" on one side and "149" on other, followed by "306/Jumeau/1939/Paris." Closed mouth, flirty or paperweight eyes. Jointed French body. No damage and nicely dressed. 20" - $2,000.00; 30" - $3,400.00.

Marked Shoes: #5 and up - $200.00 up. #7–10 - $350.00–400.00.

Left to right: 22" Tete Jumeau with closed mouth. Clothes may be original. 21" marked "1907 Jumeau" in pink. Has open mouth. 23½" Tete Jumeau with open mouth and on jointed Jumeau body. 21" Tete Jumeau with closed mouth and in blue dress. Front center: 12" Tete Jumeau, size 3. Jointed Jumeau body. 21–23" with closed mouth - $4,300.00; 21–23" with open mouth - $3,000.00. 12" with closed mouth - $3,200.00. *Courtesy Kathy Riddick.*

Kämmer and Reinhardt dolls generally have the Simon and Halbig name or initials incised along with their own name or mark, as Simon & Halbig made most of their heads. They were located in Thüringia, Germany, at Waltershausen and began in 1895, although their first models were not on the market until 1896. The trademark for this company was registered in 1895. In 1909, a character line of fourteen molds (#100–#114) was exhibited at the Leipzig Toy Fair.

Marks:

Character boy or girl: Closed or open/closed mouth. Jointed body or five-piece body. No damage and nicely dressed.

#101 ("Peter" or "Marie"): Five-piece body: 9" - $1,700.00; 11" -$2,500.00. **Fully jointed body:** 9"- $2,200.00; 11" - $2,800.00; 14" - $3,800.00; 16" - $4,200.00; 18" - $5,800.00; 22" - $6,300.00. **Glass eyes:** 14" - $6,800.00; 17" - $7,600.00; 21" - $10,000.00.

#102 ("Karl"): Extremely rare. 12" - $29,000.00 up; 15" - $34,000.00; 20" - $52,000.00. **Glass eyes:** 17" - $38,000.00 up.

#103: Closed mouth, sweet expression, painted eyes. **#104:** Open/closed mouth, dimples, mischievous expression, painted eyes. Extremely rare. 19" - $60,000.00 up; 22" - $76,000.00 up.

#105: Extremely rare. Open/closed mouth. Much modeling around intaglio eyes. 19" - $85,000.00 up.

#106: Extremely rare. Full round face, pursed closed full lips, intaglio eyes to side, and much chin modeling. 21" - $65,000.00 up.

#107: Pursed, pouty mouth. Intaglio eyes. 15" - $17,000.00 up; 22" - $42,000.00 up. **Glass eyes:** 17" - $48,000.00 up.

#108: One example sold at auction at over $240,000.00.

#109 ("Elise"): Very rare.. (See photo in Series 8, pg. 105; Series 10, pg. 105.) 9–10" - $6,500.00; 15" - $22,000.00; 20" - $30,000.00. **Glass eyes:** 20" - $35,000.00.

#112, #112X, #112A: Very rare. (See photo in Series 5, pg. 91.) 15" - $10,000.00; 18" - $24,000.00; 23" - $30,000.00. **Glass eyes:** 15" - $15,000.00; 18" - $25,000.00; 24" - $32,000.00.

#114 ("Gretchen" or "Hans"): (See photo in Series 9, pg. 108.) 8" - $1,800.00; 10" - $2,300.00; 15" - $4,600.00; 19" - $5,900.00; 23" - $8,600.00. **Glass eyes:** 18" - $12,000.00 up; 24" - $18,000.00 up.

#117: Closed mouth. 9" (on five-piece body) - $2,500.00; 12" - $3,000.00; 14" - $4,000.00; 17" - $5,200.00; 22" - $6,600.00; 25" - $7,400.00; 28" - $8,500.00; 32" - $9,850.00.

17" and 16" K✿R model #114 named "Gretchen." Both have glass eyes, closed pouty mouths, and on fully jointed bodies. Both are *very expressive.* Excellent quality. 17" - $13,500.00; 16" - $13,000.00.
Courtesy Frasher Doll Auctions.

#117A: Closed mouth. 15" - $4,200.00; 18" - $5,400.00; 22" - $6,800.00; 25" - $7,600.00; 28" - $8,700.00.

#117, 117N: Open mouth, flirty eyes. (Subtract $300.00 for sleep eyes only on #117N.) 16" - $1,500.00; 20" - $2,200.00; 23" - $2,500.00; 28" - $2,800.00; 32" - $3,2700.00.

#123, #124 ("Max & Moritz"): (See photo in Series 8, pg. 107.) 17" - $29,000.00 up each.

#127: (Also see under babies.) Molded hair, open/closed mouth. Jointed body. 16" - $2,000.00; 20" - $2,600.00; 24" - $3,300.00.

#135, child: 14" - $1,800.00; 17" - $2,200.00.

Character baby: Open/closed mouth or closed mouth on five-piece bent limb baby body, solid dome or wigged. No damage and nicely dressed.

16" K✿R #115 toddler with glass eyes and slightly open/closed mouth. This version with molded, painted hair is scarce. $4,500.00. *Courtesy Turn of Century Antiques.*

#100 ("Kaiser Baby"): Intaglio eyes, open/closed mouth. 12" - $600.00; 15" - $800.00; 18" - $950.00; 21" - $1,400.00. **Glass eyes:** 14" - $1,900.00; 19" - $2,500.00. **Black:** (See photo in Series 1, pg. 176.) 15" - $1,100.00; 17" - $1,800.00.

#115, #115a ("Phillip"): 15" - $4,200.00; 18" - $4,700.00; 24" - $5,500.00; 26" - $5,800.00. **Toddler:** 16" - $5,000.00; 18" - $5,400.00; 24" - $5,800.00.

#116, #116a: 15" - $3,800.00; 18" - $4,300.00; 25" - $5,000.00. **Toddler:** 16" - $4,500.00; 21" - $5,000.00; 25" - $5,400.00. **Open Mouth:** 16" - $1,400.00; 18" - $2,300.00. **Toddler:** 20" - $3,500.00.

#127: (Also see Child.) 12" - $850.00; 16" - $1,450.00; 21" - $2,000.00; 24" - $2,300.00. **Toddler:** 15" - $1,700.00; 20" - $2,300.00; 26" - $2,700.00.

Baby with open mouth: Sleep eyes, wigs. On five-piece bent limb baby

17" "Max" character with flirty sleep eyes and broad closed mouth grin. On jointed body with straight wrists. Modeled-on shoes and socks. Shown with "Max and Moritz" storybook by Wilhelm Busch. Doll - $29,000.00; book - $200.00. *Courtesy Frasher Doll Auctions.*

body. May have tremble tongues or "mama" cryer in body. No damage and nicely dressed. Allow more for flirty eyes.

#118a: 15" - $1,700.00; 18" - $2,500.00; 20" - $2,700.00.

#119: 16" - $4,000.00; 20" - $4,900.00; 24" - $5,400.00.

#121: (See photo in Series 10, pg. 107.) 12" - $600.00; 15" - $800.00; 18" - $1,300.00; 23–24" - $1,500.00. **Toddler:** 14"- $1,200.00; 21" - $1,700.00; 25" - $2,200.00; 28" - $2,600.00.

#122, 128: 12" - $675.00; 15" - $875.00; 18" - $1,300.00; 22" - $1,500.00. **Toddler:** 14" - $1,300.00; 18" - $1,600.00; 24" - $2,000.00; 27" - $2,500.00.

#126: 8" - $425.00; 12" - $550.00; 16" - $750.00; 20"- $900.00; 24" - $1,200.00; 28" - $1,800.00. **Toddler:** 6½–7" - $675.00; 9" - $745.00; 16" - $950.00; 21" - $1,300.00; 24" - $1,700.00; 29" - $2,000.00. **Child body:** 22" - $950.00; 34" - $1,800.00.

#135: 14" - $1,500.00; 20" - $2,500.00.

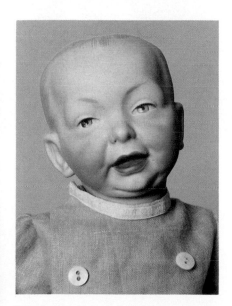

15" "Kaiser Baby," mold #100. Deeply modeled face with intaglio eyes. Wide open/closed mouth. On baby body. $895.00. *Courtesy Turn of Century Antiques.*

21" with open mouth and excellent bisque. On fully jointed body. Marked "K✿R/58." This doll belonged to the owner's mother. $900.00. *Courtesy June Murkins.*

#172, 175: Circa 1925. Five-piece baby body. 16" - $3,200.00; 20" - $3,700.00. Cloth body: 11" - $1,150.00; 16" - $3,600.00.

Child dolls: 1895–1930s. Open mouth, sleep or set eyes. Fully jointed body. No damage, nicely dressed. Most often found mold numbers are: **#109, 191, 290, 400, 403:** (See photo in Series 8, pg. 105.) Add more for flirty eyes. Add more for all original clothes. 8" - $485.00; 12" - $600.00; 15" - $725.00; 18" - $825.00; 21" - $900.00; 24" - $1,150.00; 29" - $1,400.00; 34" - $1,900.00; 39" - $2,700.00; 42" - $3,600.00.

#192: Closed mouth, sleep eyes, fully jointed body. No damage. 6–7" - $625.00; 16" - $2,500.00; 22"- $3,000.00; 25" - $3,500.00. **Open mouth:** 7–8" - $525.00; 12" - $700.00; 14" - $800.00; 20" - $1,150.00; 25" - $1,500.00; 28" - $1,900.00.

Small child doll: Open mouth, sleep eyes (some set). No damage. Five-piece body: 4½–5" - $400.00; 6" - $450.00; 8" - $550.00. Jointed body: 8" - $600.00; 10" - $685.00. **Walker:** 6–7" - $550.00.

Small child doll: Flapper style. Open mouth, painted bisque. 8" - $550.00.

Small child doll: Closed mouth. 6" - $525.00; 8" - $650.00.

Googly: See Googly section.

Needle sculptured: 1927. Characters. Each - $145.00 up.

Celluloid: See Celluloid section.

Infant: 1924 on. Molded hair, glass eyes, open mouth. Cloth body with composition hands. 14" - $1,850.00; 17" - $2,800.00.

Composition, #926: Looks like mold #260. Five-piece toddler body: Allow more for flirty eyes. 17" - $600.00; 23" - $825.00. Baby: 18" - $500.00; 24" - $700.00.

Kämmer & Reinhardt needle sculptured cloth characters representing Sherlock Holmes and Franklin D. Roosevelt. Limbs are wire and feet are wooden. From 1927. Each - $145.00.

Johannes Daniel Kestner's firm was founded in 1802, and his name was carried through the 1920s. The Kestner Company was one of the few that made entire dolls, both bodies and heads. In 1895, Kestner started using the trademark of the crown and streamers. (Also see German - All Bisque.)

Sample marks:

B MADE IN 6	**J.D.K.**
GERMANY	**208**
J.D.K.	**GERMANY**
126	

F GERMANY 11

Child doll, closed mouth: Circa 1880. Some appear to be pouties, some may have very sweet expression. Sleep or set eyes, jointed body with straight wrist. No damage and nicely dressed.

#X, XII, XV, 1003: (See photo in Series 8, pg. 111.) 15" - $3,350.00; 18" - $3,700.00; 22" - $4,000.00; 25" - $4,600.00.

#XI, 103: Very pouty. (See photos in Series 6, pg. 122; Series 7, pg. 106.) Price will be less for kid body. 11–12" - $2,800.00; 16" - $3,450.00; 18" - $3,800.00; 22" - $4,000.00; 25" - $4,300.00; 32" - $5,000.00.

#128 pouty, #169, or unmarked pouty: #128 can have sweet pouty expression. Five-piece body. (See photo of #169 in Series 10, pg. 108.) 6½–7" - $1,000.00; 10" - $1,500.00; 12" - $1,800.00; 14" - $2,500.00; 17" - $2,800.00; 19" - $3,000.00; 23" - $3,400.00; 26" - $3,800.00.

15½" Kestner with heavy feathered eyebrows, glass eyes, full closed mouth, and human hair wig. Marked "G/Made in Germany/169." $2,800.00. *Courtesy Kathy Riddick.*

15½" Kestner with large glass eyes and full closed mouth. On Schmitt type body with straight wrists. Marked "XII." $3,350.00. *Courtesy Barbara Earnshaw-Cain.*

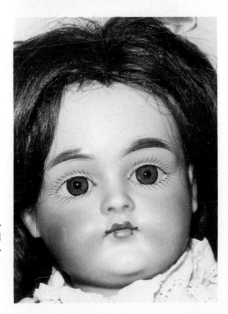

Turned shoulder head: Circa 1880s. Set or sleep eyes. Kid body with bisque lower arms. No damage and nicely dressed. (Allow more for swivel neck.) **Closed mouth:** 12" - $825.00; 16" - $1,075.00; 18" - $1,200.00; 23" - $1,800.00; 26" - $2,200.00. **Open mouth:** 16" - $600.00; 18" - $700.00; 23" - $800.00.

Early child with square cut porcelain teeth: Jointed body. Marked with number and letter. 10–11" - $650.00; 15" - $900.00; 18" - $1,200.00; 22" - $1,600.00 up; 25" - $1,900.00 up.

A.T. type: Composition jointed body with straight wrists. (See photo in Series 8, pg. 111; Series 9, pg. 113.) **Closed mouth:** 11" - $10,000.00; 13" - $14,000.00; 15" - $16,000.00; 17" - $18,000.00. **Open mouth:** 13" - $2,100.00; 15" - $2,500.00; 17" - $3,300.00.

Bru type: Open/closed mouth, modeled teeth. Bulge in back of neck looks like roll of fat. (See photo in Series

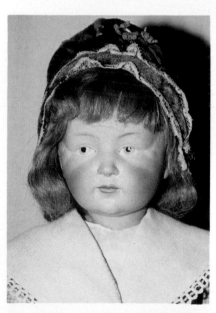

17" closed mouth character doll made by Kestner. Painted eyes have much detail around them. Original wig. On fully jointed body. Marked "187." $4,200.00.

7, pg. 107; Series 8, pg. 112.) **Composition lower arms, kid body:** 16" - $2,500.00; 22" - $3,200.00. **Bisque lower arms:** 17" - $5,200.00; 24" - $6,400.00. **Jointed composition body, straight wrists:** 18" - $4,800.00; 23" - $5,800.00; 26" - $6,400.00.

Character child: 1910 and after. Closed mouth or open/closed unless noted. Glass or painted eyes, jointed body. No damage and nicely dressed. (See photos in Series 4, pg. 102; Series 6, pg. 124, Series 9, pg. 114.)

#175, 176, 177, 178, 179, 180, 181, 182, 183, 184, 185, 187, 188, 189, 190: These mold numbers can be found on the boxed set doll that has one body and interchangable four heads. (See photos in Series 5, pg. 96; Series 6, pg. 124.) **Boxed set with four heads:** (See photo in Series 2, pg. 97.) 12–13" - $7,500.00 up. 15–16" - $10,000.00 up. **Larger size, painted eyes:** Closed or open/closed mouth: 12" - $3,000.00; 15" - $3,800.00; 17" - $4,200.00. **Larger size, glass eyes:** 12" - $3,300.00; 15" - $3,800.00; 18" - $4,900.00. Glass eyes, molded-on bonnet: 16" - $4,800.00 up.

#151: 16" - $2,600.00; 20" - $3,500.00.

#155: Five-piece body: 8–9" - $525.00. Jointed body: 8–9" - $750.00.

#206: Fat cheeks, closed mouth. (See photo in Series 8, pg. 112.) **Child or toddler:** 12" - $6,000.00; 15" - $9,000.00; 21" - $17,000.00; 25" - $20,000.00.

#208: Painted eyes: 12" - $3,700.00; 16" - $6,000.00; 19" - $9,600.00; 24" - $13,000.00. **Glass eyes:** 18" - $10,000.00; 24" - $13,000.00.

#212: 10" - $2,100.00; 15" - $3,800.00.

#239: Child or toddler. (Also see Babies.): 17" - $3,800.00; 21" - $4,800.00; 26" - $6,400.00.

#241: Open mouth, glass eyes. (See photo in Series 7, pg. 108.) 16" - $4,400.00; 22"- $5,800.00.

#249: 17" - $1,400.00; 20" - $1,800.00.

#211, 260: Open/closed mouth. Jointed or toddler body. 8" - $675.00; 12" - $975.00; 16" - $1,800.00; 22" - $2,400.00.

Child doll: Late 1880s to 1930s. Open mouth on fully jointed body, sleep eyes, some set, with no damage and nicely dressed.

#128, 129, 134, 136, 141, 142, 144, 146, 149, 152, 156, 159, 160, 161, 162, 164, 173, 174, 180, 208, 211, 215: (Allow 20% more for **#129, 149, 152, 160, 161, 173, 174.**) 10" - $485.00; 14" - $550.00; 17" - $600.00; 20" - $700.00; 22" - $800.00; 25" - $1,000.00; 30" - $1,250.00; 33" - $1,400.00; 37" - $2,000.00.

#143, 189: Character face, open mouth. (See photo in Series 6, pg. 126.) 8" - $700.00; 12" - $900.00; 16" - $1,000.00; 18" - $1,400.00; 20" - $1,600.00; 24" - $1,800.00 up.

#192: 15" - $650.00; 18" - $750.00; 21" - $950.00.

Child with kid body: Circa 1880s. "Dolly" face, open mouth, sleep or set eyes, bisque shoulder head, bisque lower arms. No damage and nicely dressed.

#145, 147, 148, 149, 155, 166, 167, 170, 195, etc.: Add more for fur eyebrows. 8" - $275.00; 12" - $350.00; 16" - $500.00; 19" - $600.00; 22" - $700.00; 25" - $900.00; 29" - $1,100.00.

#142, 144, 146, 154, 164, 167, 168, 171, 196, 214: Jointed body. Open mouth. 10" - $700.00; 14" - $775.00; 17" - $850.00; 22" - $925.00; 25" - $1,000.00; 30" - $1,200.00; 35" - $2,000.00; 42" - $3,800.00 up. **Swivel bisque head:** Bisque shoulder head, open mouth. 17" - $565.00; 21" - $800.00; 26" - $1,100.00. **Kid body:** 17" - $450.00; 21" - $525.00; 26" - $700.000.

#171 (Daisy), some #154 (see previous listing for additional sizes): Blonde, side part mohair wig. White dress, red hooded cape. 18" only. Original - $965.00; redressed - $600.00.

Character babies: 1910 and later. Bent limb baby bodies, sleep or set eyes, open mouth. Can be wigged or have solid dome with painted hair. No damage and nicely dressed.

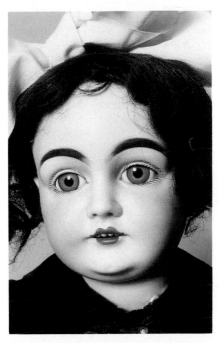

27" Kestner, mold #146, with large sleep eyes, open mouth, and very heavy feathered eyebrows. $1,050.00. *Courtesy Turn of Century Antiques.*

#121, 142, 150, 151, 152, 153, 154: Now attributed to Hertel, Schwab & Co. 10" - $425.00; 14" - $550.00; 17" - $675.00; 20" - $825.00; 24" - $975.00.

#211, 226, 236, 260, 262, 263: 9" - $500.00; 12" - $600.00; 15" - $750.00; 18" - $850.00; 20" - $1,050.00; 24" - $1,400.00.

#220: Glass eyes, open/closed mouth, deep dimples. (See photo in Series 8, pg. 109.) 15" - $4,800.00; 18" - $5,800.00. Toddler: 17" - $6,200.00; 25" - $7,000.00.

#234, 235, 238: 13" - $675.00; 16" - $900.00; 20" - $1,100.00; 24" - $1,300.00.

#237, 245, 1070 ("Hilda"): Wigged or solid dome. 12" - $2,800.00; 16" - $4,200.00; 19" - $5,000.00; 22" - $6,000.00; 24" - $7,000.00. **Toddler:** 17" - $5,300.00; 19" - $5,900.00; 24" - $6,400.00.

#239: 15" - $2,600.00; 17" - $3,500.00; 23" - $3,900.00.

#247: 12" - $1,200.00; 16" - $1,700.00; 19" - $2,000.00; 22" - $4,000.00.

#249: 13" - $1,100.00; 16" - $1,800.00; 20" - $2,000.00.

#257: 9" - $600.00; 14" - $750.00; 18" - $900.00; 21" - $1,200.00; 25" - $1,700.00. **Toddler:** 22" - $1,500.00; 27" - $2,400.00.

#272 ("Siegfried"): Closed mouth, wide spaced eyes. 9½" head circumference. $1,250.00 up.

#279, 200 (Century Doll): Molded hair with part, bangs, cloth body, composition hands. 15" - $1,100.00; 18" - $2,200.00; 23" - $4,800.00.

#281 (Century Doll): Open mouth: 20" - $1,000.00.

J.D.K. marked baby: Called **"Sally," "Jean," or "Sammy."** Solid dome, painted eyes and open mouth. 12" - $1,100.00; 17" - $1,500.00; 23" - $2,000.00; 27" - $2,900.00.

Adult doll, #162: Sleep eyes, open mouth, adult jointed body (thin waist and molded breasts) with slender limbs. No damage and very nicely dressed. 14" - $1,400.00; 17" - $1,600.00; 22" - $2,300.00.

Adult #172 ("Gibson Girl"): 1910. Bisque shoulder head with closed mouth, kid body with bisque lower arms, glass eyes. No damage and beautifully dressed. (See photo in Series 8, pg. 115.) 10–11" - $1,150.00; 14" - $2,000.00; 16" - $2,600.00; 20" - $3,800.00.

Oriental #243: Olive fired-in color to bisque. Matching color five-piece bent limb baby body (or jointed toddler-style body). Wig, sleep or set eyes. No damage and dressed in oriental style. 14" - $4,600.00; 17" - $6,000.00. Child: On jointed Kestner olive-toned body. 15" - $5,200.00; 18" - $6,800.00. Molded hair baby: 14" - $4,800.00.

Small dolls, open mouth: Five-piece bodies or jointed bodies. Wigs, sleep or set eyes. No damage and nicely dressed. 7" - $500.00; 9" - $650.00. Closed mouth: 8–9" - $950.00 up.

#133: 9" - $800.00.

#155: Five-piece body: 8–9" - $550.00. Jointed body: 8–9" - $825.00.

Beautiful 22" life-size baby with sleep eyes and open mouth. Marked "Hilda J.D.K. Jr. 1914 GesGesch 1070." $6,000.00.
Courtesy Turn of Century Antiques.

Designed by Rose O'Neill and marketed from 1913. All prices are for dolls that have no chips, hairlines or breaks. (See Modern section for composition and vinyl Kewpies.)

Labels:

All bisque: One-piece body and head, jointed shoulders only. Blue wings, painted features with eyes to one side. 2½" - $110.00; 4½" - $135.00; 6" - $200.00; 7" - $265.00; 8" - $400.00; 10" - $700.00; 12" - $1,300.00. **With any article of clothing:** 3" - $250.00; 5" - $300.00; 7" - $350.00; 9" - $650.00 up.

All bisque: Jointed at hips and shoulders. 4" - $450.00; 6" - $700.00; 9" - $900.00; 12" - $1,400.00 up. **Painted shoes and socks:** 4–5" - $525.00; 10" - $1,500.00.

Shoulder head: Cloth or stockinette body. 6–7" - $600.00. **Head only:** 3" - $175.00.

Action Kewpie: Arms folded. 4½" - $475.00.

Confederate soldier: 4½" - $475.00.

Cowboy: Big hat, gun. Made as lamp. (See photo in Series 7, pg. 11.) 10½" - $850.00.

Farmer: 4" - $425.00.
Gardener: 4" - $450.00.
Governor: 4" - $385.00.
Groom with bride: 4" - $325.00.
Guitar player: 3½" - $350.00.
Holding pen: (See photo in Series 5, pg. 100.) 3" - $400.00.

Holding cat: (See photo in Series 9, pg. 117.) 4" - $465.00.
Holding butterfly: 4" - $525.00.
Hugging: 3½" - $245.00.
On stomach: Called **"Blunderboo."** (See photo in Series 7, pg. 117.) 4" - $425.00.
Soldier: 4½" - $650.00.
Thinker: 4" - $265.00; 6" - $475.00.
Traveler: Tan or black suitcase. (See photo in Series 5, pg. 101.) 3½" - $325.00.
With broom: 4" - $475.00.
With dog, "Doodle": (See photo in Series 7, pg. 117.) 3½" - $1,200.00 up.
With helmet: (See photo in Series 5, pg. 101.) 6" - $550.00.
With outhouse: 2½" - $1,400.00.
With pumpkin: 4" - $365.00.
With rabbit: 2½" - $365.00.

Kewpie Jasperware clock, 6 x 5½", signed "O'Neill." Shown with 4½" fully jointed Kewpie and 3" Kewpie with pen. Atop clock is a cute 5" "Our Fairy," mold #222. Googly glass eyes, open/closed mouth with two teeth. Original. Clock - $350.00; 4½" Kewpie - $135.00; Kewpie with pen - $400.00; "Our Fairy" - $1,600.00. *Courtesy Turn of Century Antiques.*

With rose: 2" - $350.00.
With teddy bear: 4" - $550.00.
With turkey: 2" - $350.00.
With umbrella and dog: 3½" - $1,800.00.
Kewpie soldier and nurse: 6" - $2,300.00 up.
Kewpie tree or mountain: 17 figures. $18,000.00 up.
Kewpie driving chariot: $2,800.00 up.
Kewpie on inkwell: Bisque: 3½" - $650.00. Cast metal: (See photo in Series 9, pg. 118.) 3½" - $425.00; 6" - $650.00.
Kewpie in basket with flowers: 3½" - $750.00 up.

Kewpie with drawstring bag: 4½" - $625.00.
Buttonhole Kewpie: $165.00.
Reading book: 3½" - $825.00.
Sitting in chair: Arms crossed. (See photo in Series 8, pg. 96.) 3½" - $525.00.
At tea table: 4" - $1,800.00 up.
Kewpie and dog on bench: 4" - $3,000.00 up.
Kewpie Doodle Dog: (See photo in Series 8, pg. 117.) 1½" - $725.00; 3" - $1,500.00.
Hottentot (Black Kewpie): 3½" - $425.00; 5" - $550.00; 9" - $900.00; 12" (rare) - $4,000.00 up.

Large 12" Kewpie (at bottom) is shown with 7½", 6½", and 6" bisque Kewpies, 11" composition head Kewpie, two 8½" "Cuddle Kewpies" - one dressed in red; the other in checked outfit, and 15½" "Cuddle Kewpie" in pale blue. 12" - $775.00; 7½" - $265.00; 6–6½" - $200.00; 11" - $300.00; 8½" in red - $175.00; 8½" in checks - $200.00; 15½" - $450.00. *Courtesy Turn of Century Antiques.*

Kewpie perfume bottle: 3½" - $400.00 up; 4½" - $550.00.

Pincushion Kewpie: 2½" - $325.00.

Paperweight: 1935. Kewpie in center. (See photo in Series 10, pg. 114.) $350.00.

Celluloid Kewpies: 2" - $40.00; 5" - $85.00; 9" - $165.00. Black: 5" - $135.00. **Jointed shoulders:** 3" - $70.00; 5" - $110.00; 9" - $175.00; 12" - $250.00; 16" - $600.00 up; 22" - $900.00 up. **Soldier or Action:** 4" - $100.00 up.

Cloth body Kewpie: Bisque head, painted eyes. (See photo in Series 4, pg. 106.) 10" - $1,500.00; 14" - $1,800.00. **Glass eyes:** 12" - $2,600.00 up; 16" - $4,500.00 up. Composition head and half arms: 13" - $350.00.

Glass eye Kewpie: Chubby jointed toddler body, bisque head. Marked "Ges. Gesch./O'Neill J.D.K." 10" - $3,600.00; 12" - $4,900.00; 16" - $6,200.00; 20" - $7,900.00.

All cloth ("Cuddle Kewpie"): Made by Krueger. All one-piece with body forming clothes, mask face. (See photo in Series 7, pg. 117.) Mint condition: 7–8" - $175.00; 12" - $265.00; 15" - $450.00; 21" - $700.00; 26" - $1,200.00. Fair condition: 12" - $90.00; 15" - $150.00; 21" - $250.00; 26" - $450.00. **Plain cloth body, removable clothes:** Original, mint condition. 15" - $550.00; 21" - $800.00; 26" - $1,400.00; 21" - $2,500.00. Fair condition: 15" - $150.00; 21" - $250.00.

Kewpie tin or celluloid talcum container: Excellent condition: 7–8" - $185.00.

Kewpie soaps: 4" - $95.00 each. Boxed set of five: $525.00.

Japan: Bisque. 2" - $30.00; 3" - $50.00; 4" - $70.00; 5" - $90.00; 6" - $100.00.

KLEY & HAHN

Kley & Hahn operated in Ohrdruf, Germany from 1895 to 1929. They made general dolls as well as babies and fine character dolls.

Marks:

K & H   > **K⊀H** <

Character child: Boy or girl. Painted eyes (some with glass eyes), closed or open/closed mouth; on jointed body. No damage and nicely dressed. **#320, 520, 523, 525, 526, 531, 536, 546, 547, 548, 549, 552:** (See photos in Series 1, pg. 187; Series 3, pg. 93; Series 7, pg. 89, 115; Series 10, pg. 115.) 12" - $3,600.00; 15" - $3,500.00; 18" - $4,400.00; 22" - $5,300.00; 25" - $6,000.00. **Toddler bodies:** 16" - $2,800.00; 20" - $3,900.00; 24" - $4,900.00. **Bent limb baby body:** 14" - $1,000.00; 16" - $1,800.00; 20" - $2,600.00; 23" - $3,000.00.

10½" and 16" Kley & Hahn mold #525. The larger doll is very much like mold #538. Both have solid domes, brush painted hair, intaglio eyes, and open/closed mouths. Both are on fully jointed bodies. 10½" - $2,750.00; 16" - $3,650.00. *Courtesy Turn of Century Antiques.*

Child with glass eyes: 14" - $4,000.00; 18" - $6,500.00; 21" - $7,200.00; 25" - $8,000.00.

Character Baby: Molded hair or wig, glass sleep eyes or painted eyes. Can have open or open/closed mouth. On bent limb baby body, no damage and nicely dressed. (Allow more for flirty eyes.) **#130, 132, 138, 142, 150, 151, 158, 160, 161, 162, 167, 176, 199, 458, 522, 525, 531, 538, 585, 680:** 10" - $500.00; 16" - $625.00; 20" - $825.00; 24" - $1,100.00; 26" - $1,500.00. **Toddler bodies:** 14" - $625.00; 16" - $825.00; 20" - $1,100.00; 24" - $1,300.00; 28" - $1,800.00.

#547: Closed mouth, glass eyes. 15" - $2,4000.00; 17" - $2,750.00. Baby: 15" - $1,500.00.

#538, 568: (See photo in Series 8, pg. 118.) 15" - $725.00; 17" - $850.00; 20" - $950.00. **Toddler:** 22" - $1,500.00; 26" - $1,900.00.

#162, talker mechanism in head: 17" - $1,500.00; 23" - $2,300.00; 25" - $2,800.00.

24" Kley & Hahn, mold #680, with flirty eyes. Open mouth with tremble tongue. On five-piece bent limb baby body. $1,300.00. *Courtesy Turn of Century Antiques.*

#162, flirty eyes and clockworks in head: 18" - $1,800.00; 26" - $3,200.00.

#680: 16" - $850.00. **Toddler:** 20" - $1,500.00.

#153, 154, 157, 166, 169: Child, closed mouth. (See photo in Series 7, pg. 114.) 16" - $3,000.00; 22" - $3,800.00. **Open mouth:** 16" - $1,300.00; 22" - $1,700.00. Baby: 18" - $1,200.00.

#159, two-faced doll: (See photo in Series 4, pg. 110.) 12" - $1,900.00; 15" - $2,400.00.

#166: Molded hair , open mouth. 17–18" - $1,500.00; 25" - $1,950.00. Baby: 20" - $1,350.00. **Closed mouth:** 18" - $2,650.00.

#169: Closed mouth. (See photo in Series 8, pg. 118.) **Toddler:** 14" - $2,300.00; 18" - $3,600.00. **Open mouth:** 20" - $1,400.00.

#119: Child, glass eyes, closed mouth. 20" - $5,000.00. **Painted eyes:** 20" - $3,500.00. **Toddler, glass eyes:** 20" - $4,800.00.

24" with open mouth and sleep eyes. On fully jointed body. Marked "Wälkure/Germany." $775.00. *Courtesy Kathy Riddick.*

Child dolls, Walküre, and/or #250: Sleep or set eyes, open mouth, jointed body. No damage and nicely dressed. 8" - $365.00; 14" - $450.00; 17" - $550.00; 20" - $685.00; 24" - $775.00; 28" - $925.00; 32" - $1,050.00; 36" - $1,600.00; 42" - $2,900.00.

KNOCH, GEBRUDER

Gebruder Knoch porcelain factory operated in Neustadt, Germany, from 1887 into the 1920's. Most of their dolls have bisque shoulder heads and kid or cloth bodies, but some will be on jointed bodies and/or have kid bodies with composition jointed limbs.

Marks:

Character doll: No damage and ready to display in collection.

#206: 10" - $950.00 up; 15" - $1,450.00 up.

#216, 218: Girl or boy with modeled hairdo, wide open/closed mouth, and molded lower teeth. 14" - $2,300.00; 18" - $5,000.00.

#246: Winking, has molded cap. 13–14" - $3,250.00.

#237: Molded decorated bonnet. 9–10" - $825.00; 14" - $1,300.00.

#3920: Closed mouth. (See photo in Series 10, pg. 116.) 9½" - $850.00; 13" - $1,050.00.

Child doll: Perfect, no damage, nicely dressed. Sleep eyes, wig, open mouth, ball-jointed body. 14" - $275.00; 17" - $425.00; 20" - $525.00.

15" large-eyed child with very pale bisque shoulder head and full closed mouth. Kid body with bisque lower arms. Original mohair wig. Marked "G.K." $1,300.00. *Courtesy Kathy Riddick.*

Käthe Kruse began making dolls in 1910. In 1916, she obtained a patent for a wire coil doll, and in 1923 she registered a trademark of a double "K" with the first one reversed, along with the name Käthe Kruse. The first heads were designed after her own children and copies of sculptures from the Renaissance period. The dolls have molded muslin heads that are handpainted in oils, and jointed cloth bodies. These early dolls will be marked "Käthe Kruse" on the foot and sometimes with a "Germany" and number.

In 1911, doll had disc-jointed bodies with wide hips and a double seam down the center of the bodies. Thumbs were sewn on individually. From 1911 to 1912, the dolls had swivel heads and ball-jointed knees. The bodies were short with long legs. These dolls are rare.

Early marked dolls, Model I: 1910. Wide hips, painted hair. In excellent condition and with original clothes. (See photo in Series 7, pg. 116; Series 8, pg. 120; Series 10, pg. 117.) 17" - $3,800.00; 21" - $4,800.00. **Fair condition:** Not original. 17" - $1,500.00; 21" - $2,000.00. **Ball-jointed knees:** (See photo in Series 8, pg. 120.) 18" - $5,300.00; 22" - $6,200.00. **Later model:** Slim hips. Mint condition: 17" - $2,900.00. Fair condition: 17" - $1,900.00.

Model II: 1922–1936. Smiling baby with tricot covered body and limbs. 14" - $2,900.00.

Model III, IV: 1923 on. Serious child. (See photo in Series 7, pg. 116.) 17" - $2,200.00 up.

Model V, VI: 1925 on. Typical Kruse. (See photo in Series 8, pg. 121.) 17" - $1,500.00; 21" - $2,000.00. Baby: **"Traümchen"** has painted closed eyes; **"Du Mein"** has open eyes. Has weighted tricot-covered body and limbs with sewn on navel. 21" - $3,400.00 up.

Model VII: 1927–1952. Reduced body same as model I with wide hips. Larger size has a thin body and swivel head. (See photo in Series 7, pg. 116;

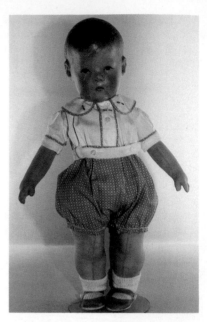

17" Käthe Kruse doll, Model I, with oil-painted features. Cloth body. Original romper suit. Marked on left foot "Käthe Kruse." $3,800.00. *Courtesy Glorya Woods.*

19" pair of Käthe Kruse #XII dolls in mint condition. They have the same face but different hairdos. Each - $1,850.00. *Courtesy Ellyn McCorkell.*

Series 8, pg. 120.) 14" - $1,900.00; 21" - $2,500.00. Fair condition: 14" - $1,000.00.

Model VIII: 1929 on. Wigged. (See series 9, pg. 123.) 16" - $1,800.00; 21" - $2,400.00. **Good condition:** 21" - $1,200.00. Ball-jointed knees: Slim hips. **Mint condition:** 17" - $2,900.00. **Fair condition:** 17" - $1,900.00.

Model IX: 1929. Wigged. 14" - $1,900.00. Good condition: 15" - $1,250.00.

Model X: 1935 on. 14–15" - $1,200.00.

1920s dolls, Model IH and others: (See photo in Series 7, pg. 116; Series 8, pg. 121.) Molded hair or wigged, hips arc wide. **Excellent condition:** Original. 16" - $2,200.00; 21" - $2,800.00. **Fair condition:** Not original. 16" - $1,300.00; 21" - $1,800.00.

U.S. Zone: Germany, 1945–1951. Has turtle mark. (See photo in Series 6, pg. 133.) 14" - $975.00; 17" - $1,100.00. Cloth head: 14" - $1,250.00.

Hard plastic dolls: 1952–1975. Glued-on wigs, sleep or painted eyes. Pink muslin body. Mint condition: 14" - $425.00; 17" - $575.00.

Celluloid: 1936–1939, 1945–1958. 12" - $300.00; 16" - $475.00.

1975 to date: Retail store prices could be higher. 9" - $185.00; 13" - $350.00; 17" - $500.00.

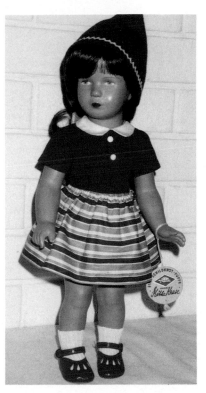

12" all celluloid Käthe Kruse with turtle mark. All original. Circa 1949–1952. Numbered "740" on head and back. $265.00. *Courtesy Pat Graff.*

KUHNLENZ, GEBRÜDER

Kuhnlenz made dolls from 1884 to 1930 and was located in Kronach, Bavaria. Marks from this company include the "G.K." plus numbers such as **31.42, 32.14, 34.32, 38.27, 41.28, 41.72, 41.77, 44.15, 44.26, 44.27, 44.30, 56.18, 56.38, 61.24.** Other marks now attributed to this firm are:

Child with closed mouth, mold #31, 32, : Bisque head in perfect condition, jointed body and nicely dressed. (See photo in Series 4, pg. 75.) 8" - $800.00, 10" - $1,000.00; 15" - $1,500.00; 19" - $1,900.00; 23" - $2,300.00.

Mold #34: Bru type. (See photo in Series 4, pg. 75.) 13" - $1,400.00; 17" - $2,800.00.

Mold #38: Kid body, bisque shoulder head. (See photo in Series 9, pg. 124.) 15" - $675.00; 22" - $1,200.00.

Child with open mouth, mold #41, 44, 56: Bisque head in perfect condition, jointed body and nicely dressed. (See photo in Series 6, pg. 134.) 15" - $700.00; 19" - $900.00; 23" - $1,200.00.

Mold #61: Shoulder head, kid body. 20" - $800.00.

Mold #165: Bisque head in perfect condition, jointed body and nicely dressed. 18" - $500.00; 24" - $700.00.

Tiny dolls, mold #44, 46 and others: Bisque head in perfect condition, five-piece body with painted-on shoes and socks, open mouth. (See photo in Series 6, pg. 134.) 8" - $200.00. Closed mouth: 8" - $450.00. Fully jointed body: 8" - $375.00 up.

Cute little 11" Gebrüder Kuhnlenz with open mouth and feathered eyebrows. On jointed body with straight wrists. Marked "41.77." $595.00. *Courtesy Barbara Earnshaw-Cain.*

LANTERNIER (LIMOGES)

A. Lanternier & Cie of Limoges, France, made dolls from about the 1890's on into the 1930s. Before making dolls, they produced porcelain pieces as early as 1855. Their doll heads will be fully marked and some carry a name such as "LaGeorgienne Favorite," "Lorraine," "Cherie," etc. They generally are found on papier maché bodies but can be on fully jointed composition bodies. Dolls from this firm may have nearly excellent quality bisque to very poor quality.

Marks:

FABRICATION FRANCAISE

AL & CIE
LIMOGES

Child: 1915. Open mouth, set eyes on jointed body. No damage and nicely dressed. Good quality bisque with pretty face. 15" - $600.00; 20" - $800.00; 24" - $1,000.00; 27" - $1,300.00. **Poor quality bisque:** Very high coloring or blotchy color bisque. 16" - $425.00; 20" - $475.00; 24" - $575.00; 27" - $700.00.

Jumeau style face: Has a striking Jumeau look. Good quality bisque. 18" - $1,300.00; 21" - $1,600.00. **Poor quality bisque:** 19" - $750.00; 23" - $950.00.

Character: 1915. Open/closed mouth with teeth, smiling fat face, glass eyes, on jointed body. No damage and nicely dressed. Marked "Toto." 17" - $950.00; 21" - $1,400.00.

Lady: 1915. Adult-looking face, set eyes, open/closed or closed mouth. Jointed adult body. No damage and nicely dressed. 14" - $850.00; 17" - $1,350.00.

16" Limoges character with set glass eyes and open mouth with two rows of teeth. On jointed French body. Can also be on baby or toddler body. $750.00. *Courtesy Turn of Century Antiques.*

LENCI

Lenci dolls are all felt with a few having cloth torsos. They are jointed at neck, shoulders and hips. The original clothes will be felt, organdy, or a combination of both. Features are oil painted and generally eyes are painted to the side. Other characteristics are sewn together middle and fourth fingers and the steam-molded head is seamless with sewn-on felt ears. Size can range from 5" to 45". (Mint or rare dolls will bring higher prices.)

Marks: On cloth or paper label "Lenci Torino Made in Italy." "Lenci" may be written on bottom of foot or underneath one arm.

Child: No moth holes, very little dirt, doll as near mint as possible and all in **excellent condition.** 14" - $850.00 up; 16" - $1,200.00 up; 18" - $1,500.00 up; 20" - $1,800.00 up. **Dirty,** original clothes in poor condition or redressed: 14" - $300.00; 16" - $450.00; 18" - $625.00; 20" - $750.00. Very pouty child: (See photo in Series 6, pg. 13.)

Baby: (See photos in Series 5, pg. 108.) 16" - $1,800.00; 20" - $2,300.00. **Fair condition:** $800.00-1,200.00.

Tiny dolls (called Mascottes): (See photos in Series 7, pg. 120; Series 8, pg. 126.) **Excellent condition:** 5" - $250.00; 8–9" - $365.00. **Dirty,** redressed, or original clothes in **poor condition:** 5" - $95.00; 8–9" - $165.00. **Unusual costume:** 8" - $400.00.

Beautiful 17" early Lenci dressed in organdy with felt collar and trim. All original. $1,250.00. *Courtesy Virginia Sofie.*

Sailor: 16" - $1,600.00.

Indians or Orientals (Thailand): (See photo in Series 2, pg. 112.) **Excellent condition:** 17" - $3,800.00. **Dirty** and poor condition: 17" - $1,000.00.

Lady with papoose: 18" - $4,100.00.

Golfer or other sports: (See photo in Series 2, pg. 112.) **Excellent, perfect condition:** 16" - $2,600.00. **Poor condition:** 16" - $900.00.

Mozart, Bach, Mendel: 17½" - $3,300.00 up.

Pinocchio: All wood and felt. Label on back. (See photo in Series 8, pg. 125.) 15" - no price known.

Pan: Has hooved feet. (See photo in Series 9, pg. 127.) 9½–10" - $2,100.00. **Dirty** and fair condition: 9½–10" - $650.00.

16" Lenci with painted features and mohair wig from 1925. Body is hollow felt with strung arms and legs. Original. $1,200.00. *Courtesy Glorya Woods.*

Ladies with adult faces: "Flapper" or "boudoir" style with long limbs. (See photos in Series 5, pg. 107, Series 6, pg. 136; Series 10, pg. 121.) **Excellent condition:** 14–15" - $950.00; 24" - $2,000.00 up; 27" - $2,400.00 up; 32" - $2,800.00; 34" - $3,000.00; 42" - $3,800.00; 48" - $5,000.00. **Dirty** or in poor condition: 24" - $900.00; 28" - $950.00.

Aviator: Girl with felt helmet. Referred to as "Amelia Earhart." 16½" - $3,800.00 up.

Characters: 1926. Tom Mix or Jack Dempsey. Both fat-faced. 17" - $3,800.00 each.

Clowns: (See photo in Series 4, pg. 99.) **Excellent condition:** 18" - $1,700.00; 27" - $2,200.00. **Poor condition:** 18" - $600.00; 27" - $950.00.

26" all original Lenci lady with long boudoir doll legs and arms. Hair done up in braids on back of head. $800.00 up.

Shirley Temple type: Excellent condition: 24" - $2,100.00. **Dirty** and poor condition: 24" - $800.00.

Bali dancer: Excellent condition: 16" - $1,800.00. **Poor condition:** 16" - $550.00. **South Seas girl:** Long thin limbs. 18" - $2,800.00 up.

Smoking doll: Painted eyes. (See photo in Series 1, pg. 192.) **Excellent condition:** 25" - $2,200.00 up. **Poor condition:** 25" - $950.00. **Glass eyes:** Excellent condition: 17" - $2,600.00; 22" - $3,200.00. Poor condition: 17" - $950.00; 22" - $1,050.00.

"Surprise Eyes" doll: Very round painted eyes and O-shaped mouth. (See photo in Series 4, pg. 99; Series 9, pg. 128.) 15" - $1,500.00; 19" - $1,900.00; 21" - $2,400.00. **Glass eyes:** 15" - $2,000.00; 19" - $2,600.00; 21" - $3,200.00. **Flirty glass eyes:** 15" - $2,600.00; 19" - $3,200.00.

Widow Allegra: Dressed in black, holds dog. (See photo in Series 9, pg. 128.) Painted eyes: 17" - $1,700.00. Glass eyes: 17" - $2,500.00.

Teenager: Long-legged child. 16–17" - $1,200.00 up; 25" - $1,700.00; 36" - $2,400.00.

Boys: Side part hairdo. **Excellent** condition: 18" - $2,200.00 up; 23" - $2,600.00. **Poor condition:** 18" - $850.00; 23" - $975.00. **In Fascist uniform:** (See photo in Series 8, pg. 124.) 17" - $1,800.00 up. **Hitler Youth:** 17" - $1,600.00 up. **Winking:** 1920s. Open/closed mouth, painted teeth. (See photo in Series 9, pg. 127.) 11" - $1,200.00; 14" - $2,000.00.

Lenci type: Can be made in Italy, Germany, France, Spain, or England. 1920s through 1940s. Felt and cloth. **Child:** Felt or cloth, mohair wig, cloth body. Original clothes. 16" - $650.00; 18" - $775.00. **Small dolls:** Dressed as child. 7–8" - $60.00; 12" - $100.00. In foreign costume: 7–8" - $45.00.

Lenci catalogs: 1920s. $900.00–1,200.00.

17" all original Lenci dressed as Dutch girl. (Has dowel rod legs that fit down into and become part of wooden shoes. Dowels are covered with flesh-toned material.) $795.00 up. *Courtesy Doris Blake.*

LIMBACH

These dolls were made mostly from 1893 into the 1920s by Limbach Porzellanfabrik, Limbach, Germany. Allow more for excellent bisque and artist workmanship.

Mark:

Child: 1893–1899, 1919 and after. Incised with clover mark. Bisque head, glass eyes, jointed body. No damage and nicely dressed. **Open mouth:** 14" - $450.00; 17" - $600.00; 21" - $775.00; 24" - $950.00. **Closed mouth:** 15" - $1,400.00; 17" - $1,800.00; 20" - $2,000.00; 23" - $2,400.00. **Incised name:** Circa 1919. Incised names such as "Norma," "Rita," "Wally," etc. 16" - $600.00; 21" - $775.00; 24" - $850.00.

16" with bisque head on fully jointed French body. Open mouth with four teeth. Marked "Norma ⬚ Limbach 1." $600.00. *Courtesy Jane Walker.*

MAROTTES

Large 16½" marotte with music box that plays when twirled. Bisque head. Maker unknown. Shown with 21" Schoenau & Hoffmeister with sleep eyes, open mouth, and on fully jointed body. Marotte - $850.00; doll - $550.00. *Courtesy Turn of Century Antiques.*

The marotte on the left is 14½" tall with glass eyes, open mouth, and has excellent music box. On the right is a 10" marotte with whistle in stick. Parian-style shoulder head. Both twirl and play music. 14½" - $795.00; 10" - $495.00. *Courtesy Turn of Century Antiques.*

MAY FRÉRES

Bébé Mascotte dolls were made by May Fréres Cie. They operated from 1890 to 1897, then became part of Jules Steiner in 1898. This means the dolls were made from 1890 to about 1902, so the quality of the bisque as well as the artist painting can vary greatly. Dolls will be marked "BÉBÉ MASCOTTE PARIS" and some will be incised with "M" and a number.

Child: Closed mouth. Excellent condition and no damage. (See photo in Series 8, pg. 128.) Marked "Mascotte": 14" - $3,300.00; 18" - $4,400.00; 21" - $5,000.00; 24" - $5,750.00; 28" - $6,200.00. Marked with "M" and a number: 14" - $2,600.00; 17" - $3,800.00; 19" - $4,300.00; 23" - $5,250.00; 27" - $5,900.00.

23½" made by May Fréres Cie. Has closed mouth and original wig. On French jointed body. Marked "M 10" and red artist marks "HX." $5,300.00. *Courtesy Frasher Doll Auctions.*

Metal heads made in Germany, 1888–on; United States, 1917 on.

Marks:

(Buschow & Beck)

(Alfred Heller)

JUNO (Karl Standfuss)

Metal shoulder head: Cloth or kid body. Molded hair, painted eyes. 14" - $140.00; 17" - $200.00. **Molded hair, glass eyes:** 14" - $175.00; 17" - $225.00. **Wig, glass eyes:** 14" - $200.00; 17" - $250.00; 21" - $300.00.

All metal child: Wig or molded hair, fully jointed. Some are also jointed at wrist, elbow, knee, and ankle. Open/closed mouth with painted teeth. Some have metal hands and feet with composition body. 15–16" - $450.00; 19–20" - $525.00.

All metal jointed dolls: Made in Switzerland. Patented 1921–1940. Metal ball joints. **Man:** 6" - $145.00; 10" - $200.00. **Comic character:** 6" - $165.00. **Hitler:** 6" - $225.00; 10" - $285.00. **Chauffeur:** 6" - $145.00; 10" - $200.00. **Animal head:** 6" - $165.00; 10" - $225.00. **With composition heads, hands, and feet:** 6" - $100.00 up; 10" - $150.00 up.

Metal baby: All metal bent baby body. Some are spring jointed. Painted features, wig or molded hair. (See photo in Series 9, pg. 134.) 13–14" - $150.00. Glass eyes: 13–14" - $200.00.

Cloth body, metal head: Composition limbs. Sleep eyes. 13" - $140.00; 18" - $200.00.

15" metal head with cloth body, open mouth, glass eyes, and wig. In mint condition; never been played with. Marked "Minerva" on front of shoulder plate. In this condition - $275.00. *Courtesy Kathy Riddick.*

The molded hair bisque dolls are just like any other flesh-toned dolls, but instead of having wigs, they have molded hair, glass set eyes or finely painted and detailed eyes, and generally they will have closed mouths. They almost always are one-piece shoulder heads on kid or cloth bodies with bisque lower arms. Some will have compostion lower legs. These dolls are generally very pretty. Many molded hair dolls are being attributed to A.B.G. (Alt, Beck & Gottschalck) but are recognizably Kling dolls. (See photo in Series 9, pg. 135.) Such dolls are from mold **#890, 1000, 1008, 1028, 1064, 1142, 1256, 1288, etc.** (See photos in Series 7, pg. 125; Series 9, pg. 135.)

Child: Closed mouth. Glass eyes: 6½" - $145.00; 10" - $225.00; 16" - $525.00; 21" - $850.00; 24" - $1,300.00; 26" - $1,700.00. **Painted eyes:** 10" - $165.00; 15" - $400.00; 21" - $600.00; 24" - $950.00.

Boy: Glass eyes: 17" - $850.00; 20" - $1,000.00; 23" - $1,500.00. **Painted eyes:** 17" - $700.00; 20" - $850.00; 23" - $1,000.00.

Decorated shoulder plate: Glass eyes, elaborate hairdo. 20" - $1,900.00 up. **Painted eyes:** 20" - $1,000.00.

Bonnet or hat: Circa 1880–1920. Molded hair and bonnet. Some with bows, ribbons or feathers. (Allow more for unusual hairdo or hat.) **Glass eyes:** 12 - $985.00; 15" - $1,600.00; 18" - $1,900.00; 22" - $2,100.00. **Painted eyes:** 8" - $600.00; 15" - $975.00; 22" - $1,400.00.

Japan: Marked 𝒯𝓎 or ⊛. Bows on sides of head. Cloth body, long legs, black silk feet, oilcloth arms. 17" - $285.00; 20" - $325.00.

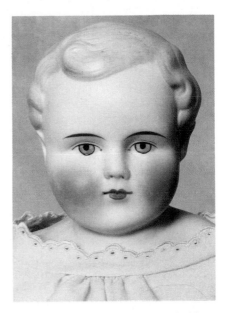

19" bisque turned head with molded hair. Unusual side part hairdo. Light flesh tone with painted features and exposed ears. $975.00. *Courtesy Turn of Century Antiques.*

17" molded hair child with full bangs, painted features, and rather downcast look. Cloth body with bisque lower limbs. $525.00. *Courtesy Turn of Century Antiques.*

Alexandre Mothereau made dolls in Paris, France from 1880 to 1895. Dolls are marked "B.M." with size number and trademarked "Bébé Mothereau." (See photos in Series 9, pg. 135; Series 10, pg. 127.) 18" - $17,000.00; 25" - $24,000.00; 30" - $29,000.00.

MOTSCHMANN (SONNEBERG TÄUFLING)

Charles Motschmann has always been credited as the manufacturer of a certain style doll, but now his work is only being attributed to the making of the voice boxes in the dolls. Various German makers such as Heinrich Stier and others are being given the credit for making the dolls. They date from 1851 into the 1880s.

The early dolls were babies, children and Orientals. They have glass eyes, closed mouths, heads of papier maché, wax over papier maché or wax over composition. They can have lightly brush stroked painted hair or come with a wig.

If the mouth is open, the doll will have bamboo teeth. The larger dolls will have arms and legs jointed at wrists and ankles. The lower torso and lower arms and legs are composition or wood; the upper torso and upper arms and legs are twill cloth. The mid-section will also be cloth. If the doll is marked, it can be found on the upper cloth of the leg and will be stamped:

Baby: Motschmann marked or type. Extremely fine condition: 13" - $1,050.00; 16" - $1,200.00; 20" - $1,800.00; 25" - $2,400.00. **Fair condition:** 13" - $500.00; 16" - $600.00; 20" - $750.00; 25" - $1,000.00.

Child: Extremely fine condition: 12" - $900.00; 15" - $1,300.00; 18" - $1,800.00; 23" - $2,300.00. **Fair condition:** 15" - $500.00; 18" - $800.00; 23" - $900.00.

Child: Bisque with cloth at waist and mid-limbs. (See photo in Series 9, pg. 136.) 18" - $6,800.00 up.

24" "Motschmann Baby" made of papier maché and composition with glass eyes. Painted curls at side of head. Swivel head, wooden shoulder plate. Arms and legs with cloth upper sections. Composition hands and feet. Papier maché torso with bellows and squeaker box. Clothes may be original. $1,300.00. *Courtesy Frasher Doll Auctions.*

Munich Art character dolls are very rare and were designed by Marion Kaulitz, 1908–1912, who had them modeled by Paul Vogelsanger. Dolls have composition or fabric heads, painted features, and are on fully jointed bodies.

Excellent condition: 13–14" - $2,600.00; 18–19" - $3,600.00.

Fair condition: 13–14" - $1,000.00; 18–19" - $1,500.00.

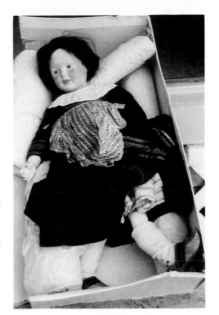

"Munich Art Doll" that is very mint. She is 18" tall with painted eyes and human hair. Made of papier maché with fully jointed body. She is all original and has never been played with. $3,600.00. *Courtesy Debbie Fellanz.*

ORIENTAL DOLLS

Bisque dolls with fired-in Oriental color and on jointed yellowish tinted bodies were made in Germany by various firms. They could be children or babies and most were made after 1900. Must be in excellent condition and in Oriental clothes with no damage to head.

All bisque, marked "Kestner": 6" - $1,250.00; 8" - $1,650.00. **S&H:** 6" - $800.00; 7½" - $1,000.00. **BSW:** 6" - $700.00. **Unknown marker:** 6" - $550.00; 8" - $700.00. Chinese man with mustache: 11" - $1,150.00.

Amusco, mold #1006: Bisque head. (See photo in Series 9, pg. 138.) 16" - $1,100.00.

Armand Marseille: Girl or boy marked only "A.M." 6" - $550.00; 8–9" - $700.00. **Painted bisque:** Excellent condition. 8" - $265.00; 12" - $475.00. **#353 baby:** 12" - $1,100.00; 15" - $1,350.00; 17" - $1,600.00. **Painted bisque:** 15" - $600.00. Cloth body: 10" - $900.00.

Belton type, #193, 206, etc.: Closed mouth. Small doll may have painted-on slippers. 10" - $2,400.00 up; 14" - $2,800.00 up; 17" - $3,800.00 up.

Bru: Olive toned bisque. Bru Jne: 18" - $26,000.00; 23" - $35,000.00. Eyebrows painted into hairline: 18" - $30,000.00; 23" - $42,000.00.

Bruno Schmidt (BSW), #220: Closed mouth. 14" - $2,700.00; 17" - $3,900.00. **#500:** 14" - $2,200.00; 16" - $2,500.00.

Jumeau: Very rare. Closed mouth, very almond-shaped angled eyes, and upward painted eyebrows. Early body with straight wrists. 20" - $47,000.00; 27" - $60,000.00 up.

Kestner (J.D.K.), #243: Baby: 14" - $4,600.00; 17" - $6,000.00. **Molded hair baby:** 14" - $4,800.00. **Child:** 15" - $5,200.00; 18" - $6,800.00.

Schoenau & Hoffmeister, #4900: Marked "S" PB in star "H." (See photo in

Series 5, pg. 116.) 9" - $700.00; 16" - $1,800.00; 20" - $2,200.00.

Simon & Halbig (S&H), #164: (See photo in Series 5, pg. 116.) 16" - $2,300.00; 19" - $2,700.00 up. **#220:** (See photo in Series 6, pg. 145.) Solid dome or "Belton" type. Closed mouth. 10–11" - $1,400.00; 16" - $3,400.00. **#1099, 1129, 1159, 1199:** (See photo in Series 7, pg. 129; Series 8, pg. 132; Series 9, pg. 138.) 15" - $3,200.00; 19" - $3,700.00. **#1329:** (See photo in Series 7, pg. 129.) 15" - $2,000.00; 20" - $3,200.00.

Unmarked: Open mouth: 14" - $1,300.00; 18" - $2,000.00. **Closed mouth:** 14" - $1,800.00; 18" - $2,600.00. All bisque: Glass eyes. 6" - $550.00; 10–11" - $885.00 up. **Tiny dolls: Glass eyes:** 6" - $475.00; 11" - $900.00. **Painted eyes:** 5" - $265.00; 9" - $500.00.

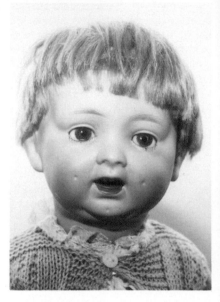

16" Morimura Brothers character baby with bisque head, dimples, open mouth, and sleep eyes. On five-piece bent limb baby body with jointed wrists. $675.00. *Courtesy Susan Giradot.*

Nippon (Caucasian dolls made in Japan): 1918–1922. Most made during World War I. These dolls can be near excellent quality to very poor quality. Morimura Brothers mark is Ⓧ, which is the *komaru* or clan crest of the family. (The Morimura family were the founders of Noritake.) Dolls marked 𝒴 were made by Yamato. Others will just be marked with NIPPON along with other marks such as "J.W."

Nippon or Japan marked baby: Good to excellent bisque, well painted, nice body and no damage. 10" - $185.00; 12" - $245.00; 15" - $350.00; 21" - $575.00; 24" - $800.00. **Poor quality:** 12" - $125.00; 16" - $175.00; 20" - $265.00; 25" - $365.00. **"Hilda" look-alike: Excellent quality:** 15" - $800.00; 18" - $1,000.00. **Medium quality:** 15" - $500.00; 18" - $745.00. **Pouty:** Closed mouth. (See photo in Series 1, pg. 119.) 13" - $600.00.

19" on French jointed body with straight wrists. Slant cut eyes and slant eyebrows. Open mouth with square cut teeth. Head marked "S.H. DEP 1099." Adult body marked "E.D.B. Paris. La Patricienne Depose." $3,600.00. *Courtesy Frasher Doll Auctions.*

11" Nippon using the "Hilda" mold. Bisque head with human hair wig. Glass eyes, open mouth with two upper teeth. Heavy body painted flesh tones. Marked: ⬚ $500.00. *Courtesy Jeannie Mauldin.*

Nippon child: Good to excellent quality bisque, no damage and nicely dressed. 14" - $300.00; 17" - $375.00; 22" - $500.00. **Poor quality:** 15" - $135.00; 19" - $225.00; 23" - $325.00. **Mold #600:** Marked 𝒯𝒴. 14" - $375.00; 17" - $475.00; 22" - $600.00.

Molded hair: 1920–1930s. Molded bows on side, cloth body, oilcloth lower arms, silk feet. Marked 𝒯𝒴 or ⊛. 14" - $300.00; 17" - $500.00.

Traditional doll: Made in Japan. Papier maché swivel head on shoulder plate, cloth mid-section and upper arms and legs. Limbs and torso are papier maché, glass eyes, pierced nostrils. The early dolls will have jointed wrists and ankles and will be slightly sexed. **Early fine quality:** Original dress, 1890s. 14" - $350.00; 19" - $550.00; 26" - $1,000.00. **Early Boy:** With painted hair. 17" - $500.00; 22" - $900.00; 26" - $1,200.00 up. **1930s or later:** 14" - $145.00; 17" - $265.00. 1940s: 13" - $85.00. **Lady:** All original and excellent quality. 1920s: 12" - $200.00; 16" - $285.00. **Later lady:** 1940s–1950s. 12" - $85.00; 14" - $100.00.

Emperor or Empress in sitting position: 1890s: 10" - $800.00 up. 1920s–1930s: (See photo in Series 10, pg. 133.) 4–5" - $150.00; 8" - $200.00 up; 12" - $375.00 up.

Warrior: 1880s–1890s. 16–18" - $800.00 up. **On horse:** 16" - $1,200.00 up. **Early 1920s:** 12" - $250.00 up. **On horse:** 12" - $900.00 up.

12" baby incised with 𝒯𝒴. Bisque head, glass eyes with no pupils. Open mouth, cute expression. Very unusual doll. $595.00. *Courtesy Turn of Century Antiques.*

Japanese baby: Bisque head, sleep eyes, closed mouth, and all white bisque. **Papier maché body:** Original and in excellent condition. Late 1920s. 8" - $75.00; 12" - $100.00. **Glass eyes:** 8" - $125.00; 12" - $225.00.

Japanese baby: Head made of crushed oyster shells painted flesh color, papier maché body, glass eyes and original. 8" - $65.00; 12" - $95.00; 16" - $145.00; 19" - $200.00.

Oriental dolls: All composition, jointed at shoulder and hips. Painted features and hair. Can have bald head with yarn braid down back with rest covered by cap, such as "Ling Ling" or "Ming Ming" made by Quan Quan Co. in 1930s. Painted-on shoes. 10" - $175.00.

Baby Butterfly: 1911–1913. E.I. Horsman. Composition and cloth. Painted hair and features. 13–14" - $450.00.

Chinese traditional dolls: Man or woman. Composition-type material with cloth-wound bodies or can have wooden carved arms and feet. In traditional costume and in excellent condition. 9" - $300.00; 12" - $475.00.

Door of Hope Dolls: Created at the Door of Hope Mission in China from 1901 to 1910s. Cloth bodies with head and limbs carved of wood by carvers who came from Ning-Po providence. Chinese costume. (See photo in Series 7, pg. 59; Series 8, pgs. 63–65; Series 9, pg. 68.) **Adult:** 9" - $600.00; 11" - $675.00 up. **Child:** 6" - $425.00; 8" - $550.00. **Mother and baby:** 11" - $700.00. **Man:** 9" - $625.00. **Carved flowers in hair:** 12" - $725.00. **Bride or bridesmaid:** 12" - $650.00. **Groom:** $600.00. **Widow:** $700.00. **Mourner:** $650.00. **Grandfather:** $700.00. **Amah (Governess):** $625.00. **Manchu:** Mandarin man or woman. Ornate clothes. 12" - $1,100.00 up.

A complete Japanese "Girl's Day" set. ("Girl's Day" is observed May 3.) First row is always the Emperor and Empress with screen behind them. Lower step figures vary but will always have servants, musicians, and can have gardeners, soldiers, etc. Sets can be extremely simple or very elaborate depending upon the finances of each family. Many pieces for these sets have been handed from generation to generation. Each piece - $100.00–500.00. *Courtesy Charlene Lopez.*

P.D. marked dolls were made in Paris, France by Petit & DuMontier, 1878–1890. (See Series 8, pg. 77; Series 10, pg. 134.)

Child: Closed mouth, jointed body, **metal hands.** No damage, nicely dressed. 15" - $9,500.00; 18" - $16,000.00; 21" - $18,000.00; 23" - $20,000.00; 27" - $24,000.00.

P.G.

Pintel & Godchaux of Montreuil, France made dolls from 1890 to 1899. They held one trademark – "Bébé Charmant." Heads will be marked "P.G."

Child, closed mouth: 16" - $2,600.00; 21" - $3,000.00; 25" - $3,900.00.
Child, open mouth: 15" - $1,300.00; 20" - $2,000.00; 23" - $2,500.00.

28" child with large glass eyes and open mouth with very tiny teeth. On French jointed body. Marked "P.G." Shown with 16" Kestner baby, mold #247. 28" - $3,000.00; 16" - $1,500.00.

Papier maché dolls were made in U.S., Germany, England, France and other countries. Paper pulp, wood and rag fibers containing paste, oil or glue are formed into a composition-like moldable material. Flour, clay and/or sand is added for stiffness. The hardness of papier maché depends on the amount of glue added.

Many so called papier maché parts were actually laminated paper with several thicknesses of molded paper bonded (glued) together or pressed after being glued.

"Papier maché" means "chewed paper" in French, and as early as 1810, dolls of papier maché were being mass produced by using molds.

Marked "M&S Superior": Made by Muller & Strassburger. Papier maché shoulder head with blonde or black

17" French papier maché jester with much character. Cloth and original. Shown with 27" Armand Marseille #390 with set glass eyes and open mouth. On fully jointed body. Jester - $450.00; doll - $600.00. *Courtesy Turn of Century Antiques.*

molded hair, painted blue or brown eyes, old cloth body with kid or leather arms and boots. Nicely dressed and head not repainted, chipped or cracked. 16" - $400.00; 18"- $600.00; 24" - $750.00. **Glass eyes:** 20" - $800.00. **With wig:** 18" - $750.00. **Repainted** nicely: 16" - $300.00; 21" - $450.00. Chips, scuffs or not repainted well: 16" - $95.00; 21" - $110.00.

French or French type: (See photos in Series 5, pg. 151; Series 7, pg. 133; Series 9, pg. 142.) Painted black hair, some with brush marks, on solid dome. Some have nailed-on wigs. Open mouths have bamboo teeth. Inset glass eyes. All leather/kid body. Very good condition, nice old clothes. 16" - $1,400.00; 19" - $1,900.00; 23" - $2,250.00; 26" - $2,500.00; 30" - $2,850.00. **Wooden jointed body:** 7–8" - $825.00. **Painted eyes:** 7" - $450.00; 15" - $900.00.

Early papier maché: 1840s–1860s. Cloth body and wooden limbs. Early hairdo with top knots, buns, puff curls or braiding. Not restored and dressed in original or very well made clothes. Very good condition; may show a little wear. (See photo in Series 6, pg. 153.) 12" - $500.00; 14" - $750.00; 18" - $1,000.00; 21" - $1,200.00; 25" - $1,300.00; 32" - $2,000.00. **Glass eyes:** 20" - $1,800.00; 24" - $2,350.00. **Flirty eyes:** 20" - $2,700.00 up; 24" - $3,000.00.

Long curls: 9" - $600.00; 13" - $700.00; 23" - $1,550.00.

Covered Wagon or Flat Top hairdo: 7" - $275.00; 11" - $400.00; 14–15" - $600.00.

Milliner's models: 1820s–1860s. (See photos in Series 6, pg. 153; Series 8, pg. 137.) **Braided bun, side curls:** 9–10" - $825.00; 13–14" - $1,350.00. **Side curls, high Apollo top knot (beehive):** 12" - $1,000.00; 17" - $1,900.00; 18" - $2,200.00. **Coiled braids over ears, braided bun:** 18" - $1,800.00; 20–21" - $2,200.00 up. **Center part:** Sausage curls. 15" - $700.00; 18" - $900.00. **Center part with molded**

bun: 7" - $550.00; 11" - $975.00. **Molded bonnet:** Very rare. Kid body, wood limbs, bonnet painted to tie under chin. 15" - $2,000.00 up. **Side curls, braided coronet, molded comb:** 16" - $3,600.00 up.

Marked Greiner: See Greiner section.

Motschmann types: With wood and twill bodies. Separate hip section, glass eyes, closed mouth and brush stroke hair on solid domes. Nicely dressed and ready to display. 15" - $685.00; 21" - $825.00; 25" - $1,250.00.

Left: 20" papier maché shoulder head with glass eyes and closed mouth. On gussetted kid body with bisque lower arms. Wig and clothes are original. Right: 19" made by Armand Marseille with sleep eyes and open mouth. On fully jointed body. All original. Marked "1894 A.M.5." 20" - $800.00; 19" - $350.00. *Courtesy Frasher Doll Auctions.*

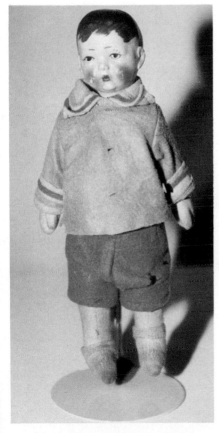

8" papier maché head with painted features and hair. On tightly stuffed body with mitt hands with free standing thumbs. Original felt clothes. Character by C. & O. Dressel. $100.00.

German papier maché: 1870–1900s. Various molded hairdos, painted eyes and closed mouth. May be blonde or black hair. Nicely dressed and not repainted. (See photos in Series 2, pg. 133, Series 4, pg. 124, Series 7, pg. 135.) 14" - $225.00; 17" - $350.00; 19" - $450.00; 23" - $500.00; 25" - $550.00; 30" - $750.00. **Glass eyes:** 14" - $525.00; 17" - $775.00. Showing **wear and scuffs,** but not touched up: 17" - $225.00; 21" - $300.00; 25" - $350.00; 30" - $450.00; 35" - $700.00.

Wax over papier maché: See Wax section.

Turned shoulder head: Solid dome, glass eyes, closed mouth. Twill cloth body with composition lower arms. Very good condition and nicely dressed. (See photo in Series 3, pg. 114.) 17" - $700.00; 22" - $900.00.

German character heads: Heads are molded just like the bisque ones. Glass eyes, closed mouth. On fully jointed body. Excellent condition and nicely dressed. (See photo in Series 6, pg. 152.) 15" - $1,000.00 up; 21" - $1,600.00 up.

Papier maché, 1920s on: Head usually has bright coloring and wigged. Usually dressed as a child or in provincial costumes. Stuffed cloth body and limbs or have papier maché arms. Excellent overall condition. (See photo in Series 5, pg. 119.) 8" - $75.00; 12" - $135.00; 14" - $185.00. Marked by maker: **German:** 8" - $95.00; 12" - $165.00. **French:** 8" - $115.00; 12" - $195.00; 14" - $275.00.

Clowns: Papier maché head with painted clown features. Open or closed mouth. Molded hair or wigged. Cloth body with some having composition or papier maché lower arms or five-piece body. (See photo in Series 10, pg. 136.) Excellent condition. 10" - $250.00; 14" - $425.00; 20" - $700.00; 26" - $825.00.

PARIAN-TYPE (UNTINTED BISQUE)

Parian-type dolls were made from the 1850s to the 1880s, with the majority being made during the 1870s and 1880s. There are hundreds of different heads, and all seem to have been made in Germany. If there is a mark, it will be found on the inside of the shoulder plate. It must be noted that the very rare and unique unglazed porcelain dolls are difficult to find and their prices will be high.

Parian-type dolls can be found with every imaginable thing applied to the head and shirt tops – flowers, snoods, ruffles, feathers, plumes, etc. Many have inset glass eyes, pierced ears and most are blonde, although some will have from light to medium brown hair, and a few will have glazed black hair.

Various fancy hairstyles: With molded combs, ribbons, flowers, head bands, or snoods. Cloth body with cloth/Parian-type limbs. Perfect condition and very nicely dressed. (See photo in Series 5, pg. 121.) **Glass eyes:** 16" - $1,700.00 up; 21" - $3,000.00 up. **Painted eyes,** unpierced ears: 18" - $900.00 up; 22" - $1,600.00 up.

Swivel neck: Glass eyes. 17" - $2,900.00; 21" - $3,400.00; 23" - $3,700.00.

Molded necklaces: Jewels or standing ruffles, undamaged. (See photo in

23" Parian with hair drawn away from face, black beaded headband, braids behind ears, and pierced ears. Fancy modeled shirtwaist top with Iron Cross necklace. Cloth body with leather arms. Circa 1870. $1,600.00 up. *Courtesy Frasher Doll Auctions.*

Series 5, pg. 121.) **Glass eyes,** pierced ears: 16" - $1,900.00 up; 21" - $2,500.00 up. **Painted eyes,** unpierced ears: 18" - $1,200.00; 22" - $1,600.00. **Necklace** with multiple large stones: scenes of Paris in them. 16" - $9,800.00 up.

Bald head: Solid dome, takes wigs, full ear detail. 1850s. Perfect condition and nicely dressed. 14" - $775.00; 18" - $995.00; 22" - $1,600.00.

Molded head band or comb (called "Alice"): (See photo in Series 5, pg. 121; Series 7, pg. 137; Series 9, pg. 146.) 14" - $445.00; 17" - $650.00; 20" - $800.00.

Very plain style: No decoration in hair or on shoulders. No damage and nicely dressed. 10" - $140.00; 15" - $300.00; 20" - $425.00; 24" - $525.00. With applied flowers: 18" - $800.00.

Men or boys: Hairdos with center or side part, cloth body with cloth/Parian-type limbs. Decorated shirt and tie. 16" - $800.00; 19" - $1,000.00. Glass eyes: 19" - $2,800.00 up.

Molded hat: Blonde or black hair. (See photos in Series 8, pg. 140.) **Painted eyes:** 15" - $2,200.00; 18" - $2,800.00 up. **Glass eyes:** 14" - $2,600.00; 16" - $3,100.00; 20" - $3,900.00.

Right: 17½ brown hair Parian with untinted bisque, apple cheeks, and painted features. Also has blue headband, decorated shoulders and cloth body. Left: 16" tinted bisque with painted features. Rare molded feather and snood accented with china glaze. Rear: 25" open mouth French marked "R.D." (made by Rabery & Delphieu.) 17½" - $1,200.00; 16" - $1,800.00; 25" - $4,500.00. *Courtesy Turn of Century Antiques.*

These dolls were made by Danel & Cie in France from 1889 to 1895. The heads will be marked "Paris Bébé" and the body's paper label will be marked with a drawing of the Eiffel Tower and "Paris Bébé/Brevete."

Paris Bébé Child: Closed mouth, no damage and nicely dressed. 16" - $4,300.00; 20" - $4,900.00; 24" - $5,200.00; 27" - $5,900.00. **Late doll:** High color to bisque, closed mouth: 17" - $2,450.00; 21" - $3,200.00; 25" - $3,800.00; 27" - $4,200.00.

Doll with large eyes and closed mouth with space between lips. On French jointed body marked with purple stamp of the Eiffel Tower and "Bébé-Barreras Brevete." Head marked "Paris Bébé/TeteDEP cc 12." 28" - $6,000.00. *Courtesy Frasher Doll Auctions.*

PHÉNIX (ALEXANDRE, HENRI)

Bébé Phénix dolls were made by Henri Alexandre of Paris who made dolls from 1885 to 1901. The company was sold to Tourel in 1892 and Jules Steiner in 1895.

Mark:

(1885–1891)

This 20" Phénix is a pull-string talker ("Mama," "Papa") dressed in original chemise generally found on Jumeau. Has closed mouth and is marked with star and "93." Also has original box. $5,000.00. *Courtesy Frasher Doll Auctions.*

Child, closed mouth: #81: 10" - $1,600.00. **#85:** 14" - $2,800.00. **#88:** 17" - $3,900.00. **#90:** 18" - $4,200.00. **#91:** 19–21" - $4,400.00. **#93:** 22" - $5,000.00. **#94:** 23-24" - $5,300.00. **#95:** 23–25" - $5,600.00.

Child, open mouth: 17" - $1,800.00; 19" - $2,100.00; 23" - $2,500.00; 25" - $2,800.00.

1885–1891: (Also see under Alexandre, Henri.) Perfect, early jointed body, beautiful clothes, closed mouth, glass eyes. Marked: H⬚A 15" - $5,000.00; 17½" - $6,250.00; 25" - $7,500.00.

PIANO BABIES

Piano babies were made in Germany from the 1880s into the 1930s. One of the finest quality makers of piano babies was Gebruder Heubach. They were also made by Kestner, Dressel, Limbach, etc. A number of these figures were reproduced in the late 1960s to late 1970s. Painting and skin tones will not be as "soft" as old ones.

Piano Babies: All bisque with molded hair and painted features.

Unjointed with molded-on clothes. Figures come in a variety of poses.

Excellent quality or marked "Heubach": Extremely good artist workmanship and excellent detail to modeling. 4" - $200.00; 6" - $450.00; 8" - $600.00 up; 12" - $750.00 up; 16" - $1,100.00 up.

Medium quality: May not have painting finished on back side of figure. 4" - $100.00; 8" - $200.00; 12" - $300.00; 16" - $425.00.

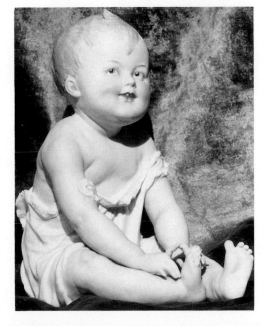

Beautiful 12" Gebrüder Heubach piano baby with excellent bisque and modeling. The arms barely rest on the legs and large toes are separate. Dimpled smile with open/closed mouth and modeled teeth. $750.00. *Courtesy Albert Fossat.*

With animal, pot, flowers, on chair, or with other items: (See photos in Series 6, pg. 158; Series 7, pg. 141.) Excellent quality. 4" - $250.00; 8" - $450.00; 12" - $825.00 up; 16" - $1,200.00 up.

Black: Excellent quality: 4" - $365.00; 8" - $475.00; 12" - $825.00; 16" - $1,200.00 up. Medium quality: 4" - $150.00; 8" - $200.00; 12" - $325.00; 16" - $750.00.

RABERY & DELPHIEU

Rabery & Delphieu began making dolls in 1856. The very first dolls have kid bodies and are extremely rare. Most of their dolls are on French jointed bodies and are marked "R.D." A few may be marked "Bébé de Paris."

Child, closed mouth: Pretty face. Body in overall good condition and nicely dressed. Excellent condition with no chips, breaks or hairlines in bisque. 12" - $2,600.00; 16" - $3,200.00; 19" - $3,500.00; 22" - $3,800.00; 24" - $4,200.00; 27" - $5,200.00. **Child, open mouth:** 15" - $1,300.00; 19" - $2,000.00; 22" - $2,500.00; 24" - $3,000.00; 28" - $3,500.00. **With two rows of teeth:** Excellent condition. 22" - $2,900.00. Bisque: 28" - $4,000.00; 36" - $5,000.00.

Child, high color: Lesser quality, poor artist workmanship. **Closed mouth:** 16" - $1,800.00; 19" - $2,300.00; 22" - $2,500.00. **Open mouth:** 15" - $700.00; 19" - $950.00; 22" - $1,100.00.

Walker: Head turns. Closed mouth: (See photo in Series 10, pg. 141.) 24" - $4,600.00. In original box: 24" - $5,000.00.

14½" French bisque with French jointed body and straight wrists. Marked "R. 2 D. Depose." $1,300.00. *Courtesy Kathy Tvrdik.*

Bernard Ravca made dolls in Paris from 1924 to the mid-1930's when he moved to New York. The dolls were stitched stockinette characters and personalities. If made in France, doll will bear a label marked "Original Ravca/Fabrication Francaise" or a wrist tag "Original Ravca" plus handwritten name of doll. Some of the dolls will be cloth and stockinette, some with cloth body and limbs, and others will be a gesso/papier maché combination. His dolls can range in size from 7" to 35."

Peasants/Old People: 7" - $90.00; 9" - $100.00; 12" - $150.00; 15" - $200.00 up.

Character from books/poems: 7" - $100.00 up; 9" - $125.00 up; 12" - $165.00 up; 15" - $200.00 up; 17" - $285.00 up.

Gesso, papier maché, and cloth dolls: Personality figures. 12" - $400.00; 15" - $565.00; 17" - $985.00; 20" - $1,425.00.

Military Figures: Such as Hitler, Mussolini. 17" - $1,000.00; 20" - $1,800.00; 27" - $4,000.00 up.

17" "Mr. Pickwick" from the Charles Dickens book. Stockinette sculptured features and hands. Cloth body and wire glasses. $285.00 up. *Courtesy Christine Perisho.*

10" lady sitting in chair made of stockinette with painted features. Paper tag reads "Original Ravca Paris." $100.00. *Courtesy Susan Giradot.*

Dolls marked with "R.A." were made by Recknagel of Alexandrinenthal, Thuringia, Germany. The R.A. dolls date from 1886 to after World War I. Bisque quality and artist workmanship can range from very poor to excellent. Prices are for dolls with good artist workmanship, such as nice lips and eyebrows painted straight, feathered, and not off center. Original or nicely dressed and no damage.

Child: 1890s–1914. Set or sleep eyes, open mouth. Small dolls have painted-on shoes and socks. 8" - $150.00; 12" - $200.00; 16" - $300.00; 20" - $450.00; 23" - $650.00. Covered with rabbit fur: (See Series 6, pg. 160.) 12" - $245.00.

#1907, 1909, 1914, etc.: 8" - $165.00; 12" - $225.00; 16" - $350.00; 20" - $500.00; 23" - $600.00.

Baby: Circa 1909–1910 on. Five-piece bent limb baby body or straight leg, curved arm toddler body and with sleep or set eyes. No damage and nicely dressed. 7" - $150.00; 9" - $185.00; 12" - $245.00; 16" - $400.00; 20" - $500.00.

Character, painted eyes: Modeled bonnet or large hair bow, and open/closed mouth. Some dolls are smiling; some have painted-in teeth. No damage and nicely dressed. (See photo in Series

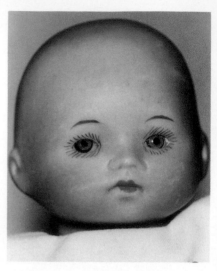

9" infant made by Recknagel. Bisque head and sleep eyes. On five-piece bent limb baby body. Marked "Germany/1924 15/0." $185.00. *Courtesy Kathy Riddick.*

9, pg. 152.) 9" - $950.00; 12" - $1,200.00. Molded ribbon and two side bows: (See photo in Series 7, pg. 146.) 14" - $725.00 up.

Character, glass eyes: Closed mouth, composition bent limb baby body. 7" - $525.00; 10" - $625.00; 14" - $850.00.

REINECKE, OTTO

Dolls marked "P.M." were made by Otto Reinecke of Hof-Moschendorf, Bavaria, Germany, from 1909 into the 1930s. The mold number found most often is the **#914** baby or toddler. (See photo in Series 7, pg. 144.)

Child: Bisque head with open mouth. On five-piece papier maché body or fully jointed body. Can have sleep or set eyes. No damage and nicely dressed. 8" $150.00; 10" - $165.00; 14" - $250.00; 17" - $385.00; 21" - $450.00.

Character child: Molded hair, open/closed or fully closed mouth. 7" - $325.00.

Baby: Open mouth, sleep eyes or set eyes. Bisque head on five-piece bent limb baby body. No damage and nicely dressed. Can be incised "DEP - P.M. - Grete." 8" - $250.00; 10" - $300.00; 12" - $375.00; 15" - $475.00; 21" - $600.00; 26" - $950.00.

Bruno Schmidt's doll factory was located in Waltershausen, Germany and many of the heads used by this firm were made by Bahr & Proschild, Ohrdruf, Germany. They made dolls from 1898 on into the 1930s.

Mark:

2033-6

Child: Bisque head on jointed body, sleep eyes, open mouth, no damage and nicely dressed. 16" - $500.00; 20" - $700.00; 25" - $950.00. **Flirty eyes:** 21" - $900.00; 29" - $1,500.00.

Character baby, toddler or child: Bisque head, glass eyes or painted eyes, jointed body, no damage and nicely dressed.

#2025, 2026: Closed mouth, glass eyes. (See photo in Series 9, pg. 146.) 20" - $4,200.00; 23" - $4,600.00. **Painted eyes:** 16" - $1,900.00; 22" - $3,900.00.

#2052: Intaglio eyes with molded eyelids, glass eyes. Closed smile mouth. Molded hair or wig. 17" - $5,600.00 up.

#2069: Closed mouth, glass eyes, sweet face, jointed body. 13" - $4,200.00; 17" - $6,700.00.

#2048, 2094, 2096 ("Tommy Tucker": Molded, painted hair. (See photo in Series 6, pg. 163; Series 8, pg. 146.) **Open mouth:** 10" - $975.00; 14" - $1,200.00; 18" - $1,500.00; 23" - $1,800.00; 26" - $2,000.00. **Closed mouth:** (See photo in Series 8, pg. 146.) 14" - $2,000.00; 18" - $2,800.00; 23" - $3,400.00. **Toddler:** 17" - $3,000.00; 20" - $3,500.00.

18" "Tommy Tucker" with molded painted hair, open mouth, and glass eyes. Marked with mold #2048. Also shown is a 6" fully jointed "Ignatz Mouse." Doll - $1,500.00; mouse - $250.00 up. *Courtesy Turn of Century Antiques.*

15" baby with set eyes, open mouth, and mohair wig. On five-piece bent limb baby body. Marked ⟨BSW⟩. $700.00. *Courtesy Glorya Woods.*

135

#2072: Closed mouth, glass eyes, wig. 20" - $4,000.00. **Toddler:** 22" - $4,350.00.

#2097, toddler: 15" - $700.00; 21" - $1,000.00. Baby: (See photo in Series 6, pg. 164.) 14" - $550.00; 18" - $850.00.

Character child: Closed mouth, painted eyes or glass eyes, jointed child body, no damage and nicely dressed.

Marked "BSW" in heart: No mold number. (See photo in Series 6, pg. 164.) 17" - $2,800.00; 21" - $3,400.00.

#529: Marked with "BSW" in heart. Closed mouth, painted eyes, molded eyelids. (See photo in Series 9, pg. 154.) 16" - $5,600.00 up; 22" - $6,800.00 up.

#2033, 531, 537 "Wendy": (See photo in Series 6, pg. 163; Series 9, pg. 154.) 11" - $8,000.00; 13" - $16,000.00; 16" - $19,000.00 up; 20" - $22,000.00 up.

28" Bruno Schmidt with sleep eyes and open mouth. On fully jointed body. Marked "Made in Germany" and ⬤. $1,350.00. *Courtesy Kathy Humphries.*

SCHMIDT, FRANZ

Franz Schmidt & Co. began in 1890 at Georgenthal, near Waltershausen, Germany. In 1902, they registered the cross hammers with a doll between and also the F.S.&Co. mark.

Mark:

1310
F.S. & Co.
Made in
Germany
10

Baby: Bisque head on bent limb baby body, sleep or set eyes, open mouth and some may have pierced nostrils. No damage and nicely dressed.

#1255, 1271, 1272, 1295, 1296, 1297, 1310: 12" - $365.00; 14" - $525.00; 20" - $800.00; 25" - $1,450.00. **Toddler:** 8–9" - $625.00; 15" - $725.00; 21" - $1,100.00; 25" - $1,500.00.

#1267: Painted eyes, open/closed mouth. (See photo in Series 5, pg. 126; Series 10, pg. 147.) 14" - $2,800.00; 19" - $3,800.00. **Glass eyes:** 16" - $3,600.00; 21" -$4,600.00.

#1270: Painted eyes, open/closed mouth with painted teeth. Bald head with very protruding ears. 16" - $800.00. With two faces: 16" - $1,400.00.

#1285: (See photos in Series 1, pg. 253; Series 4, pg. 133.) 16" - $825.00; 22" - $975.00.

Child: Papier maché and composition body with walker mechanism with metal rollers on feet. Open mouth, sleep eyes. Working and no damage to head, nicely dressed. (See photos in Series 4, pg. 173; Series 8, pg. 148.) **#1250:** 14" - $750.00; 20" - $975.00.

#1262: Child with closed mouth, almost smiling. Painted eyes, wig, jointed body. 16" - $6,600.00; 21" - $12,000.00 up.

#1263: Closed mouth, wide spaced painted eyes. Can have sweet expression or downcast expression. 20" - $9,700.00 up; 24" - $15,000.00 up. (21" at auction went for over $17,000.00.)

#1266, 1267: Child with open mouth and sleep eyes. (See photo in Series 10, pg. 147.) 22" - $2,600.00.

#1286: Molded hair, ribbon, open mouth smile, glass eyes. 15–16" - $4,100.00.

SCHMITT & FILS

Schmitt & Fils produced dolls from the 1870s to 1891 in Paris, France. The dolls have French jointed bodies and came with closed or open/closed mouths.

Mark:

Child: 1880–on. Bisque head with long, thin face. Jointed body with closed mouth or open/closed mouth. No damage and nicely dressed. Marked on head and body. (See photo in Series 8, pg. 149; Series 9, pg. 156.) 11–12" - $9,500.00; 16" - $15,000.00 up; 18" - $17,000.00 up; 22" - $21,000.00 up; 25" - $25,000.00 up; 28" - $27,000.00.

Child: Round face, full cheeks. (See photo in Series 6, pg. 166.) 11–12" - $9,200.00; 15" - $1,400.00; 18" - $16,000.00 up; 23" - $22,000.00 up.

19½" Schmitt & Fils with closed mouth and full cheeks. On jointed French body with straight wrist. Marked with crossed hammers and "SCH" in shield. $18,000.00.
Courtesy Frasher Doll Auctions.

Schoenau & Hoffmeister began making dolls in 1901 and were located in Bavaria. The factory was called "Porzellanfabrik Burggrub" and this mark will be found on many of their doll heads.

Mark:

HANNA

PORZELLANFABRIK BURGGRUB

Princess Elizabeth: Smiling open mouth, set eyes, bisque head on jointed five-piece body and marked with name on head or body. 16" - $1,950.00; 22" - $2,550.00; 25" - $3,000.00.

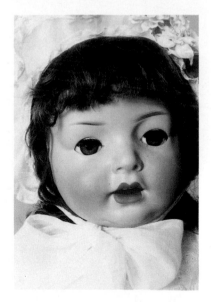

29" "Hanna" baby with sleep eyes, open mouth, and character face. On five-piece bent limb baby body. Marked with name and ⭐. $2,800.00.

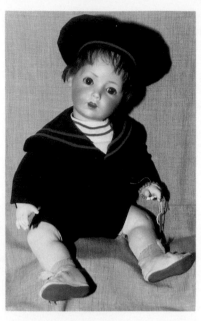

16" Schoenau & Hoffmeister baby with character face, sleep eyes, and hair lashes. On five-piece bent limb baby body. $575.00. *Courtesy Patricia Wood.*

Hanna: Child with black or brown fired-in color to bisque head. Sleep or set eyes, five-piece body or jointed body. Marked with name on head. 8" - $350.00; 14" - $650.00.

Hanna Baby: Bisque head, open mouth, sleep eyes. On five-piece bent limb baby body. 9" - $300.00; 11" - $400.00; 14" - $675.00; 15" - $725.00; 22" - $1,150.00; 24" - $1,500.00. **Toddler:** 7–8" - $385.00–425.00; 15" - $875.00; 19" - $1,200.00.

Character baby, #169, 769, 1271, etc.: 1910–on. Bisque head on five-piece bent limb baby body. Can also be marked with "Burggrub." 13" - $385.00; 16" - $500.00; 18" - $675.00; 24" - $800.00. **Toddler:** 20" - $950.00; 23" - $1,100.00.

Child, #1800, 1906, 1909, 5500, 5700, 5800, 5900, etc. Bisque head with open mouth, sleep or set eyes, jointed body. No damage and nicely dressed. 10" - $225.00; 14" - $300.00; 17" - $425.00; 21" -

$525.00; 28" - $850.00; 30" - $975.00; 34" - $1,250.00; 38" - $1,800.00; 42" - $3,200.00 up. **Kid body:** Open mouth. 14" - $225.00; 17" - $325.00; 21" - $400.00.

Character child, #4000: "Long" face, open mouth. 10–12" - $345.00; 16" - $625.00; 19" - $950.00; 23" - $1,100.00; 26" - $1,300.00.

Painted bisque: Painted head on five-piece body or jointed body. 9" - $165.00; 12" - $275.00.

Das Lachende Baby (The Laughing Baby): 23" - $2,400.00; 26" - $2,900.00.

Pouty baby: Closed mouth, very small sleep eyes, and painted hair. Cloth body with composition limbs. 12" - $775.00.

27" character Schoenau & Hoffmeister, mold #4000, with sleep eyes and open mouth. Has a short distance between lips and chin as well as a longer distance between lips and eyes. An unusual doll. $1,400.00.

SCHOENHUT

Albert Schoenhut & Co. was located in Philadephia, PA, from 1872 until the 1930's. The dolls are all wood with spring joints, have holes in the bottoms of their feet to fit in a metal stand.

Marks:

(1911–1913)   **(1913–1930)**

SCHOENHUT DOLL
PAT. JAN. 17, '11, USA
& FOREIGN COUNTRIES
(Incised 1911–on)

Child with carved hair: May have comb marks, molded ribbon, comb or bow. Closed mouth. Original or nice clothes. **Excellent condition:** 14" - $2,500.00; 21" - $2,900.00. Very good condition: **Some wear.** 14" - $1,600.00; 17" - $1,750.00; 21" - $2,200.00. **Poor condition:** With chips and dents. 14" - $600.00; 21" - $700.00.

Child (rare): 1911. Looks exactly like Kammer & Reinhardt's #101 pouty. (See photo in Series 8, pg. 152.) 21" - $5,200.00 up. **Baby, #100:** 13–14" - $1,250.00.

Man with carved hair: Mint: 19" - $2,700.00 up. **Some wear:** 19" - $1,600.00. Chips, dirty: 19" - $800.00.

Baby head: Can be on regular body or bent limb baby body. Bald spray painted hair or wig, painted decal eyes. Nicely dressed or original. **Excellent condition:** 12" - $565.00; 16" - $750.00; 18" - $850.00. **Good condition:** 16" - $400.00; 18" - $500.00. **Poor condition:** 16" - $175.00; 18" - $225.00.

Toddler: Excellent condition. 12" - $900.00; 16" - $1,000.00.

Child, character face: 1911–1930. Wig, intaglio eyes. Open/closed mouth with painted teeth. Suitably redressed or original. **Excellent condition:** 14" - $1,600.00; 17" - $1,750.00; 21" - $2,000.00. **Good condition:** 14" - $900.00; 17" - $1,100.00; 21" - $1,400.00. **Poor condition:** 14" - $325.00; 17" - $485.00; 21" - $600.00.

Cap molded to head: (See photo in Series 8, pg. 152.) 16" - $3,600.00 up.

Snickelfritz: Some wear. 15" - $2,500.00.

Tootsie Wootsie: Molded, painted hair, open/closed mouth with molded tongue and two upper teeth. Toddler or regular body. (See photo in Series 6, pg. 170.) 14" - $1,900.00; 17" - $2,100.00; 20" - $2,400.00 up.

Left: 22" with painted features and open/closed mouth with painted teeth. Original. Right: 14" pouty with carved hair. 22" - $900.00; 14" - $2,500.00. *Courtesy Turn of Century Antiques.*

"Dolly" face: 1915–1930. Common doll that is wigged. Open/closed mouth with painted teeth. Decal painted eyes. Original or nicely dressed. **Excellent condition:** 14" - $675.00; 17" - $750.00; 20" - $875.00. **Good condition:** 14" - $450.00; 17" - $625.00; 21" - $750.00. **Poor condition:** 14" - $175.00; 16" - $285.00.

Sleep eyes: 1920–1930. Has lids that lower down over the eyes. Open mouth with teeth or just slightly cut open mouth with carved teeth. Original or nicely dressed. **Excellent condition:** 13–14" - $1,200.00; 17" - $1,400.00; 22" - $1,600.00. **Good condition:** 14" - $700.00; 18" - $800.00. **Poor condition:** 17" - $225.00; 22" - $300.00.

Walker: 1919–1930. One-piece legs with "walker" joints in center of legs and torso. Painted eyes, open/closed or

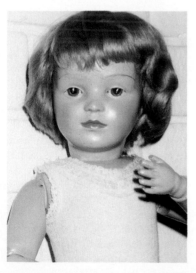

Beautiful 19" Schoenhut with original finish, wig, and teddy. Mint condition. $1,200.00. *Courtesy Pat Graff.*

closed mouth. Original or nicely dressed. **Excellent condition:** 15" - $900.00; 18" - $1,100.00; 21" - $1,400.00. **Good condition:** 15" - $550.00; 18" - $650.00; 21" - $850.00. **Poor condition:** 15" - $125.00; 18" - $185.00; 21" - $250.00.

All composition: 1924. Molded curly hair, "Patsy" style body, paper label on back. (See photo in Series 7, pg. 153.) 13" - $550.00.

Circus animals: (See photo in Series 9, pg. 161.) $95.00–500.00.

Circus parade set, #18: 1950s. Tent and all figures/animals - $1,900.00.

Circus Humpty Dumpty: Tent, figures, and animals. (See photo in Series 9, pg. 161.) $2,800.00 up.

Clowns: $150.00–300.00.

Ringmaster: $200.00–350.00.

Roly-Poly figures: 1914. Figures are marked. (See photo in Series 8, pg. 155.) $300.00 up.

Maggie and Jiggs: 9" and 7" figures from the comic, "Bringing Up Father." She has tall top knot. $450.00 up.

Dancing doll: Constructed like a marionette. Made of wood and papier maché. Attached by wire to wooden base. Excellent condition. (See photo in Series 9, pg. 160.) $600.00 up.

17" character boy, #308. Original mohair wig. Old clothes may be original. In close to mint condition. $1,100.00. *Courtesy Turn of Century Antiques.*

Great set of pick-up sticks made by Schoenhut and in original cylinder. Doll collectors like to display non-doll items with their dolls. Mint condition, full set - $60.00 up. *Courtesy Ellen Dodge.*

Schuetzmeister & Quendt made dolls from 1893 to 1898. This short term factory was located in Boilstadt, Germany.

Marks:

SQ ℚ $\begin{smallmatrix} S \\ Q \end{smallmatrix}$

Child, mold #251, 252, etc.: Can have cut pate or be a bald head with two string holes. No damage and nicely dressed, open mouth. 14" - $375.00; 20" - $485.00; 23" - $585.00.

Baby, includes mold #201, 301: Five-piece bent limb baby body. Not damaged and nicely dressed. Open mouth. 12" - $300.00; 14" - $375.00; 17" - $475.00; 22" - $650.00. **Toddler:** 16" - $800.00; 20" - $975.00; 24" - $1,200.00.

SIMON & HALBIG

Simon & Halbig began making dolls in the late 1860s or early 1870s and continued until the 1930s. Simon & Halbig made many heads for other companies and they also supplied some doll heads from the French makers. They made entire dolls, all bisque, flange neck dolls, turned shoulder heads and socket heads.

All prices are for dolls with no damage to the bisque and only minor scuffs to the bodies, well dressed, wigged and with shoes. Dolls should be ready to place in a collection.

Marks:

S ″ H
729

1279-3
DEP
SH
GERMANY

Child, #130, 530, 540, 550, 570, 600, 1039, 1040, etc: 1890 to 1930's. Open mouth. (Add more for flirty eyes.) 12" - $425.00; 16" - $600.00; 19" - $725.00; 23" - $950.00; 27" - $1,300.00; 32" - $1,800.00; 35" - $2,000.00; 40" - $2,800.00. **#1039 walker:** See end of this section.

#1049, 1059, 1069, 1078, 1079, 1099: Open mouth, jointed body. 12" -

$550.00; 15" - $650.00; 19" - $700.00; 21" - $785.00; 24" - $825.00; 26" - $1,100.00; 30" - $1,300.00; 32" - $1,600.00; 35" - $2,100.00; 42" - $3,800.00. **Pull string sleep eyes:** 19" - $950.00 up.

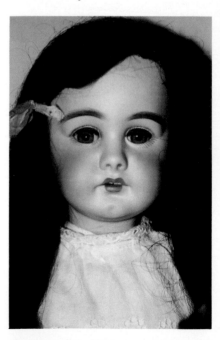

26" with deeply detailed open mouth and character face modeling. On fully jointed body. Marked "S & H 1049." $1,250.00.
Courtesy Susan Capps.

#1009: Kid body. 16" - $700.00; 19" - $900.00; 24" - $1,200.00; 26" - $1,400.00. **Jointed body:** 16" - $975.00; 19" - $1,300.00; 21" - $1,500.00; 24" - $1,800.00.

#1019, open mouth: Smiling. Jointed body. 16" - $6,300.00. Composition shoulder plate, ball-jointed arms, cloth body and upper legs. Ball-jointed lower legs. 18" - $7,500.00.

#1010, 1029, 1040, 1080, 1170, etc: Open mouth and **kid body.** 10" - $325.00; 14" - $500.00; 21" - $700.00; 25" - $800.00; 28" - $975.00.

#1109: 16" - $750.00; 23" - $1,000.00.

#1250, 1260: Open mouth, **kid body.** 16" - $500.00; 19" - $625.00; 25" - $845.00.

Characters: 1910 and after. Wig or molded hair, glass or painted eyes, with open/closed, closed, or open mouth. On jointed child bodies.

S & H, no mold number: Closed or open/closed mouth. 14" - $1,400.00; 16" - $1,650.00. Shoulder head: 10" - $975.00; 15" - $1,300.00; 17" - $1,900.00. Fashion type: 16" - $3,450.00.

#IV: 20" - $22,000.00 up. Open mouth: 16" - $20,000.00 up.

#120: 15" - $1,850.00; 23" - $2,900.00; 28" - $3,800.00.

#150: Full, closed mouth. Intaglio eyes. (See photo in Series 7, pg. 155; Series 9, pg. 163.) 16" - $14,000.00 up; 19" - $18,000.00 up; 23" - $24,000.00 up; 26" - $27,000.00.

#151, 1388: Open/closed mouth, painted teeth. (See photo in Series 7, pg. 155; Series 9, pg. 163.) 15" - $5,300.00; 20" - $7,600.00.

#153 ("Little Duke"): (See photo in Series 8, pg. 157.) 13" - $22,000.00; 15" - $30,000.00; 17" - $38,000.00; 21" - $45,000.00 up.

#540, 550, 570, Baby Blanche: 17" - $600.00; 23" - $685.00.

#600: 14" - $950.00; 18" - $1,400.00; 22" - $1,900.00. **Open mouth:** 17" - $650.00; 21" - $800.00.

22" Simon & Halbig mold #719 DEP with cute character face. Open mouth, very full cheeks. Large glass eyes. Jointed body with straight wrists. $2,250.00. *Courtesy Virginia Sofie.*

#603: 10–12" - $5,600.00.

#718, 719, 720: 16" - $2,400.00; 22" - $3,600.00. **Open mouth:** (See photo in Series 9, pg. 164.) 13" - $1,300.00; 18" - $2,000.00; 25" - $2,600.00.

#729: Slight open mouth, smiling. 16" - $3,200.00 up; 19" - $4,600.00. Closed mouth. 16" - $3,000.00; 20" - $3,700.00. **Kid body:** 16" - $1,400.00; 20" - $1,850.00; 25" - $2,200.00.

#739: 13" - $1,350.00; 18" - $2,200.00; 26" - $2,800.00. **Open mouth:** 17" - $1,250.00; 21" - $1,500.00; 26" - $1,850.00.

#740: Kid or cloth body, closed mouth. 10" - $550.00; 16" - $1,400.00; 18" - $1,600.00. **Jointed body:** 10" - $650.00; 17" - $1,800.00; 21" - $2,200.00.

#749: Closed mouth, jointed body. 18" - $2,900.00; 22" - $3,500.00. **Open mouth:** 12" - $1,350.00; 18" - $2,200.00; 25" - $2,900.00. **Kid body:** Open mouth. 17" - $2,000.00; 21" - $2,900.00.

#759: Open mouth, deep cheek dimples, rare. (See photo in Series 9, pg. 164.) 15" - $6,000.00; 18" - $7,200.00.

#769: Open mouth. 12" - $1,300.00; 18" - $2,200.00; 25" - $2,900.00.

#905, 908: (See photo in Series 6, pg. 173.) Closed mouth. 16" - $2,900.00; 19" - $3,300.00. **Open mouth:** 14" - $1,600.00; 20" - $1,800.00; 25" - $2,300.00.

#919: Open/closed mouth. 17" - $5,200.00; 21" - $7,200.00.

#929: Closed mouth. 17" - $3,500.00; 22" - $4,500.00. **Open mouth:** 18" - $2,200.00; 21" - $3,200.00.

#939: Closed mouth. (See photo in Series 6, pg. 173.) Composition body: 15" - $2,600.00; 18" - $2,900.00; 21" - $3,400.00; 26" - $4,800.00; 30" - $5,900.00. **Kid body:** Closed mouth. 18" - $2,100.00; 21" - $2,600.00; 26" - $3,000.00. **Open mouth:** 13" - $1,300.00; 18" - $2,000.00; 26" - $2,700.00; 30" - $3,600.00.

20" Simon & Halbig #940. Beautiful child with large glass eyes and closed mouth. On kid body with bisque lower arms. $2,300.00. *Courtesy Kathy Riddick.*

#939, 949: See Black or Brown Doll section.

#940, 950: Kid body. (See photo in Series 7, pg. 156.) 10" - $565.00; 15" - $1,400.00; 21" - $1,800.00. **Jointed body:** 10" - $725.00; 15" - $1,800.00; 21" - $2,400.00.

#949: Closed mouth. (See photo in Series 9, pg. 165.) 16" - $2,300.00; 21" - $2,900.00; 25" - $3,400.00; 32" - $4,200.00. **Open mouth:** (See photo in Series 9, pg. 164.) 18" - $1,600.00; 21" - $1,900.00; 26" - $2,400.00. **Kid body:** (See photo in Series 9, pg. 165.) 15" - $1,500.00; 18" - $1,800.00; 21" - $2,000.00.

#969, 970: Slighty open mouth grin, square cut teeth, puffed cheeks. 13" - $3,700.00; 17" - $6,900.00; 21" - $9,800.00.

#979: Closed mouth. (See photo in Series 8, pg. 157.) 13" - $2,500.00; 16" - $3,300.00; 19" - $3,600.00. **Open mouth:** Square cut teeth, slight smile. 16" - $1,650.00; 21" - $2,400.00; 24" - $2,750.00; 28" - $3,200.00. **Kid body:** 17" - $1,500.00; 21" - $2,200.00.

19" with swivel neck on bisque shoulder plate. Kid body with bisque lower arms. Long thin face, large eyes, and open mouth. Marked "949 S & H." $1,700.00. *Courtesy Turn of Century Antiques.*

#1247, 1248, 1249, 1250, 1260
Santa: 14" - $985.00; 17" - $1,100.00; 22" - $1,300.00; 26" - $1,600.00; 30" - $2,000.00; 34" - $2,500.00.

#1269, 1279: (See photo in Series 5, pg. 134; Series 9, pg. 166.) 12" - $1,500.00; 15" - $2,300.00; 18" - $2,900.00; 22" - $3,300.00; 25" - $3,800.00; 30" - $5,200.00; 34" - $5,600.00.

#1299: 14" - $1,200.00; 17" - $1,600.00; 21" - $2,100.00.

#1302: See Black or Brown Dolls section.

#1303: Closed mouth, thin lips. Adult body. (Also see Black or Brown Dolls section.) 18" - $7,800.00 up. Man: (See photo in Series 8, pg. 161.) 16" - $9,000.00.

#1304: 14" - $6,500.00; 17" - $8,200.00.

#1305: Open/closed mouth, long nose. 18" - $14,000.00 up.

#1308: 20" - $6,600.00 up.

#1309: Character with open mouth. 10" - $1,500.00; 16" - $2,000.00; 20" - $3,100.00.

#1310: Open/closed mouth, modeled mustache. 19½" - $19,000.00.

#1338: Open mouth, jointed body. 18" - $1,400.00; 24" - $2,500.00; 28" - $3,000.00.

#1339: Character face, open mouth. (See photos in Series 5, pg. 135; Series 7, pg. 157.) 18" - $1,600.00; 26" - $3,000.00.

#1339, 1358: See Black or Brown Dolls sections.

#1345: 15" - $2,700.00; 17" - $4,100.00.

#1388, 1398: Lady doll. 22" - $17,500.00 up.

#1428: Very character face. Open/closed mouth, glass eyes. 16" - $1,800.00; 22" - $2,800.00.

24" Simon & Halbig mold #1294 with sleep eyes, open mouth, and tremble tongue. On chunky toddler body with jointed elbows. $1,450.00. *Courtesy Turn of Century Antiques.*

27" mold #1247 "Santa" made by Simon & Halbig. Sleep eyes and open mouth. Lower lip has indent with dark painted center. On fully jointed body. $1,750.00. *Courtesy Turn of Century Antiques.*

#1448: Full closed mouth. 17" - $20,000.00 up; 21" - $25,000.00 up. **Open/ closed mouth:** Laughing. Modeled teeth. 16" - $14,000.00 up; 21" - $24,000.00 up.

#1478: 17" - $9,700.00 up.

#1488: Child, closed mouth. (See photos in Series 4, pg. 139; Series 6, pg. 175.) 16" - $3,300.00; 20" - $4,200.00; 24" - $5,300.00.

Character babies: 1909 to 1930s. Wigs or molded hair, painted or sleep eyes, open or open/closed mouth and on five-piece bent limb baby bodies. (Allow more for toddler body.)

#1294: 16" - $700.00; 19" - $825.00; 23" - $1,200.00; 26" - $1,800.00. **With clockwork** in head to move eyes: 25-26" - $2,400.00. **Toddler:** 22" - $1,500.00.

#1299: Open mouth. 10" - $585.00; 16" - $1,000.00. **Toddler:** 16" - $1,300.00; 18" - $1,500.00.

21" with sleep eyes and open mouth with four teeth. On toddler body. Marked "Erika/1489/Simon & Halbig." $4,800.00 up. *Courtesy Frasher Doll Auctions.*

#1428, toddler: (See photo in Series 7, pg. 158.) 12" - $1,500.00; 16" - $2,400.00; 20" - $2,600.00; 26" - $3,100.00. **Baby:** 12" - $1,400.00; 15" - $1,900.00; 19" - $2,400.00.

#1488, toddler: (See photo in Series 6, pg. 175.) 15" - $2,600.00; 18" - $4,200.00; 22" - $4,800.00. **Baby:** 15" - $1,800.00; 18" - $3,500.00; 22" - $4,200.00; 26" - $4,800.00.

#1489 Erika baby: (See photos in Series 6, pg. 176; Series 7, pg. 159.) 20" - $3,800.00; 22" - $4,800.00 up; 26" - $5,400.00 up.

#1498, toddler: (See photo in Series 6, pg. 175.) 16" - $5,600.00; 20" - $6,600.00. **Baby:** 16" - $5,000.00; 20" - $5,900.00.

#1039 Walker: Key wound. 16" - $1,700.00; 20" - $2,000.00; 23" - $2,400.00.

11" with dimples in both cheeks and open mouth with two upper teeth. On five-piece baby body. (The child version of this mold number has a "dolly" face and lacks the dimples.) Marked "1299/Simon & Halbig/S&H" and "5" low on neck. $850.00. *Courtesy Kathy Riddick.*

Walking/kissing: 20" - $1,600.00; 24" - $2,000.00.

Edison, Thomas: Metal body with phonograph. Uses S&H head (mold #719, etc.) Open mouth. 18" - $2,600.00 up; 24" - $3,400.00 up.

Miniature dolls: Tiny dolls with open mouth on jointed body or five-piece body with some having painted-on shoes and socks. **#1078, 1079, etc.: Fully jointed:** 7" - $500.00; 10" - $600.00. **Five-piece body:** 7" - $325.00; 10" - $425.00. **Walker:** 10–11" - $645.00.

#1160: "Little Women" type. Closed mouth and fancy wig. 5½–6½" - $400.00; 10–11" - $600.00. **Head only:** 2–3" - $85.00–145.00.

Ladies: Circa 1910. Open mouth, molded lady-style slim body with slim arms and legs. (See photo in Series 9, pg. 167.) **#1159, 1179:** 12" - $1,150.00; 15" - $1,700.00; 19" - $2,100.00; 22" - $2,400.00; 26" - $2,900.00.

Ladies: Circa 1910. Closed mouth. Adult slim limb body. **#1303:** 15" - $11,000.00; 17" - $13,000.00.

#1305: Lady with open/closed mouth and long nose. 18" - $9,600.00 up; 22" - $14,000.00 up.

#1307: Lady with long face. 18" - $15,500.00 up; 21" - $20,000.00; 24" - $22,500.00 up.

#1308, man: 13" - $5,600.00; 15" - $6,100.00.

#1388: Thin face with dimples and open/closed smile mouth. Glass eyes with heavy upper molded eyelids. Adult composition and wood body. 28" - $30,000.00 at auction.

#1398: 18" - $12,000.00 up.

#1468, 1469: Sweet expression. Closed mouth, glass eyes. 14" - $2,400.00; 16" - $2,900.00.

#1527: 18" - $9,500.00 up; 22" - $11,000.00 up.

#152, lady: Long Roman nose, molded eyelids, closed mouth. 17" - $19,000.00 up; 23" - $32,000.00 up.

13" Simon & Halbig trapeze acrobat with open mouth. Has keywind mechanism. All original. $1,800.00. *Courtesy Turn of Century Antiques.*

The Société Française de Fabrication de Bébés et Jouets (S.F.B.J.) was formed in 1899 and known members were Jumeau, Bru, Fleischmann & Bloedel, Rabery & Delphieu, Pintel & Godchaux, P.H. Schmitz, A. Bouchet, Jullien, and Danel & Cie. By 1922, S.F.B.J. employed 2,800 people. The Society was dissolved in 1958. There is a vast amount of "dolly-faced" S.F.B.J. dolls, but some are extremely rare and are character molds. Most of the characters are in the 200 mold number series.

Marks:

S.F.B.J.
239
PARIS

DÉPOSÉ
S.F.B.J.
301

S F
B J

14" S.F.B.J., mold #226, with paperweight "jewel" eyes. Open/closed mouth with sculptured upper teeth. On toddler body. $1,800.00. *Courtesy Turn of Century Antiques.*

Child: 1899. Sleep or set eyes, open mouth and on jointed French body. No damage and nicely dressed.

#60: 12" - $600.00; 14" - $650.00; 20" - $850.00; 28" - $1,350.00.

#301: 8" - $475.00; 12" - $675.00; 14" - $825.00; 20" - $1,050.00; 28" - $1,800.00; 36" - $2,900.00. Lady body: 23" - $1,600.00.

Bleuette: 1930s–1960s. Exclusively made for Gautier-Languereau and their newspaper for children, La Semaine de Suzette. (Just as "Betsy McCall" was used by McCall's magazine.) Marked "SFBJ" or "71 Unis France 149 301" with "1½" at base of neck socket. Body marked "2" and feet marked "1." Sleep eyes, open mouth. (See photo in Series 7, pg. 36.) 10" - $825.00 up.

Jumeau type: 1899–1910. Open mouth. (See photo in Series 7, pg. 163; Series 8, pg. 164; Series 9, pg. 170.) 15" - $1,150.00; 20" - $1,600.00; 24" - $2,000.00; 28" - $2,500.00. **Closed mouth:** 17" - $2,300.00; 21" - $3,000.00; 25" - $3,400.00.

Lady #1159: Open mouth, adult body. (See photo in Series 10, pg. 159.) 24" - $2,800.00 up.

Character: Sleep or set eyes, wigged, molded hair, jointed body. (Allow more for flocked hair. Usually found on mold #227, 235, 237, 266.) No damage and nicely dressed.

#211: 18" - $6,000.00 up.

#226: (See photo in Series 4, pg. 144.) **Glass eyes:** 15" - $1,700.00; 17" - $2,100.00. **Painted eyes:** 16" - $1,400.00.

#227: (See photo in Series 5, pg. 136.) 16" - $2,300.00; 20" - $2,600.00.

#229: 16" - $3,500.00.

#230: 15" - $1,500.00; 18" - $2,000.00; 20" - $2,300.00.

#233: Screamer. (See photo in Series 4, pg. 143.) 14" - $2,100.00; 17" - $3,100.00; 20" - $3,500.00.

#234: 17" - $3,000.00; 23" - $3,500.00.

#235: Glass eyes: 14" - $1,550.00; 22" - $2,200.00. **Painted eyes:** 15" - $1,400.00; 22" - $2,100.00.

#236, 262 toddler: 12" - $1,300.00; 16" - $1,750.00; 20" - $1,950.00; 24" - $2,400.00; 26" - $2,700.00. **Baby:** 14" - $900.00; 19" - $1,600.00; 25" - $2,200.00.

#237: (See photo in Series 7, pg. 161.) 15" - $2,000.00; 20" - $2,400.00.

#238: (See photo in Series 3, pg. 134.) 16" - $3,800.00; 24" - $4,300.00. **Lady:** 22" - $4,200.00.

#239 Poulbot: (See photo in Series 10, pg. 159.) 16" - $8,500.00 up.

#242: (See photo in Series 5, pg. 137.) 14" - $2,700.00; 16½" - $3,000.00 up. Nursing baby: 14" - $3,200.00.

#247 toddler: 16" - $2,500.00; 20" - $2,850.00; 26" - $3,300.00.

#248: Very pouty, glass eyes. 14" - $4,000.00; 19" - $5,600.00.

#251 toddler: 14" - $1,500.00; 18"- $1,900.00; 22" - $2,300.00; 26" - $2,750.00. **Baby:** 15" - $1,100.00; 21" $1,700.00; 25" - $2,200.00.

21" S.F.B.J. with flirty glass sleep eyes and cloth body and limbs. Painted bisque. In original box with the S.F.B.J. seal and labeled "Parlant," which means she has a cryer voice box. Mint in box - $600.00 up. *Courtesy Turn of Century Antiques.*

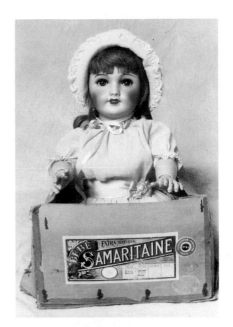

20" S.F.B.J. in original box. Has sleep eyes, open mouth, and is in unplayed with condition. Box labeled S.F.B.J. although the doll is marked UNIS. $1,500.00. *Courtesy Turn of Century Antiques.*

#252 toddler: 13" - $5,400.00; 16" - $5,800.00; 20" - $7,400.00; 26" - $8,200.00. **Baby:** 12" - $1,800.00; 16" - $5,200.00; 22" - $7,200.00; 26" - $8,300.00.

#257: 18" - $2,800.00.

#266: 22" - $4,400.00.

#306 ("Princess Elizabeth"): See Jumeau section.

Googly: See Googly section.

Kiss throwing, walking doll: (See photo in Series 5, pg. 138; Series 9, pg. 170.) Composition body with straight legs and walking mechanism. When it walks, arm goes up to throw kiss. Head moves from side to side. Flirty eyes, open mouth. In working condition, no damage to bisque head and nicely dressed. 21–22" - $2,000.00. All original - $2,600.00 up.

27" S.F.B.J. with feathered molded eyebrows and open mouth. On fully jointed French body. Wig may be original. $850.00. *Courtesy Turn of Century Antiques.*

SKOOKUMS

Skookums have mask faces with wigs. Wool blankets form the bodies that are stuffed with twigs, leaves, and grass. Wooden dowel rods form the legs and they have suede over wooden feet. They were made from 1920 to 1940s. After 1949, they have plastic feet.

Squaw with baby: 10" - $150.00; 15" - $185.00; 18" - $250.00; 22" - $385.00 up.

Portrait chief: 10" - $150.00; 15" - $200.00; 18" - $275.00; 22" - $450.00; 30" - $500.00.

Sitting squaw: 8" - $100.00; 12" - $145.00.

Child: 8" - $55.00–75.00 up.

Plastic feet: 4" - $18.00; 6" - $25.00; 12" - $50.00; 15" - $125.00; 18" - $165.00; 22" - $250.00; 30" - $350.00; 36" - $425.00.

Skookum chief, squaw with baby, boy, and girl. Mask faces with leaves and twigs inside Indian blanket covered bodies. Wood feet and legs. Chief - $145.00; squaw with baby - $135.00; children - $60.00 each. *Courtesy Mary Williams.*

SNOW BABIES

Snow babies have fired-on "pebble-textured" clothing and were made in Germany and Japan. German-made babies were made as early as the 1880s and have excellent details. These early ones had no shoes or mittens, and these "stubs" were covered with all-white pebbly "snow." In the 1890s, some snow had a blue-grey appearance. Those babies are of excellent quality but did not remain on the market long.

After 1900, the hands and feet of the snow babies became defined. Early ones had beautiful painted features, but the later ones tended to have high color and poor artist workmanship. Japan reproduced snow babies in 1971 and they are stamped "Japan."

Snow babies can be excellent to poor in quality from both countries. Many are unmarked. Prices are for good quality painted features, rareness of pose, and no damage to the piece.

Single figure: 1½" - $50.00; 3" - $100.00–125.00.

Two figures: Molded together. 1½" - $95.00–100.00; 3" - $150.00–195.00.

Three figures: Molded together. 1½" - $145.00–185.00; 3" - $195.00–245.00.

One figure on sled: 2–2½" - $185.00. With reindeer: $200.00 up. Pulled by dogs: 3" - $265.00.

Two figures on sled: 2–2½" - $200.00.

Three figures on sled: (See photo in Series 6, pg. 180.) 2–2½" - $265.00.

Jointed shoulders and hips: (See photo in Series 5, pg. 139.) 3¼" - $185.00 up; 5" - $365.00 up; 7" - $465.00 up.

Shoulder head: Cloth body with china limbs. 5" - $195.00; 9" - $345.00; 12" - $425.00.

On sled in glass: "Snow" scene. $225.00 up. Sled/dogs: 3–4" - $285.00.

With bear: Child or baby. $200.00 up.

With snowman: 2½" - $130.00.

With musical base: $185.00 up.

Laughing child: 3" - $150.00 up.

Snow bear: 2" - $85.00 up. With Santa: $365.00.

With reindeer: $250.00

Snow baby riding polar bear: 3" - $245.00.

Snow angel: White texturing. Pink feathered smooth bisque wings. 3" - $300.00 up.

Snowman alone: 3" - $110.00.

Tumbling figure: 3" - $175.00.

Sliding on cellar door: 2½" - $250.00.

Dog with Santa: 2½" - $250.00.

Santa going down chimney: $300.00.

Igloo: $90.00.

Ice skater: 3" - $185.00 up.

In airplane: 4½" - $365.00.

Mother: Pushing two babies in red sled carriage. 4½" - $365.00 up.

Rolling snowball: 5" - $225.00.

Pushing carriage with twins: $325.00.

Snow babies, new: Presently being produced but they have a different look and color than old ones. Majority of new figures are not doing the same activities as the old ones. Many marked "Dept. 56."

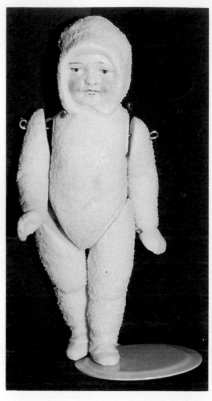

Large 5" Snow Baby with pebbled clothes, painted features, and jointed at shoulders and hips. Made in Germany. $365.00.
Courtesy Ellen Dodge.

STEIFF

Steiff started business in 1894. This German maker is better known for their well-crafted plush stuffed animals than for their dolls.

Steiff dolls: Felt, velvet or plush with seam down middle of face. Button-style eyes, painted features and sewn-on ears. The dolls generally have large feet so they stand alone. Prices are for dolls in excellent condition and with original clothes. Second prices are for dolls that are soiled and may not be original.

Adult dolls: (See photo in Series 7, pg. 165.) 18" - $2,400.00 up; 22" - $2,900.00 up.

Military men or uniforms: Policemen, conductors, etc. (See photo in Series 7, pg. 165.) 15" - $3,500.00 up; 17" - $4,000.00 up; 21" - $5,200.00 up.

Children: (See photo in Series 6, pg. 181.) 12" - $1,000.00 up; 15–16" - $1,600.00; 18–19" - $1,900.00 up.

Made in U.S. Zone Germany: Has glass eyes. 12" - $800.00 up; 16" - $1,000.00 up.

Comic characters: Such as chef, musician, etc. 14" - $2,500.00 up; 16" - $3,300.00 up.

Golliwog: 16" - $4,000.00.

Mickey Mouse: 9–10" - $1,200.00 up. **Minnie Mouse:** 9–10" - $1,800.00 up.

Clown: 16" - $2,300.00 up.

Leprechaun, elf, or gnome: All felt, straw stuffed, carries felt cloverleaf. Red mohair beard. 12" - $800.00 up; 17" - $1,500.00.

Max and Moritz: Circa 1960. "Bendy" type with felt costumes. Each - $185.00. All felt: 15" - $5,500.00 pair.

11" Dutch fisherfolk, "Harry and Helen." Glass eyes, inset mohair wigs, and felt shoes. Both are fully jointed with mitten hands. (The 1913 Steiff catalog shows them in a 14" and 17" size also.) In this condition - $2,400.00 pair. *Courtesy Margaret Mandel.*

STEINER, HERM

Hermann Steiner of Sonneburg, Germany made dolls from 1921 on. Dolls come in various sizes, but are usually small.

Marks:

$\overset{15}{)S(}$
Germany
240

Herm Steiner
$)S($
Germany

Child: Sleep eyes, open mouth, composition body. Perfect condition. 8" - $185.00; 15" - $345.00. Molded hair: 7" - $265.00. **#128:** Special eye movement. 14" - $385.00 **#401:** Shoulder head. 15" - $465.00.

Baby: Bisque character head with sleep eyes and open mouth. Cloth or composition body. All in good condition. 10" - $285.00; 15" - $375.00. **#240:** 16" - $600.00; 19" - $800.00.

Infant: Bisque head with molded hair, sleep eyes, and closed mouth. Cloth or composition body. All in good condition. 8" - $235.00; 10" - $285.00. **#246:** Holds pacifier and when bounced, hand moves to open mouth. 15" - $600.00.

19" Herm Steiner baby with sleep eyes and closed mouth. Has five-piece cloth stuffed body. Marked "3" with "S" inside "H" followed by "Germany/240." $800.00.

STEINER, JULES

Jules Nicholas Steiner operated from 1855 to 1892 when the firm was taken over by Amedee LaFosse. In 1895, this firm merged with Henri Alexandre, the maker of Phenix Bébé and a partner, May Freres Cie, the maker of Bébé Mascotte. In 1899, Jules Mettais took over the firm and in 1906, the company was sold to Edmond Daspres.

In 1889, the firm registered the girl with a banner and the words "Le Petit Parisien" and in 1892, LaFosse registered "Le Parisien."

Steiner body: All fingers are nearly same length. (See photo in Series 8, pg. 167.)

Marks:

J. STEINER	STE C3
STE. S.G.D.G.	J. STEINER
FIRE A12	B. S.G.D.G.
PARIS	

Bourgoin

"A" Series child: 1885. Has paperweight eyes, jointed body, and cardboard pate. No damage and nicely dressed. (Also see "Le Parisien – "A" Series in this listing.) Closed mouth: 8" - $3,200.00; 10" - $3,300.00; 15" - $4,400.00; 22" - $6,300.00; 25" - $6,700.00; 28" - $7,400.00. **Open mouth:** 8" - $1,450.00; 10" - $1,600.00; 14" - $1,700.00; 18" - $2,500.00; 22" - $2,900.00.

"B" Series: Closed mouth. 24" - $6,500.00; 30" - $8,700.00.

"C" Series child: Circa 1880. Round face, paperweight eyes. No damage, nicely dressed. (See photo in Series 9, pg. 173.) Closed mouth: 18" - $5,400.00; 22" - $6,400.00; 27" - $8,600.00; 30" - $9,200.00. **Open mouth:** Two rows teeth. 22" - $5,800.00.

Bourgoin Steiner: 1870s. With "Bourgoin" incised or in red stamp on head along with the rest of the Steiner mark. No damage, nicely dressed. Closed mouth: 16" - $5,000.00; 20" - $6,000.00; 25" - $7,200.00.

Wire-eye Steiner: Closed mouth, flat glass eyes that open and close by moving wire in back of the head. Jointed body, no damage and nicely dressed. **Bourgoin:** 17" - $5,400.00; 21" - $6,200.00; 26" - $7,600.00. **"A" series:** 17" - $5,200.00; 21" - $6,100.00; 26" - $7,400.00. **"C" series:** 17" - $5,200.00; 21" - $6,100.00; 26" - $7,500.00.

11" Series A-3 Jules Steiner with closed mouth. On marked jointed body with straight wrists. Shown with all original sedan chair with glass panels (14" x 8" x 7½") Doll - $4,200.00; chair - $650.00.
Courtesy Frasher Doll Auctions

"Le Parisien" - "A" Series: 1892. Closed mouth: 8–9" - $2,800.00; 13–14" - $4,100.00; 17" - $5,200.00; 21" - $6,400.00; 24" - $7,300.00; 28" - $8,000.00. **Open mouth:** 16" - $2,400.00; 22" - $2,700.00; 25" - $3,500.00.

Mechanical and Kicking Steiner: Composition torso, chest, and lower limbs. Kid or twill covered sections between parts of body. Open mouth with two rows of teeth. Key wound. Cries, head moves, legs kick. 17" - $2,400.00; 24" - $3,000.00.

Bisque hip Steiner: Bisque head, Motschmann-style body with shoulders, lower arms and legs and bisque torso sections. No damage anywhere. 18" - $6,800.00 up.

29" Jules Steiner that is a fine example of an A Series doll with closed mouth. On Steiner jointed body with label. Marked "A-19." $7,800.00. *Courtesy Frasher Doll Auctions.*

Early white bisque Steiner: Round face, open mouth with two rows of teeth. On jointed Steiner body. Pink wash over eyes. Unmarked. No damage, nicely dressed. (See Series 8, pg. 167; Series 9, pg. 174.) 16" - $4,800.00; 20" - $5,800.00.

SWAINE & CO. (LORI BABY)

The "Lori Baby" was made by Swaine & Co. and can be marked "232," "DIP," "DV," "DI," "Geschutz S & Co." with green stamp or incised "D Lori 4." It has lightly painted hair, sleep eyes, open/closed mouth, and is on five-piece bent limb baby body.

Incised "Lori": 1910. Open/closed mouth, glass eyes. 12" - $1,000.00; 16" - $1,500.00; 20" - $2,450.00; 23" - $3,000.00; 26" - $3,500.00.

Intaglio eyes: (See photo in Series 6, pg. 138.) 20" - $2,000.00; 24" - $2,500.00.

Flocked hair: 16" - $1,850.00; 20" - $2,700.00; 25" - $3,400.00.

#232: Open mouth. (See photo in Series 9, pg. 130.) 13" - $975.00; 20" - $1,650.00.

DIP: Closed mouth, wig, and glass eyes. 12" - $775.00; 16" - $1,350.00. **Toddler:** 19" - $2,400.00.

DV: Open/closed mouth, molded hair, glass eyes. 12" - $1,300.00; 15" - $1,500.00.

DI: Intaglio eyes, molded hair, open/closed mouth. 14" - $1,300.00.

S&C child with B.P.: Made for Bahr & Proschild. Smiling open/closed mouth. Very character face. (See photo in Series 10, pg. 165.) 14" - $6,000.00 up; 17" - $7,500.00 up; 21" - $8,700.00 up.

Marked "S&C": 7" - $345.00; 14" - $500.00; 17" - $675.00; 22" - $750.00; 25" - $875.00; 30" - $1,200.00; 38" - $2,200.00.

23" "Lori Baby" with painted hair, sleep glass eyes, and open/closed mouth. On five-piece bent limb baby body made by Swaine & Co. Marked "Lori" and stamped "Geschutz S & Co. Germany." $3,000.00. *Courtesy Frasher Doll Auctions.*

"Tynie Baby" was made for Horsman Doll Co. in 1924. Doll will have sleep eyes, closed pouty mouth and "frown" between eyes. Its cloth body has celluloid or composition hands. Markings will be "1924/E.I. Horsman/Made in Germany." Some will also be incised "Tynie Baby." Doll should have no damage and be nicely dressed.

Bisque head: 11" - $400.00; 13" - $475.00; 16" - $750.00. Original with pin: 16" - $925.00.

Composition head: 15–16" - $295.00.

All bisque: Glass eyes, swivel neck. 6" - $1,200.00; 9" - $1,800.00. Painted eyes: 6" - $600.00.

Vinyl/cloth: 1949. Crying face. 15" - $90.00–110.00.

Vinyl/cloth (J.C. Penney's): 1993. Sleep eyes. 13" - $80.00 (retail).

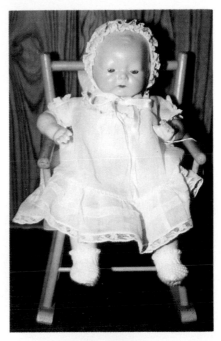

14" Horsman "Tynie Baby" from 1924. Made of composition head and limbs and cloth body. Tin sleep eyes. Original dress. $295.00. *Courtesy Jeannie Mauldin.*

UNIS

"UNIS, France" was a type of trade association or a "seal of approval" for trade goods to consumers from the manufacturers. This group of businessmen, who were to watch the quality of French exports, often overlooked guidelines and some poor quality dolls were exported. Many fine quality UNIS marked dolls were also produced.

UNIS began right after World War I and is still in business. Two doll companies are still members, Poupee Bella and Petitcollin. Other manufacturers in this group include makers of toys, sewing machines, tile, and pens.

Marks:

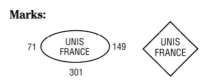

#60, 70, 71, 301: Bisque head, composition jointed body. Sleep or set eyes, open mouth. No damage, nicely dressed. (Allow more for flirty eyes.) 8–9" - $445.00; 15" - $625.00; 18" - $700.00; 22" - $850.00; 25" - $975.00. **Closed mouth:** 16" - $2,400.00; 20" - $3,000.00. **Composition head:** 12" - $165.00; 19" - $400.00. **Black or brown:** See that section.

#60, 70, 71, 301 with glass eyes: On five-piece body. 6½" - $250.00; 12" - $365.00; 14" - $465.00.

Bleuette: See S.F.B.J section.

Provincial costume doll: Bisque head, painted, set or sleep eyes, open mouth (or closed on smaller dolls.) Five-piece body. Original costume, no damage. 6" - $225.00; 12" - $400.00; 14" - $550.00.

#272 baby: Glass eyes, open mouth, cloth body, celluloid hands. (See photo in Series 5, pg. 143.) 15" - $575.00; 18" - $975.00. Painted eyes: Composition hands. 16" - $375.00; 19" - $565.00.

#251 toddler: 15" - $1,400.00 up; 24" - $2,200.00. Composition head: 22" - $725.00.

Princess Elizabeth: (See photo in Series 6, pg. 185.) 1938. Jointed body, closed mouth. (Allow more for flirty eyes.) 18" - $1,800.00; 23" - $2,400.00; 32" - $3,600.00 up.

Princess Margaret Rose: 1938. Closed mouth. 18" - $1,900.00; 23" - $2,500.00; 32" - $3,700.00.

34" "Princess Margaret Rose" and "Princess Elizabeth" marked "UNIS." Both are original and unplayed with. Each has flirty eyes and closed mouth. Both dolls came together in original box. Each - $3,800.00; pair in box - $9,400.00. *Courtesy Ellen Dodge.*

Closed mouth: 16" - $700.00; 21" - $1,050.00; 24" - $1,300.00; 27" - $1,600.00.

Open mouth: 16" - $450.00; 21" - $565.00; 24" - $675.00; 27" - $850.00.

Harald: Closed mouth. (See photo in Series 1, pg. 202.) Bisque head: 14" - $700.00. Celluloid head: 14" - $300.00 up.

Max, Hansi, Inge: Incised. 14" - $850.00.

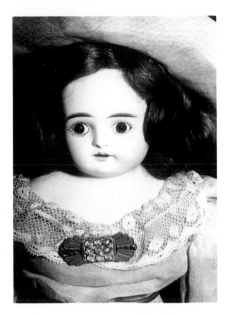

15½" early turned shoulder head with glass eyes and open mouth. Very pale bisque. Flat under sides to eyebrows. Kid body with bisque lower arms. $450.00.

WAX

Poured wax: Cloth body with wax head, limbs and inset glass eyes. Hair is embedded into wax. Nicely dressed or in original clothes, no damage to wax, but wax may be slightly discolored evenly all over. Not rewaxed. (See photos in Series 5, pg. 144; Series 7, pg. 174.) 16" - $1,300.00; 19" - $1,800.00; 22" - $2,000.00; 25" - $2,300.00. **Lady:** 20" - $2,600.00 up; 24" - $3,600.00. **Man:** Mustache embedded into wax. 17" - $1,750.00.

Wax over papier maché or composition: Cloth body with wax over papier maché or composition head and with wax over composition or wood limbs. Only minor scuffs with no chipped out places, good color and nicely dressed. (See photo in Series 6, pg. 189.)

Early dolls: 1860 on. **Sleep eyes:** Pull string to move eyes. 16" - $850.00. **Molded hair:** 14" - $285.00; 21" - $485.00; 24" - $565.00. **Squeaker body:** 14" - $325.00; 17" - $575.00.00. Motschmann: See that section.

29" poured wax doll with cloth body, sleep eyes, closed mouth, and original clothes. Body signed "Montanari/180 Soho Bazaar London." Perfect condition - $2,450.00; with repair - $1,000.00. *Courtesy Turn of Century Antiques.*

"Alice": Headband hairdo: 14" - $475.00; 17" - $550.00. **With wig:** Excellent quality. Heavy wax. 12" - $265.00; 16" - $425.00; 21" - $550.00; 24" - $650.00; 29" - $800.00. **Lever-operated eyes:** 1850s. 17" - $800.00. **Common quality:** Wax worn or gone. 12" - $150.00; 16" - $325.00; 21" - $350.00; 24" - $465.00.

Later dolls: 12" - $225.00; 16" - $400.00.

Bonnet or cap: 1860–1880. (See photo in Series 6, pg. 190.) **Hat** molded on forehead: 16" - $2,600.00. **Derby-type** hat: 22" - $2,100.00. **Bonnet-style** hat: 20" - $2,250.00. Round face, **poke bonnet:** 22" - $3,200.00. **Baby:** $16" - $1,400.00.

Pumpkin: Hair laced over ridged raised front area. 16" - $425.00; 20" - $525.00.

Slit head wax: English, 1830–1860s. Glass eyes, some open and closed by an attached wire. (See photo in Series 6, pg. 189.) 14" - $600.00 up; 18" - $900.00; 21" - $1,000.00; 25" - $1,300.00 up.

Two-faced doll: 1880–1890s. Body stamped "Bartenstein" (Fritz). One side laughing, other crying. 15–16" - $1,050.00.

21" poured wax doll in glass inset eyes, molded eyelids, and human hair inserted into scalp. Muslin body with poured wax lower limbs and bare feet. All original. $2,600.00. *Courtesy Frasher Doll Auctions.*

WELLINGS, NORAH

Norah Wellings's designs were made for her by Victoria Toy Works in Wellington, Shropshire, England. These dolls were made from 1926 into the 1960's. The dolls are velvet as well as other fabrics, especially felt and velour. They will have a tag on the foot "Made in England by Norah Wellings."

Child: All fabric with stitch jointed hips and shoulders. Molded fabric face with oil-painted features. Some faces are papier maché with a stockinette covering. All original felt and cloth clothes, clean condition. (See photo in Series 2, pg. 132.) **Painted eyes:** 12" - $375.00; 17" - $650.00; 21" - $925.00; 23" - $1,250.00. **Glass eyes:** 14" - $600.00; 17" - $800.00; 21" - $1,200.00.

Babies: Same description as child and same condition. (See photo in Series 4, pg. 158.) 15" - $600.00; 22" - $985.00.

Black islander ("Tak-uki") and Scots: These are most commonly found dolls. Must be in same condition as child. 8" - $85.00 up; 12" - $165.00 up; 14" - $200.00 up.

Characters: Mounties, Bobbies (policemen), and others. 12" - $425.00; 16" - $625.00; 23" - $1,050.00. **Glass eyes:** 16" - $875.00.

Characters from novels: Man: 24" - $795.00. **Woman:** 22" - $600.00. **Child:** 16" - $475.00.

Glass Eyes: White: 14" - $300.00; 17" - $450.00. **Black:** 14" - $250.00; 20" - $400.00; 26" - $650.00.

Left: 24" Dickens character with mutton chops and curly mohair wig. All original. Tagged "Norah Wellings." Right: 14" islander with glass eyes. Made by Norah Wellings. 24" - $795.00; 14" - $185.00. *Courtesy Turn of Century Antiques.*

WISLIZENUS, ADOLF

The Adolf Wislizenus doll factory was located at Waltershausen, Germany, and the heads he used were made by Bahr & Proschild, Ernst Heubach of Koppelsdorf, and Simon & Halbig. The company was in business starting in 1851, but it is not known when they began to make dolls.

Marks:

GERMANY
A. W.

Child: 1890s into 1900s. Bisque head on jointed body, sleep eyes, open mouth. No damage and nicely dressed. Average quality: 12" - $165.00; 14" - $285.00; 17" - $400.00; 22" - $500.00; 25" - $625.00. **Excellent quality:** 12" - $400.00; 15" - $525.00; 17" - $600.00; 22" - $750.00; 27" - $1,100.00.

Walker: Open mouth, one-piece legs. Head turns as legs move. 20" - $650.00.

Baby: Bisque head in perfect condition and on five-piece bent limb baby body. No damage and nicely dressed. 16" - $475.00; 19" - $585.00; 25" - $950.00.

#110, 115: 16" - $1,100.00. Glass eyes: 16" - $3,800.00 up.

English, William & Mary Period, 1690s–1700: Carved wooden head, eyes. Eyebrow and eyelashes are painted with tiny lines. Colored cheeks, human hair or flax wig. Wood body, carved wood hands shaped like forks. Legs are wood and jointed. Upper arms are cloth. In medium to fair condition: 15–18" - $55,000.00 up.

English, Queen Anne Period. Early 1700s: Eyebrows and lashes made of dots. Glass pupiless eyes (some painted). Carved wooden egg-shaped head. Jointed wooden body, cloth upper arms. Back (including hips) was planed flat. Nicely dressed, in overall good condition. 14" - $9,700.00 up; 18" - $18,000.00 up; 24" - $25,000.00 up.

English, Georgian Period, 1750s–1800: Round wooden head with gesso coating, inset glass eyes. Eyelashes and eyebrows made of dots. Human or flax wig. Jointed wood body with pointed torso. Medium to fair condition. 13" - $2,950.00; 16" - $4,600.00; 18" - $5,200.00; 24" - $6,550.00.

English, 1800s–1840s: Gesso coated wooden head, painted eyes. Human hair or flax wig. Original gowns generally longer than wooden legs. 12–13" - $1,450.00; 15" - $1,950.00; 20" - $2,900.00.

German, 1810s–1850s: Hair is delicately carved and painted with little spit curls around face. Some have decorations carved in hair such as yellow tuck comb. Features are painted. All wood doll with pegged or ball-jointed limbs. 7" - $765.00; 12-13" - $1,400.00; 16-17" - $1,700.00. **Exceptional:** All original. 17" - $3,200.00.

German, 1850s–1900: All wood with painted plain hairstyle. Some may have spit curls around face. 5" - $135.00; 8" - $200.00; 12" - $350.00. **Wooden shoulder head:** Same but with more elaborate carved hair such as buns. Wood limbs and cloth body. 9–10" - $400.00; 16–17" - $600.00; 23" - $875.00.

German, after 1900: Turned wood head with carved nose. Hair painted and painted lower legs with black shoes. Peg jointed. 10–11" - $60.00. **Child:** All wood, body is fully jointed. **Glass eyes, open mouth:** 14–15" - $425.00; 18" - $600.00; 23" - $825.00.

Nesting Dolls ("Matryoshka"): Prices are for the set. Old: 1930s and before. 3" - $60.00 up; 6" - $100.00 up; 8" - $150.00 up. New: 4" - $10.00; 6" - $20.00. Political: Includes Gorbachev, Yeltsin. 4½" - $25.00; 6½" - $40.00.

Swiss: Carved wooden dolls. Dowel jointed all wood bodies. Jointed elbows, hips, and knees. 8" - $400.00.

Fortune tellers: Wooden half or full doll with multi-folded papers for skirt. Paper pulled outward to allow fortune to be read. 17" - $2,400.00; 20" - $3,000.00.

Old 13" all wood, jointed mannikin with glass eyes. Maker unknown. Fully articulated, including ankles and knees. Looks hand carved. May have been early artist's model. $450.00. *Courtesy Ellen Dodge.*

Modern Dolls

21" "Nancy Lee" by Arranbee. All composition with sleep eyes. All original. $465.00. 8" "Debby" with painted eyes, and wrist tag. Mint in blue box, from 1950. $150.00. 8" painted eye "Ginny" as "Easter Girl" in green skirt and lace top. From 1950. $350.00. 8" "Ginny Indian" with painted eyes. All original and mint in box. $350.00. "Ginny Red Riding Hood" with painted eyes and all original. $350.00. "Ginny" as "Tiny Miss Series" from 1952. Dress in yellow with flowers in her hair, all original. $350.00.
Courtesy Frasher Doll Auctions.

17" "Yasmin" made by Adanta Corp. Has one-piece body and head and sleep eyes. Marked on head "P-$\frac{5}{23}$ with "A" on body. Circa 1955. In box - $65.00. *Courtesy David Spurgeon.*

MADAME ALEXANDER – ALEXANDER-KINS

The author's separate price guide covering over 1,000 Madame Alexander dolls is available from book dealers or Collector Books.

1953–1954: 7½–8" straight leg non-walker. Heavy hard plastic. **Party dress:** Mint, all correct - $600.00 up. Soiled, dirty hair, mussed, or parts of clothing missing - $95.00. **Ballgown:** Mint and correct - $800.00 up. Soiled, dirty, bad face color, not original - $150.00. **Nude:** Clean, good face color. $200.00. Dirty, bad face color - $40.00.

1955: 8" straight leg walker. **Party dress:** Mint, all correct - $425.00 up. Soiled, dirty, parts of clothes missing - $65.00. **Ballgown:** Mint, all correct - $800.00 up. Dirty, part of clothing missing,

etc. - $95.00. **Basic sleeveless dress:** Mint - $175.00. Dirty - $40.00. **Nude:** Clean, good face color - $200.00. Dirty, not original, faded face color - $35.00.

1956–1965: Bend knee walker. **Party Dress:** Mint, all correct - $350.00 up. Dirty, part of clothes missing, etc. - $50.00. **Ballgown:** Mint, correct - $800.00 up. Soiled, dirty, parts missing, etc. - $150.00. **Nude:** Clean, good face color - $200.00. Dirty, faded face color - $40.00. **Basic sleeveless dress:** Mint - $175.00. Dirty, faded face color - $40.00. **Internationals:** $65.00–265.00. Dirty, parts missing - $50.00.

1965–1972: Bend knee non-walker. **Party Dress:** Mint, original - $225.00 up. Dirty, missing parts - $40.00. **Internationals:** Clean, mint - $60.00. Dirty or soiled -

8" Alexander-kins dolls from 1955. Both are straight leg non-walkers and all original. On the left is "Victoria" and on the right is a bride doll. "Victoria" - $1,800.00; bride - $350.00. *Courtesy Turn of Century Antiques.*

$25.00. **Nude:** Clean, good face color - $85.00. Dirty, faded face color - $25.00.

1973–1976 ("Rosies"): Straight leg non-walker. Rosy cheeks. Marked "Alex." $45.00. **Bride or ballerina:** Bend knee walker - $200.00 up. Bend knee only - $150.00. Straight leg - $50.00. **Internationals:** $45.00. **Storybook:** $50.00.

1977–1981: Straight leg non-walker. Marked "Alexander." **Ballerina or bride:** $40.00–50.00. **International:** $50.00–60.00. **Storybook:** $45.00–55.00.

1982–1987: Straight leg non-walker. Deep indentation over upper lip that casts a shadow, makes doll look like it has mustache. **Bride or ballerina:** $45.00–55.00. **International:** $45.00–55.00. **Storybook:** $45.00–55.00.

1988–1989: Straight leg, non-walker with new face. Looks more like older dolls but still marked with full name "Alexander." **Bride or ballerina:** $45.00–55.00. **International:** $45.00–55.00. **Storybook:** $50.00–60.00.

MADAME ALEXANDER – BABIES

Prices are for mint condition dolls.

Baby Brother or Sister: 1977–1982. 14" - $75.00; 20" - $75.00.

Baby Ellen: 1965–1972. 14" - $100.00.

Baby Lynn: (Black "Sweet Tears") 1973–1975. 20" - $100.00.

Baby McGuffey: Composition. 22" - $300.00. Soiled - $150.00.

Bonnie: 1954–1955. Vinyl. 19" - $80.00. Soiled - $25.00.

Genius, Little: Composition. 18" - $150.00. Soiled - $50.00.

Genius, Little: Vinyl. May have flirty eyes. 21" - $185.00. Soiled - $65.00.

Genius, Little: 8" - $225.00 up. Soiled - $35.00.

Happy: 1970 only. Vinyl. 20" - $200.00. Soiled - $60.00.

Honeybun: 1951. Vinyl. 19" - $175.00. Soiled - $40.00.

Huggums, Big: 1963–1979. 25" - $95.00. **Lively:** 1963. 25" - $125.00.

Kathy: Vinyl. 19" - $100.00; 26" - $150.00. Soiled: 19" - $35.00; 26" - $50.00.

Kitten, Littlest: Vinyl. 8" - $175.00 up. Soiled - $35.00.

Mary Cassatt: 1969–1970. 14" - $150.00; 20" - $225.00.

Mary Mine: 14" - $75.00. Soiled - $25.00.

Pinky: Composition. 23" - $250.00. Soiled - $95.00.

Precious: Composition. 12" - $225.00. Soiled - $60.00.

Princess Alexandria: Composition. 24" - $225.00. Soiled - $80.00.

Pussy Cat: Vinyl. 14" - $95.00. Soiled - $25.00. Black: 14" - $110.00. Soiled - $40.00.

Rusty: Vinyl. 20" - $350.00. Soiled - $85.00.

Slumbermate: Composition. 21" - $500.00. Soiled - $185.00.

Sweet Tears: 9" - $50.00. Soiled - $15.00. With layette: $135.00.

Victoria: 20" - $75.00. Soiled - $35.00.

17½" "Lively Kitten" made of vinyl and cloth. Doll moves when knob in back is wound. Marked "Alexander 1962." $100.00. *Courtesy Lee Crane.*

8" "Littlest Kitten" all vinyl pay doll that had a varied wardrobe available. Sleep eyes and rooted hair. $175.00. *Courtesy Marge Meisinger.*

This 10–11" doll with high heel feet was made from 1957 to 1963, but the mold was used for other dolls later. She is made of hard plastic, and clothes will be tagged "Cissette."

The first price is for mint condition dolls and the second price is for soiled, dirty or faded clothes, tags missing and hair messy.

Street dresses: $275.00, $80.00
Ballgowns: $400.00, $125.00.
Ballerina: $325.00, $100.00.
Gibson Girl: $800.00, $250.00.
Jacqueline: $500.00 up, $145.00.
Margot: $400.00 up, $150.00.
Portrette: $450.00, $160.00.
Wigged in case: $850.00 up, $300.00.

10" "Queen" from 1957–1959. Dressed in gold brocade gown. $350.00. *Courtesy Flip Phelps.*

"Cissy" was made 1955–1959 and had hard plastic with vinyl over the arms, jointed at elbows, and high heel feet. Clothes are tagged "Cissy." Prices are for excellent face color and clean dolls.

Street dress: $350.00.
Ballgown: $775.00 up.
Bride: $500.00 up.
Queen: $825.00.
Portrait: "Godey," etc. 21" - $950.00 up.
Scarlett: $1,100.00.
Flora McFlimsey: Vinyl head, inset eyes. 15" - $650.00.

20" "Cissy" in ballgown from 1958. Mint with beautiful face color. $775.00. *Courtesy Shirley's Doll House.*

The Alexander Company made cloth/plush dolls and animals and oil cloth baby animals in the 1930s, 1940s and early 1950s. In the 1960s, only a few were made.

First prices are for mint condition dolls; second prices are for ones in poor condition, dirty, not original, played with or untagged.

Animals: $300.00 up, $85.00.

Dogs: $275.00, $95.00.

Alice in Wonderland: $650.00, $200.00.

Clarabelle The Clown: 19" - $350.00, $100.00.

David Copperfield or other boys: $650.00 up.

Funny: $65.00, $10.00.

Little Shaver: 7" - $275.00 up; 10" - $400.00.

Little Women: Each - $600.00 up, $150.00.

Muffin: 14" - $55.00, $25.00.

So Lite Baby or Toddler: 20" - $300.0 up, $100.00.

Susie Q: $650.00, $175.00.

Tiny Tim: $675.00, $250.00.

Teeny Twinkle: Has disc floating eyes. $450.00 up, $100.00.

16" "Alice in Wonderland" made of all cloth. This is an early model with flat face. Later ones have molded facial features. All original. $800.00. *Courtesy Green Museum.*

MADAME ALEXANDER – COMPOSITION

First prices are for mint condition dolls; second prices are for dolls that are crazed, cracked, dirty, soiled clothes or not original.

Alice in Wonderland: 9" - $350.00, $85.00; 14" - $450.00, $100.00; 21" - $950.00, $200.00.

Babs Skater: 1948. 18" - $750.00, $175.00.

Baby Jane: 16" - $850.00, $300.00.

Brides or bridesmaids: 7" - $225.00, $60.00; 9" - $250.00, $75.00; 15" - $325.00, $80.00; 21" - $525.00, $150.00.

Dionne Quints: 8" - $160.00, $50.00. Set of five - $1,200.00. 11" - $300.00, $100.00. Set of five - $2,000.00. Cloth Baby: 14" - $800.00, $175.00; 16" - $800.00, $200.00.

Dr. DeFoe: 14–15" - $1,400.00 up, $500.00.

Fairy Princess: 1939. 15" - $600.00; 21" - $950.00 up.

Flora McFlimsey: Has freckles. Marked "Princess Elizabeth." 15" - $500.00, $150.00; 22" - $800.00, $250.00.

Flower Girl: 1939–1947. Marked "Princess Elizabeth." 16" - $550.00,

$125.00; 20" - $750.00, $200.00; 24" - $900.00, $400.00.

Internationals/Storybook: 7" - $225.00, $50.00; 9" - $285.00, $75.00.

Jane Withers: 13" - $950.00 up, $400.00; 18" - $1,200.00, $500.00.

Kate Greenaway: Very yellow blonde wig. Marked "Princess Elizabeth." 14" - $600.00, $145.00; 18" - $850.00, $250.00.

13" closed mouth "Jane Withers." All composition with sleep eyes. All original in white dress and red/white coat. $950.00. *Courtesy Kathy Riddick.*

Little Colonel: 9" (rare size) - $700.00, $250.00; 13" - $600.00, $185.00; 23" - $850.00, $350.00.

Madelaine DuBain: 1937–1944. 14" - $475.00, $150.00; 17" - $575.00, $200.00.

Margaret O'Brien: 15" - $700.00, $250.00; 18" - $850.00, $250.00; 21" - $975.00, $425.00.

Marionettes by Tony Sarg: 12" - $325.00, $95.00. Disney: $325.00, $165.00. Others: 12" - $245.00, $95.00.

McGuffey Ana: Marked "Princess Elizabeth." 13" - $600.00, $185.00; 20" - $800.00, $350.00.

Military dolls: 1943–1944. 14" - $750.00, $300.00.

Nurse: 1936–1940. 14–15" - $525.00 up.

Portrait dolls: 1939–1941, 1946. 21" - $2,600.00 up, $1,000.00.

Princess Elizabeth: Closed mouth. 13" - $500.00, $175.00; 18" - $700.00, $250.00; 24" - $850.00, $350.00.

Beautiful "Sonja Henie" that is all original and in mint condition with wrist tag. Deep cheek dimples, open mouth, and sleep eyes. $950.00. *Courtesy Martha Sweeney.*

Scarlett: 9" - $550.00, $165.00; 14" - $800.00, $200.00; 18" - $1,100.00, $500.00; 21" - $1,500.00, $650.00.

Snow White: 1939–1942. Marked "Princess Elizabeth." 13" - $400.00, $135.00; 18" - $625.00, $200.00.

Sonja Henie: 17" - $950.00, $350.00; 20" - $1,100.00, $450.00. Jointed waist: 14" - $700.00, $250.00.

Wendy Ann: 11" - $500.00, $175.00; 15" - $600.00, $200.00; 18" - $750.00, $300.00.

MADAME ALEXANDER – HARD PLASTIC

First prices are for mint condition dolls; second prices are for dolls that are dirty, played with, soiled clothes or not original.

Alice in Wonderland: 14" - $600.00, $200.00; 17" - $675.00, $250.00; 23" - $800.00, $325.00.

Annabelle: 15" - $500.00, $175.00; 18" - $650.00, $200.00; 23" - $750.00, $275.00.

18" all hard plastic "Babs Skater" is original and has wonderful face color. Uses "Margaret" face. $750.00. *Courtesy Turn of Century Antiques.*

Babs: 20" - $750.00, $250.00.

Babs Skater: 18" - $750.00, $200.00; 21" - $800.00, $275.00.

Ballerina: 14" - $450.00, $175.00.

Brenda Starr: 1964 only. Dress: 12" - $175.00. Gown: $300.00 up. Bride: $300.00.

Binnie Walker: 15" - $135.00, $40.00; 25" - $450.00, $165.00.

Cinderella: In ballgown: 14" - $700.00, $200.00. "Poor" outfit: 14" - $650.00, $185.00.

Cynthia: Black doll. 15" - $750.00, $300.00; 18" - $950.00, $400.00; 23" - $1,200.00, $500.00.

Elise: In street dress: 16½" - $300.00, $90.00. Ballgown: $600.00 up, $200.00.

Bride: 16" - $325.00, $165.00.

Fairy Queen: 14½" - $675.00,

Godey Lady: 14" - $950.00, $300.00.

Man/Groom: 14" - $1,000.00, $400.00.

Kathy: 15" - $550.00, $175.00.

Kelly: 12" - $375.00, $125.00.

Lissy: Street dress: 12" - $285.00, $125.00. Bride: $400.00, $175.00. Ballerina: $325.00, $150.00.

Little Women: 8" - $135.00, $60.00. Set of five with bend knees - $700.00; Set of five with straight legs - $350.00. Using Lissy doll: 12" - $300.00, $100.00. Set of five - $1,500.00. 14" - $425.00. Set of five - $1,500.00. **Laurie:** Bend knee. 8" - $145.00 up, $60.00; 12" - $350.00, $150.00.

Madeline: 1950–1953. Jointed knees and elbows. 18" - $950.00 up, $300.00.

Maggie: 15" - $450.00, $150.00; 17" - $625.00, $225.00; 23" - $750.00, $300.00.

Maggie Mixup: 8" - $425.00 up, $150.00; 16½" - $375.00, $145.00. Angel: 8" - $675.00, $175.00.

Margaret O'Brien: 14½" - $875.00, $400.00; 18" - $1,000.00, $500.00; 21" - $1,250.00, $575.00.

Marybel: 16" - $350.00, $125.00.

Mary Martin: Sailor suit or ballgown. 14" - $850.00 up, $450.00; 17" - $1,000.00, $450.00.

McGuffey Ana: 1948–1950. Hard plastic. 21" - $850.00, $375.00.

Peter Pan: 15" - $800.00 up, $375.00.

Polly Pigtails: 14" - $525.00, $175.00; 17" - $650.00, $200.00.

Prince Charming: 14" - $775.00, $275.00; 18" - $875.00, $300.00.

Queen: 18" - $750.00 up, $325.00.

Shari Lewis: 14" - $400.00, $165.00; 21" - $600.00, $250.00.

Sleeping Beauty: 16½" - $550.00, $150.00; 21" - $950.00, $425.00.

Wendy (Peter Pan set): 14" - $700.00, $300.00.

Wendy Ann: 14½" - $725.00, $250.00; 17" - $875.00, $400.00; 22" - $925.00, $425.00.

Winnie Walker: 15" - $165.00, $60.00; 18" - $250.00, $80.00; 23" - $350.00, $95.00.

18" "Glamour Girl" using the "Maggie" face doll with large round eyes. All original except missing tafetta hat. $1,300.00 up. *Courtesy Kris Lundquist.*

18" "Miss 1950" from the very rare "Century of Fashion" series. All hard plastic. Doll and gown in near mint condition (hair has been combed). $1,500.00 up. *Courtesy Kris Lundquist.*

First prices are for mint condition dolls; second prices are for dolls that are played with, soiled, dirty and missing original clothes.

Bellows' Anne: 1987 only. 14" - $75.00.

Bonnie Blue: 1989 only. 14" - $95.00.

Bride: 1982–1987. 17" - $135.00.

Caroline: 15" - $285.00, $100.00.

Cinderella: Pink: 1970–1981. Blue: 1983–1986. 14" - $75.00.

Edith The Lonely Doll: 1958–1959. 16" - $245.00; 22" - $325.00.

Elise: Street dress: Made in 1966. 17" - $200.00. Formal: 1966, 1976–1977. $175.00. Bride: 1966–1986. $175.00.

First Ladies: First set of six - $700.00. Second set of six - $550.00. Third set of six - $475.00. Fourth set of six - $550.00. Fifth set of six - $475.00. Sixth set of six - $600.00.

Grandma Jane/Little Granny: 1970–1972. 14" - $225.00, $80.00.

Ingres: 1987 only. 14" - $75.00.

Isolde: 1985 only. 14" - $70.00.

Jacqueline: Street Dress: 21" - $650.00, $250.00. Ballgown: $800.00 up, $350.00. Riding Habit: $650.00, $225.00.

Janie: 12" - $285.00, $100.00.

Joanie: 36" - $450.00, $185.00.

Leslie: Black doll. Ballgown: 17" - $350.00, $200.00. Ballerina: $350.00, $200.00. Street dress: $375.00, $165.00.

Little Shaver: 1963 only, vinyl. 12" - $300.00, $100.00.

Nancy Drew: 1967 only. 12" - $375.00, $100.00.

Napoleon: 1980–1986. 12" - $60.00.

Marybel: 16" - $250.00, $90.00. In case: $350.00 up; $175.00.

Mary Ellen: 31" - $600.00 up, $275.00.

Melinda: 14" - $375.00, $150.00; 16" - $425.00, $175.00.

Michael with bear: Peter Pan set. 11" - $350.00, $125.00.

Peter Pan: 14" - $300.00, $100.00.

Polly: 17" - $325.00, $125.00.

29" "Barbara Jane" made in 1952 only. Vinyl with rooted hair, sleep eyes. All original and in exceptional condition. $450.00 up. *Courtesy Cris Johnson.*

Renoir Girl: 14" - $100.00–50.00. With watering can: 1986–1987. $85.00–35.00. With hoop: 1986–1987. $85.00–35.00.

Scarlett: White gown, green ribbon. 1969–1986. 14" - $145.00, 70.00.

Smarty: 12" - $365.00, $145.00.

Sound of Music: Small set: $1,400.00. Large set: $1,700.00. **Liesl:** 10" - $200.00, $95.00; 14" - $225.00, $95.00. **Louisa:** 10" - $265.00, $125.00; 14" - $300.00, $145.00. **Brigitta:** 10" - $225.00, $95.00; 14" - $225.00, $95.00. **Maria:** 12" - $350.00, $150.00; 17" - $375.00, $160.00; **Marta:** 8" - $225.00, $75.00; 11" - $200.00, $145.00. **Gretl:** 8" - $225.00, $95.00; 11" - $200.00, $145.00. **Friedrich:** 8" - $225.00, $95.00; 11" - $200.00, $100.00.

Wendy: Peter Pan set. 14" - $300.00, $100.00.

18" "Kelly" using the "Marybel" doll of 1958. All vinyl with jointed waist and sleep eyes. All original. $450.00. *Courtesy Floyd and Gracie James.*

14" "Elise-Leslie" made in 1989 for one year only. All original. $95.00. *Courtesy Roger Jones.*

Prices are for mint condition dolls. There are many 21" portrait dolls and all use the Jacqueline face. The early ones have jointed elbows; later dolls have one-piece arms. All will be marked "1961" on head.

Agatha: 1967–1980. $500.00.

Bride: 1965. $900.00 up.

Coco: 1966. Portrait: 21" - $2,000.00. Street Dress: $2,200.00. Ballgown: Other than portrait series. $2,400.00.

Cornelia: 1972–1978. $225.00–475.00.

Gainsborough: 1968–1978. $425.00–650.00.

Godey: 1965, 1967–1977. $550.00, $275.00–550.00.

Jenny Lind: 1969. $1,300.00.

Lady Hamilton: 1968: $475.00.

Madame Pompadour: 1970. $1,200.00.

Magnolia: 1977: $475.00. 1988: $275.00.

Manet: 1982–1983. $250.00.

Melanie: 1967–1989. $300.00–600.00.

Mimi: 1971. $525.00.

Monet: 1984. $285.00.

Morisot: 1985–1986. $225.00.

Queen: 1965. $700.00 up.

Renoir: 1965–1973. $525.00–850.00.

Scarlett: 1965–1989. $300.00–950.00 up.

Toulouse-Lautrec: 1986–1987. $200.00.

21" "Queen" dolls made by Madame Alexander. Left: Dressed in gold brocade. From 1968. Right: Dressed in white and very hard to find, especially in this condition. From 1965. Each - $950.00. *Courtesy Turn of Century Antiques.*

22" "Snow Baby" made for B. Altman & Co. in association with American Heritage Books. Flannel type material with fur trim and has B. Altman name on bodice. Attached pants, removable jacket. Vinyl head, painted eyes, and molded hair. Marked "Made exclusively for B. Altman. 1988." $125.00 up. *Courtesy Kathy Tvrdick.*

AMERICAN CHARACTER DOLL COMPANY

All American Character dolls are very collectible and all are above average in quality of doll material and clothes. Dolls marked "American Doll and Toy Co." are also made by American Character, and this name was used from 1959 until 1968 when the firm went out of business. Early dolls will be marked "Petite." Many will be marked "A.C."

First prices are for mint dolls; second prices are for dolls that have been played with, dirty, with soiled clothes or not original.

"A.C." marked child: Composition. In excellent condition. 14" - $175.00, $60.00; 20" - $275.00, $115.00.

Annie Oakley: 1955. Hard plastic. Original. 7" - $425.00, $160.00.

Betsy McCall: See Betsy McCall section.

Butterball: 1961. 19" - $150.00, $75.00.

Campbell Kid: 1929–1931. Composition toddler. Curl in middle of forehead. Marked "Petite." (Allow more for original dress with tag.) 12" - $300.00.

Carol Ann Beery: Daughter of Wallace Beery. All composition, sleep eyes, closed mouth. Mohair wig with braid over top of head. Marked "Petite Sally" or "Petite." 13" - $500.00; 16½" - $725.00; 19½" - $975.00.

Cartwrights: Ben, Hoss, Little Joe: 1966. 8" - $125.00, $50.00.

Chuckles: 1961. 23" - $165.00, $75.00. Baby: 18" - $125.00, $50.00.

Composition babies: 1930s–1940s. Cloth bodies, marked "A.C." In excellent condition. 16" - $200.00, $90.00. 24" - $325.00, $70.00. Marked **"Petite":** 1920s–

1930s. 14" - $150.00, $60.00; 22" - $225.00, $90.00.

Cricket: 1964. 9" - $30.00, $15.00. Growing hair: $35.00, $12.00.

Eloise: 1950s. Cloth character with yarn hair and crooked smile. (See photo in Series 7, pg. 212.) 14–15" - $250.00; 21" - $375.00 up. Christmas dress: 15" - $350.00; 21" - $475.00.

Freckles: 1966. Face changes. 13" - $30.00, $15.00.

Hedda-Get-Betta: 1960. 21" - $95.00, $45.00.

Miss Echo, Little: Talker, 1964. (See photo in Series 8, pg. 190.) 30" - $250.00, $95.00.

"Petite" marked child: Composition. 16" - $250.00, $85.00; 20" - $300.00, $100.00; 24–25" - $375.00, $165.00.

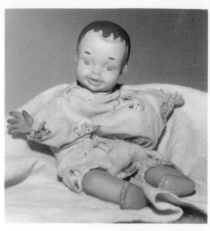

11" "Ricky Jr." with cloth puppet body and blanket attached to the body. Vinyl head with painted and molded features. Vinyl arms and legs. Has tag identifying as "Ricky Jr." from the *I Love Lucy Show.* Head is unmarked but made by Zany Toys, Inc. in 1953. $35.00 up. *Courtesy Susan Giradot.*

Preteen: 14" child marked "AM. Char. 63." (1963) **Grow hair:** $35.00, $15.00.

Puggy: 1929–1931. All composition, painted eyes, frown. Has pug nose. Marked "Petite." 12–13" - $500.00, $165.00.

Ricky, Jr.: 1955–1956. 13" - $50.00, $35.00; 20" - $100.00, $50.00. Hand puppet: $25.00.

Sally: 1929–1935. Composition, molded hair in "Patsy" style. Painted eyes. 12" - $200.00, $75.00; 14" - $225.00, $80.00. 16" - $285.00, $85.00; 18" - $325.00, $145.00. **Sally Joy:** 24" - $385.00 up.

Sally: Shirley Temple look-alike with full bangs and ringlet curls around head. Composition/cloth. Sleep eyes, open mouth. 16" - $250.00; 18" - $300.00; 24" - $365.00.

Sally Says: 1965. Talker, plastic/vinyl. 19" - $75.00, $35.00.

Sweet Sue/Toni: 1949–1960. Hard plastic, some walkers, some with extra joints at knees, elbows and/or ankles,

21" "Eloise" cloth doll with face mask, painted features, and yarn hair. Wearing her tagged Christmas dress. Doll and outfit are original and mint. $475.00. *Courtesy Susan Giradot.*

some combination hard plastic and vinyl. Marked "A.C. Amer. Char. Doll," or "American Character" in circle. **Must have excellent face color and be original. Ballgown:** 1958. 10½" - $150.00, $75.00; 15" - $265.00, $85.00; 18" - $325.00, $125.00. **Street dress:** 1958. 10½" - $125.00, $50.00; 15" - $225.00, $70.00; 18" - $300.00, $100.00; 22" - $350.00, $125.00; 24" - $375.00, $150.00; 30" - $550.00, $200.00. **Vinyl:** 10½" - $150.00, $50.00; 14" - $165.00, $60.00; 17" - $225.00, $60.00; 21" - $325.00, $100.00; 25" - $400.00, $175.00; 30" - $550.00 up, $200.00. **Groom:** 20" - $425.00, $150.00. **Mint in box:** 14" - $325.00 up; 17–18" - $400.00 up; 20" - $450.00.

30" all hard plastic "Sweet Sue Bride" with vinyl one-piece arms. Legs are jointed at knees. Original. $250.00 up.

A beautifully kept 13" "Ricky Jr." that is all original and the childhood doll of owner Theo Lindley. $50.00.

20" all heavy vinyl "Toodles Baby." All original including the cute gloves. $225.00. *Courtesy Christine McWilliams.*

Talking Marie: 1963. Record player in body, battery operated. Vinyl/plastic. 18" - $95.00, $40.00.

Tiny Tears: 1955–1962. **Hard plastic/vinyl:** 8" - $50.00, $20.00; 13" - $150.00, $45.00; 17" - $200.00, $90.00. **All vinyl:** 1963. 8" - $30.00, $15.00; 12" - $40.00, $20.00; 16" - $55.00, $25.00. **Mint in box:** 13" - $300.00 up.

Toodles: 1956–1960. **Baby:** 14" - $125.00, $50.00; 18" - $225.00, $85.00. **Tiny:** 10½" - $165.00, $50.00. **Toddler:** With "follow me eyes." 22" - $225.00, $80.00; 24" - $250.00, $95.00; 28" - $300.00, $130.00; 30" - $325.00, $165.00. **Mint in box:** 28–30" - $400.00 up.

24" "Toodles" with open/closed mouth, painted teeth, and large sleep eyes with lashes. All original. Marked "American Doll & Toy Corp. 19©60" on head. $250.00. *Courtesy private collection.*

10" "Toni" marked "American Character" and is mint with original box. These dolls could be purchased as shown and extra packaged clothes were available for them or they could be purchased wearing clothes. Mint condition - $225.00; near mint - $150.00. *Courtesy Karen Stephenson.*

Toodle-Loo: 1961. 18" - $165.00, $65.00.

Tressy: 12½". **Grow Hair:** 1963–1964. (#1 heavy makeup). $55.00, $20.00. **#2 Mary/Magic Makeup:** 1965–1966. Pale face, no lashes, bend knees. $30.00, $10.00. **Miss America:** 1963. $50.00 up.

Whimette/Little People: 1963. 7½" - $20.00, $10.00.

Whimmsie: 1960. 19" - $95.00, $40.00. **Hilda the Hillbilly or Devil:** $125.00.

13" "Tiny Tear" with rooted hair, hard plastic head, and vinyl body and limbs. Open mouth nurser. All original and mint in case with wardrobe. Mint in case - $300.00; doll only - $125.00. *Courtesy Ellyn McCorkell.*

One of the most difficult "Whimmsie" dolls to find – "Hilda the Hillbilly." All original, including tears in apron. $125.00. *Courtesy Ellyn McCorkell.*

The first Annalee tags were red woven lettering on white linen tape. Second tags were made of white rayon with red embroidered lettering. The third tags, around 1969, were red printing on white satin tape. The fourth tags, about 1976, had red printing on gauze-type cloth. The hair on dolls from 1934–1963 was made of yarn. From 1960–1963, it was made of orange or yellow chicken feathers. Since 1963, the hair has been made of synthetic fur.

Animals became part of the line in 1964. On the oldest models, tails were made of the same materials as the body. During the mid-1970s, cotton bias tape was used and the ones made during the 1980s are made of cotton flannel.

Child: 1950s: 10" - $1,200.00 up. **1960s:** 10" - $600.00 up. **1970s:** 10" - $300.00 up. **1980s:** $175.00 up.

Adults: 1950s: 10" - $2,500.00 up. 1970s: 7" - $800.00.

Babies: Usually angels. 1960s: 7–8" - $325.00. 1970s: 7" - $275.00. 1980s: 7" - $200.00.

Old clown by Annalee has satin tag. Round tummy and large round red nose. Hand signed by maker. $95.00. *Courtesy Kris Lundquist.*

12" gnome from 1978 came in four colors – red, kelly green, white, and mint green. (10,140 were made.) Shown with 1980 gnome. (13,238 were made.) 1978 - $300.00; 1980 - $135.00. *Courtesy Bette Todd.*

Clowns: 1970s. 18" - $450.00; 10" - $125.00. 1978: Baggy pants. 42" - $700.00.

Elf/Gnome: 1970s: 7" - $225.00; 12" - $300.00. 1980s: 7" - $85.00; 12" - $135.00; 16" - $185.00; 22" - $225.00.

Indians: 1970s: 7" - $225.00. 1980s: 8" - $175.00 up; 18" - $250.00 up.

Monks: 1970s: 8" - $85.00 up.

Santa/Mrs. Claus: 1970s: 7" to 26" - $75.00-200.00. 1980s: 7 to 30" - $45.00-450.00.

Skiers: 1960s: 7" - $600.00 up. 1970s: 7" - $300.00. 1980s: 7" - $95.00 up.

Bears: 1970s: 7" - $150.00 up; 10" - $185.00 up; 18" - $265.00 up. 1980s: 7" - $80.00 up; 10" - $150.00 up; 18" - $175.00 up.

Mice: 1970s. Fireman: $350.00. Groom: $200.00. Desert Storm: 1991. $90.00.

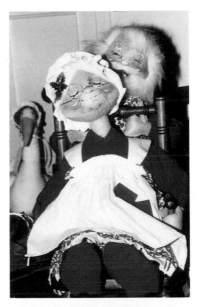

30" "Santa and Mrs. Claus" by Annalee. Very posable. Made in the 1970s. Each - $450.00. *Courtesy Nell Hudson.*

Large 18" elves from the 1980s. Note different facial expressions. Original. $200.00.

Tiny Annalee Santa mouse that is old and has a satin tag. $85.00. *Courtesy Kris Lundquist.*

The Arranbee Doll Company began making dolls in 1922 and was purchased by the Vogue Doll Company in 1958. Vogue used the Arranbee marked molds until 1961. Arranbee used the initials "R & B."

First prices are for mint condition dolls; second prices are for dolls that have been played with, are cracked, crazed, dirty or do not have original clothes.

Babies: Bisque heads. See Armand Marseille section.

Babies: Original. 1930s–1940s. Composition/cloth bodies. 16" - $125.00, $50.00; 22" - $150.00, $60.00.

Bottletot: 1932–1935. Has celluloid bottle molded to celluloid hand. 18" - $265.00, $95.00.

Debu-Teen: 1940. Composition girl with cloth body. 12" - $175.00, $65.00; 14" - $185.00, $65.00; 18" - $245.00, $80.00; 21" - $300.00, $110.00.

Dream Baby, My: (See Armand Marseille section for bisque heads.) **Composition:** 1934–1944. 14" - $250.00 up, $95.00; 16" - $300.00 up; 19" - $450.00 up. **Vinyl/cloth:** 1950. 16" - $65.00, $30.00; 23" - $140.00, $50.00.

Kewty: 1934–1936. Original. Composition "Patsy" style molded hair. Marked "R&B." (Kewty marked with name on back made by Domec toy Co., 1930.) 10" - $145.00, $45.00; 16" - $225.00, $85.00.

Littlest Angel: 1956. All hard plastic. 10" - $50.00, $20.00. **Vinyl head:** 10" - $30.00, $10.00. **Red hair/freckles (Lil Imp):** 1960. 10" - $70.00, $30.00.

11" "Debu-Teen Ice Skater" with sleep eyes. Made of all composition. Very rare size and outfit. All original. $000.00. *Courtesy Patricia Wood.*

21" all hard plastic "Nancy Lee" by Arranbee. Beautiful face color. Has replaced socks. $325.00. *Courtesy Kris Lundquist.*

24" composition "Nanette" with human hair wig, glassene sleep eyes, cloth body, and swivel head on composition shoulder plate. Paper tag pinned to dress. Original and in extremely mint condition. Mint - $650.00; near mint - $450.00. *Courtesy Susan Giradot.*

Miss Coty: 1958. Vinyl, marked " Ⓟ ." (" Ⓟ " dolls also dressed and marketed by Belle Doll Co.) 10" - $100.00, $30.00.

My Angel: 1961. Plastic/vinyl. 17" - $45.00, $20.00; 22" - $75.00, $40.00; 36" - $185.00, $90.00. Walker: 1957–1959. 30" - $200.00. Oil cloth body/vinyl: 1959. 22" - $65.00.

Nancy: 1936–1940. Composition, molded hair or wig. Sleep eyes, open mouth. 12" - $200.00, $85.00; 17" - $300.00, $125.00; 19" - $375.00, $140.00. **Hard plastic:** Vinyl arms/head: 1951–1952 only. **Wig:** 14" - $135.00, $70.00; 18" - $200.00, $90.00. **Walker:** 24" - $250.00, $100.00. **Cloth body:** Rest is composition. Molded

wavy hair combed to side. 12" - $200.00; 14" - $250.00; 17" - $300.00.

Nancy Lee: 1939. **Composition:** 12" - $180.00; 14" - $235.00, $95.00; 17" - $300.00, $125.00; 20" - $365.00, $150.00. **Hard plastic:** 1950–1959. 14" - $265.00, $100.00; 20" - $465.00, $150.00.

Nancy Lee: 1934–1939. Baby with composition head and limbs, open mouth with upper and lower teeth. 25" - $265.00, $100.00.

Nancy Lee: 1952. Baby, painted eyes, "crying" look. 15" - $145.00, $70.00.

Nancy Lee: 1954. Unusual eyebrows/vinyl. 15" - $160.00, $70.00.

Nanette: 1949–1959. Hard plastic or composition. 14" - $225.00, $80.00; 17" - $275.00, $95.00; 21" - $325.00 up, $125.00; 23" - $425.00, $150.00. **Walker:** 1957–

14" all hard plastic "Nanette" in dress designed by Schiaparelli. Hem is tight around legs and dress "balloons" out. Missing shoes and hoses. Floss-like wig is "high style." $265.00.

1959. Jointed knees. 18" - $300.00, $125.00; 25" - $465.00, $200.00. **Plastic/vinyl walker:** 1955–1956. 30" - $195.00, $95.00. **Hard plastic:** Mint in box. 17" - $450.00 up.

Sonja Skater: 1945. Composition. Some have "Debu-Teen" tag. 10–12" - $175.00; 14" - $245.00, $80.00; 17" - $285.00, $90.00; 21" - $350.00, $100.00.

Storybook dolls: 1930–1936. All composition. Molded hair, painted eyes. 9–10" - $165.00, $45.00. **Mint in box:** $250.00 up.

Taffy: 1956. Looks like Alexander's "Cissy." 23" - $80.00, $40.00.

14" all hard plastic "Nanette Bride" with mohair wig and sleep eyes. All original. Early 1950s. $225.00. *Courtesy Pat Graff.*

18" composition "Sonja Skater" with sleep eyes. All original and in mint condition. In this mint condition - $450.00; near mint condition - $325.00 up. *Courtesy Kris Lundquist.*

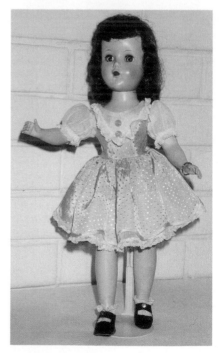

14" all hard plastic "Nanette" walker. All original. From 1954. $200.00. *Courtesy Pat Graff.*

First prices are for mint dolls; second prices are for dolls in average condition, dirty, soiled, or not original.

Alfred E. Newman: Vinyl head. 20" - $200.00, $125.00.

Captain Kangaroo: 19" - $125.00, $80.00; 24" - $225.00, $95.00.

Christopher Robin: 18" - $145.00, $60.00.

Daisy Mae: 14" - $200.00, $55.00; 21" - $285.00, $100.00.

Emmet Kelly (Willie the Clown): (See photo in Series 10, pg. 199.) 15" - $165.00, $45.00; 24" - $250.00, $85.00.

Lil' Abner: 14" - $200.00, $55.00; 21" - $285.00, $100.00.

Mammy Yokum: 1957. (See photo in Series 9, pg. 203.) Molded hair: 14" - $200.00, $100.00; 21" - $300.00, $125.00. **Yarn hair:** 14" - $250.00, $100.00; 21" - $350.00, $135.00. **Nose lights up:** 23" - $400.00, $150.00.

Pappy Yokum: 1957. 14" - $150.00; 21" - $300.00, $125.00. Nose lights up: 23" - $400.00, $150.00.

Close-up of 14" "Mammy Yokum" with both eyes open. Most have eye over pipe squinted closed. Vinyl and cloth. Pipe is removable. Marked "Baby Berry 1957." (For full-length view of doll, see photo in Series 9, pg. 203.) $200.00. *Courtesy Phyllis Houston-Kates.*

Prices are as accurate as possible, but one must remember a price guide is just a "guide," and prices vary from coast to coast. These prices are based on mint in box doll and accessories. (Must be *mint*, but may have been removed from box.) Second price, when indicated, is for doll only.

Barbie® is a registered trademark of Mattel Inc. See related dolls, such as "Midge," "Ken," etc. in Mattel section.

Mattel's # 3 "Barbie" with brunette hair. Mint and dressed in "Wedding Day." $625.00. *Courtesy Susan Giradot.*

Angel Face: $30.00.

Astronaut: $50.00.

Baby Sits: 1963–1965: $250.00. 1974–1976: $55.00.

Baggies: Doll in plastic bag. $55.00–95.00.

Ballerina: $30.00.

Beautiful Bride: $200.00. With hair lashes: $250.00.

Beauty Secrets: $40.00.

Bendable legs: 1965: $700.00. 1966: $1,200.00.

Bild Lilli: German. Mint - $400.00 up.

Black: $45.00.

Bubble cut: $275.00.

Busy: $200.00.

Busy Talking: $275.00.

Color Magic: $1,400.00, $600.00 up.

Crystal: $30.00.

Day to Night: $25.00.

Dream Date: $30.00.

Dream Glow: $20.00.

Dreamtime: $15.00.

Dressed boxed doll: $300.00 up. Pink Silhouette: $800.00 up. Wedding Day set: $1,500.00 up.

Eskimo: $150.00.

Fashion Jeans: $20.00.

Fashion Photo: $65.00.

Fashion Queen: $500.00.

Feelin' Groovy: $140.00.

Free Moving: $65.00.

Fun Time: $15.00.

Gift Giving: $15.00.

Gift Sets: NRFB prices. **Barbie Hostess:** $2,000.00 up. **Barbie & Ken Little Theatre:** $2,800.00. **Barbie, Ken & Midge Pep Rally:** $1,700.00. **Barbie, Ken & Midge on Parade:** $2,000.00. **Barbie Movie Groovy (Sears):** $350.00. **Barbie Perfectly Plaid (Sears):** $350.00. **Barbie Round The Clock:** $950.00. **Barbie Sparkling Pink:** $950.00. **Barbie Travels In Style (Sears):** $700.00. **Barbie & Ken Tennis:** $1,500.00. **Barbie Color Magic (Sears):** $1,500.00. **Fashion Queen & Friends:** $700.00. **Fashion Queen & Ken Trousseau:** $1,800.00. **Mix & Match (ponytail or bubble cut):** $1,000.00. **Party Set:** $1,800.00. **Trousseau Set:** $3,000.00.

German: $75.00.

Golden Dream: $40.00.

Gold Medal: $90.00. Skater: $35.00. Skier: $15.00.

Great Shape: $15.00.

Growing Pretty Hair: 1971: Pink. $295.00. 1972: Blue. $295.00.

Hair Fair: $85.00.

Hair Happenin's: $80.00.

Happy Birthday: White or pink. $25.00.

Hawaiian: $40.00.

Hispanic: $60.00.

Rare Barbie Hostess Set still mint in the box. "Barbie entertains! You help her be a perfect hostess with 2 fashion ensembles and complete 46 piece Cook 'n Serve set." $2,000.00 up. *Courtesy Susan Giradot.*

Horse Lovin': Formerly Western. $30.00.
India: $125.00.
Italian: $195.00.
Japanese: $100.00.
Jewel Secrets: $20.00.
Kissing: $45.00. With bangs: $60.00.
Live Action: $150.00. On stage: $175.00.
Living: $175.00.
Loving You: $60.00.
Magic Curl Moves: $25.00.
Malibu: 1971. $30.00.
Miss Barbie: $1,500.00.
My First: $25.00.
Newport: $125.00.
Oriental: $150.00.
Parisian: $125.00.
Peaches & Cream: $30.00.
Pink & Pretty: $35.00.
Plus Three: $50.00.
Ponytail: M.I.B. with second price for doll only. **#1:** Blonde: $3,400.00, $2,200.00. Brunette: $3,800.00; $2,400.00. **#2:** Blonde: $3,200.00, $2,400.00. Brunette: $3,500.00, $2,600.00. **#3:** $800.00, $600.00. **#4:** $500.00, $325.00. **1962–1965:** $400.00, $200.00.
Pretty Changes: $35.00.
Quick Curl: $60.00. Deluxe: $75.00.
Rocker Barbie: 1986–1987. $30.00.
Roller Skating: $50.00.
Royal: $250.00.
Scottish: $150.00.
Sears Celebration: $60.00.
Standard: 1967–1972. $325.00.
Spanish: $115.00.
Sun Gold Malibu: $18.00.
Sun Lovin': $25.00.
Sunsational: $25.00.
Sun Valley: $150.00.
Super Hair: $20.00.
Super Size: Bridal: $175.00. Super Hair: $150.00.
Super Star: $150.00. Fashion Change Abouts: $90.00. In The Spotlight: $70.00.
Swedish: $75.00.
Sweet Sixteen: $65.00.

Swirl Ponytail: $425.00.
Talking: $275.00. Spanish speaking: $300.00.
Spanish: $300.00.
Tropical: $15.00.
Twirly Curls: $25.00.
Twist N' Turn: $300.00.
Walk Lively: $195.00.
Ward's Anniversary: $600.00.
Western: $20.00.
Wig Wardrobe: $195.00.
Barbie items: Travel trailer: $50.00. **Silver Vette:** $65.00. **Roadster:** $200.00 up. **Sports car:** $175.00 up. **Sports car:** Orange. $85.00. **Ferrari:** White. $40.00. **Motor bike:** Pink. $45.00. **Splash cycle:** $50.00. **Speed boat:** $200.00 up. **Dune buggy:** $90.00 up. **Airplane:** $900.00 up. **"Dancer":** Brown horse. $200.00. **"Prancer":** All white

"Star Dream Barbie" was a Sears exclusive in 1987. $75.00. *Courtesy Shirley's Doll House.*

horse. $165.00. **"Dallas":** Palomino horse. $60.00. **"Dixie":** Pony. $45.00. **"Blinking Beauty":** All white horse with extremely long mane and tail. $40.00. **"Midnight":** All black horse. $50.00.

Special editions and store specials: Does not include all, just ones that are most likely to increase in value at a steady rate.

1988: Equestrienne: Toys 'Я Us. $45.00. **Lilac & Lovely:** Sears. $45.00. **Mardi Gras:** $85.00. **Tennis Barbie & Ken:** Toys 'Я Us. $40.00. **Sweet Dreams:** Toys 'Я Us. $35.00.

Barbie dressed as "Little Debbie" was advertised as a mail-in offer from Little Debbie Cakes in 1992. There was such a demand for this doll that the company couldn't fill all their first orders. Long brown hair, blue eyes. Blue gingham country dress trimmed in white eyelet. Straw hat. $50.00. *Courtesy Beth Summers.*

1989: Army: $30.00. **Dance Club:** Child's World. $45.00. **Denim Deluxe:** Toys 'Я Us. $25.00. **Evening Enchantment:** Sears. $45.00. **Golden Greeting:** FAO Schwarz. $150.00. **Gold n' Glitter:** Target. $35.00. **Lavender Look:** Wal-Mart. $25.00. **Party Lace:** Hills. $25.00. **Party Pink:** Winn-Dixie. $20.00. **Peach Pretty:** K-Mart. $40.00. **Pepsi Set:** Toys 'Я Us. $35.00. **Pink Jubilee:** $1,500.00. **Special Expressions:** Woolworth. $18.00. **Sweet Roses:** Toys 'Я Us. $25.00. **Sweet Treats:** Toys 'Я Us. $35.00. **UNICEF:** Four nations. Each - $35.00.

1990: Air Force: $35.00. **Barbie Style:** Applause. $35.00. **Dance Magic set:** $45.00. **Disney's Barbie:** Child's World. $35.00. **Dream Fantasy:** Wal-Mart. $25.00. **Evening Sparkle:** Hills. $30.00. **Party Sensation:** Wholesale Clubs. $75.00. **Pink Sensation:** Winn-Dixie. $20.00. **Special Expressions:** Woolworth. $15.00. **Summit:** Four nations. Each - $35.00. **Wedding Fantasy:** $30.00. **Western Fun-Sun Runner Gift Set:** $55.00. **Winter Fantasy:** FAO Schwarz. $150.00.

1991: All American: Wholesale Clubs. $55.00. **Ballroom Beauty:** Wal-Mart. $20.00. **Barbie Collector Doll:** Applause. $35.00. **Barbie & Friends Gift Set:** Disney and Toys 'Я Us. $55.00. **Blossom Beauty:** Shopko/Venture. $25.00. **Blue Rhapsody:** Service Merchandise. $25.00. **Cute & Cool:** Target. $20.00. **Dream Bride:** $40.00. **Enchanted Evening:** J.C. Penney. $25.00. **Golden Evening:** Target. $20.00. **Jewel Jubilee:** Sam's Club. $35.00. **Moonlight & Roses:** Hills. $20.00. **Navy:** $20.00. **Night Sensation:** FAO Schwarz. $135.00. **Party In Pink:** Ames. $20.00. **School Fun:** Toys 'Я Us. $25.00. **Southern Beauty:** Winn-Dixie. $20.00. **Southern Belle:** Sears. $35.00. **Star Stepper Gift Set:** Wholesale Clubs. $55.00. **Sterling Wishes:** Spiegel. $95.00. **Swan Lake Gift Set:** Wholesale Clubs. $55.00. **Sweet Romance:** Toys 'Я Us. $25.00.

1992: Anniversary Star: Wal-Mart. $35.00. **Barbie For President:** Toys 'Я Us. $20.00. **Blossom Beauty:** Sears. $55.00. **Blue Elegance:** Hills. $20.00. **Cool Look:** Toys 'Я Us. $20.00. **Cool 'N Sassy:** Toys 'Я Us. $20.00. **Dazzlin' Date:** Target. $25.00. **Denim 'N Lace:** $30.00. **Evening Flame:** Home Shopping Club. $00.00. **Evening Sensation:** J.C. Penney. $28.00. **Dr. Barbie:** Toys 'Я Us. $20.00. **Fantastica:** Pace. $35.00. **Hot Looks:** Ames. $25.00. **Little Debbie:** Little Debbie Cakes. $50.00. **Madison Avenue:** FAO Schwarz. $75.00. **Marine Corps:** $20.00. **Marine Barbie & Ken Gift Set:** $45.00. **My Size:** Three feet tall. $140.00. **Nutcracker:** $110.00. **Party Premiere:** Supermarkets. $20.00. **Party Perfect:** Shopko/Venture. $27.00. **Peach Blossoms:** Sam's Club. $25.00. **Picnic Pretty:** Osco. $20.00. **Pretty in Plaid:** Target. $25.00. **Pretty in Purple:** K-Mart. $22.00. **Radiant in Red:** Toys 'Я Us. $35.00. **Regal Reflections:** Spiegel. $95.00. **Royal Romance:** Price Clubs. $50.00. **Satin Nights:** Service Merchandise. $35.00. **School Fun:** Toys 'Я Us. $20.00. **Something Extra:** Meijers. $20.00. **Special Expressions:** Woolworth. $25.00. **Special Parade:** Toys 'Я Us. $20.00. **Sweet Lavender:** Woolworth. $23.00. **Very Violet:** Pace. $40.00. **Wild Style:** Target. $20.00.

1993: Army Desert Storm: $22.00. **Army Barbie & Ken Gift Set:** $45.00. **Back To School:** Supermarkets. $20.00. **Baseball:** Target. $20.00. **Country Looks:** Ames. $25.00. **Disney Fun:** Disney. $30.00. **Festiva:** Ames. $30.00. **Gibson Girl:** $60.00. **Golf Date:** Target. $20.00. **Golden Winter:** J.C. Penney. $25.00. **Holiday Hostess:** Supermarkets. $20.00. **Hollywood Hair Gift Set:** Wholesale Clubs. $30.00. **Island Fun Gift Set:** Wholesale Clubs. $20.00. **Love To Read:** Toys 'Я Us. $25.00. **Malt Shop:** Toys 'Я Us. $20.00. **Moonlight Magic:** Toys 'Я Us. $35.00. **1920s Flapper:** $60.00. **Paint 'n

Dazzle Gift Set: Wholesale Club. $30.00. **Police Officer:** Toys 'Я Us. $20.00. **Radiant In Red:** Toys 'Я Us. $30.00. **Rockette:** FAO Schwarz. $85.00. **Romantic Bride:** $35.00. **Royal Invitation:** Spiegel. $50.00. **School Spirit:** Toys 'Я Us. $20.00. **Secret Hearts Gift Set:** Wholesale Clubs. $20.00. **Shopping Fun:** Meijer. $22.00. **Special Expressions:** Woolworth. $18.00. **Sparkling Splendor:** Service Merchandise. $35.00. **Spring Bouquet:** Supermarkets. $20.00. **Spots 'n Dots:** Toys 'Я Us. $22.00. **Super Star:** Wal-Mart. $20.00. **Western Horse Gift Set:** Toys 'Я Us. $50.00. **Western Stampin' Gift Set:** Wholesale Clubs. $50.00. **Winter Royal:** Wholesale Clubs. $20.00. **Winter Princess:** Home Shopping Club. $70.00.

Bob Mackie collection: Designer Gold: 1990. $500.00. **Platinum:** 1991. $200.00. **Starlight Splendor:** 1991. $150.00. **Empress Bride:** 1992. $220.00. **Neptune's Daughter:** 1992. $150.00.

1988 "Holiday Barbie" in bright red. There was another one in burgundy a couple of years later, but this is the first in the series. $400.00. *Courtesy Kathy Tvrdik.*

Masquerade Ball: 1993. Harlequin costume. $200.00.

Other designers: Benefit Ball: 1992, Carol Spencer. $60.00. Opening Night: 1993, Janet Goldblatt. $60.00. City Style: 1993, Janet Goldblatt. $60.00.

Happy Holiday Barbie: 1988: $400.00. 1989: $110.00. 1990: White - $95.00; Black - $75.00. 1991: White - $75.00; Black - $55.00. 1992: White - $65.00; Black - $50.00. 1993: White or Black - $38.00.

Clothing, early years (1959–1963): After 5: $100.00. Apple print sheath: $125.00. American Airlines: $175.00. Ballerina: $150.00. Barbie Baby Sits: With apron - $250.00. With layette - $300.00. Barbie-Q outfit: $125.00. Bride's Dream: $175.00. Busy Gal: $300.00. Busy Morning: $225.00. Candy Striper: $350.00. Career Girl: $250.00. Cheerleader: $175.00. Commuter set: $600.00. Cotton Casual: $125.00. Cruise Stripe dress: $125.00. Dinner at Eight: $200.00. Drum

"American Girl Barbie" wearing "Saturday Matinee" outfit. A beautiful doll. $785.00.
Courtesy Susan Giradot.

Majorette: $150.00. Easter Parade: $2,000.00. Enchanted Evening: $250.00. Evening Splendor: $175.00. Fancy Free: $95.00. Fashion undergarments: $125.00. Floral petticoat: $125.00. Friday Night: $200.00. Garden Party: $95.00. Gay Parisienne: $1,600.00. Golden Elegance: $200.00. Golden Girl: $195.00. Graduation: $50.00. Icebreaker: $125.00. It's Cold Outside: $125.00. Knitting Pretty: Blue - $350.00; pink - $300.00. Let's Dance: $125.00. Masquerade: $150.00. Mood For Music: $125.00. Movie Date: $100.00. Nighty-Negligee: $125.00. Open Road: $250.00. Orange Blossom: $100.00. Party Date: $150.00. Peachy Fleecy coat: $95.00. Picnic Set: $250.00. Plantation Belle: $300.00. Red Flair: $125.00. Registered Nurse: $150.00. Resort Set: $125.00. Roman Holiday: $1,800.00. Senior Prom: $175.00. Sheath Sensation: $100.00. Silken Flame: $125.00. Singing in the Shower: $75.00. Ski Queen: $125.00. Solo in the Spotlight: $275.00. Sophisticated Lady: $250.00. Sorority Meeting: $175.00. Stormy Weather: $75.00. Suburban Shopper: $200.00. Sweater Girl: $125.00. Sweet Dreams: $175.00. Swingin' Easy: $125.00. Tennis Anyone: $50.00. Theatre Date: $125.00. Wedding Day Set: $350.00. Winter Holiday: $175.00.

Clothing, 1964–1966: Aboard Ship: $250.00. Beautiful Bride: $800.00. Beau Time: $225.00. Benefit Performance: $850.00. Black Magic: $250.00. Brunch Time: $250.00. Campus Sweetheart: $600.00. Caribbean Cruise: $150.00. Club Meeting: $250.00. Country Club Dance: $300.00. Country Fair: $125.00. Crisp 'n Cool: $140.00. Dancing Doll: $350.00. Debutante Ball: $450.00 up. Disc Date: $225.00. Dogs 'n Suds: $250.00. Dreamland: $125.00. Evening Enchantment: $475.00. Evening Gala: $275.00. Fabulous Fashion: $475.00. Fashion Editor: $300.00. Fashion

Luncheon: $600.00 up. **Floating Gardens:** $400.00. **Formal Occasion:** $450.00. **Fraternity Dance:** $425.00. **Fun At The Fair:** $230.00. **Fun 'n Games:** $230.00. **Garden Tea Party:** $125.00. **Garden Wedding:** $370.00. **Golden Evening:** $185.00. **Golden Glory:** $295.00. **Gold 'n Glamour:** $800.00. **Here Comes The Bride:** $900.00. **Holiday Dance:** $395.00. **International Fair:** $375.00. **Invitation To Tea:** $350.00. **Junior Designer:** $250.00. **Junior Prom:** $425.00. **Knit Hit:** $125.00. **Knit Separates:** $125.00. **Little Theater:** Arabian Nights - $275.00; Cinderella - $295.00; Guinevere - $225.00; Red Riding Hood/Wolf - $400.00. **London Tour:** $295.00. **Lunch Date:** $90.00. **Lunch on the Terrace:** $250.00. **Lunchtime:** $200.00. **Magnificence:** $450.00. **Matinee Fashion:** $350.00. **Midnight Blue:** $500.00. **Miss Astronaut:** $750.00. **Modern Art:** $325.00. **Music Center Matinee:** $500.00. **On the Avenue:** $400.00. **Outdoor Art Show:** $375.00. **Outdoor Life:** $200.00. **Pajama Party:** $85.00. **Pan Am Airways:** $2,000.00. **Poodle Parade:** $550.00. **Pretty as a Picture:** $350.00. **Reception Line:** $385.00. **Riding In The Park:** $400.00. **Satin 'n Rose:** $250.00. **Saturday Matinee:** $700.00. **Shimmering Magic:** $1,500.00. **Skater's Waltz:** $285.00. **Skin Diver:** $100.00. **Sleeping Pretty:** $200.00. **Sleepytime Gal:** $225.00. **Slumber Party:** $200.00. **Sorority Tea:** $175.00. **Student Teacher:** $275.00. **Sunday Visit:** $350.00. **Travel outfits:** Hawaii - $200.00; Holland - $200.00; Japan - $375.00; Mexico - $200.00; Switzerland - $200.00. **Underfashions:** $350.00. **Vacation Time:** $200.00. **White Magic:** $185.00.

The Mederato Era (1967–1971): An overwhelming amount of outfits was produced during these years, but many of them are beginning to increase in value at a fast pace. This era of clothing is broken down as follows:

Plain street length dresses that have only a few accessories such as Knit Hit, Midi Magic, Snap Dash, etc. $75.00 up.

Elaborate dresses with lots of accessories that have a "mod" look such as Zokko, All That Jazz, Sparkle Squares, etc. $125.00 up.

Formals and brides such as Romatic Ruffles, Silver Serenade, Winter Wedding, Let's Have A Ball, etc. $175.00 up.

The Years of Fears (1972–1976): During these years the quality of Barbie clothes was poor. The outfits that will continue to climb in value are the ones that reflect the times, such as granny dresses, bell bottoms, peasant dresses, and clothing with a "flower child" look. Most are priced between $20.00 and $45.00.

The Vigorous Era (1980–1990): Most are only worth what you purchased them for, but you should try to keep your collection current and they will rise in value as time goes by. The following have increased in value. Collector series: $45.00 up. Oscar de la Renta collector series: $45.00 up.

BETSY McCALL

First prices are for mint condition dolls; second prices are for played with, dirty, soiled or not original dolls.

8": All hard plastic, jointed knees. Made by American Character Doll Company in 1958. **Street dress:** $165.00, $70.00. **Ballgown:** $200.00 up, $90.00. **Bathing suit** or romper: $100.00, $40.00. **Ballerina:** $200.00; $65.00. **Riding** $200.00, $80.00.

11½": Vinyl/plastic with bro' eyes, and reddish rooted hair.

Made by Uneeda but unmarked. $95.00, $30.00.

13": Made by Horsman in 1975, but doll is marked "Horsman Dolls, Inc. 1967" on head. $65.00, $35.00.

14": Vinyl with rooted hair, medium high heels, and round sleep eyes. Made by American Character Doll Company in 1961. Marked "McCall 1958." $265.00 up, $95.00.

14": Vinyl head, hard plastic body and limbs. Rooted hair. Marked "P-90" body. Made by Ideal Doll Company. $250.00 up, $90.00.

14" "Betsy McCall" with vinyl head and hard plastic body. Made by Ideal Doll Corp. Body marked "P-90." $250.00. *Courtesy Susan Giradot.*

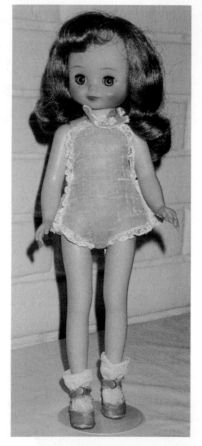

14" American Character "Betsy McCall" made of hard plastic with vinyl head. All original. From 1950. $00.00. *Courtesy Pat Graff.*

22": Extra joints at waist, ankles, wrists and above knees. Unmarked. Made by American Character Doll Company. $250.00, $80.00.

20": Vinyl with rooted hair and slender limbs. Made by American Character Doll Company. (Allow more for flirty eyes.) $300.00, $100.00.

22": Vinyl/plastic with extra joints. Made by Ideal Doll Company. $275.00 up, $100.00.

29-30": All vinyl with rooted hair. Made by American Character Doll Company. $400.00, $165.00.

29": Extra joints at ankles, knees, waist and wrists. Made by American Character Doll Company. Marked "McCall 1961." $400.00 up, $140.00.

29": Marked "B.M.C. Horsman 1971." $175.00, $60.00.

36": All vinyl with rooted hair. Made by American Character Doll Company. $550.00 up, $250.00.

36": Made by Ideal Doll Company. Marked "McCall 1959." $550.00 up, $225.00.

39": Boy called "Sandy McCall." Made by Ideal Doll Company. Marked "McCall 1959." $650.00 up, $300.00.

In background is a 14" "Betsy McCall" along with two 8" "Betsy McCall" dolls in the right foreground. All three are original. Shown with an all original 10½" "Sweet Sue Sophisticate Bride." 14" - $265.00; 8" - $200.00 each; 10½" - $225.00. *Courtesy Frasher Doll Auctions.*

29" "Betsy McCall" with painted blue eyes, open/closed mouth, painted teeth, and rooted hair. She is all original. Marked on head "B.M.C. Horsman 1971." Her 20" dog is plush with felt eyes and pom-pom nose. Came in black or white. Tagged "Knickerbocker Toy Co., Inc. New York. U.S.A. Betsy McCall's Puppy. McCall Corp." Doll - $175.00; dog - $250.00. *Courtesy Jeannie Mauldin.*

Right: 12" "Betty Boop" made of composition and wood. Made by Cameo Doll Co. Clothes are painted on. (Some chipping; dress is all black.) Left: Unusual composition head "Betty Boop" with silk body that is actually a purse. Tagged "Paramount Star Copyright Fleischer Studios." 12" in mint condition - $625.00; fair condition - $285.00. Purse - $550.00 up. *Courtesy Marcia Jarmush.*

BUDDY LEE

"Buddy Lee" dolls were made in composition to 1949, then changed to hard plastic and discontinued in 1962–1963. "Buddy Lee" came dressed in two Coca-Cola® uniforms. The tan with green stripe outfit matched the uniforms worn by delivery drivers while the white with green stripe uniforms matched those of plant workers. (Among Coca-Cola employees the white uniform became more popular and in warmer regions of the country, the white outfit was also worn by outside workers.)

"Buddy Lee" came in many different outfits.

Engineer: $275.00 up.

Gas station attendant: $250.00 up.

Cowboy: $300.00 up.

Coca-Cola uniform: White with green stripe - $450.00 up. Tan with green stripe - $500.00 up.

Other soft drink companies uniforms: $285.00 up.

Hard plastic: Original clothes. $300.00 up.

All hard plastic "Buddy Lee" from 1949. Original with gun and holster belt. $350.00 up. *Courtesy Jeannie Mauldin.*

Babyland General Hospital:
Cleveland, Georgia. Original dolls. (See photos in Series 5, pg. 173; Series 6, pg. 222; Series 7, pg. 203.)

"A" blue edition: Made in 1978. $1,500.00 up.

"B" red edition: Made in 1978. $1,200.00 up.

"C" burgundy edition: Made in 1979. $900.00 up.

"D" purple edition: Made in 1979. $800.00 up.

"X" christmas edition: Made in 1979. $1,200.00 up.

"E" bronze edition: Made in 1979. $600.00 up.

Preemie edition: Made in 1980. $650.00 up.

Celebrity edition: Made in 1980. $500.00 up.

Christmas edition: Made in 1980. $600.00 up.

Grand edition: Made in 1980. $750.00 up.

Rose edition "Baxter Joseph" and "Sheli Qyiana" from Babyland General Hospital. From 1984. Each - $100.00.

Left: 1986 brunette #10 with two bottom teeth, popcorn hairdo, and holding toothbrush. Right: 1986 #11 with dark gold popcorn hair, exposed tongue, and original clown suit. #10 - $45.00; #11: $50.00. *Courtesy Betty Chapman.*

New ears edition: Made in 1981. $125.00.
Ears edition: Made in 1982. $150.00 up.
Green edition: Made in 1983. $400.00 up.
"KP" dark green edition: Made in 1983. $550.00 up.
"KPR" red edition: Made in 1983. $550.00.
"KPB" burgundy edition: Made in 1983. $200.00.
Oriental edition: Made in 1983. $850.00.
Indian edition: Made in 1983. $850.00.
Hispanic edition: Made in 1983. $750.00.
"KPZ" edition: Made in 1983–1984. $175.00.
Champagne edition: Made in 1983–1984. $900.00.
"KPP" purple edition: Made in 1984. $250.00.

Porcelain "Cabbage Patch" was put on market in 1984. They looked exactly like the vinyl ones, but quality of clothes was much better. Made by Shaders China Doll, Inc. for Applause. Cost in 1984 was $227.00 plus tax.

Sweetheart edition: Made in 1984. $250.00.
Bavarian edition: Made in 1984. $250.00.
World Class edition: Made in 1984. $175.00 up.
"KPF," "KPG," "KPH," "KPI," "KPJ" editions: Made in 1984–1985. $100.00–150.00 up.
Emerald edition: Made in 1985. $100.00 up.

Coleco Cabbage Patch Dolls:
1983: Have powder scent and black signature stamp. Boys or girls: $95.00. Bald babies: $100.00 up. With pacifiers: $50.00–175.00. With freckles: $100.00 up. Black boys or girls with freckles: $175.00 up. Without freckles - $75.00 up. Red hair boys: Fuzzy hair. $175.00 up.

1984–1985: Green signature stamp in 1984; blue signature stamp in 1985. Only a few dolls of these years are worth more than retail prices. Single tooth: Brunette with ponytail. $165.00 up. Popcorn hairdos: Rare. $200.00. Gray-eyed girls: $165.00 up. Freckled girl with gold hair: $95.00 up.

Valued from retail to $65.00: From collectible years. Includes baldies, popcorn curl with pacifier, red popcorn curls with single tooth, and freckled girls with gold braided hair.

Valued slightly higher than retail: There are many various types and molds that are collected due to personal preferences. These include ringmaster, clown, baseball player, astronaut, travelers, twins, babies, talking Preemie, Splash Kid, Cornsilk Kid, etc. The value for these dolls is not more than $30.00–50.00. These dolls and others are easily attainable for collectors.

Annie Rooney, Little: 1926. All composition, legs painted black, molded shoes. 12" - $450.00 up; 17" - $750.00 up.

Baby Bo Kaye: 1925. Bisque head: See Antique section. **Celluloid head:** 12" - $350.00; 15" - $550.00. **Composition head:** Mint: 14" - $500.00. Light craze: Not original. 14" - $150.00.

Baby Mine: 1962–1964. Vinyl/cloth, sleep eyes. **Mint:** 16" - $100.00; 19" - $125.00. **Slightly soiled:** Not original. 16" - $40.00; 19" - $60.00. On "Miss Peep" hinged body: 16" - $145.00.

Bandy: Wood/composition. Ad doll for General Electric. Large ears. Painted-on majorette uniform. Non-removable tall hat. 17" - $425.00 up.

Betty Boop: See that section.

Champ: 1942. Composition with freckles. **Mint:** 16" - $500.00. **Light craze:** Not original. 16" - $175.00.

Giggles: 1946. Composition with molded loop for ribbon. **Mint:** 11" - $300.00; 14" - $565.00. **Light craze:** 11" - $145.00; 14" - $200.00.

Ho-Ho: 1940. **Plaster:** Excellent condition. 4" - $50.00. **Vinyl:** Excellent condition: 4" - $10.00.

Joy: 1932. Composition with wood jointed body. **Mint:** 10" - $275.00; 15" - $425.00. **Slight craze:** 10" - $125.00; 15" - $150.00.

Kewpie: See Kewpie section.

Margie: 1935. **Composition:** Mint condition. 6" - $165.00; 10" - $250.00. **Slight craze:** Not original. 6" - $100.00; 10" - $145.00. **Segmented wood/composition:** 1929. Mint. 9½" - $285.00, 125.00.

Miss Peep: 1957 and 1970s. Pin-jointed shoulders and hips. **Vinyl:** Mint condition and original. 1960s. 15" - $45.00; 18" - $60.00. **Black:** 18" - $75.00. Slightly soiled, not original. 18" - $28.00. Black, from 1972: 18" - $35.00. **Ball-jointed** shoulders and hips: 1970s–1980s. 17" - $55.00; 21" - $90.00.

Miss Peep, Newborn: 1962. Vinyl and plastic. **Mint:** Original. 18" - $35.00. Slight soil: Not original. 18" - $15.00.

15" "Baby Mine" with sleep eyes and molded hair. Open/closed mouth with molded tongue. $100.00. *Courtesy Phyllis Teague-Kates.*

Pete the Pup: 1930–1935. Composition with wood jointed body. **Mint:** 9" - $235.00. Slight craze: Few paint chips. 9" - $95.00.

Pinkie: 1930–1935. Composition: Mint: Original. 10" - $285.00. Slight craze: 10" - $145.00. **Wood jointed body:** 10" - $375.00. **Vinyl/plastic:** 1950s. Mint condition: 10–11" - $150.00. Slight soil: Not original. 10–11" - $75.00.

Scootles: 1925, 1930s. **All cloth** with fat legs, yarn hair, and dimples. No toe detail. **Composition:** Mint condition: Original. 8" - $365.00 up; 12" - $475.00 up; 15" - $625.00 up; 20" - $700.00; 22–23" - $785.00 up. Light craze: Not original. 8" - $100.00; 12" - $225.00; 15" - $285.00; 20" - $350.00; 22" - $385.00. **Composition/sleep eyes:** Mint condition: 15" - $700.00; 21" - $850.00 up. Slight craze: 15" - $300.00; 21" - $385.00. **Black, composition:** Mint: 15" - $775.00. Slight craze: 15" - $300.00. **Vinyl:** 1964. Mint: Original. 14" - $165.00

up; 19" - $325.00 up; 27" - $485.00 up. Lightly soiled: Not original. 14" - $80.00; 19" - $125.00; 27" - $200.00. **All bisque:** See that section.

Pretty Bettsie: Composition one-piece body and limbs. Separate wooden neck joint. Has molded hair. and smile mouth. Molded-on yellow, pink, or blue short dress with white ruffles at hem. Painted-on shoes and socks. Chest paper label marked "Pretty Bettsie/Copyright J. Kallus." 9" - $225.00; 14" - $300.00 up.

17" rare "Scootles" that is all cloth with chubby limbs, face mask, cheek dimples, and tight yarn hair. Replaced romper suit of the period. He may have been made by Georgene Averill rather than Cameo. $700.00 up. *Courtesy Jeanne Venner.*

CHADWICK-MILLER

8" "Sad Eyes" made of plastic and vinyl with large painted eyes. Made in Hong Kong for Chadwick-Miller. $25.00. *Courtesy Kathy Tvrdik.*

14" "Little Lulu" with painted mask face and made of all cloth. Made in 1950s by Georgene Averill. $400.00. *Courtesy Carol Turpen.*

11½" "New York Yankees" is all printed cloth. $25.00. *Courtesy Sandra Cummins.*

COSMOPOLITAN

8" "Pam" and her monkey. Monkey has stapled on clothes and may have been made by Krueger. Has full mitt hands. (The monkey made for "Terri Lee" by Steiff has cutout thin hands.) Doll made by Cosmopolitan. Doll - $65.00; monkey - $85.00 up.

17" "Marylee" made by Dee & Cee of Canada in 1967. All excellent quality rigid vinyl with rooted long hair and sleep eyes. Bears an uncanny resemblance to Madame Alexander's "Marybel." All original except shoes. $300.00. *Courtesy Pat Graff.*

DELUXE TOPPER, READING, PREMIUM

This company also used the names Topper Toys and Topper Corp. They were well known for making dolls that did things and were battery operated during the 1960s and 1970s. These dolls have become highly collectible as they were well played with and not many dolls survived.

Baby Boo: Battery operated, 1965. 21" - $45.00.

Baby Catch A Ball: Battery operated, 1969. 18" - $55.00.

Baby Magic: 1966. 18" - $50.00.

Baby Peek 'N Play: Battery operated, 1969. 18" - $35.00.

Baby Tickle Tears: 14" - $35.00.

Betty Bride: Also called "Sweet Rosemary." 1957. One-piece vinyl body and limbs. 30" - $125.00.

Dawn: 6". Mint - $20.00. In original box - $27.00. Played with - $6.00 up.

Dawn Model Agency dolls: Mint - $35.00. In box - $45.00. Played with - $18.00.

Dawn Series, boys: Mint - $28.00. In box - $35.00. Played with - $15.00.

Lil' Miss Fussy: Battery operated. 18" - $35.00.

Party Time: Battery operated, 1967. 18" - $45.00.

Penny Brite: 8" child. (See photo in Series 10, pg. 216.) Mint - $28.00. Played with - $8.00 up.

Private Ida: One of "Go Go's" from 1965. (See photo in Series 9, pg. 217.) Mint condition. 6" - $35.00.

Smarty Pants and other mechanicals: Battery operated, 1971. 19" - $35.00.

Suzy Cute: Move arm and face changes expressions. (See photo in Series 10, pg. 216.) 7" - $20.00.

Tom Boy: One of the "Go-Go's" in 1965. (See photo in Series 10, pg. 216.) Mint condition. 6" - $35.00.

22" "Susie Homemaker" made of plastic and vinyl with jointed knees. Marked "Deluxe Reading Co. 1964/43." $40.00.
Courtesy Kathy Tvrdik.

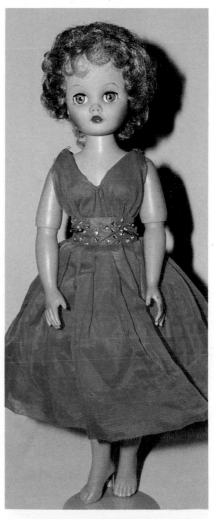

21" "Candy Fashion" made by Deluxe Premium, a division of Deluxe Reading, in 1958. Doll sold through grocery stores. Came with three dress forms, additional outfits, and accessories. Has extra joints. $85.00 up. *Courtesy Kathy Tvrdik.*

17", 16", and 10" "Punch and Family" made of resin and composition. First limited edition by artist Rosemary Volpi. Limited to 60 sets. No price available. *Courtesy Turn of Century Antiques.*

13" limited edition "Pouty Shirley" by artist Karen Bruser. Mohair wig, painted eyes, composition head painted in oils. Flesh color felt limbs and cloth body. Original "Bright Eyes" tagged Shirley Temple dress. Head marked "K.B. 9 1980." $600.00. *Courtesy Glorya Woods.*

14" "Little Black Sambo" made by artist Wendy Lawton in 1991. This porcelain doll is faithful to each detail in Mrs. Bannerman's 1889 original text – right down to his purple shoes with crimson soles and linings. Limited edition of 500. $800.00 up. *Courtesy The Lawton Doll Company.*

5" South African "Ready For Safari" made by artist Chaye Arotsky. Made of gesso resin and painted. Marked "Sara." $25.00.

Below: 3" and 4" tall "Snow White and Seven Dwarfs." Made of gesso resin and painted by artist Chaye Arotsky. Marked "Sara." Each - $35.00.

18" "Danny Heartfelts" made by Carla Thompson in 1987. Felt with oil-painted features. $600.00. *Courtesy Turn of Century Antiques.*

14" "China" made same as a Chase doll. Designed and made by Kathy Tvrdik. $95.00.

DURHAM

11" "Skinny" made of all flat vinyl. Fully jointed; will fold up. Marked with picture of the world and "I" inside "D/No. 1550/Durham Ind." $8.00. *Courtesy Kathy Tvrdik.*

The "Eegee" name was made up from the name of company founder E.G. Goldberger. Founded in 1917, the early dolls were marked "E.G.", then "E. Goldberger." Now the marks "Eegee" and "Goldberger" are used.

Andy: Teen type. (See photo in Series 9, pg. 221.) 12" - $30.00.

Annette: Teen type. 11½" - $55.00. Child: 1966, marked "20/25M/13." (See photo in Series 9, pg. 221.) 19" - $50.00. Walker: 1966. Plastic/vinyl. 25" - $55.00; 28" - $75.00; 36" - $100.00.

Baby Luv: 1973. Cloth/vinyl. Marked "B.T. Eegee." 14" - $35.00.

Baby Susan: 1958. Name marked on head. 8½" - $20.00.

Baby Tandy Talks: 1960. Pull string talker. Foam body/vinyl. $65.00.

Babette: 1962. Barbie look-alike. 11½" - $70.00 up.

Ballerina: 1958. Hard plastic/vinyl head. 20" - $45.00.

Ballerina: 1964. Hard plastic/vinyl head. 31" - $100.00.

Ballerina: 1967. Foam body and limbs, vinyl head. 18" - $30.00.

Boy dolls: Molded hair, rest vinyl. 13" - $40.00; 21" - $55.00 up.

Cartland, Barbara: Painted features, adult. (See photo in Series 9, pg. 222.) 15" - $52.00.

Composition: Open mouth child. Sleep eyes. 14" - $140.00 up; 18" - $185.00 up. **Babies:** Cloth/composition. 16" - $85.00 up; 20" - $125.00 up.

Debutante: 1958. Vinyl head, rest hard plastic. Jointed knees. 28" - $90.00.

Flowerkins: 1963. Plastic/vinyl. Marked "F-2" on head. Seven in set. 16", in box - $70.00. Played with, no box - $25.00.

Gemmette: 1963. Teen type. (See photo in Series 8, pg. 216.) 14" - $50.00 up.

Georgie or Georgette: 1971. Cloth/vinyl red-headed twins. (See photo in Series 10, pg. 221.) 22–23" - $50.00.

Gigi Perreaux: 1951. Hard plastic, early vinyl head. Open/closed smile mouth. 17" - $550.00 up.

Granny: Old lady modeling. Grey rooted hair, painted or sleep eyes. From "Beverly Hillbillies." 14" - $80.00.

Miss Charming: 1936. All composition Shirley Temple look-alike. (See photo in Series 10, pg. 222.) 19" - $450.00 up. Pin - $40.00.

Miss Sunbeam: 1968. Plastic/vinyl, dimples. 17" - $30.00.

Musical baby: 1967. Key wind music box in cloth body. 17" - $20.00.

20" "Puppetrina" made in 1963–1965. Cloth and vinyl with open/closed mouth and two lower teeth. Sleep eyes and lashes, rooted hair. Place in back for hand to make her a puppet. $35.00. *Courtesy Kathy Tvrdik.*

My Fair Lady: 1956. Adult type. All vinyl, jointed waist. 10½" - $45.00; 19" - $75.00.
Parton, Dolly: 1980. 12" - $25.00; 18" - $50.00.
Posey Playmate: 1969. Foam and vinyl. 18" - $20.00.
Puppetrina: 1963. 22" - $35.00.
Shelly: 1964. "Tammy" type. Grow hair. 12" - $18.00.

Sniffles: 1963. Plastic/vinyl nurser. Marked "13/14 AA-EEGEE." 12" - $20.00.
Susan Stroller: 1955. Hard plastic with vinyl head. (See photo in Series 9, pg. 222.) 15" - $45.00; 20" - $50.00; 23" - $60.00; 26" - $70.00.
Tandy Talks: 1961. Pull string talker. Plastic with vinyl head and freckles. 20" - $50.00.

EFFANBEE DOLL COMPANY

First prices are for mint condition dolls; second prices for dolls that are played with, soiled, dirty, cracked or crazed or not original. Dolls marked with full name or "F & B."
Alice In Wonderland (Honey): Hard plastic. 16" - $425.00, $165.00.
Alyssia: 1958–1962. All hard plastic **walker** with vinyl head. 20" - 225.00, $90.00. (**Alicia** has rigid vinyl unjointed arms.)
American Children: (See photo in Series 8, pgs. 217–218.) 1938. All composition. Painted or sleep eyes. Marked with that name. Some have "Anne Shirley" marked bodies; others are unmarked. Closed mouth girls: Sleep or painted eyes. 19–21" - $1,400.00. Closed mouth boy: 15" - $1,000.00; 17" - $1,300.00. **Barbara Joan:** Open mouth girl. 15" - $625.00. **Barbara Ann:** Open mouth. 17" - $725.00. **Barbara Lou:** Open mouth. 21" - $875.00 up.
Animals: Uses "Patsyette" body. Wolf, sheep, etc. $150.00 up.
Anne of Green Gables: 1937. Composition. 14" - $450.00.
Anne Shirley: 1936–1940. All composition. Marked with name. 15" - $275.00; 17" - $300.00; 21" - $400.00; 27" - $500.00.
Armstrong, Louis: 1984–1985 only. 15½" - $80.00.
Babyette: 1946. Cloth/composition sleeping baby. 12" - $265.00, $125.00; 16" - $350.00; $175.00.

Babykin: 1940. All composition: 9–12" - $175.00, $85.00. All vinyl: 10" - $30.00.

22" "Alyssia" made by Effanbee, 1958–1962. Vinyl head and arms and the rest hard plastic. Jointed at elbows. Rooted hair, sleep eyes. All original and unplayed with. $350.00. *Courtesy Pat Graff.*

Baby Cuddleup: 1953. Oil cloth body. Vinyl head/limbs. Two lower teeth. 20" - $55.00, $20.00; 23" - $85.00, $40.00.

Baby Dainty: 1912–1922. Cloth/composition. Marked with name. 15" - $245.00, $80.00; 17" - $285.00, $100.00.

Baby Effanbee: 1925. Marked on head. 12–13" - $165.00.

Baby Evelyn: 1925. Composition/cloth. Marked with name. 17" - $250.00, $100.00.

Baby Grumpy: See Grumpy.

Baby Tinyette: 1933–1936. Composition. 7–8" - $245.00, $100.00. Toddler: 7–8" - $265.00; $100.00.

Betty Brite: 1933. All composition. Fur wig, sleep eyes. Marked with name. 16–17" - $300.00, $100.00.

Bright Eyes: 1938, 1940s. Composition/cloth, flirty eyes. Same doll as "Tommy Tucker" and "Mickey." 16" - $300.00; 18" - $350.00; 22–23" - $400.00.

11" "Brazil" made in 1980 and is one of the International Series. Marked "Effanbee/1976/1170" and on back "EFF & BEE." $30.00 up. *Courtesy Renie Culp.*

Brother or Sister: 1943. Composition head and hands, rest cloth. Yarn hair, painted eyes. 12" - $150.00, $50.00; 16" - $200.00, $80.00.

Bubbles: 1924. Composition/cloth. Marked with name. 15" - $325.00, $125.00; 19" - $365.00, $130.00; 22" - $450.00, $175.00; 25" - $500.00, $175.00. **Black:** 16" - $550.00; 20" - $865.00.

Button Nose: 1936–1943. (See photo in Series 8, pg. 218.) **Composition:** 8–9" - $225.00, $80.00. **Vinyl/cloth:** 1968. 18" - $45.00, $25.00.

Candy Kid: 1946. All composition. 12" - $265.00, $95.00. Black: 12" - $350.00, $95.00.

Champagne Lady: From Lawrence Welk's Show. "Miss Revlon" type. 19" - $265.00.

Churchill, Sir Winston: 1984. $75.00.

16" "Brother" and 12" "Sister" with composition heads and hands. Body and limbs are cloth. Yarn hair and painted eyes. Matching outfits. Made during World War II. 16" - $200.00; 12" - $150.00. *Courtesy Susan Giradot.*

Charlie McCarthy: 1929–1934. Composition/cloth. Mint condition. 15" - $500.00; 19–20" - $700.00.

Coquette: Composition with molded hair. Some have loop for hair ribbon. Painted eyes, smile. 10" - $225.00; 14" - $300.00.

Composition dolls: 1930s. All composition. Jointed neck, shoulders and hips. Molded hair. Painted or sleep eyes. Open or closed mouth. Original clothes. Marked "Effanbee." Perfect condition. 9" - $150.00, $85.00; 15" - $200.00, $100.00; 18" - $250.00, $100.00; 21" - $325.00, $125.00.

Composition dolls: 1920s. Composition head/limbs with cloth body. Open or closed mouth. Sleep eyes. Original clothes. Marked "Effanbee." Perfect condition. 18" - $165.00, $80.00; 22" - $200.00, $100.00; 25" - $300.00, $125.00; 27–28" - $375.00, $145.00.

Currier & Ives: Plastic/vinyl. 12" - $45.00, $12.00.

Disney dolls: 1977–1978. "Snow White," "Cinderella," "Alice in Wonderland" and "Sleeping Beauty." 14" - $185.00 up, $90.00.

Dydee Baby: 1933 on. Hard rubber head; rubber body and ears. Later versions had hard plastic head. Perfect condition. 14" - $125.00 up, $30.00.

Dydee Baby: 1950 on. Hard plastic/vinyl. 15" - $125.00 up, $40.00; 20" - $200.00 up, $100.00.

Emily Ann and other character puppets: 1937. Composition puppet. 13" - $160.00, $40.00.

Fields, W.C.: 1938. Composition/cloth. 22" - $650.00, $150.00. **Plastic/vinyl:** See Legend Series.

Fluffy: 1954. All vinyl. 10" - $35.00, $15.00. **Girl Scout:** 10" - $50.00, $20.00. **Black:** 10" - $45.00, $15.00. **Katie:** 1957. Molded hair. 8½" - $50.00, $20.00.

Garland, Judy: See Legends Series.

Gumdrop: 1962 on. Plastic/vinyl. 16" - $35.00, $20.00.

Grumpy: 1912. Frowns. Cloth/composition. Painted features. German molds #172 through #176. 12" - $250.00, $85.00; 14" - $300.00, $100.00. Others: 14" - $250.00. **Black:** 12" - $325.00, $165.00; 14–15" - $400.00, $175.00.

Hagara, Jan: Designer. **Laurel:** 1984. 15" - $135.00. **Cristina:** 1984 only. $185.00. **Larry:** 1985. 15" - $85.00. **Lesley:** 1985. $80.00. **Originals:** George Washington, Uncle Sam, Amish, etc. 12" - $200.00 up.

Half Pint: 1966 on. Plastic/vinyl. 10" - $35.00, $15.00.

Happy Boy: 1960. All vinyl. Molded tooth and freckles. 10½" - $40.00, $15.00.

Hibel, Edna: Designer. 1984 only. **Flower girl:** $150.00. **Contessa:** $175.00.

11" "Contessa" designed by Edna Hibel for Effanbee in 1984. All vinyl and original. $175.00 up. *Courtesy Pat Graff.*

Historical Dolls: 1939. Painted eyes, all composition. Original. 14" (uses "Little Lady" doll) - $565.00, $185.00; 21" (uses "American Child" doll) - $1,350.00, $700.00.

Honey: 1949–1955. All hard plastic, closed mouth. Must have excellent face color. (Add more for unusual, original clothes.) 14" - $250.00, $90.00; 18" - $345.00, $150.00; 21" - $485.00, $160.00.

Honey: 1947–1948. Composition, flirty eyes: 14" - $225.00, $95.00; 21" - $365.00, $125.00; 27" - $500.00, $200.00. **Walker:** 14" - $245.00, 19" - $345.00. **Jointed knees:** 19" - $365.00.

Howdy Doody: 1949: Composition/cloth. String operated mouth. 16–17" - $185.00. **Puppet on string:** Composition head/limbs. 17" - $185.00; 20" - $250.00. **1947–1949:** Composition/cloth, puppet mouth formed but not moveable. 18" - $250.00. 1950s: Hard plastic/cloth doll. 18" - $200.00.

Humpty Dumpty: 1985. $85.00 up.

Ice Queen: 1937. Skater outfit. Composition with open mouth. 17" - $800.00 up, $200.00.

Lamkins: 1930. Composition/cloth. (See photo in Series 9, pg. 226.) 15" - $365.00 up; 18" - $500.00 up; 22" - $650.00.

Legend Series: 1980: W.C. Fields - $265.00. **1981:** John Wayne as soldier. $185.00. **1982:** John Wayne as cowboy. $185.00. **1982:** Mae West - $95.00. 1983: Groucho Marx - $85.00. **1984:** Judy Garland dressed as "Dorothy" from *Wizard of Oz.* $80.00. **1985:** Lucille Ball. $70.00. **1986**: Liberace - $75.00. **1987:** James Cagney - $60.00.

Lil Sweetie: 1967. Nurser with no lashes or brow. 16" - $55.00, $25.00.

Limited Edition Club: 1975: Precious Baby - $450.00. **1976:** Patsy - $325.00. **1977:** Dewees Cochran - $150.00. **1978:** Crowning Glory - $125.00. **1979:** Skippy - $285.00. **1980:** Susan B. Anthony - $125.00. **1981:** Girl with watering can - $100.00. **1982:** Princess Diana - $100.00.

18" and 14" "Honey Bridesmaids." All hard plastic and both original with original tags. Both have closed mouths and saran wigs. 14" - $300.00; 18" - $400.00.
Courtesy Kris Lundquist.

1983: Sherlock Holmes - $150.00. **1984:** Bubbles - $100.00. **1985:** Red Boy - $95.00. **1986:** China head - $65.00.

Little Lady: 1939–1947. All composition. (Add more for original clothes.) 15" - $275.00, $90.00; 17" - $375.00, $125.00; 21" - $450.00, $150.00; 27" - $550.00, $200.00.

Little Lady: 1943. **Cloth body:** Yarn hair. 21" - $365.00 up. **Pink cloth body:** Wig. 17" - $250.00 up. **Magnets** in hands: 15" (doll only) - $300.00. Doll/accessories - $385.00.

Lovums: 1928. Composition/cloth. Open smiling mouth. Marked with name. 15" - $250.00, $100.00. 20" - $365.00, $150.00; 23" - $425.00.

Mae Starr: Record player in torso. Composition/cloth. Marked with name. 30" - $465.00, $200.00.

Marionettes: Composition/wood. 14" - $145.00 up.

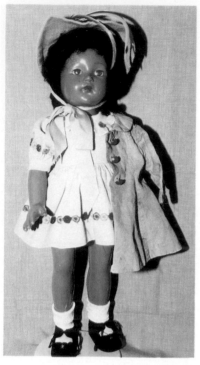

21" extremely rare Black "Little Lady-Anne Shirley." All composition with sleep eyes and floss wig. Marked on head and body. $750.00. *Courtesy Patricia Wood.*

21" "Little Lady" marked "Anne Shirley." Rare gown. All composition. Original hairdo. Mint condition and original. This doll - $650.00. *Courtesy Patricia Wood.*

27" "Harem Girl" using "Little Lady" mold. All composition with sleep eyes. Everything about the doll is very professional and looks factory made, but she could have been a belly dancer made for a special occasion. No matter, she is a super doll. $525.00 up. *Courtesy Virginia Sofie.*

Martha and George Washington: 1976. 11", pair - $125.00.

Mary Ann or Lee: 1928–1937. Open smile mouth. Composition and cloth or all composition. Marked with name. 16" - $265.00, $95.00; 18" - $285.00, $125.00; 20" - $325.00, $150.00; 24" - $425.00, $175.00.

Marilee: 1920s. Composition/cloth. Open mouth. Marked with name. 13" - $250.00, $100.00; 16" - $300.00, $125.00; 23" - $365.00, $150.00; 28" - $475.00; $200.00.

Mary Jane: 1917–1920. Composition. Jointed body or cloth. "Mama" type. 20–22" - $285.00.

Mary Jane: 1960. Plastic/vinyl walker with freckles. 31" - $225.00, $95.00. Flirty eye walker: 30" - $285.00.

Mickey: 1946. Composition/cloth with flirty eyes. (Also Tommy Tucker and Bright Eyes.) 16" - $300.00; 18" - $350.00, $100.00; 22–23" - $400.00, $125.00.

Mickey: 1956. All vinyl. (Some have molded-on hats.) 11" - $95.00, $25.00.

Miss Chips: 1965 on. Plastic/vinyl. White: 18" - $40.00. **Black:** 18" - $50.00.

Pat-O-Pat: Composition/cloth with painted eyes. Press stomach and hands pats together. 13–14" - $175.00, $80.00.

Patricia: 1932–1936. All composition. 14" - $400.00, $165.00. Original: $450.00 up.

Patricia-kin: 1929–1930s. 11" - $325.00, $125.00.

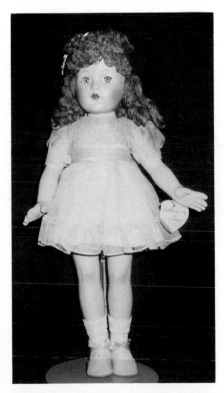

21" "Little Lady" from World War II era. All composition with yarn hair and sleep eyes. In beautiful mint condition. $525.00. *Courtesy Martha Sweeney.*

Hard to find "Mickey" as a boxer with black eye and vinyl boxing gloves. All original. $85.00. *Courtesy Patricia Wood.*

18" "Night Time" made of vinyl and plastic with sleep eyes. All original. From 1986. $45.00 up. *Courtesy Pat Graff.*

Patsy: 1927–1930s. All composition: 14" - $375.00, $160.00. **Composition/ cloth:** 14" - $395.00, $175.00. Original: $425.00 up.

Patsy look-alike: Composition arm bent at elbow. Excellent quality, original: $250.00. Medium quality: $175.00. Poor quality: $100.00.

Patsy Baby: Cloth body. Can have straight legs. 11" - $265.00, $100.00. Black: $445.00.

Patsy Babyette: 1930s, 1940s. 9" - $245.00, $90.00. Original: $300.00 up.

Patsyette: 1930s. 9" - $325.00, $125.00. Original: $400.00 up. Black: $450.00.

Patsy Ann: 1930s. 19" - $465.00, $165.00. Original: $525.00 up. Vinyl: 1959.

15" - $165.00, $60.00. Original: $200.00 up. Vinyl with jointed wasit: 15" - $185.00.

Patsy Joan: 1927–1930. Reissued 1946–1949. 16" - $450.00, $175.00. Original: $500.00 up. **Black:** 16" - $625.00 up, $225.00. Original: $550.00 up.

Patsy Junior.: 11" - $300.00, $100.00. Original: $350.00 up.

Patsy Lou: 1929–1930s. 22" - $485.00, $175.00. Original: $575.00 up.

Patsy Mae: 1932. 30" - $785.00, $325.00. Original: $865.00 up.

Patsy Ruth: 1935. 26–27" - $765.00, $325.00. Original: $850.00 up.

Patsy, Wee: 1930s. 5–6" - $300.00, $125.00. Original: $365.00 up.

Polka Dottie: 1953. 21" - $165.00, $60.00.

Portrait Dolls: 1940. All composition. "Bo Peep," "Ballerina," "Bride," "Groom," "Gibson Girl," "Colonial," etc. 12" - $250.00, $95.00.

11" "Patsy Junior" that is all composition with molded hair and sleep eyes. All original with box. She was called a "New Playmate" and the text on the box tells the child to have fun choosing a new name for her. With box - $425.00. Doll only, original - $300.00. *Courtesy Gloria Anderson.*

All dolls are composition. 15" "Majorette" using the "Little Lady" doll and 19" "Patsy Ann" have sleep eyes. Shown with 8" "Amish Baby Tinyette" toddlers. 15" - $325.00; 19" - $465.00; 8" $185.00 each. *Courtesy Turn of Century Antiques.*

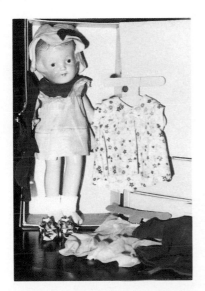

Two "Patsy" look-alike dolls. Left: 12" all composition "Nancy" made by Arranbee. Molded hair and painted eyes. Original with trunk and wardrobe. Right: 13–14" "Kewty" made by Domec in 1930. All composition with sleep eyes and bent left arm. One of the best quality copies. "Nancy" doll only - $250.00; with trunk/wardrobe - $375.00. "Kewty" - $350.00. *Kewty doll courtesy Glorya Woods.*

Presidents: 1984. Lincoln: 18" - $60.00. Washington: 16" - $55.00. Teddy Roosevelt: 17" - $65.00. F.D. Roosevelt: 1985. $60.00.

Prince Charming or Cinderella (Honey): All hard plastic. 16" - $425.00 up, $165.00.

Pum'kin: 1966 on. All vinyl with freckles. 10½" - $30.00, $15.00.

Rootie Kazootie: 1953. 21" - $165.00, $60.00.

Roosevelt, Eleanor: 1985. 14½" - $60.00.

Rosemary: 1925 on. Composition/cloth. Marked with name. 13" - $250.00, $125.00; 16" - $300.00, $150.00; 23" - $365.00, $150.00; 28" - $475.00, $200.00.

Santa Claus: 19" composition with molded beard and hat. (See photo in Series 8, pg. 223.) $1,200.00 up.

Skippy: 1929, 1940s. All composition. 14" - $445.00, $165.00. **Soldier:** $500.00. **Sailor:** $565.00.

Suzanne: 1940. All composition. Marked with name. 14" - $275.00, $125.00.

Suzie Sunshine: 1961 on. Has freckles. 17–18" - $50.00-20.00. **Black:** 17–18" - $70.00, $40.00.

Suzette: 1939. Marked with name. All composition. 12" - $250.00, $95.00.

Sweetie Pie: 1938–1940s. Composition/cloth. 14" - $175.00, $60.00; 19" - $285.00, $90.00; 24" - $365.00, $150.00.

Tommy Tucker: 1946. Composition/cloth with flirty eyes. (Also Mickey and Bright Eyes.) 16" - $300.00, 18" - $350.00, 22–23" - $400.00, $125.00.

Twain, Mark: 1984. 16" - $70.00.

Witch: Designed by Faith Wick. 18" - $75.00 up.

GATABOX

10" twins by Gatabox, a division of Horsman, in 1981. Cloth and vinyl. Both are original and tagged. Each - $32.00 up. *Courtesy Pat Graff.*

1936: 8" all printed cloth doll. Holds can of baby food and toy dog. Rare. $400.00.

1954: 12" rubber doll made by Sun Rubber Co. Mint - $95.00 up; Mint in box - $225.00 up.

1966: 14" soft vinyl doll made by Arrow Industries. Has lopsided smile. $65.00 up.

1972: 10" plastic/vinyl doll made by Uneeda Doll Co. $45.00 up.

GIBBS, RUTH

Ruth Gibbs of Flemington, New Jersey, made dolls with and without china glaze heads and limbs. They had pink cloth bodies and were between 7" and 13" tall. Dolls are marked "R.G." on back shoulder plate. Boxes state "Godey Little Lady Dolls" but not all dolls represent Godey ladies. Dolls were designed by Herbert Johnson.

7-8": In box - $185.00. Doll only: $125.00.

10-12": In box - $245.00. Doll only: $150.00.

10" wigged: $175.00.

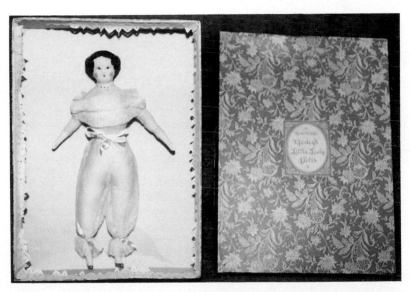

13" Ruth Gibbs doll with china glazed head and limbs and cloth body. Painted gold necklace and 14K gold slippers. Comes in net chemise to be dressed by owner. Marked "RG" on shoulder. In box - $185.00. *Courtesy Susan Giradot.*

Hartland Industries made many figures with horses during the mid to late 1950s. These are extremely collectible as they are rare, especially when the horses have saddles. Most came from the Warner Brothers television productions. The figures included:

James Arness as "Matt Dillon" on *Gunsmoke.* (Sept. 1955–Sept. 1975)

James Garner as "Bret Maverick" on *Maverick.* (See photo Series 8, pg. 228.)

John Lupton as "Tom Jeffords" on *Broken Arrow.* (Sept. 1956–Sept. 1960)

Gail Davis as "Annie Oakley" on *Annie Oakley* (April 1953–Dec. 1956)

Hugh O'Brien as "Wyatt Earp" on *Life and Legend of Wyatt Earp* (Sept. 1955– Sept. 1961)

Dale Robertson as "Jim Hardie" on *Tales of Wells Fargo.* (March 1957–Sept. 1962)

Hartland's "Hoby Gilman" (Robert Culp) from TV's *Trackdown* (October 1957–September 1958.) Note horse has ears laid down and back legs in a running stop position. $375.00. *Courtesy Steve Humphries.*

This Hartland figure is that of Jim Bowie and his horse, Blaze. $300.00. *Courtesy Steve Humphries.*

Pat Conway as "Clay Hollister" on *Tombstone Territory.* (Oct. 1957–Oct. 1959)

Wayde Preston as "Capt. Chris Colt" on *Colt .45.* (Oct. 1957–Sept. 1960)

Richard Boone as "Paladin" on *Have Gun Will Travel.* (Sept. 1957–Sept. 1963)

John Payne as "Vint Bonner" on *The Restless Gun.* (Sept. 1957–Sept. 1959)

Clint Walker as "Cheyenne Bodie" on *Cheyenne.* (Sept. 1955–Sept. 1963)

Ward Bond as "Major Seth Adams" on *Wagon Train.* (Sept. 1957–Sept. 1965)

Chief Thunderbird with his horse "Northwind."

Robert E. Lee with his horse "Traveler."

General George Custer and his horse "Bugler."

Brave Eagle with his horse "White Cloud."

General George Washington with his horse "Ajax."

"Lone Ranger" with his horse "Silver."

"Tonto" with his horse "Scout."

Jim Bowie with his horse "Blaze."

"Sgt. Preston of the Yukon" with his horse.

Roy Rogers with his horse "Trigger."

Dale Evans with her horse "Buttermilk."

Cochise with pinto horse.

Buffalo Bill with horse.

Other figures made by the company include baseball notables Mickey Mantle, Ted Williams, Stan Musial, Henry Aaron, Ed Mathews, and George "Babe" Ruth.

Figure and horse: Mint condition. $300.00 up.

Figure in box with horse and accessories: $500.00 up.

Figure alone: $125.00.

Horse alone: $175.00.

Baseball figure: $325.00 up.

Rare "MacKenzie's Raiders" character, "Colonel Ronald MacKenzie" (Richard Carlson.) The TV show ran for only 39 episodes and only 5,000 figures were made, compared to 200,000 figures for other shows. His rearing horse is also rare. $375.00. *Courtesy Kathy Humphries.*

HASBRO

All prices are for mint condition dolls.

Adam: 1971. Boy for World of Love series. 9" - $18.00.

Aimee: 1972. Plastic/vinyl. 18" - $50.00.

Charlie's Angels: 1977. 8½" Jill, Kelly or Sabrina. $20.00 each.

Defender: 1974. One-piece arms and legs. 11½" - $85.00 up.

Dolly Darling: 1965. 4½" - $10.00.

Flying Nun: Plastic/vinyl, 1967. 5" - $40.00.

(Add $50.00 more in mint in box on G.I. Joe.)

G.I. Joe Action figures: 12" doll. 1964: Marked on right lower back: "G.I. Joe™/Copyright 1964/By Hasbro ®/Patent Pending/Made in U.S.A." 1965: Slight change in marking. G.I. Joe®/Copyright 1964/By Hasbro ®/Patent Pending/Made in U.S.A." (This mark appears on all four armed service branches, excluding the Black action figures.) Hard plastic head with facial scar, painted hair, and no beard. **Soldier:** Flocked hair. $450.00. Painted hair: $275.00. Black painted hair: $1,300.00. **Marine:** $350.00. **Sailor:** $350.00. **Pilot:** $600.00. **Dolls only:** $50.00–95.00. With black painted hair: $325.00.

G.I. Joe Action Soldiers of the World (1966): Figures in this set may have any hair and eye color combination.

No scar on face. Hard plastic heads. Same markings as 1965. **Russian infantry:** In box: $600.00. Doll only: $200.00. **German soldier:** In box: $600.00. Doll only: $200.00. **Japanese Imperial soldier:** In box: $800.00. Doll only: $275.00. **British commando:** In box: $250.00. Doll only: $200.00. **Australian jungle fighter:** In box: $400.00. Doll only: $150.00. **French resistance:** In box: $500.00. Doll only: $200.00.

G.I. Joe Navy military policeman with missing arm band. $125.00 up. *Courtesy Kathy Tvrdik.*

G.I. Joe, Talking (1967–1969): Marked "G.I. Joe ®/Copyright 1964/By Hasbro ®/Pat. No. 3,277,602/Made In U.S.A. Talking mechanism added, excluding Black figure. Semi-hard vinyl head. **Talking action soldier:** No scar, blonde, brown eyes. $185.00 up. **Sailor:** $575.00. **Marine:** $475.00. **Pilot:** $800.00.

G.I. Joe Nurse (1967): The only female in this action series. Hard plastic jointed body, vinyl head. Rooted short blonde hair. Blue/green painted eyes. Marked across back waist: "Patent Pending ®/1967Hasbro/Made in Hong Kong. In box: $1,800.00. Doll, dressed: $800.00. Doll, nude: $150.00.

G.I. Joe, Man of Action (1970–1975): Marked "G.I. Joe ®/Copyright 1964/By Hasbro ®/Pat. no. 3,277,602/Made in U.S.A." Flocked hair, scar on face. Dressed in fatigues with Adventure Team emblem on shirt. Plastic cap. $60.00 up. Talking: $175.00.

G.I. Joe Adventure Team (1975–1976): Marked in small of back "© 1975 Hasbro ®/Pat. Pend., Pawt. R.I." Six team members. Flocked hair and beard. **Team Commander (talking):** Olive fatigues. $450.00 up. **Land Adventurer (Black):** Tan fatigues. No beard. $350.00 up. **Land Adventurer (talking):** Camouflage fatigues. $450.00 up. **Sea Adventurer:** Light blue shirt, navy pants. $265.00 up. **Air Adventurer:** Orange flight suit. $285.00 up. **Astronaut (talking):** White flight suit. $450.00 up.

G.I. Joe with kung fu grip: Adventure Team: $200.00 up. Black talking: $450.00.

G.I. Joe, "Mike Powers, Atomic Man": $95.00 up.

"Eagle Eye" G.I. Joe: $125.00.

G.I. Joe Secret Agent: Unusual face, mustache. $450.00 up.

Boxed G.I. Joe with uniform: Mint condition. Fighter pilot: $625.00. Tank G.I. Joe: $625.00. Action Soldier Sabotage: $475.00. Air Force dress uniform: $275.00.

Airborne military police: Green or tan outfits. $1,000.00.

Adventures of G.I. Joe sets: No doll included. Deep sea diver: "Eight Ropes of Danger." $300.00 up. Scuba diver: "Jaws of Death." $300.00 up. Safari: "White Tiger Hunt." $300.00 up. Test pilot: $650.00 up. Jungle explorer: "Mouth of Doom." $300.00 up. Secret agent: "Secret Mission To Spy Island." $250.00 up. Astronaut: "Space Walk Mystery." $450.00 up. "The Hidden Missile" $450.00 up. Polar explorer: "Fight For Survival." $465.00 up. "Shark's Surprise": $350.00 up. Pilot: "Fantastic Free Fall": $275.00.

Packs or boxed uniforms and accessories: Green Beret: $450.00. Secret Agent: $150.00. Marine mine detector: $275.00. Marine jungle fighter: $850.00. Action sailor: $350.00. Frogman demolition set: $375.00. Military police: $325.00. Landing signal officer: $250.00. Rescue diver: $350.00. Crash crew fire fighter: $275.00. Deep sea diver: $250.00. Annapolis, West Point, Air Force Academy cadet: Each - $200.00. Astronaut: $250.00. Marine dress parade: $225.00. Pilot scramble set: $275.00. Shore patrol: $300.00. Ski patrol: $350.00. Deep Freeze with sled: $250.00.

G.I. Joe accessories: Armored car: 20" - $150.00 up. **Motorcycle and side car:** By Irwin. $200.00 up. **Desert jeep:** Tan. $250.00 up. **Turbo swamp craft:** $185.00 up. **Space capsule:** $225.00 up. **Footlocker:** $30.00 up. **Sea sled:** $75.00 up. **Tank:** $175.00 up. **Jeep:** Olive green. $145.00 up. **Helicopter:** $275.00 up. **All terrain vehicle:** $165.00 up.

Leggie: 1972. (See photo in Series 9, pg. 236.) 10" - $30.00. Black: $40.00.

Little Miss No Name: 1965. 15" - $85.00.

Mamas and Papas: 1967. (See photo in Series 8, pg. 230.) $35.00 each.

Show Biz Babies: 1967. $45.00 each. Mama Cass: $50.00.

Monkees: Set of four. 4" - $95.00 up.

Storybooks: 1967. 3" dolls. Complete set: Sleeping Beauty: $50.00. Rumplestilskin: $55.00. Goldilocks: $50.00. Snow White and Dwarfs: $75.00. Prince Charming: $60.00. Doll only: $20.00–30.00.

Sweet Cookie: 1972. 18" - $35.00.

That Kid: 1967. 21" - $85.00.

World of Love Dolls: 1971. (See photo in Series 10, pg. 236.) White: 9" - $15.00. Black: 9" - $20.00.

12" "Jem" on stage and "Jerrica" off stage (in second outfit). Jointed wrists and waist. 1½ volt batteries operate earring that becomes stars and sparkle. Marked "1985 Hasbro." $00.00.

First prices are for mint condition dolls; second prices for ones that have been played with, are dirty and soiled or not original. Marked "Horsman" or "E.I.H."

Angelove: 1974. Plastic/vinyl. Made for Hallmark. 12" - $25.00.

Answer Doll: 1966. Button in back moves head. 10" - $15.00, $8.00.

Billiken: 1909. Composition head, slant eyes, plush or velvet body. 12" - $345.00, $125.00; 16" - $425.00.

Baby Bumps: 1910. Composition/cloth. 12" - $185.00, $65.00; 14" - $245.00, $95.00. **Black:** 11" - $265.00, $90.00; 15" - $300.00, $125.00.

Baby Butterfly: Oriental: 12" - $225.00. Black: 12" - $300.00.

15" "Bright Star" that is all hard plastic with open mouth and sleep eyes. Completely original and never been played with. Has original box. With box - $450.00. Doll only - $275.00. *Courtesy Patricia Wood.*

Baby First Tooth: 1966. Cloth/vinyl. Cry mouth with one tooth. Tears on cheeks. 16" - $35.00, $18.00.

Baby Tweaks: 1967. Cloth/vinyl, inset eyes. 20" - $30.00, $15.00.

Ballerina: 1957. Vinyl, one-piece body and legs, jointed elbows. 18" - $50.00.

Betty: All composition. 16" - $225.00, $90.00. All vinyl: 1951. One-piece body and limbs: 14" - $60.00. **Plastic/vinyl:** 16" - $25.00, $15.00.

Betty Jo: All composition. 16" - $225.00, $90.00. **Plastic/vinyl:** 1962. 16" - $25.00, $15.00.

Betty Ann: Add more for original clothes. All composition: 19" - $275.00, $125.00. **Plastic/vinyl:** 19" - $60.00, $25.00.

Betty Jane: All composition. 25" - $350.00, $150.00. **Plastic/vinyl:** 25" - $75.00, $40.00.

Blink: (Also called "Happy.") 1916 Gene Carr designed character. Cloth body, composition head and limbs. Painted eyes are almost closed. Watermelon-style open/closed mouth with one lower tooth. Very prominent ears, painted hair. 14–15" - $345.00 up.

Bye-Lo Baby: 1972. Made for 100th anniversary for Wards. Cloth/vinyl. 14" - $55.00. Reissued: 1980–1990s. 14" - $25.00.

Body Twist: 1929–1930. All composition. Top of body fits down into torso. 11" - $225.00, $85.00.

Bright Star: 1937–1946. (See photo in Series 8, pg. 233.) All composition: 18–19" - $295.00, $125.00. **All hard plastic:** 1952. 15" - $275.00, $100.00.

Brother: Composition/cloth. 22" - $250.00 up, $100.00. Vinyl: 13" - $45.00, $20.00.

Campbell Kids: Circa 1911. Cloth/composition with painted features. Marked "E.I.H." 14" - $325.00 up. "Dolly Dingle" style face: 1930–1940s. All composition. 13" - $325.00 up.

Celeste portrait doll: In frame. Eyes painted to side. 12" - $35.00, $15.00.

Christopher Robin: 11" - $35.00, $15.00.

Child dolls: 1930–1940s. All composition: 14" - $165.00, $60.00; 16" - $235.00, $80.00; 18" - $300.00, $95.00. All hard plastic: 14" - $145.00, $50.00; 18" - $250.00 up, $100.00. **Toddler:** All composition, very chubby. 14" - $125.00, $50.00; 17" - $150.00, $85.00.

Cindy: 1950s. Marked "170." All hard plastic: 15" - $175.00 up, $50.00; 17" - $200.00 up, $100.00. All early vinyl: 1953. 18" - $60.00, $18.00. Lady type with jointed waist: 1959. 19" - $75.00, $40.00. Walker: 16" - $225.00.

Cindy Kay: 1950–on. All vinyl child with long legs. (See photo in Series 9, pg. 239.) 15" - $85.00, $40.00; 20" - $125.00; 27" - $225.00.

Cinderella: 1965. Plastic/vinyl. Painted eyes to side. 11½" - $30.00, $15.00.

Composition dolls: 1910s–1920s. "Can't Break 'Em" composition/cloth body. Marked "E.I.H." 12" - $175.00, $60.00; 16" - $200.00, $100.00. 1930s: 16" - $140.00, $70.00; 18" - $185.00, $90.00; 22" - $225.00, $115.00.

Crawling Baby: 1967. Vinyl. 14" - $25.00, $10.00.

Dimples: 1928–1933. Composition/cloth. (See photo in Series 9, pg. 238.) 16" - $250.00, $90.00; 20" - $325.00, $125.00; 24" - $350.00, $145.00. **Toddler:** 20" - $385.00, $145.00; 24" - $425.00, $165.00. **Laughing:** Painted teeth. 22" - $425.00, $185.00.

Disney exclusives: "Cinderella," "Snow White," "Mary Poppins," "Alice in Wonderland." 1981. 8" - $40.00 each.

Gold Medal doll: 1930s. Composition/cloth. Upper & lower teeth. 21" - $200.00, $90.00. Vinyl/molded hair: 1953. 26" - $185.00, $85.00. Vinyl Boy: 1954. 15" - $75.00, $30.00.

Ella Cinders: 1925. Comic character. Composition/cloth. Marked "1925 MNS." 14" - $400.00; 18" - $650.00.

Elizabeth Taylor: 1976. 11½" - $45.00, $20.00.

14" "Jackie Coogan" with cloth body and legs. Composition shoulder head and lower arms. Molded hair and painted features. All original. Tagged "Jackie Coogan Kid. Licensed by Jackie Coogan. Patent Pending" on pants. Shoulder marked "E.I.H. Co. 1921." $465.00 up. *Courtesy Jeannie Mauldin.*

Floppy: 1965. Foam body and legs, rest is vinyl. 18" - $25.00.

Flying Nun: (Sally Field) 1965. (See photo in Series 9, pg. 240.) Original: 12" - $50.00, $15.00. M.I.B.: $125.00.

Hansel & Gretel: 1963. Sleep eyes, unusual faces. (See photo in Series 7, pg. 238.) Each - $200.00.

Hebee-Shebee: 1925. All composition. 10½" - $500.00, $275.00

Jackie Coogan: 1921. Composition/cloth, painted eyes. 14" - $465.00, $165.00.

Jackie Kennedy: 1961. Marked "Horsman J.K." Adult body, plastic/vinyl. 25" - $125.00, $60.00.

Jeanie Horsman: 1937. All composition: 14" - $225.00, $90.00. Composition/cloth: 16" - $185.00, $80.00.

Jojo: 1937. All composition. 12" - $200.00, $95.00. 16" - $265.00, $125.00.

Life-size baby: Plastic/vinyl. 26" - $225.00, $100.00.

Lullabye baby: 1964, 1967. Cloth/vinyl. Music box in body. 12" - $20.00, $8.00. All vinyl: 12" - $15.00, $5.00.

Mary Poppins: 1964: 12" - $35.00, $15.00; 16" - $70.00, $30.00; 26" (1966) - $200.00, $100.00; 36" - $350.00, $175.00. In box with "Michael" and "Wendy": 12" and 8" - $150.00.

Mama style babies: 1920s– 1930s. Composition/cloth. Marked "E.I.H" or "Horsman." 14" - $185.00, $85.00; 18" - $250.00, $100.00. Girl dolls: 14" - $250.00, $90.00; 18" - $325.00, $125.00; 24" - $385.00, $165.00. Hard plastic/cloth: 16" -

$85.00; $45.00; 22" - $110.00, $50.00. Vinyl/cloth: 16" - $25.00, $10.00; 22" - $35.00, $20.00.

Michael: (Mary Poppins) 1965. 8" - $25.00, $15.00.

Mousketeer: 1971. Boy or girl. 8" - $30.00, $15.00.

Patty Duke: 1965. Posable arms. 12" - $45.00, $18.00.

Peek-A-Boo: Designed by Grace Drayton. Cloth and composition. 7½–8" - $150.00 up.

Peggy: 1957. All vinyl child. One-piece body and legs. 25" - $125.00, $50.00.

Peggy Ann: 1930. Composition/cloth. (See photo in Series 9, pg. 240.) Mint condition. 28" - $165.00.

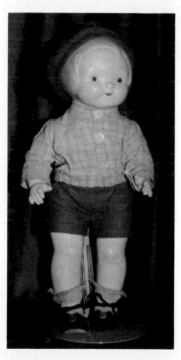

13½" "Peterkin" with cloth body with composition head and limbs. Molded "Campbell Kid" hairstyle. Original clothes. Tagged "Peterkin, E.I.H." on back of head and "Horsman Doll Mfg. U.S.A." on shirt. $425.00 up. *Courtesy A. "Pidd" Miller.*

14" "Ruthie" that is plastic and vinyl with sleep eyes and rooted hair. Open hands with wide spread fingers. Original. From 1960. $28.00.

Peggy Pen Pal: 1970. Multi-jointed arms. Plastic/vinyl. 18" - $35.00, $20.00.

Peterkin: 1915–1930. All composition. Painted googly-style eyes. 10" - $300.00, $115.00; 14" - $425.00 up.

Pippi Longstocking: 1972. Vinyl/cloth. 1972. 18" - $35.00, $20.00.

Polly & Pete: 1957. All vinyl Black dolls with molded hair. 13" - $225.00, $60.00.

Poor Pitiful Pearl: 1963, 1976. 12" - $50.00, $25.00; 17" - $100.00, $50.00.

Pudgie Baby: Plastic/vinyl. 1978: 12" - $30.00, $15.00. 1980: 24" - $40.00, $20.00.

Pudgy: 1974. All vinyl, very large painted eyes. 12½" - $30.00, $10.00.

Roberta: 1928: All composition. 1937: Molded hair or wigs. 14" - $250.00, $90.00; 20" - $325.00, $125.00. 24" - $325.00, $150.00.

Rosebud: 1928. Composition/cloth. Dimples and smile. Sleep eyes and wig. Marked with name. 14" - $250.00, $90.00; 18" - $300.00, $125.00. 24" - $385.00, $165.00.

Ruthie: 1958–1966. All vinyl or plastic/vinyl. 14" - $20.00, $8.00; 20" - $32.00, $12.00.

Sleepy Baby: 1965. Vinyl/cloth. Eyes molded closed. 24" - $40.00, $25.00.

Tuffie: 1966. All vinyl. Upper lip molded over lower. 16" - $35.00, $15.00.

Tynie Baby: See that section.

"Poor Pitiful Pearl" dolls. All have cloth bodies and vinyl heads and limbs. All original. Left to right: 17" and 10" made in 1976 by Tri-Star. 18" made by Horsman in 1963. 17" - $95.00; 10" - $40.00; 18" - $100.00. *Courtesy Kathy Tvrdik.*

Large black "Softee" doll with hard plastic head, cloth body, and early vinyl limbs. Glassene sleep eyes with hair lashes. Not original. From 1952. Black - $45.00; white - $30.00. *Courtesy Ellyn McCorkell.*

18" "Tessie Talks" made of plastic and vinyl with freckles. Pull string in back of neck operates mouth. Marked "3660 Horsman Dolls Inc., 1974." $40.00. *Courtesy Kathy Tvrdik.*

HOYER, MARY

The Mary Hoyer Doll Mfg. Co. operated in Reading, Pennsylvania, from 1925. The dolls were made in all composition, all hard plastic, and last ones produced were in plastic and vinyl. Older dolls are marked in a circle on back "Original Mary Hoyer Doll" or "The Mary Hoyer Doll" embossed on lower back.

First price is for perfect doll in tagged factory clothes. Second price for perfect doll in outfits made from Mary Hoyer patterns and third price is for redressed doll in good condition with only light craze to composition or slight soil to others.

Composition: Early dolls have left arm bent at elbow and can have extra joints just below breast line or at waist. ("Blanks" purchased from Knickerbocker Toy Co.) 14" - $425.00, $345.00 up, $165.00.

Hard plastic: 14" - $425.00 up, $400.00, $195.00; 17" - $565.00 up, $500.00, $250.00. Boy: 14" - $525.00–450.00.

Plastic/vinyl (Margie): 14–15". Marked "AE23." 12" - $145.00, $70.00, $15.00; 14" - $200.00, $95.00; $30.00.

14" Mary Hoyer dolls that are all original and mint. Both are all hard plastic. Earlier one in skater's outfit has mohair wig. The other one has a beautiful saran wig. Skater - $475.00; ballerina - $525.00. *Courtesy Patricia Wood.*

Close-up of 14" Mary Hoyer doll's face. All hard plastic with sleep eyes and original hair set. $425.00. *Courtesy Peggy Millhouse.*

14" Mary Hoyer doll that is all composition with mohair wig. Eyes painted to side. In original outfit made from Hoyer pattern. $345.00. *Courtesy Susan Giradot.*

18" marked Mary Hoyer "Gigi." Rare doll in original short dress. Has thick saran braids. Mint and original. $650.00–800.00. *Courtesy Patricia Woods.*

First prices are for mint condition dolls. Second prices are for cracked, crazed, dirty, soiled or not original dolls.

April Showers: 1968. Battery operated. Splashes with hands and head turns. (See photo in Series 7, pg. 242.) 14" - $28.00, $15.00.

Belly Button Babies: 1970. Plastic/vinyl. White: 9½" - $18.00, $7.00. Black: 9½" - $25.00, $12.00.

Baby Crissy: 1973–1975. Pull string to make hair grow. White: 24" - $85.00, $35.00. Black: 24" - $100.00, $45.00. Reissued in 1981: No grow hair. 24" - $40.00, $15.00.

14" early Ideal child with composition head and short arms. Cloth body and chubby legs. "Mama" cryer box in body. Tin sleep eyes, open mouth. Mint - $200.00. *Courtesy Gloria Anderson.*

Baby Snooks: See Flexies.

Bam-Bam: 1963. Plastic/vinyl or all vinyl. 12" - $15.00, $8.00; 16" - $25.00, $10.00.

Betsy McCall: See that section.

Betsy Wetsy: 1937 on. Composition head. Excellent rubber body. 13" - $110.00, $20.00; 16" - $135.00, $35.00. Hard plastic/vinyl: 12" - $75.00, $20.00; 14" - $125.00, $45.00. All vinyl: (See photo in Series 9, pg. 243.) 12" - $25.00, $9.00; 18" - $55.00, $20.00.

Betty Big Girl: 1968. Plastic/vinyl. (See photo in Series 10, pg. 243.) 32" - $285.00, $105.00.

Betty Jane: 1930s–1944. Shirley Temple type. All composition, sleep eyes, open mouth. 14" - $265.00, $100.00; 16" - $300.00, $125.00; 24" - $365.00, $145.00.

Blessed Event: 1951. Also called "Kiss Me." Cloth body with plunger in back to make doll cry or pout. Vinyl head with eyes almost squinted closed. (See photo in Series 9, pg. 246.) 21" - $135.00, $50.00.

Bonny Braids: 1951. Hard plastic/vinyl head. (See photo in Series 7, pg. 245.) **Mint:** 13½" - $155.00, $45.00. **Baby:** 13" - $135.00; $25.00.

Bonnie Walker: 1956. Hard plastic. Pin-jointed hips. Open mouth, flirty eyes. Marked "Ideal W-25." 23" - $90.00, $40.00.

Brandi: 1972. Of Crissy family. 17½" - $50.00, $20.00.

Brother/Baby Coos: 1951. Cloth/composition with hard plastic head. 25" - $125.00, $60.00. Composition head/latex: 24" - $100.00, $35.00. Hard plastic head/vinyl: 24" - $65.00, $20.00.

Bizzie Lizzie: 1971. 18" - $30.00, $15.00.

Bye-Bye Baby: 1960. Lifelike modeling. 12" - $175.00, $50.00; 25" - $365.00, $150.00.

Captain Action: 1966. Extra joints. (Add $50.00 if mint in box.) Complete, no box: 12" - $225.00 up. As Batman, etc.: $250.00 up.

Cinnamon: 1971. Of Crissy family. 13½" - $45.00, $20.00. **Black:** $60.00, $30.00. Hair Doodler: $35.00. Curly Ribbons: $40.00.

Comic heroines: Batgirl, Mera, Queen of Atlantis, Super Girl, Wonder Woman. Vinyl. (See photo in Series 7, pg. 243.) 11½" - $150.00, $60.00 up.

Composition baby: 1930s–1940s. (Also see "Mama Dolls.") Composition head and limbs with cloth body. Closed mouth. Sleep eyes, allow more for flirty eyes. Original. In excellent condition. 16" - $250.00, $95.00; 18" - $300.00, $100.00; 22" - $325.00, $125.00; 25" - $375.00, $150.00. **Flirty eyes:** 16" - $285.00, $100.00; 18" - $365.00, $125.00.

Composition child: All composition girl with sleep eyes, some flirty. Open mouth. Original clothes. Excellent condition. Marked "Ideal" and a number or "Ideal" in a diamond. 14" - $175.00, $70.00; 18" - $265.00, $90.00; 22" - $325.00, $100.00. **Cloth body:** With straight composition legs. 14" - $125.00, $45.00; 18" - $185.00, $70.00; 22" - $200.00, $80.00.

Composition/wood segmented characters: 1940s. Composition head and wooden segmented body. 9" - $235.00; 13" - $365.00. **Jiminy Cricket:** 9" - $345.00, $145.00. **Pinnochio:** 10" - $285.00; 12" - $325.00.

Cricket: 1970–1971. Of Crissy family. 15½" - $40.00, $15.00. **Black:** $50.00, $20.00. Look-a-round: $45.00, $20.00.

Crissy: 1968–1971. 17½" - $45.00, $15.00. Black: $60.00, $30.00. Look-a-round: 1972. $40.00, $20.00. Talking: 1971. $50.00, $30.00. **Floor length hair:** First issue in 1968. $145.00, $60.00. Moving: $45.00, $20.00. Swirls Curler: 1973. $40.00, $20.00. Twirly Beads: 1974. $35.00, $15.00. Hair Magic: 1977. No ponytail. $35.00, $15.00.

Daddy's Girl: 1961–1962. 29" - $650.00 up, $200.00. 42" - $850.00 up, $300.00 up.

Deanna Durbin: 1939. All composition. (See photo in Series 10, pg. 245.) 14" -

Rare 25" "Deanna Durbin" made of all composition with human hair wig and blue sleep eyes. Mint and original. The gown goes to floor with plain hem. Marked only "Ideal Doll 25" on back. This condition and size - $1,500.00 up. *Courtesy Patricia Wood.*

$500.00, $200.00; 17" - $700.00, $250.00; 21" - $775.00, $275.00; 24" - $925.00, $325.00; 27" - $1,050.00 up, $400.00. "Gulliver's Travels": Tight pants, boots, full sleeves, black wig. 21" - $1,000.00, $450.00.

Diana Ross: Plastic/vinyl. 17½" - $165.00, $80.00.

Dina: 1972. Of Crissy family. 15" - $50.00, $20.00.

Doctor Evil: 1965. Multi-jointed. Came with face masks. 11" - $50.00 up, $20.00.

Dodi: 1964. Of Tammy family. Marked "1964-Ideal-D0-9E." 9" - $40.00, $10.00.

Dorothy Hammill: 1977. 11½" - $25.00, $8.00.

Electro-Man: 1977. Switch sets off alarm. Activated by beam of light. 16" - $200.00 up.

Eric: 1976. Tuesday Taylor's boyfriend. 12" - $35.00, $15.00.

Flatsy: 1968–1970. Set of nine in frames. (See photo in Series 9, pg. 244.) 5" - $20.00 each, $6.00 each. With train, bicycle, etc.: $25.00 each, $6.00 each. Fashion: 1969. 8" - $20.00 each, $7.00 each.

Flexies: Wire and composition. **Baby Snooks (Fannie Brice), Mortimer Snerd:** 1938. Dolls include a Black figure (1938–1942), soldier (1938), clown (1938), and **Sunny Sue or Sam** (1938). 12" - $265.00 up, $100.00.

Flossie Flirt: 1938–1945. Cloth/composition. Flirty eyes: 20" - $275.00, $95.00; 24" - $350.00, $125.00. **Black:** $400.00, $150.00. Boy: 17" - $265.00, $100.00.

Giggles: Plastic/vinyl. 16" - $48.00, $20.00; 18" - $55.00, $35.00. **Black:** 18" - $125.00, $75.00. Baby: 15" - $35.00, $15.00.

Goody Two Shoes: 1965. 19" - $165.00, $45.00. Walking/talking: 19" - $100.00, $45.00; 27" - $225.00, $70.00.

Harmony: 1971. Battery operated. (See photo in Series 10, pg. 246.) 21" - $45.00, $25.00.

13" "Ginger" by Ideal. All composition and on Shirley Temple body. All original and mint. Marked "13." This doll - $375.00. *Courtesy Patricia Wood.*

15" "Jackie" by Ideal. Vinyl head with sleep eyes and upsweep hairdo. Hard plastic body. Plaid hat missing. Box says 1961. This doll was used for several dolls by Ideal and the only known "Jackie" is in this outfit. $425.00. *Courtesy Pat Graff.*

Harriet Hubbard Ayer: 1953. Hard plastic/vinyl. 15" - $200.00 up, $70.00; 17" - $300.00 up, $125.00.

Honey Moon: 1965. From "Dick Tracy." White yarn hair, Magic Skin body. (See photo in Series 9, pg. 245.) 15" - $50.00, 10.00. With helmet: $65.00. Cloth/vinyl: $65.00, $30.00.

Howdy Doody: 1940s. Composition head/cloth body. Floating disc eyes. Mouth moves by string in back of head. Original cowboy clothes. (See photo in Series 8, pg. 240.) 20" - $225.00 up.

Joan Palooka: 1952. 14" - $85.00, $45.00.

Joey Stivic (baby): 1976. One-piece body and limbs. Sexed boy. 15" - $35.00, $15.00.

Jiminy Cricket: 1939–1940. Composition/wood. 9" - $345.00, $145.00.

Judy Garland: 1939. All composition. Original: 14" - $1,000.00, $400.00; 18" - $1,400.00 up, $500.00. Replaced clothes: 14" - $825.00. Marked with backward "21": From 1941. 14" - $350.00, $125.00; 21" - $500.00, $165.00.

Judy Splinters: 1951. Cloth/vinyl/latex. Yarn hair, painted eyes. 18" - $165.00, $45.00; 22" - $235.00, $75.00; 36" - $400.00, $125.00.

Katie Kachoo: 1968. Raise arm and she sneezes. 17" - $30.00; $15.00.

Kerry: 1971. Of Crissy family. 17½" - $45.00, $15.00.

King Little: 1940. Composition/wood. 14" - $245.00, $95.00.

Kiss Me: 1951. See "Blessed Event."

18" "Judy Garland" as "Dorothy" from *The Wizard of Oz.* All composition with large sleep eyes and open mouth. 18" "Scarecrow" of cloth and yarn. Both are mint and original. Both made by Ideal Toy and Novelty Co. Dorothy - $1,400.00; Scarecrow - $800.00. *Courtesy Martha Sweeney.*

24" "Magic Lips" with oil cloth body and early vinyl head and limbs. Squeeze and her mouth presses shut. The mouth is open/closed with two lower modeled teeth. Mint and original with original box. $50.00. *Courtesy Jeannie Mauldin.*

Kissy: 22" - $55.00, $35.00. **Black:** $100.00, $50.00. Cuddly: 1964. Cloth/vinyl. 17" - $35.00, $15.00.

Kissy, Tiny: 1962. 16" - $30.00, $15.00. **Black:** $75.00, $30.00. Baby: 1966. Kisses when stomach is pressed. 12" - $25.00, $10.00.

Liberty Boy: 1918. 12" - $325.00, $90.00.

Little Lost Baby: 1968. Three-faced doll. (See photo in Series 7, pg. 249.) 22" - $65.00, $30.00.

Magic Lips: 1955. Vinyl coated cloth/vinyl. Lower teeth. 24" - $50.00, $25.00.

Magic Skin Baby: 1940s. Composition or hard plastic head. Stuffed latex rubber body and limbs. Good condition. 14" - $100.00; 17" - $165.00.

Mama style dolls: 1920–1930s. Composition/cloth: 14" - $200.00, $70.00; 16" - $250.00, $95.00; 18" - $300.00, $100.00; 24" - $350.00, $125.00. **Hard plastic/cloth:** 18" - $100.00, $45.00; 23" - $145.00, $55.00.

Mary Hartline: 1952 on. All hard plastic. (See photo in Series 8, pg. 241.)

8" "Mary Hartline" with one-piece body and legs. Painted-on boots over molded shoes with bows. Long blonde wig with side part. Felt heart glued to one side of head. Body marked "Ideal" in oval but was actually made by Duchess Doll Co. The set came with two cut-outs – "This is Mary Hartline, Band Leader for Super Circus" and "This is Cliffie, The Big Clown for Super Circus." On the back sides of cut-outs are advertisements for children's Weatherbird Shoes. Mint in box - $125.00. *Courtesy Ann Wencel.*

15" - $365.00, $100.00; 21–23": $575.00 up, $200.00. White dress: 15" - $400.00, $100.00. 8" in box: $125.00. Doll only: $75.00.

Mary Jane or Betty Jane: All composition, sleep eyes, open mouth. (Allow more for flirty eyes.) Marked "Ideal 18": 18" - $265.00 up, $100.00. 21" - $350.00, $150.00.

Mia: 1970. Of Crissy family. 15" - $45.00, $20.00.

Mini Monsters: (Dracky, Franky, etc.) 8½" - $20.00, $15.00.

Miss Clairol (Glamour Misty): 1965. Marked "W-12-3." 12" - $35.00, $15.00.

Miss Curity: 1952 on. Hard plastic: 8" - $90.00; 14" - $300.00 up, $100.00. Composition: 21" - $450.00, $125.00.

Miss Ideal: 1961. Multi-jointed. (See photo in Series 10, pg. 247.) 25" - $375.00 up, $100.00; 28" - $425.00, $165.00.

Miss Revlon: 1956–on. Mint. 10½" - $85.00, $35.00; 17" - $185.00 up, $65.00. 20" - $250.00, $95.00. In box/trunk: (See photo in Series 9, pg. 247.) 20" - $450.00 up; $125.00.

Mitzi: 1960. Teen. 12" - $165.00 up, $30.00.

Patti Playpal: 1960–on. 30" - $250.00, $100.00; 36" - $300.00, $150.00. **Black:** 30" - $350.00, $125.00; 36" - $425.00, $185.00. 1970s: (See photo in Series 10, pg. 247.) 15" - $45.00.

Pebbles: 1963. Plastic/vinyl and all vinyl. 8" - $15.00, $8.00; 12" - $25.00, $10.00; 16" - $35.00, $15.00.

Penny Playpal: 1959. 32" - $185.00, $80.00.

Pepper: 1964. Freckles. Marked "Ideal - P9-3." 9" - $35.00, $15.00.

Pete: 1964. Freckles. Marked "Ideal - P8." 7½" - $40.00, $25.00.

16" "Marion" made of composition with cloth body and legs. Short arms with lower part made of composition. Celluloid over tin sleep eyes. Mohair wig in original set. Marked "Ideal" in diamond on head. Circa 1918. $250.00. *Courtesy Glorya Woods.*

18" "Mary Jane" by Ideal. All composition child with happy face and flirty eyes. Deep dimple in chin. Original aqua dress and attached panties. Marked on body "18." $265.00. *Courtesy Kathy Riddick.*

This cute "Mortimer Snerd" Flexie is only 13" tall and is one of the early "action figures." He has composition head, hands, and feet. The rest is flexible metal cable. Painted features. Original two-piece brown striped suit with blue striped shirt and black tie. $265.00 up. *Courtesy Kathy Riddick.*

Peter Playpal: 1961. 36-38" - $375.00, $150.00.

Pinocchio: 1938–1941. Composition/wood. (See photo in Series 8, pg. 243.) Mint condition: 10" - $285.00; 12" - $325.00. Near mint: 10" - $200.00; 12" - $275.00, $100.00; 21" - $500.00, $250.00.

Pixie: 1967. Foam body. 16" - $20.00, $10.00.

Plassie: 1942. Composition and cloth body. 14" - $150.00, 22" - $265.00. Magic Skin body: 1950s. 14" - $95.00; 22" - $185.00.

Posie Walker: 1953–1956. Hard plastic with vinyl head. Jointed knees. Marked "Ideal VP-17." 17" - $90.00, $40.00.

Real Live Baby: 1965. Head bobs. 20" - $30.00, $15.00.

Sally-Sallykins: 1934. Composition/cloth. Flirty eyes, two upper and lower teeth. 14" - $135.00, $60.00; 19" - $200.00, $80.00; 25" - $265.00, $100.00.

Samantha The Witch: 1965. Green eyes. Marked "M-12-E-2." (See photo in Series 9, pg. 248.) 12" - $145.00, $50.00.

Sandy McCall: See Betsy McCall section.

Sara Ann: 1952 on. Hard plastic. Marked "P-90." (See photo in Series 7, pg. 248.) Saran wig: 14" - $285.00 up, $95.00. Marked "P-93": 21" - $385.00 up, $125.00.

Saralee: 1950. Cloth/vinyl. **Black:** 18" - $285.00, $145.00.

Sara Stimson: (Little Miss Marker) 1980. Marked "1979." $20.00, $8.00.

Saucy Walker: 1951 on. 16" - $85.00, $30.00; 17" - $125.00, $50.00; 22" - $195.00, $85.00. **Black:** 18" - $200.00, $80.00.

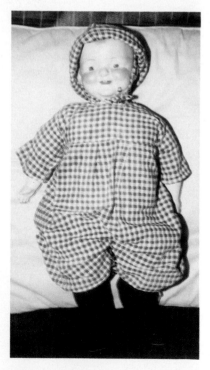 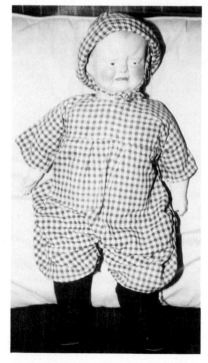

15½" "Snoozie Smiles - The Surprise Baby" has composition head with two faces. Cloth body and legs. Cloth upper arms and composition lower arms. Painted features. Original romper which also came in pink. Mint - $365.00. *Courtesy Jeannie Mauldin.*

Seven Dwarfs: Composition: 12" - $350.00 each; 16" - $425.00 each. Cloth body, composition head: 16" - $550.00 each; 18–20" - $625.00 each. Puppet: Cloth/composition. Pull string operates mouth. 20" - $425.00.

Shirley Temple: See that section.

Snoozie: 1933. Composition/cloth. Molded hair, sleep eyes, open yawning mouth. Marked "B Lipfert." 13" - $150.00, $50.00; 16" - $250.00, $100.00; 20" - $355.00, $125.00.

Snow White: 1937 on. All composition. Black wig. Sleep and/or flirty eyes. On marked Shirley Temple body. (See photo in Series 10, pg. 248.) 12" - $475.00, $200.00; 18" - $575.00, $225.00. **Molded hair:** 1939. Eyes painted to side. 14" - $200.00, $85.00; 18" - $375.00, $125.00.

Sparkle Plenty: 1947. Hard plastic and vinyl. 15" - $100.00, $30.00. Magic Skin: 15" - $50.00, $20.00.

Suzy Playpal: 1960–1961. Chubby vinyl body and limbs. Marked "Ideal O.E.B. 24-3." 24" - $150.00, $60.00.

Tabitha: 1966. Cloth/vinyl. Eyes painted to side. Marked "Tat-14-H-62" or "82." 15" - $40.00, $20.00.

Tara: 1976. Black doll with growing hair. 16" - $40.00, $20.00.

Tammy: 1962. 12" - $50.00, $20.00. **Black:** Marked "BS-12-Ideal." $300.00. Grown-up: 1965. 12" - $45.00, $20.00. Black: $75.00. Sun Tan: $30.00, $15.00.

Tammy's mom: 1963. Eyes to side. Marked: "Ideal W-18-L." 12" - $55.00, $30.00.

Ted: 1963. Tammy's brother. Molded hair. Marked "Ideal B-12-U-2." (See photo in Series 9, pg. 249.) 12½" - $55.00, $30.00.

Thumbelina: 1962 on. **Kissing:** 10½" - $20.00, $8.00. **Tearful:** 15" - $30.00, $12.00. **Wake Up:** 17" - $45.00, $20.00. **Black:** 10½" - $50.00, $20.00.

Tickletoes: 1930s. Composition/cloth. 15" - $150.00, $85.00; 21" - $225.00, $100.00. Magic Skin body: 1948. Hard plastic head. 15" - $60.00, $15.00.

13" all composition "Snow White" with red bodice and red print on skirt. Marked "Ideal." (See Series 10, pg. 248 for same doll with blue bodice and skirt printing.) $475.00. *Courtesy Susan Giradot.*

Tiffany Taylor: 1973. Top of head swivels to change hair color. 19" - $45.00, $15.00. **Black:** 19" - $45.00, $20.00.

Tippy or Timmy Tumbles: 16" - $20.00, $15.00. **Black:** $30.00, $20.00.

Toni: 1949–on. (Allow more for mint in box.) 14" P-90; 14" - $300.00 up, $85.00. P-91: 15" - $325.00 up, $95.00. P-92: 17–18" - $400.00 up, $100.00. P-93: 21" - $475.00 up, $145.00. P-94: 23" - $525.00 up, $200.00. Walker: $300.00 up, $75.00.

Tressy: Of Crissy family. 17½" - $45.00, $20.00. Black: $60.00, $30.00.

Trilby: 1940s. (See photo in Series 9, pg. 251.) Composition: Mint and original. 15" - $250.00. **Three-faced baby:** 1951. Cloth/vinyl. 20" - $55.00, $25.00.

Tubsy: 1966. Plastic/vinyl. Battery operated. 18" - $30.00, $10.00.

Tuesday Taylor: 1977. 11½" - $35.00, $15.00.

Uneeda Kid: 1914–1919. Looks like Schoenhut doll. Cloth body, composition head/limbs. Bent right arm. Painted eyes and hair. Yellow rain slicker and hat. Molded-on black boots. (See photo in Series 9, pg. 251.) 16" - $450.00, $150.00; 24" - $675.00, $225.00.

Upsy Dazy: 1972. Foam body. Stands on head. 15" - $20.00, $8.00.

Velvet: 1970–1971. Of Crissy family. 15" - $45.00, $15.00. **Black:** $85.00, $30.00. Look-a-round: $50.00, $20.00. Talking: $50.00, $30.00. Moving: $45.00, $15.00. Beauty Braider: 1973. $40.00, $15.00. Swirly Daisies: 1974. $40.00, $15.00.

Wingy: Hard plastic body, vinyl head. From Dick Tracy comics. (See photo in Series 8, pg. 247.) 14" - $145.00 up, $50.00.

15" "Toni" that is extremely pretty and in mint condition. All hard plastic. Original dress. Marked "P-91." $300.00 up. *Courtesy Glorya Woods.*

Three P-90 "Toni" dolls made of all hard plastic with nylon wigs. All original except for shoes and socks. Each - $300.00. *Courtesy Susan Giradot.*

20" "Tina Toddler" Imperial Doll Company. (Some are marked "IMPCO" or "IMCO.") This doll has never been played with and is mint with original tag. All hard plastic. Built just like Ideal's "Saucy Walker." Unmarked. $85.00. *Courtesy Kris Lundquist.*

First prices are for mint condition dolls; second prices are for played with, dirty or missing clothing and accessories.

Baby Bundles: 16" - $15.00, $10.00. Black: $22.00, $15.00.

Baby Yawnie: 1974. Cloth/vinyl. 15" - $20.00, $8.00.

Big Foot: All rigid vinyl. (See photo in Series 7, pg. 253.) 13" - $15.00, $6.00.

Bionic Woman: 12" - $25.00, $9.00.

Butch Cassidy or Sundance Kid: 4" - $20.00, $9.00 each.

Blythe: 1972. Pull string to change the color of eyes. (See photo in Series 9, pg. 254.) 11½" - $40.00, $10.00.

Charlie Chaplin: 1973. All cloth with walking mechanism. 14" - $60.00, $25.00.

Cover Girls: 1978. 12½" dolls with bendable elbows and knees. **Dana: Black** doll. $40.00, $12.00. **Darci:** Blonde hair. $35.00, $12.00. **Erica:** Red hair. (See photo in Series 10, pg. 252.) $35.00, $12.00.

Crumpet: 1970. Plastic/vinyl. 18" - $30.00, $18.00.

Dusty: 12". $20.00, $8.00.

Gabbigale: 1972. 18" - $40.00, $15.00. **Black**: $45.00, $20.00.

Garden Gals: 1972. Hand bent to hold watering can. 6½" - $10.00, $4.00.

Hardy Boys: 1978. Shaun Cassidy and Parker Stevenson. 12" - $20.00, $8.00.

International Velvet: 1976. Tatum O'Neill. 11½" - $25.00, $10.00.

Jenny Jones and Baby: 1973. All vinyl. 9" Jenny and 2½" baby. $15.00, $6.00. Set - $25.00, $8.00.

Oscar Goldman: 13" - $25.00, $9.00.

Six Million Dollar Man: Lee Majors. 13" - $22.00, $8.00.

Skye: Black doll. 12" - $25.00, $10.00.

Star Wars: 1974–1978. Large size figures. **R2-D2:** 7½" - $150.00 up, $40.00. **C-3PO:** 12" - $150.00 up, $50.00. **Darth Vader:** 15" - $175.00 up, $25.00. **Boba Fett:** 13" - $250.00 up, $50.00. **Jawa:** 8½" - $65.00, $20.00. **IG-88:** 15" - $375.00 up, $65.00. **Stormtrooper:** 12" - $200.00 up,

9½" "Bob Scout" in extra packaged outfit. (White doll was "Steve Scout.") Multi-jointed. Marked "1972 G.M.F.G.I./Kenner Prod./Cinncinati/No. 7005/Made in Hong Kong. $32.00. *Courtesy Kathy Tvrdik.*

12" "Skye" with multi-jointed vinyl body. Open/closed smile mouth. Wears an original outfit. Made in 1976. $25.00.

$40.00. Leia: 11½" - $145.00 up, $25.00.
Han Solo: 12" - $145.00, $25.00. **Luke Skywalker:** 13½" - $195.00, $25.00. **Chewbacca:** 15" - $125.00 up, $40.00. **Obi Wan Kenobi:** 12" - $195.00, $45.00. **Yoda:** 9" - $90.00 up. **Star Wars characters, MIB:** Sealed box. Any of above - $595.00 up.

Strawberry Shortcake: 1980s. 4½–5". Each - $12.00 up. **Sleep eyes:** Each - $30.00. **Sour Grapes, etc.:** 9" characters. $15.00. Mint in box: 4½–5". Each - $18.00.

6" "Reed Smith" (Chuck Norris) and 6" "Kimo" from the Karate Kommando set made in 1986 by Kenner. Clothes are molded on. Each - $25.00. *Courtesy Don Tvrdik.*

13" "Maskatron," robot enemy of the Bionic Man. Has human mask disguises. (His own face is a computer.) From 1977. Complete set - $45.00. *Courtesy Kathy Tvrdik.*

11½" "Miss America - Raquel" that was part of a series of dolls. Excellent quality. Marked "Kenner/Div. of Tonka. 1991." $30.00. *Courtesy Kathy Tvrdik.*

Steve Scout: 1974. 9" - $20.00, $9.00. **Bob Scout: Black.** $25.00, $10.00.

Sweet Cookie: 1972. 18" - $30.00, $12.00.

KEWPIE

First prices are for mint condition dolls; second prices are for dolls played with, crazed or cracked, dirty, soiled or not original.
Bisque Kewpies: See antique Kewpie section.
All composition: Jointed shoulder only. 9" - $165.00, $70.00; 12" - $235.00, $85.00; 14" - $285.00, $100.00. Jointed hips, neck and shoulder: 9" - $250.00, $100.00; 14" - $375.00, $150.00. **Black:** 12" - $400.00.
Talcum powder container: 7-8" - $175.00.

Celluloid: (See photo in Series 8, pg. 253.) 2" - $35.00; 5" - $75.00; 9" - $125.00. **Black:** 5" - $150.00.
Bean bag body: Must be clean. 10" - $35.00, $10.00.
Cloth body: Vinyl head and limbs. 16" - $185.00, $95.00. Composition head: $325.00.
Kewpie Gal: With molded hair/ ribbon. 8" - $40.00, $20.00.
Hard plastic: 1950s. One-piece body and head. 8" - $125.00, $30.00; 12" - $200.00, $95.00; 16" - $285.00, $125.00.

14" "Kewpie" with composition socket head and limbs, cloth stuffed body. Painted features. $325.00. *Courtesy Susan Giradot.*

12" and 13" plush and vinyl "Kewpies" made by Knickerbocker. The white one is very scarce and earlier than the red one. Both are scarce in this condition because these made extremely fine play dolls and sleeping mates. Red - $45.00; white - $60.00. *Courtesy Glorya Woods.*

Fully jointed at shoulder, neck and hips: 12–13" - $400.00, $175.00; 16" - $500.00, $225.00.

Ragsy: 1964. Vinyl. One-piece molded-on clothes with heart on chest. 8" - $40.00, $20.00. Without heart: 1971. 8" - $20.00, $10.00.

Thinker: 1971. One-piece vinyl. Sitting down. 4" - $20.00, $8.00.

Kewpie, vinyl: Hinge jointed: (Miss Peep body) 16" - $225.00, $95.00. Jointed at shoulder only: 9" - $40.00, $10.00; 12" - $65.00, $20.00; 14" - $80.00, $30.00. Jointed at neck, shoulders and hips: 9" - $80.00, $25.00; 12" - $135.00, $35.00; 14" - $185.00, $50.00; 27" - $350.00, $165.00. **No joints:** 9" - $25.00, $10.00; 12" - $45.00, $15.00; 14" - $60.00, $20.00. **Black:** 9" - $50.00, $15.00; 12" - $75.00, $25.00; 14" - $125.00, $45.00. Bean bag type body: 1970s. Vinyl head. 10" - $40.00, $15.00.

Ward's Anniversary: 1972. 8" - $60.00, $20.00.

All cloth: Made by Kreuger. All one-piece: Including clothing. 12" - $185.00, $90.00; 16" - $350.00, $100.00; 20" - $485.00, $175.00. Removable dress and bonnet: 12" - $265.00, $85.00; 16" - $400.00, $145.00; 20" - $600.00, $200.00; 25" - $1,200.00, $500.00.

Kewpie Baby: 1960s. With hinged joints. 15" - $185.00, $80.00; 18" - $265.00, $95.00.

Kewpie Baby: One-piece stuffed body and limbs. 15" - $225.00, $85.00; 18" - $300.00, $70.00.

Plush: 1960s. Usually red body with vinyl face mask. Made by Knickerbocker. 6" - $45.00, $20.00; 10" - $60.00, $30.00.

11½" Klumpe look-alike with hard stuffed cloth body, painted mask face, and mohair wig. Clothes sewn to doll. Tagged "Layna/Spain." $50.00. *Courtesy Marie Ernst.*

10½" Klumpe figure that is all cloth over wire frame. Flannel and cotton clothes. Holding fishing pole wrapped in yarn. Painted features. Hand tag printed "I am a Klumpe Doll." Hand made in Spain and distributed by Effanbee. $95.00. *Courtesy Patricia Wood.*

KNICKERBOCKER TOY COMPANY

First prices are for mint condition dolls; second prices are for dolls played with, crazed or cracked, dirty, soiled or not original.

Alexander: Comic character from "Blondie." All composition, painted hair and features. 9" - $375.00 up, $145.00.

Bozo Clown: 14" - $25.00; 24" - $65.00.

Cinderella: With two heads – one is sad; the other with tiara. 16" - $20.00.

Clown: Cloth. 17" - $20.00.

Composition child: 1938–on. Bent right arm at elbow. 15" - $225.00 up.

Daddy Warbucks: 1982. 7" - $18.00, $9.00.

Dagwood: Composition, painted hair and features. 14" - $650.00, $275.00.

Disney: 1930s. Donald Duck, Mickey Mouse, etc. All cloth. $500.00 up, $200.00.

Flintstones: 6" - $8.00 each; 17" - $35.00 each.

Jiminy Cricket: All composition. 10" - $465.00, $200.00.

Kewpie: See Kewpie section.

Little House on the Prairie: 1978. 12" - $22.00 each.

Little Orphan Annie: 1982. 6" - $20.00, $8.00.

Mickey Mouse: 1930–1940s. Composition and cloth. 18" - $1,200.00 up.

Miss Hannigan: 7" - $16.00, $9.00.

Molly: 5½" - $15.00, $7.00.

Pinocchio: All plush and cloth. 13" - $250.00 up. All composition: 13" - $285.00 up.

Punjab: 7" - $15.00, $9.00.

Scarecrow: Made of cloth. 23½" - $250.00 up.

Seven Dwarfs: 10" all composition. Each - $245.00 up. All cloth: 14" - $275.00 each.

Sleeping Beauty: 1939. All composition. Bent right arm. 15" - $400.00 up; 18" - $525.00.

Snow White: 1937. All composition. Bent right arm. Black wig. (See photo in Series 10, pg. 257.) 15" - $350.00 up; 20" - $465.00 up. Molded hair and ribbon: 13" - $300.00. All cloth: 16" - $365.00.

Soupy Sales: 1966. Vinyl and cloth. Non-removeable clothes. 13" - $125.00.

Two-headed dolls: 1960s. Vinyl face masks – one crying, one smiling. 12" - $18.00.

15" "Snow White" with molded hair, ribbon, and bow. Left arm bent at elbow. Marked "Walt Disney/1937/ Knickerbocker." Redressed - $300.00. *Courtesy Glorya Woods.*

7" "Glamour Cowgirl" (Laurie Anders) that appeared on the Ken Murray Show, 1950–1953. She wears short pants under chaps so legs are bare in back. Across back of belt is "Ah love the wide open spaces." All hard plastic, jointed hips and shoulders. Made by Marcie in 1953. $20.00. *Courtesy Glorya Woods.*

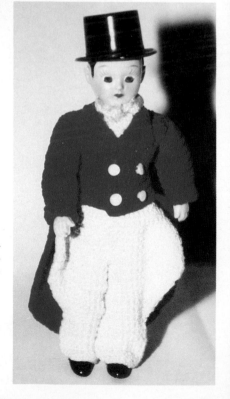

7" all hard plastic man made by Marcie. Jointed at shoulder only. Painted-on shoes. Crocheted riding habit may be original. Plastic top hat. $20.00.

18" "Miss Toddler" was also called "Miss Marx." Battery operated walker has a rod between feet. She laughs as she walks. Modeled-on shoes and socks and molded-on clothes. Has painted features. She is not excellent quality, but value is high because she is rare and very unusual. $75.00. *Courtesy Randy Numley.*

MATCHBOX

26" "PeeWee Herman" that is a puppet and made of vinyl and cloth. Made by Matchbox in 1989. Shown with a 11" all vinyl with maker and year unknown. 26" - $65.00, 11" - $30.00. *Courtesy David Spurgeon.*

First prices are for mint condition dolls; second prices are for dolls that have been played with, are dirty, soiled, not original and/or do not have accessories. Except for Barbie family dolls, these prices are for mint dolls.

Allan: Bendable legs: 12" - $200.00. Straight legs: $95.00. Dressed boxed doll: $750.00 up.

Baby First Step: 1964. 18" - $25.00, $15.00. Talking: $30.00, $15.00.

Baby Go Bye Bye: 1968. 12" - $12.00, $7.00.

Baby's Hungry: 1966. 17" - $25.00, $15.00.

Baby Love Light: 1970. Battery operated. 16" - $20.00, $10.00.

Baby Pataburp: 13" - $25.00, $15.00.

Baby Play-A-Lot: 1971. 16" - $20.00, $10.00.

Baby Say 'n See: 1965. 17" - $20.00, $10.00.

Baby Secret: 1965. 18" - $30.00, $15.00.

A fantastic 20" "Chatty Cathy" with perfect face color, condition, and original clothes. Mint condition; value exceeds "book price." $150.00. *Courtesy Susan Giradot.*

Baby Small Talk: 1967. 11" - $15.00, $8.00. **Cinderella:** $20.00, $10.00. **Black:** $25.00, $10.00.

Baby Tenderlove: 1969. Newborn: 13" - $15.00, $5.00. Talking: 1969. 16" - $20.00, $10.00. Living: 1970. 20" - $30.00. Molded hair piece: 1972. 11½" - $35.00. Brother: 1972. Sexed. 13" - $40.00.

Baby Teenie Talk: 1965. 17" - $25.00, $12.00.

Baby Walk 'n Play: 1968. 11" - $15.00, $8.00.

Baby Walk 'n See: 18" - $20.00, $15.00.

Barbie: See that section.

Bozo: 18" - $30.00, $15.00.

Brad: 1971. Bend knees. $125.00. Talking: 1970. $135.00.

Bucky Love Notes: 1974. Press body parts for tunes. 12" - $16.00.

Buffie: 1967. With Mrs. Beasley. 6" - $60.00, $20.00; 10" - $150.00, $45.00.

Capt. Lazer: 1967. (See photo in Series 9, pg. 259.) 12½" - $265.00 up, $60.00.

Cara: 1975. Black doll. Free Movin': $25.00. Ballerina: $25.00. Quick Curl: $25.00.

Casey: 1975. 11½". Packaged in baggie: $40.00. Twist 'n Turn: $250.00.

Casper The Ghost: 1964: 16" - $30.00, $10.00. 1971: 5" - $15.00, $6.00.

Charlie's Angels: 1978. Marked "1966." 11½" - $20.00, $8.00.

Charmin' Chatty: 1961. 25" - $145.00, $50.00.

Chatty Brother, Tiny: 1963. 15" - $30.00, $10.00. **Baby:** 1962. $25.00, $10.00. **Black:** $40.00, $15.00.

Chatty Cathy: 1962 on. 20" - $75.00, $40.00. Brunette: Brown eyes. $95.00, $45.00. **Black:** $200.00, $55.00.

Cheerleader: 1965. 13" - $20.00, $9.00.

Cheerful Tearful: 1965. 13" - $20.00, $8.00. Tiny: 1966. 6½" - $20.00, $8.00.

Chris: 1967–1968. 6" - $150.00.

Christie: 1968. Black doll. 11½" - $75.00 up. Talking: 1969. $175.00 up.

Super Star: 1976. $75.00 up. Kissing: 1979. $45.00. Golden Dream: 1980. $35.00. Live Action: $140.00. Beauty Secrets: $25.00. Fashion Photo: $55.00. Pink & Pretty: $55.00. Supersize: $95.00. Twist 'n Turn: $195.00.

Curtis: Free Movin': 1976. $45.00.

Cynthia: 1971. 20" - $45.00, $20.00.

Dancerina: 1968. 24" - $50.00, $20.00. Black: $70.00, $30.00. Tiny: Not battery operated. 16" - $35.00, $15.00. Black: $50.00, $25.00. Teeny: 12" - $30.00.

Debbie Boone: 1978. (See photo in Series 9, pg. 261.) 11½" - $45.00, $15.00.

Dick Van Dyke: 25" - $70.00, $30.00.

Donny Osmond: 1978. Marked "1968." 12" - $45.00, $12.00.

Drowsy: 1966. Pull string talker. 15" - $18.00, $6.00.

Dr. Doolittle: 1967. Talker. Cloth/ vinyl: 22½" - $65.00, $25.00. All vinyl: 6" - $25.00, $7.00.

Fluff: 9" - $135.00.

14" "Tiny Chatty Baby" that is in mint condition and never played with. Rare Black version. $40.00 up. *Courtesy Cris Johnson.*

Three sizes of "Dancerina" with the tallest being 24" and battery operated. The other two, "Teeny Dancerina" and "Tiny Dancerina," are hand operated and hard to find. All are original. All have plastic crown and knob on top of head so child could rotate them. "Dancerina" - $50.00; "Tiny" - $35.00; "Teeny" - $30.00.

Francie: 1966. (See photo in Series 8, pg. 265.) 11½" - $100.00 up. No bangs: $850.00. **Black:** 1967. $950.00 up. Twist n' Turn: 1967. $325.00. Quick Curl: 1973. $65.00. Malibu: 1978. $45.00. Grow Pretty Hair: $150.00. Hair Happening: $295.00. Packed in baggie: $100.00. Bendable legs: $200.00. Straight legs: $150.00. Busy: $275.00.

Grandma Beans: 11" - $12.00, $5.00.

Gorgeous Creatures: 1979. Mae West style body with animal heads. Each - $20.00, $8.00.

Grizzly Adams: 1971. 10" - $45.00, $15.00.

Guardian Goddesses: 1979. 11½" in mint condition. Each - $145.00 up, $45.00.

Herman Munster: 16" - $30.00, $15.00.

Heros In Action: 1975. Set of 14. Marked "Mattel Hong Kong. Pat Pending." 3" - $65.00 each.

Hi Dottie: 1969. 17" - $30.00, $15.00.

Honey Hill Bunch: 1975. Set of six. 6" - $10.00, $3.00.

How West Was Won: 1971. 10" - $45.00. Indians: 10" - $50.00.

Hush Lil Baby: 15" - $18.00, $8.00.

Jamie, Walking: 1969. With dog. (See photo in Series 8, pg. 265.) 11½" - $200.00 up.

Jimmy Osmond: 1979. 10" - $65.00, $9.00.

Julia: 1969. 11½" nurse from TV show by same name. One-piece uniform: $125.00 up. Two-piece uniform: $175.00. Talking: $125.00 up.

Kelley: 11½". Quick Curl: $75.00. Yellowstone: $175.00.

Ken: Bendable legs: $250.00. Busy: $150.00. Busy Talking: $125.00. Crystal: $25.00. Day To Night: $25.00. Dream Date: $25.00. Dressed boxed doll: $300.00.

14" "Mariko Drama" made of cloth and bisque. made by Sekiguchi of Japan for Mattel in 1983. There were four limited edition dolls in the set. $200.00. *Courtesy Gloria Anderson.*

Fashion Jeans: $30.00. Flocked hair: $150.00. Free Movin': $40.00. Gold Metal Skier: $80.00. Horse Lovin': $25.00. Live Action: $95.00. Live Action On Stage: $135.00. Mod Hair: $150.00. Now Look: $55.00. Painted hair, straight legs: $115.00. Super Star: $75.00. Talking: $125.00. Walk Lively: $75.00.

Kiddles: 1966–on. Doll only: Mint condition. (Add $10.00 more for Black dolls.) $25.00 up. With cars: $50.00 up. With planes: $55.00 up. In ice cream cones: $25.00 up. In jewelry: $35.00 up. In perfume bottles: $20.00 up. In bottles: $35.00 up. With lollipops: $35.00. With cup and saucer: $100.00 up. **Storybooks:** With accessories. $125.00. **Mint in box -** $200.00 up. Baby Beddle: In carriage. $165.00 up. **Peter Paniddle:** Made one year. With accessories. $150.00. Mint in box - $300.00. **Santa:** Complete - $125.00 up. **Tinkerbelle:** Mint - $80.00. Fair condition - $30.00. **Animals:** $40.00 up. **Circus necklace:** 1968. $60.00 each.

Kitty O'Neill: 1978. (See photo in Series 9, pg. 261.) 11½" - $25.00, $9.00.

Lil Big Guy: 13" - $15.00, $8.00.

Midge: 1963. Freckles. 11½" - $150.00 up. 1965: Bendable legs. $550.00 up. Dressed boxed doll: $800.00 up. Wig wardrobe: $200.00.

Miss America: 1972. Walk Lively. White gown. $175.00. 1974: Quick Curl - $150.00.

Mother Goose: 20" - $25.00, $10.00.

Mrs. Beasley: Talking. 16" - $35.00, $15.00.

Peachy & Puppets: 1972. 17" - $20.00, $8.00.

P.J.: 11½" - $50.00 up. Talking: $125.00 up. Live Action: 1971. $95.00. Gold Medal: 1975. $75.00. Deluxe Quick Curl: 1976. $65.00. Free Movin': $45.00. Twist 'N Turn: $225.00. Fashion Photo: $45.00. Sweet Roses: $35.00.

Randy Reader: 1967. 19" - $45.00, $18.00.

Real Sister: 14" - $20.00, $10.00.

Ricky: 1965. Has red hair and freckles. (See photo in Series 9, pg. 262.) $125.00 up.

Rockers: 1986–1987. Dana, Dee-Dee, Derek, Diva. 11½" - $25.00 each.

Rockflowers: 1970. 6½" - $25.00, $10.00.

Rose Bud Babies: 6½" - $15.00 up, $10.00.

Saucy: 1972. 15" - $55.00. Black: $75.00.

Scooby Doo: 1964. Vinyl and cloth girl. Mint: 21" - $65.00, $25.00.

Shaun: 1979. 12" - $22.00, $10.00.

Shogun Warrior: 23½". All plastic. Battery operated. Each - $250.00 up.

Shrinking Violet: 1962. Pull string talker, features move. Cloth, yarn hair. (See photo in Series 7, pg. 265.) 15" - $45.00 up, $15.00.

Singing Chatty: 1964. Pull string. 17" - $30.00, $10.00.

Sister Belle: 1961. 17" - $35.00, $15.00.

Skediddles: 1966–on. (See photo in Series 9, pg. 264.) 4" - $40.00 up. Disney: $85.00 up. Cherry Blossom: 1967. $85.00. Cartoon: $60.00.

Skipper: 1963. (See photo in Series 9, pg. 263.) $100.00 up. Growing up: 1976. $65.00 up. Living: $55.00. Funtime: 1967. Bend knees. $75.00. Pose 'N Play: 1970. $50.00; Super Teen: 1979. $30.00. Western: 1981. $25.00. Malibu: $30.00. Bendable legs: $225.00. Dressed boxed doll: $300.00 up. Quick Curl: $65.00. Twist 'N Turn: $175.00.

Skooter: 1964. Freckles. (See photo in Series 9, pg. 263.) $125.00 up. Bendable legs: $285.00.

Small Talk: 1967. Pull string. 11" - $20.00, $8.00. Sister: 1967. 10" - $20.00, $8.00. Cinderella: 1968. $25.00, $10.00.

Small Walk, Sister: 1967. 11!/2" - $25.00, $10.00.

Stacey: Talking: $275.00. Twist 'N Turn: 1968. $275.00. Short turned-up hair: $295.00.

15" "Saucy" made of rigid vinyl and vinyl. Move arm to make face change expressions. All original. $55.00. *Courtesy Shirley's Doll House.*

Star Spangled Dolls: 1976. Uses Sunshine Family adults. Marked "1973." Regina & Richard Stanton, Southern Belle, New England Girl, Pioneer Daughter, etc. Each - $45.00.

Steffie: 1972. Busy or Talking: $175.00 up. Walk Lively: $150.00.

Swingy: 20" - $30.00, $12.00.

Tatters: 10" - $40.00, $15.00.

Teachy Keen: 1966. 17" - $35.00, $15.00.

Teeners: 4" - $30.00, $10.00.

Tiff: Pose 'N Play: $250.00.

Timey Tell: (Chatty Tell) 1964, watch attached to wrist. 17" - $30.00, $10.00.

Tinkerbelle: 19" - $25.00, $12.00.

Tippy Toes: 1967. 16" - $20.00, $9.00. Tricycle or horse: $20.00, $5.00.

Truly Scrumptious: 11½", original. Doll only: $175.00 up. Straight legs: $350.00 up. Talking: 1968. $375.00.

Tutti: 1965. 6" - $150.00 up. Packaged sets: Cookin' Goodies: $350.00. Me and My Dog: $400.00. Melody in Pink:

$350.00. Night, Night: $250.00. Sundae Treat: $450.00. Swing-A-Ling: $350.00. Walkin' My Dolly: $275.00.

Todd: 1965. 6" - $150.00 up. Sundae Treat: $450.00.

Twiggy: 1967. 11½" - $225.00 up.

Upsy-Downsy: 1969. 3" - $20.00, $8.00.

Welcome Back Kotter: 1973. 9" figures. $12.00–20.00.

Zython: 1977. Has glow-in-dark head. Enemy in "Space 1999" series. $75.00, $20.00.

"Styla Blue" is a friend of "Spectra" and has blue and silver hair. Marked "Mattel/1986." Mint condition - $40.00. *Courtesy Kathy Tvrdik.*

MEGO

First prices are for mint condition dolls; second prices are for ones that are dirty or not original. For full Mego listing, see *Modern Collector Dolls, Volume 4,* page 172–177.

Action Jackson: 1971–1972. Beard and no beard. 8" - $165.00 up.

Batman: 1974. Action figure. 8" - $20.00, $8.00. Arch enemy set: Four figures in series. 8" - $25.00, $8.00.

Camelot: 1974. Five figures in series. 8" - $65.00, $20.00.

Captain & Tenille: 1977. 12" - $25.00, $10.00.

Cher: 12" - $20.00 up, $6.00. Dressed in Indian outfit: $25.00, $10.00.

CHiPs: Ponch and Jon, 1977. 8" - $15.00, $6.00.

Diana Ross: 12½" - $50.00 up, $20.00.

Dinah Mite: 1973. 7½" - $12.00, $5.00. Black: $15.00, $7.00.

Haddie Mod: 1971. Teen type. 11½" - $15.00, $6.00.

Happy Days Set: 1974. (See photo in Series 9, pg. 267.) **Fonzie:** $15.00, $6.00. Others: $10.00, $3.00.

Jaclyn Smith: 1975. 12½" - $25.00, $10.00.

Joe Namath: 1971. 12" - $60.00, $20.00.

KISS: 1978. Four figures in series. 12½" - $60.00, $20.00.

Kojack: 1977–1978. (See photo in Series 9, pg. 267.) 9" - $25.00, $9.00.

Lainie: 1973. Jointed waist. Battery operated. 19" - $40.00, $15.00.

Laverne & Shirley: 1977. 11½" - $25.00, $9.00. **Lenny & Squiggy:** 12" - $30.00, $10.00.

One Million BC: 1974–1975. Five figures in series. 8" - $20.00, $8.00.

Our Gang set: 1975. Six figures in series. Mickey: 5" - $22.00, $10.00. Others: 5" - $12.00, $6.00.

Planet of Apes: 1974–1975. Five figures in series. 8" - $20.00, $8.00.

Pirates: 1971. Four figures in series. 8" - $75.00, $30.00.

Robin Hood set: 1971. Four figures in series) 8" - $65.00, $30.00.

Soldiers: 8" - $25.00 up, $10.00.

Sonny: Smiling in 1977; not smiling in 1976. 12" - $25.00 up, $9.00.

Starsky or Hutch: 1975. 8" - $15.00, $6.00. **Captain or Huggy Bear:** $20.00, $8.00. **Chopper:** $22.00, $10.00.

Star Trek set: 1974–1975. Six figures in series. (See photo in Series 8, pg. 269, Series 10, pg. 263.) 8" - $45.00, $25.00.

Star Trek aliens: 1974–1977. Mugatu, Romulan, Talos, Andorian, Cheron, The Gorn, The Keeper, and Neptunian. 8" - $25.00, $9.00.

Super Women: 1973. Four action figures in series. 8" - $18.00, $6.00.

Suzanne Somers: 1975. 12½" - $30.00, $12.00.

Waltons: 1975. Six figures in series. 8" - $15.00, $6.00.

Wild West set: 1974. Six figures in series. 8" - $50.00, $20.00.

Wonder Woman: (Lynda Carter) 1975. 12½" - $25.00, $10.00.

8" "King Arthur" from "Camelot" series. Made by Mego and will be marked "1974." $65.00.

8" "Friar Tuck," "Will Scarlett," and "Little John" made by Mego in 1975. Will be marked "1971." Each - $65.00.

MEGO

World's Greatest Super Heros:
1974–1975. Eight figures in series. (See
photo in Series 9, pg. 267.) 8" - $20.00,
$8.00. **Arch Enemy set:** Eight figures in
series. 8" - $20.00, $8.00.
World's Greatest Super Heros:
1975–1976. Second set with six figures in
series.) **Isis:** 1977. 8" - $14.00. **Teen Titans:**
6" "Aqua Lad," "Kid Flash," "Wonder Girl,"
or "Speedy." Each - $12.00, $6.00.
Wizard of Oz: 1974. (See photo in
Series 5, pg. 224.) Dorothy: $30.00, $9.00.
Munchkins: $18.00, $6.00. Wizard: $25.00,
$8.00. Others: $15.00 - $6.00. 15" size:
Cloth/vinyl. Each - $145.00, $45.00.

4" "Captain Stubing" from the "Love Boat"
TV series. Plastic and vinyl. Marked "Mego
1981 - Aaron Spelling Productions." Each -
$12.00. *Courtesy Don Tvrdik.*

MOLLYE DOLLS

Mollye Goldman of International
Doll Company and Hollywood Cinema
Fashions of Philadephia, PA made dolls
from cloth, composition, hard plastic,
and plastic/vinyl. Only the vinyl dolls
will be marked with her name. The rest
usually have paper wrist tag. Mollye purchased unmarked dolls from many other
firms and dressed them to be sold under
her name. She designed clothes for
many other makers, including Eegee
(Goldberger), Horsman, and Ideal.

First prices are for mint condition
dolls; second prices are for crazed,
cracked, dirty dolls or ones without
original clothes.

17" all hard plastic "Coronation Queen"
from 1953–1954. Saran wig, sleep eyes, original gown and cape. Dressed and marketed
by Mollye. Fair condition - $350.00. *Courtesy
Patricia Wood.*

Airline doll: Hard plastic. 14" - $200.00 up, $85.00; 18" - $300.00 up, $110.00; 23" - $385.00 up, $100.00.

Babies, composition: 15" - $150.00, $65.00; 21" - $225.00, $95.00. Composition/cloth: 18" - $85.00, $35.00. **Toddler:** All composition. 15" - $200.00, $65.00; 21" - $275.00, $80.00.

Babies, hard plastic: 14" - $85.00, $50.00; 20" - $125.00, $75.00. Hard plastic/cloth: 17" - $80.00, $40.00; 23" - $125.00, $60.00.

Babies, vinyl: 8½" - $15.00, $7.00; 12" - $20.00, $8.00; 15" - $35.00, $12.00.

18" "Bridesmaid" dressed and marketed by Mollye International. All hard plastic. Doll may have been purchased as a "blank" from the same source that Nancy Ann Storybook Doll Co. purchased their "Style Show" dolls. $425.00. *Courtesy Kris Lundquist.*

14" "Sara Lou" that is all hard plastic with turned-up nose and sleep eyes. Doll purchased by Mollye as a "blank" to be dressed and marketed. From 1954. $385.00. *Courtesy Kris Lundquist.*

Cloth, children: 15" - $135.00, $50.00; 18" - $155.00, $60.00; 24" - $200.00, $70.00; 29" - $265.00, $90.00.

Cloth, young ladies: 16" - $195.00, $80.00; 21" - $285.00, $100.00.

Cloth, Internationals: 13" - $85.00, $40.00; 15" - $125.00 up, $50.00; 27" - $275.00 up, $85.00.

Composition, children: 15" - $165.00, $55.00; 18" - $225.00, $85.00.

Composition, young ladies: 16" - $365.00, $100.00; 21" - $525.00, $150.00.

Jeanette McDonald: Composition. (See photo in Series 1, pg. 225.) 27" - $800.00 up, $250.00.

Thief of Bagdad dolls: Composition. (See entire set in Series 1, pg. 223.) 14" - $550.00, $125.00; 19" - $650.00, $150.00. Sultan: 19" - $650.00, $200.00. Sabu: 15" - $600.00, $200.00.

Vinyl children: 8" - $25.00, $10.00; 11" - $45.00, $20.00; 16" - $75.00, $25.00.

Hard plastic, young ladies: 17" - $285.00 up, $95.00; 20" - $350.00 up, $100.00; 25" - $400.00, $125.00.

Little Women: Vinyl. 9" - $35.00, $15.00.

Lone Ranger or Tonto: Hard plastic/latex. 22" - $200.00, $75.00.

Raggedy Ann or Andy, Beloved Belindy: See Raggedy Ann section.

17" doll on revolving musical stand. (Total height - 20") All hard plastic and unmarked with sleep eyes. Tagged "No. 6973/Cathy/Has Dynel Hair/The Latest Rage." Banner across dress reads "Dancing Deb." Dress tagged "Created by Mollye." This is an exceptionally beautiful doll. Mint condition - $385.00. *Courtesy Martha Sweeney.*

8½" "Tyrolean Girl" that is mint in box. All vinyl with sleep eyes and rooted hair. Made by Mollye Creations (International). $110.00. *Courtesy Patricia Wood.*

Monica Dolls were made from late 1930s and early 1940s. They were all composition with painted eyes. Human hair rooted into composition heads made these doll very unique.

11" dolls: Mint condition: $275.00. Played with: $175.00.
15" dolls: Mint condition: $485.00. Played with: $385.00.
18" dolls: Mint condition: $700.00. Played with: $500.00.
21" dolls: Mint condition: $950.00. Played with: $600.00.

21" "Monica" that is all composition with painted eyes. Human hair is embedded into composition. Dressed in original pink/blue floor length gown and wide brim bonnet of same material. $950.00.

Three things stand out in a Naber Kid – humor, happiness, and a smile of tolerance. Even if that Naber Kid disagrees or looks different than his or her Naber, the smile shows that no intolerant words are spoken.

Harold Naber began carving wooden figures of Eskimos while living and working mainly as a bush pilot for 22 years in Alaska. The early works of this very talented man are highly prized by those who own them. (See photo in Series 9, pg. 271.) Many of his early carvings were done for his Native American friends and some were sold in Naber's own store called Fur Traders in Anchorage. This was during the 1970s. "Jake," "Molli," and "Max" were his first production dolls to be introduced in 1984.

In 1988, Prescott, Arizona, became the site of a new doll factory. The "Arizona finish" was perfected and used mostly for "Peter" and "Darina." This finish shows very little wood grain and has a satin surface. As of January 1, 1994, production of Naber Kids ended. Naber will continue to make his Wild Wood Babies and in 1994, he will begin a new chapter in his doll career.

There is a newspaper called Naber Kids News Report put out by the company that can be ordered from Naber Kids News Report Subscription Service, 8915 S. Suncoast Blvd., Homosassa, FL 32646. Included in the newspaper are dolls for sale or trade, plus new information, list of dealers, and list of places Mr. Naber will be visiting.

"Big Nuni" was the first doll ever created by Mr. Harold Naber and was sold through his store, Fur Traders, in Anchorage, Alaska, in the 1970s. To date, none have reached the secondary market that we are aware of, but it is certain that rarity will make prices extremely high. *Courtesy Naber Gestalt Corp.*

Retirement dates:

06-21-87:	Molli - $3,500.00 up.
01-16-88:	Jake - $1,200.00 up.
05-04-88:	Max - $1,100.00–1,500.00.
03-04-89:	Ashley - $800.00. (See photo in Series 9, pg. 271.)
07-15-89:	Milli - $400.00.
09-28-90:	Maurice - $600.00 up.
03-04-90:	Maxine - $450.00 up.
19-28-90:	Sissi - $700.00. (Arizona finish - 39 made)
11-30-90:	Frieda - $650.00. (Arizona finish - 28 made)
12-17-90:	Walter - $650.00 up. (Arizona finish - 67 made)
05-03-91:	Peter - $450.00. (Arizona finish - 325 made)
05-03-91:	Pam - $450.00. (Arizona finish - 289 made)
07-28-91:	Darina - $450.00. (Arizona finish - 224 made)
03-09-92:	Henry * - $800.00 up.

* as Pirate - $800.00 up.
* as Diver (yellow) - $1,000.00 up.
* as Diver (green) - $1,000.00 up.
* as Diver (beige) - $1,100.00 up. (See photo in Series 10, pg. 269.)
* as Farmer - $800.00 up.
* as Carpenter - $800.00 up. (See photo in Series 9, pg. 271.)

04-13-92:	Sami and Samantha, each - $300.00.
04-20-92:	Freddi - $300.00.
06-28-92:	Amy - $300.00.
12-08-92:	Heide ** - $400.00.

** Without braces - $625.00 up.

05-27-93:	Mishi - $250.00.
05-27-93:	Hoey - $250.00.
07-25-93:	Paula - $250.00. (See photo in Series 10, pg. 268.)
11-07-93:	Willi - $250.00.
11-13-93:	Eric - $250.00. (See photo in Series 10, pg. 268.)
11-21-93:	Denise - $250.00.
12-31-93:	Elsi - $250.00.
12-31-93:	Benni - $250.00. (See photo in Series 10, pg. 269.)
12-31-93:	Posi - $250.00.

12-31-94:	Sarah, Joseph, Josi, Tony, Juanita, Christina, Rita Witch, Richie & Flink, Marcie. $250.00 each.

17½" "Alice" is the first in new 1994 line of Naber Teens. She has ball-jointed shoulders and hips. Jointed elbows and waist. Very posable. Sculptured hair with cloth headband. Shoes with slight detail of toes. A delightful addition to any collection. $250.00 up.

Early handcarved figures: Marked on head or foot. $900.00 up.

Later 1980s figures: Marked, plus tag. $250.00 up.

Specialty dressed: Alpine, Baker, Cheerleader, Detective, Doctor, Eskimo, Farmer, Gangster, Golfer, Indian, Nurse, Pilot, Waitress. Each - $200.00 up.

Specials: Phil Racer - $500.00. Sarah and Benni Indians (20 sets made) - $500.00 up.

This is 38" "Micki" with a mischievous "Clarence," one of the "Wild Wood Babies." "Micki" - $1,500.00 up; "Clarence" - $250.00. *Courtesy Naber Gestalt Corp.*

Left is "Iko" and right is "Micki". Both are 38" tall. These Naber sculptured dolls are unique and destined to be rare because only 101 of each were produced in 1993. The collector who owns one of these is very fortunate. Each - $1,500.00 up. *Courtesy Naber Gestalt Corp.*

The painted bisque Nancy Ann dolls will be marked "Storybook Doll U.S.A." and the hard plastic dolls marked "Storybook Doll U.S.A. Trademark Reg." The only identity as to who the doll represents is a paper tag around the wrist with the doll's name on it. The boxes are marked with the name, but many of these dolls arc found in the wrong box. Dolls were made 1937–1948.

First prices are for mint condition dolls; second prices are for played with, dirty dolls.

Bisque: 1937–1948. 5" - $125.00 up, $35.00; 7½–8" - $175.00 up, $45.00. Black: 5" - $175.00 up, $60.00; 7½–8" - $225.00 up, $75.00. With white painted socks: $200.00 up.

Bisque with jointed hips (slim): 5" - $145.00 up, $40.00; 7½–8" - $185.00 up, $50.00. Jointed hips (pudgy): $195.00 up.

Bisque with swivel neck: 5" - $165.00 up, $50.00; 7½–8" - $200.00 up, $55.00. Swivel neck, jointed hips: 5" - $165.00, $50.00; 7½–8" - $200.00, $55.00.

Bisque bent leg baby: 1936–1948. (See photo in Series 8, pg. 275.) 3½–4½" - $125.00 up, $35.00.

Plastic: (1947–1953) 5" - $55.00 up, $15.00; 7½–8" - $65.00, $20.00. Black: $85.00, $30.00.

Plastic bent leg baby: 1948–1953. 3½–4½" - $85.00 up, $20.00.

Judy Ann: Name incised on back. 5" - $325.00 up, $100.00.

Audrey Ann: Heavy doll with toddler legs. Marked "Nancy Ann Storybook 12." 6" - $1,000.00 up, $300.00.

Lori Ann: All vinyl. (See photo in Series 4, pg. 17.) 7½" - $165.00.

Margie Ann: Bisque. In school dress. 6" - $150.00 up, $45.00.

Debbie: Hard plastic in school dress. Name on wrist tag/box. 10" - $145.00 up, $40.00.

Debbie: Hard plastic, vinyl head. 10" - $100.00, $40.00.

Debbie: All hard plastic walker in dressy Sunday dress. 1950s. 10½" - $150.00, $45.00. Same, vinyl head: $85.00, $25.00.

Left: "To Market" with jointed hips. Pudgy with no molded bangs or painted-on socks. Circa 1941. Center: "Swedish" with molded socks and bangs. "Storybook USA" (crude mark). Circa 1938. Right: "Portuguese" marked on back "Judy Ann USA." Circa 1938. Each - $200.00–275.00 up. *Courtesy Margaret Mandel.*

Teen type (Margie Ann): All vinyl. Also called "Miss Nancy Ann." Marked "Nancy Ann." 10½" - $125.00 up, $40.00.

Muffie: All hard plastic. (If strung, add $50.00.) **Walker:** $175.00 up. Dress: 8" - $175.00 up, $85.00. Ballgown: $300.00 up, $95.00. Riding Habit: $225.00 up, $95.00. **Poodle:** Made by Steiff. (See photo in Series 9, pg. 273.) $80.00. In box - $100.00 up.

Muffie: Hard plastic. Reintroduced doll. 8" - $95.00 up, $25.00.

Nancy Ann Fairytale Dolls: All vinyl. From 1960s. In box: 5½" - $65.00. Doll only: $40.00.

Nancy Ann Style Show Doll: All hard plastic. All dressed in ballgowns. Unmarked. (See photo in Series 8, pg. 273.) 17–18" - $500.00 up, $200.00.

10" "Debbie" by Nancy Ann Storybook. All hard plastic and all original. $150.00. *Courtesy Susan Giradot.*

10½" "Miss Nancy Ann" with high heel feet and vinyl head with rooted hair. Body and limbs are made of rigid vinyl. All original outfit. Marked on head. $125.00 up. *Courtesy Susan Giradot.*

"Little Miss Pattycake" is painted bisque with star-shaped hands. Wearing dress-up coat and bonnet #234. Shown with original box. $250.00 up. *Courtesy Susan Giradot.*

5½" "Nancy Ann Fairytale Dolls" with vinyl heads, rooted hair, and painted features. Plastic slip-on shoes. Made in Hong Kong in late 1960s. There are 12 dolls listed on back of box. In box - $65.00; doll only - $40.00. *Courtesy Susan Giradot.*

5½" painted bisque "Chinese" with jointed hips. From Nancy Ann Storybook's "Around the World Series," #33. Original box. $750.00 up. *Courtesy Susan Giradot.*

This "Nancy Ann Style Show Doll" has beautiful face color. All hard plastic. $500.00 up. *Courtesy Jeannie Nespoli.*

Close-up of "Jeanie Set The Table," #708, shown in top photo.

8" strung "Muffie" dolls with painted eyelashes and mohair wigs. Marked "Storybook Dolls Calif." All original. Each - $250.00 up. *Courtesy Glorya Woods.*

RAGGEDY ANN & ANDY

Designed by Johnny B. Gruelle in 1915, these dolls are still being made. Early dolls will be marked "Patented Sept. 7, 1915." All cloth, brown yarn hair, tin or wooden button eyes, thin nose, painted lashes far below eyes and no white outline around eyes. Some are jointed by having knees or elbows sewn. Features of early dolls are painted on cloth.

Gruelle had three children. Marcella, the only girl, suffered a long illness caused by a contaminated smallpox vaccine. During her illness, Marcella found a rag doll with worn off features, and her father painted a face on it. The doll was named by combining two James Whitcomb Riley poem-titles, "The Raggedy Man" and "Orphan Annie." Gruelle made up stories about the doll's adventures to entertain his sick child. Marcella died at the age of 12.

First prices are for mint condition dolls; second prices are for played with, dirty, missing clothes or redressed dolls.

Marked with patent date: 15–16" - $1,500.00 up; 23–24" - $2,200.00 up; 30" - $3,000.00. Worn and dirty: 15-16" - $625.00; 23–24" - $900.00; 30" - $1,000.00. Pair in mint condition: 16" - $3,500.00 up. Camel with the Wrinkled Knees: $1,500.00.

Applause dolls: Will have tag sewn in seam. 1981. 12" - $25.00; 17" - $40.00; 25" - $60.00; 36" - $100.00 up.

Averill, Georgene: Mid-1930s. Red yarn hair, painted features. Sewn cloth label in side seam of body. (See photo in Series 9, pg. 275.) 15" - $350.00, $150.00 up; 19" - $625.00; 22" - $750.00. **Asleep/ Awake:** Early doll. 13–14" - $650.00 up. Worn and dirty: $200.00 up. 1940s: 18" - $250.00. 1950s: 18" - $200.00. 1960–1963: 15" - $95.00; 18" - $125.00.

Black outlined nose: Any early maker. Pair - $700.00.

Beloved Belindy: Knickerbocker. 1965. Black doll. (See photo in Series 7, pg. 276.) 15" - $750.00 up, $300.00. **Volland Co.:** Smile mouth, two rows of teeth, button eyes. Red/white legs, red feet. (See photo in Series 8, pg. 278.) 13" - $2,000.00, $600.00; 15" - $2,400.00, 800.00. **Averill:** (See photo in Series 8, pg. 276; Series 9, pg. 277.) 15" - $1,500.00 up. **Mollye:** 15" - $1,300.00; 17" - $1,500.00.

Hasbro: 1983 to date. Under Playskool label. Still available.

Knickerbocker Toy Co.: 1963–1982. Printed features, red yarn hair. Tag sewn to seam. 1960s: 12" - $145.00; 16" - $200.00; 23–24" - $300.00; 30–36" - $400.00–500.00. 1970s: 12" - $45.00; 16" - $60.00; 23–24" - $100.00; 30–36" - $195.00– 250.00. 1980s: 16" - $25.00; 23–25" - $60.00; 30–36" - $85.00–125.00. Talking: 1974. 12" - $45.00. 1960s - $265.00. Camel with the Wrinkled Knees: $165.00.

19" "Raggedy Ann" made by Georgene Novelties with black outlined nose and brown hair. Original, from 1940. $625.00 up. *Courtesy Candy Brainard.*

Rarest of all the Raggedys is this one manufactured by Exposition Doll & Toy Mfg. Co. in 1935. All original. Value unknown. *Courtesy Candy Brainard.*

Group of 1920s Volland dolls – 13" "Beloved Belindy" in mint condition and a pair of 23" "Raggedy Ann & Andy" dolls. Pair - $2,200.00 each. "Belindy" - $2,000.00. *Courtesy Candy Brainard.*

Mollye Dolls: Red yarn hair and printed features. Heavy outlined nose. Lower lashes closer to eyes. Most will have multicolored socks and blue shoes. Will be marked in printed writing on front of torso "Raggedy Ann and Andy Doll/ Manufactured by Mollye Doll Outfitters." First company to imprint solid red heart on chest. (See photo in Series 8, pg. 278; Series 9, pg. 275.) 15" - $900.00 up, $200.00; 22" - $1,100.00 up, $300.00. "Baby": 16" - $850.00.

Nasco/Hobbs-Merrill: 1973. Plastic/ vinyl with rooted yarn hair. 24" - $165.00, $60.00.

Vinyl dolls: 8½" - $12.00, $3.00; 12" - $18.00, $6.00; 16" - $22.00, $8.00; 20" - $28.00, $10.00.

16" "Baby Raggedy Ann" by Mollye Doll Outfitters in 1935. Has been reintroduced in 1993 by Applause in limited edition. The reproduction is very well done so caution is advised. Old "Baby" - $850.00.
Courtesy Candy Brainard.

A group of Knickerbocker products from 1960s–1970s. "Raggedy Ann & Andy," "Beloved Belindy," "The Camel with Wrinkled Knees," and "Raggedy Arthur." "Ann or Andy" - $200.00 each, "Belindy" - $750.00, camel - $50.00, dog - $60.00.
Courtesy Candy Brainard.

Volland Co.: 1920–1934. Lashes low on cheeks. Feet turn outward. Can have brown yarn hair. Some have oversized hands with free-standing thumbs. Long thin nose, lines low under eyes. Different mouth appearances are:

(See photo in Series 8, pg. 277–278; Series 9, pg. 276.) 15" - $1,700.00 up; 18" - $1,850.00 up; 22" - $2,000.00 up; 24" - $2,300.00 up; 29" - $2,800.00 up.

Uncle Clem: Has center face seam, prominent nose. Red yarn hair and mustache. Red/white stripe socks and black shoes. Scots costume. 16–17" - $2,500.00.

16" Volland "Raggedy Ann" dolls with cardboard hearts inside their chests and brown yarn hair. Marked "Pateneted Sept. 7, 1915." Each - $1,500.00 up. *Courtesy Candy Brainard.*

REMCO

"The Littlechap Family" dressed in terry cloth towel wraps and robe. The stands are made just like the early Barbie stands. Set - $400.00 up.

First prices are for mint condition dolls; second prices are for played with, dirty or not original dolls.

Addams Family: 5½" - $20.00, $8.00.

Baby Crawlalong: 1967. 20" - $15.00, $8.00.

Baby Grow A Tooth: 1969. 14" - $25.00, $10.00. Black: $30.00, $12.00.

Baby Know It All: 1969. 17" - $15.00, $8.00.

Baby Laugh A Lot: 1970. (See photo in Series 7, pg. 277.) 16" - $20.00, $7.00. Black: $30.00, $15.00.

Baby Sad or Glad: 1966. 14" - $20.00, $10.00.

Baby Stroll-A-Long: 1966. 15" - $15.00, $8.00.

Dave Clark 5: 1964. 4½", each - $50.00, $20.00.

Heidi: 1965. (See photo in Series 9, pg. 279.) 5½" - $9.00, $3.00. **Herby:** 4½" - $12.00, $5.00. **Spunky:** Has glasses. 5½" - $14.00, $5.00. **Jan:** Oriental. 5½" - $14.00, $5.00.

Winking Heidi: 1968. $10.00, $4.00.

Jeannie, I Dream Of: 6" - $18.00, $5.00.

Jumpsy: 1970. (See photo in Series 7, pg. 277.) 14" - $20.00, $8.00. Black: $22.00, $10.00.

Laura Partridge: 1973. 19" - $65.00, $25.00.

Lindalee: 1970. Cloth/vinyl. 10" - $25.00, $10.00.

L.B.J.: 1964. Portrait. 5½" - $35.00, $15.00.

Littlechap Family: 1963. Set of four. $300.00, $100.00. **Dr. John:** 14½" - $75.00, $25.00. **Lisa:** 13½" - $50.00, $15.00. **Libby:** 10½" - $50.00, $15.00. **Judy:** 12" - $50.00, $15.00.

Mimi: 1972–1973. Battery-operated singer. (See photo in Series 9, pg. 279.) 19" - $50.00, $20.00. Black: $60.00, $20.00.

Orphan Annie: 1967. Plastic/vinyl. 15" - $35.00, $12.00.

Sweet April: 1971. All vinyl baby. 5½" - $10.00, $3.00. Black: 5½" - $15.00, $3.00.

Tippy Tumbles: 1966. 16" - $20.00, $8.00.

Tumbling Tomboy: 1969. 16" - $20.00, $8.00.

RICHWOOD

The 8" "Sandra Sue" doll has a slim body and limbs. She is a walker, but the head does not turn as she walks. The doll and her clothes are of excellent quality and she was first made in the late 1940s and into the 1950s. A large wardrobe of clothing was available for the doll along with accessories and scaled furniture of the finest quality. She is unmarked except for a number under an arm or leg.

"Sandra Sue" with flat feet. Fewer came with high heel feet. Has replaced shoes. Came in box with silhouette on front. Many beautiful outfits could be purchased for this doll. $125.00. *Courtesy Susan Giradot.*

Prices are for excellent condition dolls.

Nude: $50.00 up.
School/street dress: $100.00 up.
Dress, coat & hat: $125.00 up.
Ballgown: $150.00 up.
Sports clothes: Cheerleader, baseball, etc. $165.00 up. (Add $40.00 if in box.)

Basic "Sandra Sue" with high heel feet that is mint in box. Has different style box. $125.00. *Courtesy Maureen Fukushima.*

9" "Walking Princess" made of all light weight hard plastic with inset eyes. Head sits on body loosely and moves as doll is led by hands to walk. Original box. Note stuffed animals and golliwogs along with maker's name, Roddy of England. $20.00. *Courtesy Gloria Anderson.*

12" "Tina Cassini" designed by Oleg Cassini. Made by Ross Products Co. Mid-heel feet. Clothes are tagged "Made in British Crown Colony of Hong Kong." Back marked with name. Head is unmarked. This is #3002A Platinum/The Tina Church Set. In box - $250.00. Doll only - $165.00. *Courtesy Ann Wencel.*

Close-up of mark on "Tina Cassini" doll's back.

7½" and 4½" cavemen made of all rigid vinyl. They came both sexed and unsexed. Hair is same as used on "trolls." Marked "Mo-Pets by Sarco. S. Rosenberg Co. Japan." and "K" inside a triangle. 7½" - $30.00; 4½" - $15.00. *Courtesy Kathy Tvrdik.*

SASHA

Sasha dolls were manufactured by Trenton Toys, Ltd., Reddish, Stockport, England from 1965 to 1986, when they went out of business. The original designer of these dolls was Sasha Morgenthaler of Switzerland. All dolls are 16" tall and are made of all rigid vinyl with painted features. The only marks will be a wrist tag.

From 1963 to 1964 only, Sasha dolls were made by Gotz of Germany and marked on head "Sasha Serie" inside a circle.

Gotz girl or boy: $1,300.00 up.

Boy or girl in box: $225.00. No box: $200.00.

Boy or girl in cylinder: $350.00

Boy: "Gregor" - $200.00.

Girl: $200.00.

Black boy: "Caleb" - $300.00.

Black baby: $275.00

Cora: #119 (Black) - $300.00; #111 (White) - $250.00.

White baby: $185.00

Sexed baby: Pre-1979. $285.00

Early dolls: Tube/sack packaging. Girl or boy. $350.00 each.

Sasha dolls were first made by Gotz, 1963–1964 only. Due to production problems, the license went to Trenton of England. Back of head is marked "Sasha Serie" in a circle. Same mark appears within three non-concentric circles on back. These first production dolls are rare. There is a slight painting difference such as eye iris arched, longer eyebrows, and lips painted only in middle, plus an overall slight "thinness." $1,300.00 up. *Courtesy Pat Graff.*

Limited edition dolls: Limited to 5,000. Incised #763. Dressed in navy velvet. 1981: $350.00. 1982: Pintucks dress. $365.00. 1983: Kiltie plaid. $375.00. 1985: "Prince Gregor." $400.00. 1986: "Princess." $1,800.00. 1986: Dressed in sari from India. $1,400.00 up.

Made by Morgenthaler: 1950s. Mint: 20" - $5,000.00 up. Fair: $2,700.00.

Early "Gregor" made by Sasha. Original. Retail price tag is $17.98. $225.00 up. *Courtesy Shirley's Doll House.*

SHIRLEY TEMPLE

First prices are for *mint condition* dolls; second prices are for played with, dirty, cracked or crazed or not original dolls. Allow extra for special outfits such as "Little Colonel," "Cowgirl," "Bluebird," etc. (Allow 25% to 50% more for mint in box dolls. Price depends upon clothes.)

All composition: All composition child made from 1934 to late 1930s. Marked head and body or can be marked only on head or the body. **11"** - $900.00, $450.00. **11" cowgirl:** $850.00, $500.00.

Marks:

U S
IDEAL
of A (Head)

SHIRLEY TEMPLE
13 (Back)

SHIRLEY TEMPLE
13 (Head or Back)

13" - $700.00, $400.00. **15–16"** - $800.00, $450.00. **17–18"** - $950.00, $500.00. **20"** - $1,100.00, $565.00. **22"** - $1,250.00, $600.00. **25"** - $1,400.00, $650.00. **25" cowgirl:** $1,500.00, $700.00. **27"** - $1,400.00, $650.00. **27" cowgirl:** $1,600.00, $700.00.

Vinyl of 1950s: Allow more for flirty eyes in 17" and 19" sizes. **12"** in box - $200.00. Mint, not in box - $165.00. Played with, dirty - $40.00. **15"** in box - $325.00. Mint, not in box - $265.00. Played with, dirty - $85.00. **17"** in box - $400.00. Mint, not in box - $325.00. Played with, dirty - $95.00. **19"** in box - $450.00. Mint, not in box - $400.00. Played with, dirty - $125.00. **36"** in box. (See photo in Series 9, pg. 283.) $2,000.00. Mint, not in box - $1,600.00. Played with, dirty - $850.00.

1972: Reissue from Montgomery Ward. Came in plain unmarked box. 17" in box: $200.00. Mint, not in box - $165.00; Dirty - $45.00.

1973: Has box with many pictures of Shirley on it. Doll in red polka dot dress. 16" in box - $165.00. Mint, no box - $125.00. Played with, dirty - $45.00.

1982–1983: Plastic/vinyl. Made by Ideal. (See photo in Series 9, pg. 284.) 8" - $30.00, 12" - $35.00.

1984: Marked "Dolls, Dreams & Love." Henry Garfinkle Co. 36" - $300.00.

Shirley display stand: Mechanical doll. $2,800.00 up. At organ: $3,500.00.

"Hawaiian": Marked Shirley Temple, but not meant to be a Shirley Temple. (See photo in Series 6, pg. 291.) 18" - $950.00, $400.00.

Japan: All bisque: Painted. With molded hair. 6" - $250.00. **Composition:** 7–8" - $300.00. **All celluloid:** 5" - $185.00; 8" - $245.00.

German: 1936. All composition, sleep eyes, open mouth smile. Marked "GB42." 16" - $600.00 up.

Left: 10" celluloid "Shirley Temple" with one-piece body, head, and limbs. Center: 13" "Happy Shirley" marked "S.T. 5/0 Germany." Composition and a painted bisque-like material. Right: 9" doll referred to as the first Ideal "Shirley" made. All composition and marked "Ideal." 10" - $165.00; 13" - $500.00; 9" - $125.00. *Courtesy Martha Sweeney.*

Mold #480, 510X: German. Sleep, flirty eyes. Open mouth. 13" - $575.00 up.

Babies: Open mouth with upper and lower teeth. Flirty, sleep eyes. Marked on head. 16" - $1,000.00, $600.00; 18" - $1,100.00, $650.00; 22" - $1,300.00, $700.00; 25" - $1,500.00, $800.00; 27" - $1,800.00, $900.00.

Look-alike dolls: Composition, with dimples. 16" - $200.00; 20" - $350.00; 27" - $600.00. Vinyl: 36" - $800.00.

Shirley Temple accessories: Script name pin: $25.00–35.00. Pin button: Old 1930s doll pin. $135.00; others - $20.00. Charm bracelet: 1930s. $250.00.

18" "Curly Top" in pleated print organdy dress with rayon label. Fully marked on head and body. An exceptionally pretty doll. $950.00. *Courtesy Glorya Woods.*

Very rare all rubber "Shirley Temple" squeeze toy. She is holding dog "Corky" in her arms. Fair condition - $165.00. *Courtesy Pat Sparks.*

36" vinyl and plastic "Shirley Temple" with original clothes and name pin on sash. Has jointed wrists. From 1960. Mint condition - $1,600.00. *Courtesy Ellen Dodge.*

15" composition "Stand Up and Cheer Shirley Temple" doll. Very rare. Marked only with "Ideal" on head. From 1934. $1,000.00. *Courtesy Marge Mesisinger*

Boxed outfits: 1950s: $50.00 up. 1970s: $35.00 up.

Tagged 1930s dress: $165.00 up.

Purse with name: $15.00–25.00.

Buggy: Made of wood. (See photo in Series 7, pg. 283.) 20" - $550.00; 26" - $400.00 up; 32" - $450.00 up; 34" - $500.00 up. Wicker: 26" - $500.00 up.

Trunk: No doll: $165.00 up. Gift set: 1950s. Doll and clothes. $450.00 up.

Statuette: Chalk in dancing dress. 7–8" - $225.00; 4½" - $165.00.

8" and 9" "Shirley Temple" dolls. Two have painted-on shoes and socks; two have original crepe paper dresses. The doll on left has molded hair ribbon and bow and original clothes. Each - $265.00. *Courtesy Lea Nell Hayes.*

Three 5" and 8" "Shirley Temple" dolls made of celluloid and dressed in original clothes. 5" - $185.00; 8" - $245.00. *Courtesy Jo Keelen.*

13" "Sunbabe" by the Sun Rubber Co. in 1951. Hard plastic head with sleep eyes and open nurser mouth. Mint condition rubber body. $45.00 up. *Courtesy Pat Graff.*

Three 17" "Lady Luminous" (Duex-L) fashion dolls made by Takara in Japan. Left: "Regular" model with very long hair. All original. Center: This suntanned model is one of the most beautiful fashion dolls made in the 1980s and 1990s. Right: All original black "Lady Luminous Bride." Each - $300.00–350.00 up. *Courtesy Marie Ernst.*

15" hard hat version of the "Bell Doll" designed exclusively for Telephone Pioneers of America. All original. Dolls were available in black or white. $25.00. *Courtesy Gloria Anderson.*

TERRI LEE

First prices are for mint condition dolls, which could be higher due to the outfit on the doll. Second prices are for soiled, poor wig or not original.

Terri Lee: Composition: $350.00 up, $100.00. **Hard plastic:** Marked "Pat. Pend." $285.00 up, $100.00. Majorette, cowgirl, etc: $400.00 up. In original box: $500.00 up. Others: $285.00 up, $100.00. **Vinyl:** $250.00, $75.00. **Talking:** $450.00, $185.00. Mint in box: $550.00 up.

"Terri Lee" made of painted hard plastic with wiry mannequin style wig and side glancing painted eyes. Wearing taffeta party dress. Made in Lincoln, Nebraska. $350.00 up. *Courtesy Susan Giradot.*

Jerri Lee: Hard plastic. Caracul wig. 16" - $300.00, $185.00. Mint in box: $500.00 up.

Tiny Terri Lee: 10" - $175.00, $70.00.

Tiny Jerri Lee: 10" - $200.00, $85.00.

Patti Jo, Bonnie Lou: Black dolls. (See photo in Series 8, pg. 285.) $550.00 up, $250.00.

Benjie: Black doll. (See photo in Series 8, pg. 285.) $575.00, $275.00.

Connie Lynn: 19" - $365.00 up, $150.00.

Gene Autry: 16" - $1,800.00 up, $700.00.

Linda Baby (Linda Lee): 10–12" - $185.00 up, $80.00.

So Sleepy: 9½" - $300.00 up, $100.00.

Clothes: Ballgown: $100.00 up. Riding habit: $100.00 up. Skater: $100.00 up. School dresses: $50.00 up. Coats: $35.00 up. Brownie uniform: $40.00 up.

Clothes for Jerri Lee: Two-piece pants suit: $100.00 up. Short pants suits: $100.00 up. Western shirt and jeans: $70.00 up.

Mary Jane: Plastic walker. Terri Lee look-alike with long molded eyelids. (See photo in Series 9, pg. 285.) 16" - $285.00 up.

Ginger Girl Scout: 8" - $125.00–165.00.

Monkey: Tony and Penelope. Made by Steiff. 8" - $125.00 each.

Poodle with Terri Lee blanket: Made by Steiff. 5½" long, 3" tall. $135.00.

16" hard plastic "Terri Lee" with brunette braids wearing one of the Heart Fund costumes. Shown with original box. Made in Apple Valley, California. All original. Mint in box - $500.00 up. *Courtesy Susan Giradot.*

"Terri Lee" with soft hair. All original including her hair ribbon. Celluloid doll from 1930s has been added. Mint condition - $285.00 up. *Courtesy Margaret Madel.*

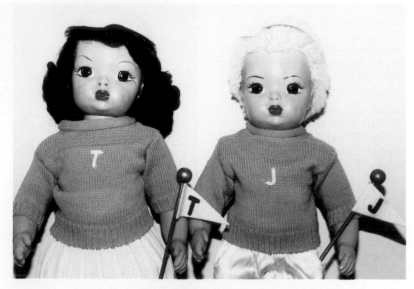

16" "Terri and Jerri Lee" dressed in matching cheerleader outfits. These outfits could be ordered in your school colors. Each - $300.00 up. *Courtesy Susan Giradot.*

"Tiny Terri and Jerri Lee" in matching romper and dress. He has caracul wig. Each - $185.00 up. *Courtesy Susan Giradot.*

All original "Terri Lee" and her poodle dog. The 5" dog was originally called "Snobby" by Steiff. It was purchased by the Terri Lee Co. and sold as her dog. The poodle came with an autographed blanket which was made at the Terri Lee factory. This blanket has rhinestones, but they also came plain. The gold leash was also added by the company. The dog came in various colors, but it is unknown if any other color except gray was used for Terri Lee's pet. Doll - $285.00 up. Poodle - $135.00. *Courtesy Susan Giradot.*

"Tiny Terri Lee" with chick yellow hair wearing pet dress and holding pet monkey, "Penelope." All original down to daisy on her wrist and pink bows in hair. Her 4¾" monkey, shown at right, was made by Steiff and dressed by Terri Lee Co. (In the general Steiff line, the monkey was called "Jocko." It has felt cut-out hands and feet.) Doll - $185.00 up. Monkey - $125.00. *Courtesy Susan Giradot.*

TROLLS

Trolls: 2½–3" - $15.00 up; 5" - $20.00–25.00; 7" - $30.00–40.00; 10" - $50.00; 12" - $60.00; 15" - $80.00 up.

Troll animals: Large size: cow - $65.00; donkey - $80.00; ape - $80.00; turtle - $55.00; giraffe - $70.00. Small size: cow - $20.00; donkey - $50.00; ape - $35.00; turtle - $30.00.

9" troll with jointed neck and shoulder. Has inset eyes looking upward. Hair is long, just combed back. This rare troll has a painted mustache. Marked "Thomas Dam Made in Denmark. 1977" on back. Shown with a small troll that was made in China. 9" - $60.00; other - $15.00. *Courtesy Gloria Anderson.*

UNEEDA

First prices are for mint condition dolls; second prices are for soiled, dirty or not original dolls.

Baby Dollikins: 1958. 21" - $45.00, $20.00.

Baby Trix: 1964. 16" - $30.00, $15.00.

Ballerina: Vinyl. 14" - $25.00, $7.00.

Blabby: 1962. $28.00, $12.00.

Bare Bottom Baby: (See photo in Series 7, pg. 289.) 12" - $20.00, $12.00.

Bob: 1963. 10½" - $25.00, $10.00.

Coquette: 1963. 16" - $28.00, $12.00. Black: 16" - $35.00.

Dollikins: 1957. (See photo in Series 9, pg. 288.) 8" - $30.00, $10.00; 11" - $35.00, $10.00; 19" - $50.00, $25.00.

Fairy Princess: 32" - $110.00, $40.00.

Freckles: 1960. 32" - $100.00, $45.00.

Freckles Marionette: 30" - $65.00, $30.00.

16" Black "Coquette" made of plastic and vinyl. Has sleep eyes and rooted hair. All original. Hard to find doll. From 1961. $35.00. *Courtesy Pat Graff.*

Grannykins: 1974. Painted-on half-glasses. 6" - $10.00, $4.00.

Lucky Lindy: (Charles Lindbergh) Composition. 14" - $400.00, $235.00.

Magic Meg, Miss Deb: 1971. Grow hair. 16" - $25.00, $12.00.

Pollyanna: 1960. 10½" - $35.00, $10.00; 17" - $55.00, $20.00; 31" - $125.00, $50.00.

Pri-Thilla: 1958. 12" - $20.00, $9.00.

Purty: 1961. Press stomach to make eyes squint. (See photo in Series 7, pg. 289.) 15" - $25.00, $15.00.

Rita Hayworth: 1948. Composition. 14" - $500.00, $185.00.

Serenade: 1962. Battery-operated singer. 21" - $55.00, $20.00.

Suzette: 1959–1960, 1962. 10½" - $50.00, $25.00; 11½" - $50.00, $25.00. Sleep eyes: 11½" - $75.00, $40.00. **Blue Fairy:** (See photo in Series 9, pg. 288.) $65.00, $25.00.

Tiny Teens: 1957. 5" - $10.00.

18" "Jennifer" made of plastic and vinyl with painted features. Original except for missing shoes. Marked "Uneeda Doll Co./ MCMLXXI/Made in Hong Kong." $25.00. *Courtesy Kathy Tvrdik.*

Left: 32" Black version of "Princess." Made of vinyl and plastic with short curly hair. Original clothes. $135.00. *Courtesy Pat Graff.*

The last year Ginny dolls were made in America was 1969. Tonka purchased the Vogue name in 1973 and continued to make dolls. The dolls and clothes did not sell well though, due greatly to inferior designs and materials and poor manufacturing. In 1977, Tonka sold the Vogue rights to Lesney of England which made a tall slender Sasson Ginny for three years. During the first two production years, the Sasson Ginny had sleep eyes. The last issue had painted eyes. Although the Sasson Ginny did not look like the earlier Ginny versions, she was dressed and made better.

In 1983, Lesney sold its rights to the Meritus Corporation. With much work, Walter Reiling, owner of Meritus, made a public impact once more with Ginny. In 1986, Dakin purchased the Vogue rights and are the current manufacturer of Ginnys. Dolls manufactured now closely resemble the original 1950s rigid vinyl dolls. One person responsible for the "Ginny Renewal" through her wonderful clothes designs and calendars is Sue Nettlingham Roberts.

First prices are for mint condition dolls. Second prices are for dirty, crazed, or played with dolls, those with messed up wigs, or doll that are not original.

Baby Dear: 1960–1961. 12" - $50.00, $20.00; 17" - $85.00, $40.00. 1964: 12" - $40.00, $20.00. **Newborn:** 1960. Sleep eyes. $75.00.

Baby Dear One: 25" - $185.00, $85.00. **Baby Dear Two:** 27" - $225.00, $85.00.

Baby Wide Eyes: 1976. Very large brown sleep eyes. All vinyl. 16" - $40.00, $12.00.

Composition doll (Betty Ann, Mary Jane): Clothes tagged "Vogue." 12" - $225.00 up; 15" - $300.00 up.

Brickette: 1960. 22" - $65.00, $25.00. Reissued: 1979–1980. 18" - $40.00.

Ginny (Toodles): 1948–1949. Composition 7½–8" - $375.00 up, $90.00.

8" composition "Toodles" as "Robin Hood." Has painted features. Mint and original. Has Vogue sticker on costume. $375.00 up. *Courtesy Susan Giradot.*

Ginny: 1950–1953. Hard plastic, strung, painted eyes. 8"- $325.00 up, $100.00. Outfits: $85.00 up.

Ginny: Hard plastic, sleep eyes, painted lashes and strung. 8" - $325.00 up, $100.00.

Ginny: Caracul (lamb's wool) wig. Child, not baby. $375.00 up, $150.00. Outfits: $65.00 up.

Ginny: 1954. Painted lashes, sleep eyes, hard plastic walker. $275.00 up, $90.00. Outfits: $35.00 up.

Ginny: 1955–1957. Hard plastic molded lash walker. $185.00 up, $85.00. Outfits: $45.00 up.

8" "Debutante Ginny" of 1953. Beautifully mint with wrist tag. Strung body. Painted lashes. $325.00 up. *Courtesy Margaret Mandel.*

Very beautiful 17" composition doll dressed by Vogue. Clothes tagged on back neck seam. One-piece body suit of yellow and red. Jacket has yellow dog on side. Pull string purse attached to wrist. Original, although hat may be missing. This mint - $475.00.

8" all vinyl Vogue "Ginnette" baby with molded hair and sleep eyes. All original in original box. In box - $65.00. *Courtesy Susan Giradot.*

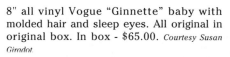

Ginny: 1957–1962. Hard plastic, jointed knee, molded lash walker. $150.00 up, $60.00. Outfits: $40.00 up.

Ginny Hawaiian: Brown/black doll. 8" - $700.00 up, $365.00.

Ginny Queen: $850.00 up, $300.00.

Ginny Crib Crowd: Bent leg baby with caracul (lamb's wool) wig. $650.00 up, $300.00.

Crib Crowd Easter Bunny: $1,400.00 up, $600.00.

Ginny: 1977. All vinyl with round face. Internationals: $40.00 up. Other: $50.00 up.

Sasson Ginny: 1978–1979. Thin bodied doll with thin limbs. Sleep eyes: 8" - $25.00 up. Painted eyes: 8" - $35.00.

Ginny Exclusives: 1986–1991. **Shirley's Doll House:** Ginny Goes Country (1985) - $90.00. Ginny Goes To Country Fair (1986) - $90.00; Black Ginny in swimsuit (1987) - $95.00; Santa/Mrs. Claus (1988) - $80.00; Babysitter: $65.00; Sunday Best (1989). Black boy or girl - $60.00.

Meyers Collectables: All birthday specials designed by Anne Cottrell. Gigi's Favorite (1985) - $80.00. Fairy Godmother (1986) - $165.00. Cinderella and Prince Charming (1987) - $175.00. Clown (1988) - $80.00. Cowgirl (1989) - $80.00. Storytime Ginny (1992), limited - $100.00. Sweet Violet Ginny (1993), limited - $150.00.

Little Friends: Alaska (1991) - $60.00.

A wonderful "Ginny" in her original red trunk with many of her outfits. The doll and some outfits came in the fitted trunk. From 1952. In trunk - $950.00 up. *Courtesy Kris Lundquist.*

Toy Village: Lansing, Michigan. Ashley Rose - $60.00.
Enchanted Doll House: Enchanted Ginny (1988) - $135.00.
Modern Doll Conventions: Rose Queen (1986) - $250.00. Ginny At Seashore (1987) - $85.00. Ginny's Claim (1988) - $80.00. Ginny in Nashville (1989) - $125.00. Ginny in Orlando (1990) - $80.00.
U.F.D.C.: Miss Unity (1987) - $175.00. Luncheon Ginny (1988) - $145.00.
Vogue Review Luncheon: 1989 - $150.00. 1990 - $85.00. 1991 - $70.00.
Vogue Doll Club: Member Special, 1990 - $95.00.

Ginny Accessories: Ginny gym: $275.00 up. Ginny pup: Steiff. $165.00 up. Luggage Set: $100.00 up. Shoes/shoe bag: $40.00 up. Furniture: Chair, bed, dresser, wardrobe, rocking chair. $55.00 each. Name pin: $50.00. Book: *Ginny's First Secret* - $125.00. Parasol: $15.00. School bag: $75.00.

Hug A Bye Baby: 1975. 16" - $20.00, $10.00. Black: $30.00, $15.00.

Jan: 1957. Rigid vinyl body and limbs with vinyl head and swivel waist. 12" - $135.00, $50.00.

Jeff: 1957. 10" - $85.00 up, $35.00.

A porcelain souvenir "Ginny" from 1984 Modern Doll Convention. She has glass eyes and is original. $145.00. *Courtesy Kris Lundquist.*

10" all vinyl "Pink Lipstick Jill." Sleep eyes, rooted hair, and high heel feet. Scarce, made in 1962 only. Bride gown original to a 1950s Jill (veil missing). $100.00 up *Courtesy Kris Lundquist.*

Jill: 1957. All hard plastic. 10" - $165.00, $55.00. In box with ballgown: $300.00 up.
Lil Imp: 11" - $50.00, $20.00.
Love Me Linda: 15" - $25.00, $10.00.
Miss Ginny: 1967–1970s. Young lady type. 11–12" - $25.00, $15.00; 15" - $45.00, $25.00.

Star Bright: 1966. 18" - $125.00, $40.00. Baby: 18" - $75.00, $25.00.
Welcome Home or Welcome Home Baby Turns Two: 20–24" - $70.00, $35.00.
Wee Imp: Has red wig. 8" - $350.00 up, $80.00.

WOODS, ROBIN

The dolls designed and made by the Robin Woods Company over the years have been some of the finest quality dolls available in their price range. These dolls stand out in a crowd because Robin Woods used imagination and creative talent that bears her signature. The dolls are beginning to show up on the secondary market and more will appear as time goes on. The last "pure" Robin Woods doll appeared on the market during 1991. In 1992, Robin Woods became the creative designer for the Alexander Doll Company and will be designing dolls under the name of "Alice Darling."

The following are dolls that can be found on the secondary market.

1986: Associated Dollmakers: Adults sculpted by Avigail Brahms. "Dancers In Action," "Great Women In The Arts." Children sculpted by Yolanda Bello. "Little Miss Deb" series. All are rare. Prices are not available.

1987: Cathryn: 15" - $450.00 up. Christmas dolls: 14" - $350.00 each.

1988: Merry Carol: 14" - $350.00 up. Scarlett Christmas: 14" - $300.00 up.

1989: Hope: $300.00. Lorna Doone: $250.00. Heidi: $265.00. William Noel: $250.00. Elizabeth St. John: $250.00. Dickens Boy: $250.00 up. Mary of Secret Garden: 14" - $265.00 up.

1990: "Camelot Series." Kyliegh Christmas: $245.00; Melanie Phebe: $225.00; Tess Circus: $225.00; Bobbi: $250.00; Marjorie: $250.00; Meaghan: $300.00; Tess of the D'urbervilles: $300.00.

1991: "Shades of Day" collection. 5,000 pieces each. Dawn, Glory, Stormy, Joy, Sunny Veil, Star, Serenity. 14" - $300.00 each.

17" "Kate Greenaway" from 1988. Part of the "Great Women In The Arts" series. Limited edition of 1,200. Doll designed by Avigail Brahms. $425.00. *Courtesy Pat Graff.*

1991: Laurel, Lily, Bouquet, Rosemary, Rose, Violet: 14" - $200.00 each. Delores: $225.00. Victoria: $185.00. Miss Muffet: $160.00. Sleeping Beauty: Set - $385.00. Pumpkin Eaters: 8" - $100.00. Eliza Doolittle: $200.00. Mistress Mary: 8" - $125.00. Bette Jack: $300.00. Alena: $275.00. Tennison: $300.00.

Robin Woods Limited Editions: Merri: 1991 Doll Convention, **Disney World.** Limited edition. 14" - $450.00 up. **Mindy:** Made for **Disney's "Robin Woods Day."** Limited to 300. 14" - $300.00 up. **Rainey:** 1991 **Robin Woods Club** doll. Limited to 300. 14" - $250.00 up.

J.C. Penney: Angelina: 1990 Christmas angel. Limited edition. 14" - $550.00. Noelle: Limited edition Christmas angel. 14" - $250.00 up. Julianna: 1991. Little girl shopping for holidays. Limited edition. 14" - $300.00.

14" "Dawn" from the "Shades of the Day" collection. Limited edition of 500. From 1991. *Courtesy of Robin Woods catalog.*

14" Robin Woods "David" from 1991. All vinyl. Dressed up for his Valentine. $285.00. *Courtesy of Robin Woods catalog.*

14" "Dani" is all dressed up to play. A charmer from the Robin Wood's 1991 catalog. $300.00.

Robin Woods exclusives: Gina, The Earthquake Doll: For Ann's of Burlingame, CA. $650.00. Camelot Castle collection: 1989–1990. 14" - $250.00 each. 1991: 8" - $100.00–130.00 each. Christmas Tree Doll: Doll becomes the tree. For Disney. $675.00.

The child is Jordon and the doll is Robin Woods's "Alice In Wonderland." Jordon's grandmother made the matching dress from a Victorian wedding dress with 9 yards of material and 61 yards of lace. Even the headpieces are the same. That loving grandmother is Patty Grady. *Priceless!*

Index

INDEX

NUMBERS

LETTERS AND SYMBOLS

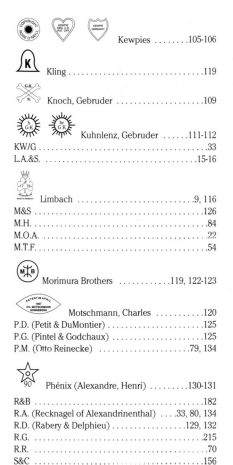

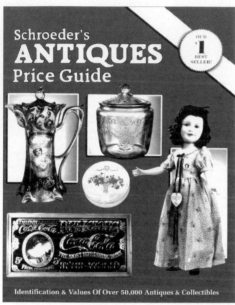